GREAT AND NOBLE JAR

EST. 75 YEARS 1938
THE UNIVERSITY OF GEORGIA PRESS 2013

GREAT & NOBLE JAR

Traditional Stoneware of South Carolina

CINDA K. BALDWIN

McKissick Museum   The University of South Carolina
The University of Georgia Press   Athens & London

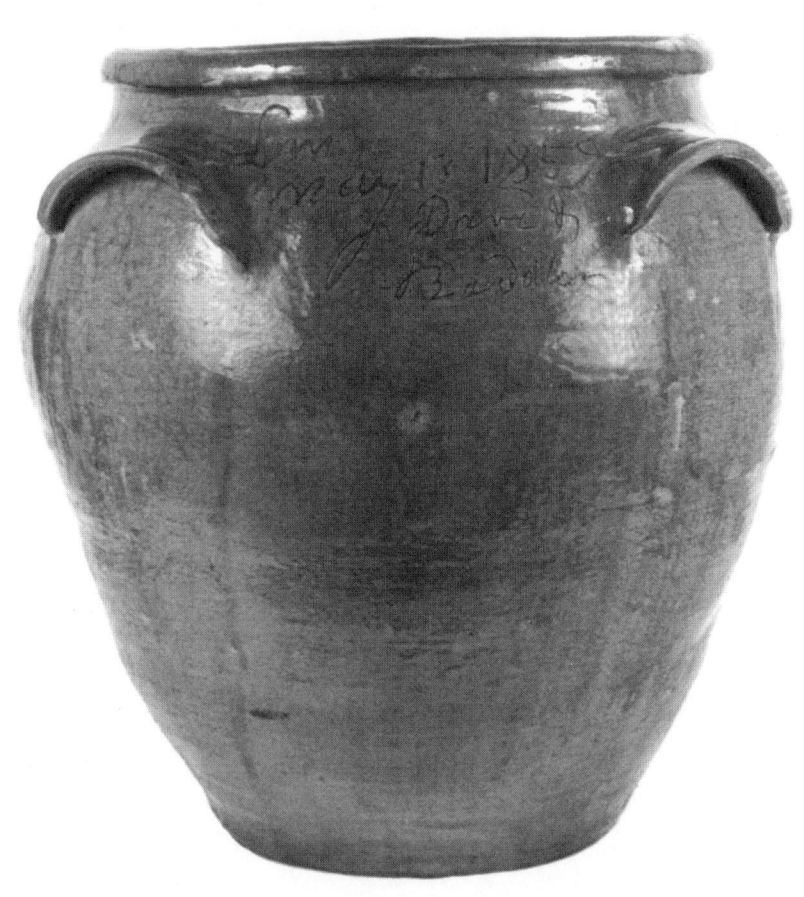

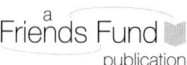
a
Friends Fund
publication

Publication of this work was made possible, in part, by a
generous gift from the University of Georgia Press Friends Fund.

Paperback edition, 2014
© 1993 by the University of Georgia Press
Athens, Georgia 30602
www.ugapress.org
All rights reserved
Designed by Sandra Strother Hudson
Set in 10 on 13 Linotype Walbum by
Tseng Information Systems Inc.
Printed and bound by Thomson-Shore

The paper in this book meets the guidelines for permanence and
durability of the Committee on Production Guidelines for Book
Longevity of the Council on Library Resources.

Most University of Georgia Press titles are
available from popular e-book vendors.

Printed in the United States of America

14 15 16 17 18   P   5 4 3 2 1

The Library of Congress has cataloged the hardcover
edition of this book as follows:
Baldwin, Cinda K.
Great & noble jar : traditional stoneware of South Carolina /
Cinda K. Baldwin.
xiii, 234 p., [8] p. of plates : ill. (some col.) ; 27 cm.
Includes bibliographical references (p. 209–215) and index.
ISBN 0-8203-1371-8 (alk. paper)
1. Stoneware—South Carolina—History. I. Title.
NK4364.B35 1993
738.3′09757—dc20   92-12029

Paperback ISBN 978-0-8203-4616-8

British Library Cataloging-in-Publication Data available

TO PETE CLAYTON AND BILLY HENSON,
the last and first of the South Carolina folk potters
AND TO JOHN,
whose love and emotional support made it all possible

Contents

Preface

It all began in the summer of 1984 when I came to South Carolina to conduct research on the southern alkaline-glazed stoneware tradition. I arrived in South Carolina after having just completed a master's program in anthropology at the University of Arkansas at Fayetteville. As a graduate assistant at the university museum I had participated in an inventory of the prehistoric ceramics collection, thereby gaining hands-on experience in the study of ceramics. My first exploration into the field of American folk pottery took place during my final semester at the University of Arkansas in the spring of 1984. At that time I was enrolled in a historical archaeology course taught by George Sabo. My research project for that class involved documentation of a nineteenth-century salt-glazed stoneware kiln site in the northwestern Arkansas community of Cane Hill. This project provided me with a general understanding of the processes involved in stoneware production.

In 1983 the National Endowment for the Humanities awarded a grant to McKissick Museum to support research into the development and diffusion of the alkaline-glazed stoneware tradition in South Carolina and the South. The following year I was hired as research investigator on the project. The project director, George D. Terry, then director of McKissick Museum, originally planned to complete the research and produce an exhibition and monograph within three years. The scope of the research was later broadened and the proposed three-year project lengthened considerably.

The major goal of the original research project was the collection of archival and survey information concerning the development of the alkaline-glazed stoneware tradition in order to determine the influence of the nineteenth-century Edgefield District potteries of South Carolina upon the spread of the folk pottery tradition throughout the lower South.

One of my earliest field trips was to the Pottersville Museum in Edgefield, South Carolina. Local historian Carlee McClendon and I walked across a plowed field located adjacent to the museum and site of his parents' home. As we walked along, Carlee stooped to pick up a handful of stoneware fragments bearing the characteristically green alkaline glaze. He told of finding similar sherds on the property as a child and of incorrectly thinking that these broken pottery pieces were made by Indians. Years later, while conducting local genealogical research, Carlee discovered that his family's property was located on the former site of Pottersville, one of the earliest stoneware factories established in South Carolina's Edgefield District. This was my first introduction to the secrets and mysteries of the Edgefield District stoneware tradition. In the next six years I traveled throughout the state in search of information and documentation on South Carolina's stoneware tradition. I visited state and local archives, county courthouses, administrative buildings, museums, antique shops, general stores, and private homes and interviewed people throughout the state and surrounding region.

The research design focused upon two major objectives: library and archival research into the origins and development of the alkaline-glaze tradition, and a descriptive and photographic survey of alkaline-glazed stoneware vessels in public and private collections. My first task was to create files of biographical information on South Carolina stoneware potters. I accomplished this goal by systematically examining primary documents regarding stoneware potters and pottery operations within the state and surrounding region, thereby establishing files on approximately 250 South Carolina potters. The second phase of the project involved the compilation of photographs and documentation on surviving stoneware vessels. Over two thousand stoneware vessels were documented through the survey.

The results of the South Carolina stoneware project confirmed the conclusions reached earlier by folk pottery scholars on the significance of the Edgefield District as the birthplace of the southern alkaline-glazed stoneware tradition. The research also documented the significance of African-American involvement in the Edgefield District stoneware tradition as well as the unique entrepreneurial approach of the Edgefield factory owners to stoneware production in the district.

Additional areas of study emerged as the project developed. For example, the Edgefield research led to an investigation of the location and spatial distribution of stoneware pottery sites in the area of the old Edgefield District. In 1987 the McKissick Museum and the South Carolina In-

stitute of Archaeology and Anthropology received funding from the United States Department of the Interior (administered through the Historic Preservation Office of the South Carolina Department of Archives and History) to conduct mapping and archaeological testing of the Edgefield District pottery sites. The findings of this survey were published in a lengthy report, the first of several publications based upon the research. Pottery sherds collected through the Edgefield District pottery site survey were compared to sherds from other alkaline-glazed stoneware sites throughout the region by means of X-ray fluorescence analysis. Also, additional South Carolina pottery centers outside the Edgefield District were documented through the stoneware project. Most of these late-nineteenth-century pottery centers were located in the up-country, where the demand for utilitarian stoneware continued well into the twentieth century.

In March 1990 the exhibition "Crossroads of Clay: The Southern Alkaline-Glazed Stoneware Tradition" opened at McKissick Museum. This major traveling exhibition and accompanying catalog, funded in part by grants from the National Endowment for the Humanities, marked the culmination of nearly ten years of research by the staff of McKissick Museum. Since the project staff believed that the exhibition and catalog should appeal to a general audience and focus upon the origins and dissemination of the alkaline-glaze tradition, additional funding was sought from the National Endowment for the Humanities to support the preparation of this more comprehensive survey of the South Carolina stoneware tradition.

Acknowledgments

Any project of this scope would not be possible without the contributions of others. I wish to acknowledge the following individuals and institutions for their assistance:

The following respondents—many of them members of pottery families—without whom this book could not have been written: Hugh Baynham, Claude Bab, Thomas Gentry Bab, Major Baynham, Mrs. Clarence Belcher, Kye Boyle, Rochelle Boyle, B. F. Buie, R. Paul Byars, Mr. and Mrs. Jones Clayton, Irene Gingrey, Elbert Duke Harley, Dewey Henson, Allie Wilson Henson, Billy Henson, David Hoffman, Robert Lee, E. C. Mathis, Mrs. H. E. Mays, Rosa Henderson Murray, Maude Stork Shull, Harold Steele, Sr., Kenneth and Clarice Tapp, Frances Thompson, Lucinda Thurmond, Boomer Williams.

McKissick Museum volunteer Hugh Wilson for endless hours spent searching the records of the South Carolina Department of Archives and History, the South Caroliniana Library, and numerous county courthouses. Hugh has been a great friend and companion during research trips.

The following scholars, genealogists, museum professionals, and private individuals went out of their way to assist with the research:

O. Holt Allen, Violet Henderson Anderson, Samuel A. Angulo (Sam Houston Memorial Museum), Dorothy and Walter Auman, Hurley Badders (Pendleton District Historical and Recreation Commission, Pendleton, South Carolina), Orin Brady, Daisy Wade Bridges, Charlie Brown, Evan Brown, B. F. Buie, Orville Vernon Burton, Mr. and Mrs. Sam Burton, Mr. and Mrs. Paul Carpenter, Edward Carter, Irene Trapp Chafin, Jake Clayton, Lewis Clayton, Robert Cogswell (Tennessee Arts Commission), Mr. and Mrs. LeGrande Cooper, Tom Cowan, William L. Cox, Mr. and Mrs. Burlon Craig, Edward C. Cushman, Jr., Melanie Delhom, Keith Derting (South Carolina Institute of Archaeology and Anthropology, University of South Carolina), Mr. C. E. Dreher, Richard Dunn, Jack J. Efurd, William Davies Eve, Sheila Tabakoff (Mint Museum of Art, Charlotte, North Carolina), Risher Fairey, Leland Ferguson (Department of Anthropology, University of South Carolina), Paul Figueroa (Gibbes Art Gallery, Charleston, South Carolina), Mr. and Mrs. W. Harold Fleming, Roy and Kathleen Garrett, Sarah Gibbes, Lloyd G. Gibbs, Anita Gregory (Museum of Florida History), Eleanor M. Hanson, Horace Harmon (Lexington County Museum, Lexington, South Carolina), Nathan Harsh, Bryding Adams Henley (Birmingham Museum of Art), Robert M. Hicklin, Jr., Beth Holley (The Houston Museum, Chattanooga, Tennessee), Graham Hood (Institute of Early American Culture, The College of William and Mary and The Colonial Williamsburg Foundation), Laurel Horton, Mr. and Mrs. Allen Huffman, Harold Hutto, Bill Hynds, Mr. and Mrs. William W. Ivey, Kevin Karl, Stacey Keisler, John Kemp, Elise Key, Keith Landreth, Sharon Lawson, Bennie Lee and Don

Lewis, Chris Loblein (Charleston Museum), Carl MacIntosh, Charles R. ("Randy") Mack (Department of Art, University of South Carolina), James Martin, Tom McCain, Betsy Alman McCall, Carlee McClendon, Keith McCurry, William McKie, Jr., Linda Carnes McNaughton (North Carolina Division of Archives and History), Vivian Milner, Nancy Crockett Mims, W. W. Mims (publisher and editor of the *Edgefield Advertiser*), R. E. Neville, Jr., Rickey Newton, Mrs. W. L. Norton, Winnie Owens-Hart, David S. Parker, William Patterson, Sharon Peckrul (South Carolina Institute of Archaeology and Anthropology, University of South Carolina), Kate Plowden, Bradford Rauschenberg (Museum of Early Southern Decorative Arts, Winston-Salem, North Carolina), Patricia H. Rhodes, Quincy Jennings Rountree, Alice Sanders, Stuart Schwartz, Willard E. Sharp (Department of Geology, University of South Carolina), Theresa Singleton, W. M. Sloan, Howard Smith, Marion Smith, Samuel D. Smith, Stanley South (South Carolina Institute of Archaeology and Anthropology, University of South Carolina), Gary Stanton (Center for Historic Preservation, Mary Washington College), Linda Steigleder (Georgia Museum of Art, Athens), Leroy Stephens, Carol Stephenson, Maria Stork, Nancy Sweezy, Harvey Teal, Raymond Timmerman, John Vlach (Department of American Studies, George Washington University), Ralph Willoughby (South Carolina Geological Survey), Mrs. D. L. Wise.

The following individuals and institutions for granting me access to their stoneware collections:

Ackland Art Museum (University of North Carolina at Chapel Hill, North Carolina), Aiken County Historical Museum (Aiken, South Carolina), Augusta-Richmond County Museum (Augusta, Georgia), Thomas Gentry Bab, Mrs. Clarence Belcher, Stan Borden, Kye Boyle, Thomas Bracco, Matt Bramblett, Alton Brant, John Burrison, Elizabeth Buxton, Sallie T. Cade, Larry Carlson, Charles Cauthran, Charleston Museum (Charleston, South Carolina), Mr. and Mrs. Oliver Jones Clayton, Charles Comolli, Dove P. Connelly, Sam Crouch, Marie Dorn, John Evans Elliot, John C. Feltham, Mr. and Mrs. William P. Ferguson, Sr., Terry and Stephen Ferrell, Gladys L. Frick, Betty Sue Gandy, Donnie Garrett, L. A. Garrett, C. N. Gignilliat, John Gordon, Georgeanna H. Greer, William Griffin, Paul Guerry, Michael Hall, Mrs. Henry Harris, Sally Hawkins, Billy Henson, George D. Henson, Harold Hines, David Hoffman, Frank Horton, Betty Jennings, J. Walter Joseph, Guy F. Kennedy, Rodney Leftwich, Robert McDonald, Lori McGraw, McKissick Museum (University of South Carolina, Columbia, South Carolina), Mississippi State Museum (Jackson, Mississippi), Mr. and Mrs. H. E. Mays, Pottersville Museum (Edgefield, South Carolina), Julian Landrum Mims, Roddy and Sally Moore, Pearl Morgan, Frances Baynham Moseley, Mr. and Mrs. Walker Murray, The Museum (Greenwood, South Carolina), Museum of Early Southern Decorative Arts (Winston-Salem, North Carolina), National Museum of American History (Division of Ceramics and Glass, Smithsonian Institution, Washington, D.C.), Richard Pearce, Doug Penland, Susie E. Ramsey, Mr. and Mrs. Levon C. Register, Danny Riddle, Jim Riddle, Jim Robertson, George V. Rosenberg, Tony and Marie Shank, Mrs. Broddus Shull, Mrs. M. T. Shull, Dr. and Mrs. James K. Smith, South Carolina State Museum (Columbia, South Carolina), Kathie and Jerry Stallworth, Leslie Stork, Clarice and Kenneth Tapp, Harvey Teal, Gary Thompson, Mary Jo and Eugene Vick, Dr. and Mrs. Charles M. Webb, Nancy White, Phil Wingard, Dr. B. J. Wood, Charles Wright, Tina Yarborough, James Yates, Charles G. ("Terry") Zug III.

The United States Department of the Interior and the South Carolina Historic Preservation Office for funding and administering the Edgefield District stoneware sites survey. George Castille and Carl Steen for conducting the archaeological research for the site survey.

The staffs of the South Caroliniana Library, University of South Carolina, and the South Carolina Department of Archives and History for assistance with archival and manuscript research.

Folk pottery scholars Joey Brackner, folk arts/crafts coordinator, Alabama State Council on the Arts, Montgomery, Alabama; John A. Burrison, director of the Folklore Program, Georgia State University, Atlanta, Georgia; Georgeanna H. Greer of San Antonio, Texas; Charles G. ("Terry") Zug III, Curriculum in Folklore, University of North Carolina at Chapel Hill for reading earlier versions of the manuscript.

The preparation of this material was made possible in part by a grant from the National Endowment for the Humanities, an independent federal agency. The findings and conclusions presented here do not necessarily represent the views of the Endowment.

This work was partially supported by a grant from the University of South Carolina Venture Fund.

To the staff of McKissick Museum for valuable support. Specifically, I would like to thank Peggy Nunn for proofreading and formatting the text to publisher specifications. For photographic assistance Susan Dunlap, Grace McElroy, Darcy Wingfield and Gordon Brown. A special thank you to Gordon Brown for his photographic expertise in the darkroom, in the studio, and on the road. Tina Yarborough for assisting with the research, and Pam Martin, Majken Blackwell, Tracey Thompson, Lilli Roberts, and Sherry Robinson for the maps, drawings, and illustrations. Catherine Wilson Horne for writing the original research proposal for the stoneware project, for providing valuable administrative and supervisory support, and for reading a draft of the manuscript; and George David Terry and Lynn Robertson Myers for their vision, direction, and support. I am especially grateful to George Terry for giving me the opportunity to tell the story of South Carolina folk pottery.

Finally, I would like to thank my children, Harmony ("Anne") and Cody, my husband John, and my parents, Joseph and Frances Red, for their patience, love, and emotional support.

GREAT AND NOBLE JAR

CHAPTER ONE

Carolina Clay:
Early Influences on the Stoneware
Tradition in South Carolina

During the 1840s and 1850s potters in the Edgefield District of South Carolina developed a distinctive type of stoneware characterized by highly refined alkaline glazes, symmetrical and often sensual forms, and trailed- and brushed-slip decoration, which they sold to merchants, planters, and farmers throughout the state and in northern and eastern Georgia. At the height of Edgefield pottery production in 1850 a total of five large-scale stoneware factories were operating in the district, employing thirty male and five female laborers. Well over a hundred potters were involved in stoneware production in the Edgefield area during the nineteenth and early twentieth centuries. The distinctive stoneware tradition that emerged in South Carolina's Edgefield District in the first quarter of the nineteenth century influenced pottery production throughout the lower South.

Southern stoneware was the product of an agricultural society. This utilitarian ware, used mainly for food preservation, preparation, and serving, was produced from local stoneware clays and glazed with a mixture of slaked wood ash or lime, clay, and most often an additional silica source, typically in the form of sand, flint, crushed glass, or iron cinders. By utilizing readily available ingredients, the southern folk potter was able to produce clean, inexpensive, and impermeable containers for local use.

A few standard vessel forms—the storage jar, smaller preserve jar, jug, churn, clabber bowl, and pitcher—were produced by folk potters throughout the lower South. This ware was generally bulbous or ovoid-shaped during the first half of the nineteenth century, with sharply defined forms and highly refined glazes. Other features that characterized early southern alkaline-glazed stoneware included the use of horizontally placed slab or ear-lug handles on storage and preserve jars, and tie-down rims with a flared or rounded lip protruding outward to hold in place a cloth cover tied with string. As mass-produced glass and metal containers became more widely available in the late nineteenth century, craftsmanship declined. However, a few folk potters, such as Burlon Craig in the Catawba Valley of North Carolina and the Meaders family of White County, Georgia, are still making southern alkaline-glazed folk pottery today.

The old Edgefield District (present-day Edgefield, Aiken, and Greenwood counties) is recognized as the earliest center for the production of alkaline-glazed stoneware in the southern United States (see Figure 1.1). Potters trained in the Edgefield District during the early decades of the nineteenth century followed the westward mi-

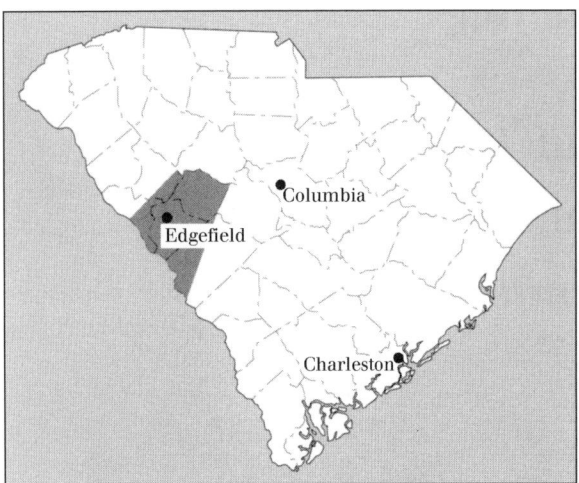

1.1   Map of South Carolina illustrating the location of the old Edgefield District, early center of alkaline-glazed stoneware production.

gration into the lower South, thereby diffusing the tradition throughout the region. Edgefield-trained potters introduced the alkaline-glazed stoneware tradition into Georgia, North Carolina, Alabama, Florida, Mississippi, and Texas. A number of alkaline-glazed stoneware pottery centers evolved within the region and are characterized by variations in form, detailing, and glaze formulas.

The domain of the alkaline-glazed stoneware tradition is the lower South, the area below Virginia and extending as far west as Texas. The old Edgefield District of South Carolina represented a core area or cultural hearth for the diffusion of the southern alkaline-glazed stoneware tradition, a unique regional pottery tradition with roots in Europe and Asia. An analysis of the stoneware tradition in South Carolina and its impact upon the development of folk pottery throughout the lower South yields larger patterns that provide a greater understanding of the nature of nineteenth-century southern society and culture.

South Carolina Clays

The principle ingredient used in the production of all pottery is clay. Clay is "generally understood to be a natural, earthy, fine-grained material which exhibits plasticity when wet."[1] Resulting from the weathering of granite, it is composed of silica, alumina, and other mineral and organic ingredients. Stoneware clays, deposited along river banks and old stream beds, were the principle materials used in pottery manufacture in the South.[2] Higher percentages of alumina and silica and fewer impurities characterize stoneware and kaolin clays.

The specific characteristics of clays are determined by their place of origin and the processes by which they are formed. South Carolina may be divided into five landform regions based upon relief, rock types, and geologic history: Blue Ridge, Piedmont, Sandhills, Coastal Plain (which can be divided into Inner and Outer Coastal plains), and Coastal Zone (see Figure 1.2). Of these five regions, the Piedmont and Coastal Plain occupy the largest area and are the principle clay-producing

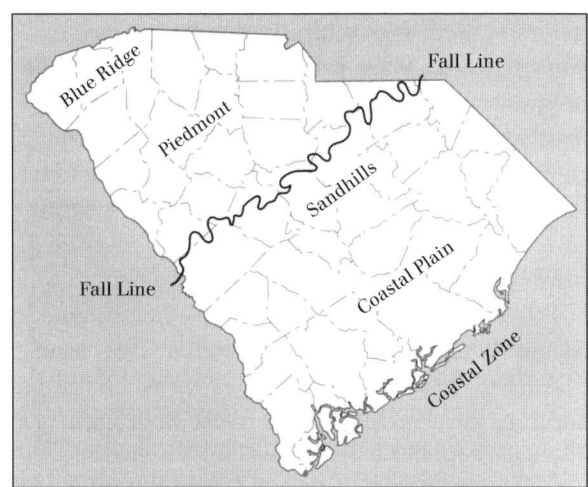

1.2   Map illustrating the five landform regions of South Carolina.

regions. The Piedmont, extending from the Sand-hills to the foothills of the Blue Ridge Mountains, constitutes a third of the state, covering approximately 10,500 square miles (27,195 square kilometers). The underlying rock structure of the Piedmont region includes crystalline or granitic rocks. The second major clay region is the Coastal Plain, covering the southern and eastern sections of the state. A sedimentary rock structure characterizes the Coastal Plain since it was covered by the ocean at least one hundred million years ago. Sea level was located adjacent to the southern edge of the Sandhills, which dominate Aiken, Lexington, Richland, Kershaw, and Chesterfield counties. Over the last eighty million years the sea level retreated from this position, exposing the Coastal Plain. The basic structure of sedimentary rocks resulted from the deposition of materials on the ocean floor during the Cretaceous period. The geologic boundary separating the Piedmont and Coastal Plain, known as the Fall Line, constitutes the dividing line between these two rock types.[3]

Two basic types of clays are found in South Carolina—residual clays and transported or sedimentary clays. Residual clays are found in the Piedmont and result from the in situ decomposition of granitic or feldspathic rock. These clays are characterized by impurities such as mica, quartz, or sand that are released when the granitic or feldspathic rock decomposes and converts to clay. Iron oxide resulting from the intense leaching of the clay gives them a reddish hue. These weathered Piedmont clays, or saprolites, are found in the northern portion of the Edgefield District.

Sedimentary clays also originate from the feldspathic rocks of the Piedmont but are formed by the transportation of clay particles by running water into streams and rivers flowing out of the region. Kaolin, white clay that has few of the impurities typical of the clays found in the Piedmont, is among the most famous of the sedimentary clays. Aiken County, South Carolina, is well known for its rich kaolin deposits. These Eocene-era clays, extending from the Bath-Langley area to Horse Creek Valley, lie within the Huber Formation. Commercial kaolin mining operations are still active in the Bath-Langley area between Augusta, Georgia, and Aiken, South Carolina. The appearance of these kaolin-rich clays in South Carolina greatly influenced the development of the stoneware tradition in the state. Kaolin-rich clays were used extensively in the Edgefield area in stoneware bodies and glazes. Edgefield stoneware made from these clays produces a resonant tone when struck similar to that of porcelain and may be classified technically as nontranslucent porcelain. During the period from approximately 1840 through the mid-1850s some Edgefield-area potters also used a kaolin-based slip, a type of liquefied clay, to decorate their ware. Geologist M. Tuomey recognized the importance of South Carolina kaolin in pottery production. He wrote that "common pottery is much improved, both in quality and appearance by the addition of this earth [kaolin], and from its abundance, were a little more taste and skill combined in the manufacture, the pottery of this State would be unrivaled."[4]

High-alumina kaolinitic clay deposits occur in a belt that extends from South Carolina across Georgia, central Alabama, northeastern Mississippi, western Tennessee and Kentucky, southern Arkansas, and the eastern and southern parts of Texas. The path of westward movement of the southern stoneware tradition in the nineteenth century followed this zone, lying along the interior boundary of the Coastal Plain and roughly paralleling the Fall Line.[5]

The stoneware potter often added nonplastic materials such as sand or flint or a highly feldspathic clay to the stoneware clay for added silica content or to improve drying/shrinkage. Other important properties that the potter sought in stoneware clays included high dry strength and retention of form during firing. The clay had to be able to withstand handling and stacking in the kiln in the dry condition. Dry strength and plasticity are related, so the more plastic clays usually also exhibited high dry strength. The rate of shrinkage during drying and firing was also an important property. Shrinkage had to be kept to a minimum in order to produce standard forms and capacities. Increased shrinkage of ware during drying also increased the dangers of cracking or warping. Stoneware potters called very plastic clays with high drying shrinkage "fat" and sandy clays with a low drying shrinkage "lean." This variation is related to grain size, the fine-grained being more plastic. Both fat and lean clays were used in stoneware manufacture.[6]

Stoneware bodies, which are much easier to shape by hand and less brittle and fragile than porcelain bodies, were preferred for the production of utilitarian ware. The higher firing temperatures required in porcelain production, and the two-step firing process for glazed ware, necessitated a greater degree of control than that required in the production of stoneware. Temperatures from 1,140 to 1,300 degrees Celsius are required for the maturation of the porcelain clay body or biscuit, and temperatures from 1,080 to 1,300 degrees for glazed porcelain. Stoneware is also high-fired, but it is usually fired only once, after glazing, with temperatures of 1,150 degrees Celsius being sufficient for the production of most true stoneware.[7]

Stoneware is impervious to liquids and resistant to corrosion. These features make it more desirable than earthenware for the storage and preservation of acidic foods and liquids. Its plasticity in shaping and toughness when fired, as well as the economic benefits arising from standardized production methods and cheaper raw materials (especially clay) used in its manufacture, have made stoneware preferable to porcelain for many uses.

"Cherokee Clay": Early South Carolina Potters

A strong pottery tradition existed among the indigenous population of South Carolina long before Europeans appeared on the scene. Pre-Colombian potters handbuilt their ware using coiling and "annular ring building" techniques (building from a long coil or series of individual rings of clay) and fired them in open hearths. Decorative techniques included cord and fabric marking, incising, punctating, or stamping with a carved wooden paddle. Native American potters were mainly women. Girls apprenticed themselves to their mothers or grandmothers in order to learn the skills and secrets of pottery production.[8]

Although the native ceramic tradition has largely disappeared in the region, the Catawba Indians of York County, South Carolina, continue to produce traditional southeastern Indian pottery. The pottery trade has served to hold Indian families together and to reinforce community social bonds. Catawba pottery represents the last vestiges of the aboriginal ceramic traditions of the eastern United States.[9]

The availability of good stoneware clays was the single most important factor leading to the establishment of the nineteenth-century stoneware tradition in South Carolina. South Carolina's reputation for fine clays became well known in Europe in the mid to late eighteenth century as British potters imported clay from the Cherokee Indian Territory. During the same period some potters began to view South Carolina as an opportunity to establish a pottery factory that would supply the entire region. These early attempts to establish a pottery factory in South Carolina provide important clues to the origins and development of the nineteenth-century stoneware tradition in the state.

In a journal written in 1767 Thomas Griffiths told of a journey that he made to North Carolina

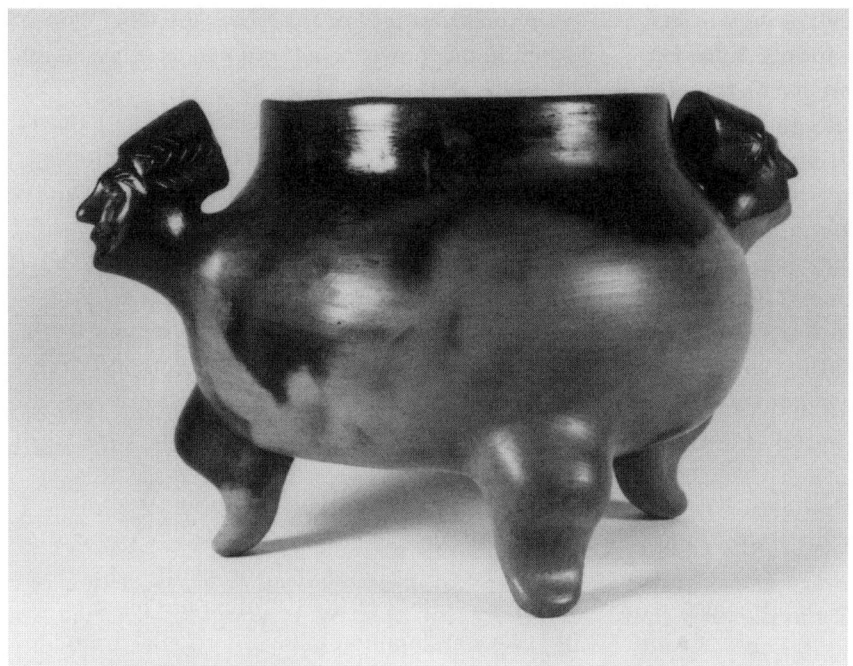

1.3 Earthenware bowl with applied decoration, 1986, Georgia Harris, York County, S.C. H 6¾″, C 28¾″. Collection of McKissick Museum, The University of South Carolina, Columbia.

to obtain clay for Josiah Wedgwood. Wedgwood had heard that the Cherokee Indian Territory in North Carolina had produced a fine white earth used by the Indians for pipe-making. Through much difficulty and expense Griffiths managed to procure five tons of the clay from a site in what is today Macon County, North Carolina. Wedgwood judged the Cherokee clay to be of fairly good quality but found the expense of obtaining it to be prohibitive and noted that he had found the recently discovered Cornish clays to be superior for his manufactures.

Other potters apparently had experimented with the Cherokee clay before Wedgwood. William Cookworthy, the first English potter to develop true hard-paste porcelain, wrote a letter in 1745 regarding his experimentation with "an earth, the product of the Cherokee Nation in America, called by the natives *Unaker*." Cookworthy later applied for a patent to produce "a kind of porcelain newly invented, composed of moorstone or growan, and growan clay, the stone

giving the ware transparence and the clay imparting whiteness and infusibility."[10] It appears that hard-paste porcelain, while first produced in Germany thirty-five years earlier, was developed in England by Cookworthy through experiments with Carolina clay.

Cookworthy was one of a number of English earthenware potters in search of the Chinese secrets of porcelain manufacture. The biggest obstacle to the development of true hard-paste porcelain in England was lack of knowledge regarding the ingredients used in its manufacture. Kaolin clays were unfamiliar to European potters. Earlier, they had developed soft paste or "artificial" porcelains made with sand, pipe clay, and glass; and later, "bone china," of bone ash, china clay, and feldspar. Cookworthy learned of the Chinese techniques and materials used in porcelain manufacture by reading the letters of Pere d'Entrecolles. D'Entrecolles, a French Jesuit who had been living in Kyang-si Province in southeastern China, wrote an account of the porcelain and stoneware manufactures at Ching-te-chen including descriptions of the mining of the raw materials and of how they were purified and processed, the location of the mines and means of transporting the raw materials, and the processes of throwing, trimming, glazing, decorating, and firing. He wrote that "the material of porcelain is composed of two kinds of clay, one called *pe-tun-tse* [feldspar]" and the other kaolin.[11] The letters were published and translated into English before the mid-eighteenth century. Since local kaolin was unknown to English potters at this time, the Cherokee clay was viewed as a valuable commodity.

The location of the clay in Carolina must have been widely known because "Tassih, the Clay Pits," were mentioned in reference to a skirmish fought between the Cherokees and the local militia during the Cherokee Expedition of 1760 and 1761. Also, when Griffiths requested permission from the Cherokee chiefs to remove clay from the pit, several mistrustful tribal leaders noted that they had been "troubled with some young men long before who made great holes in their land, took away their fine white Clay, and gave them only Promises for it."[12] Once Griffiths was permitted to take the clay, he described how his party labored for three days to clear rubbish from the old pit.

The first recorded references to the fine quality of Carolina clay for ceramic production were in a 1740s patent application by Edward Haylyn and Thomas Frye, the proprietors of the Bow factory, for the production of porcelain in England. The proprietors claimed in their application that the earth used to produce this material was "the produce of the Chirokee nation in America, called by the natives '*unaker.*'"[13] This "Cherokee clay" was shipped from Charleston to London in 1743–44. Evidently, the practice was continued periodically because in January 1757 a Charleston merchant wrote a Liverpool trading company that "we will send by the first opportunity that shall present for

2 or 300 lb. weight of the Cherokee clay. 'Tis not often in our power to get it down as it lyes at the distance of 3 or 400 Miles."[14]

Charleston merchant Caleb Lloyd sent clay to Bristol and Worcester pottery factories in 1765. That year Lloyd wrote to his brother-in-law, Richard Champion: "I now request your care of a box of porcelain earth which I have sent you by this vessel to be forwarded to Worcester to the proprietors of the China Manufactory there, to have a few pieces of china made of it for me, agreeably to a list I enclose." He added that "it was at considerable pains and expense this earth was procured. It comes from the internal part of the Cherokee Nations, 460 miles from hence, on mountains scarcely accessible."[15] A year later another Charleston merchant, Henry Laurens, wrote a resident of the Carolina backcountry that he was "applied to be a particular friend to procure a Specimen of our Cherokee Clay for making potters fine Ware. Can you help me at any reasonable expense & soon to the quantity of a Flower Borrell [barrel] full."[16] Six months later three casks of Cherokee clay were shipped to London on Laurens's ship *Two Friends*. In a letter written to his friend William Williamson in November 1771 Laurens explained that he had given two kegs of clay (one belonging to Williamson and the other to Laurens) to George Morris of the Philadelphia china firm of Bonnin and Morris "to make an Essay on each Material, and to inform me of the Quality respectively."[17] Laurens went on to mention that Morris had experimented with the clay and found it to be very fine. This interest in the clays near South Carolina drew a number of potters to the area.

Eighteenth-century earthenware manufacture was centered primarily in port cities where concentrated populations created a demand for the product and coastal traffic provided ready access to a wider market.[18] The earliest pottery establishments in South Carolina were located in the coastal region in and around Charleston. Andrew Duche, the third son of Anthony Duche of Philadelphia, an English-born potter of Huguenot descent, was the first potter to establish a pottery factory in South Carolina. In 1730 the elder Duche petitioned the Pennsylvania House of Representatives for support in "the Art of making Stoneware," an endeavor to which he claimed to have been applying himself "for severall Years past." Anthony Duche produced salt-glazed stoneware patterned on both German and English types and marked with the initials AD. His fourth son, James, contributed to the production of the first New England stoneware.[19]

Andrew Duche worked with his father and brothers in their Philadelphia "Pot-House" until the early 1730s when he and his wife, Mary, moved to Charleston, South Carolina. On 5 April 1735 Duche announced the establishment of his Charleston pottery in the following *South Carolina Gazette* advertisement: "This is to give notice to all Gentlemen, Planters and others, that they may be supplied with Butter pots, milk-pans and all other sorts of Earthen ware of this Country make, by whole sale or retail, at much cheaper rate than can be imported into this Province from England or any other Place, by ANDREW DUCHE Potter, next door but one to Mr. *Yeomans,* or at his Pot-house on the Bay."[20] Soon thereafter Duche moved to the newly formed township of New Windsor, located on the Savannah River near present-day North Augusta, South Carolina. Ample stoneware and kaolin clays were available at this site. For a year or two Duche stayed at New Windsor, where he became involved in the Indian trade. Although documentation on Duche's activities at New Windsor is sketchy, he may have experimented with the local kaolin there in an effort to produce the first American porcelain.

At the suggestion of Roger Lacy, Georgia's agent to the Cherokee Indians, Duche obtained support from the English Trustees of Georgia for the establishment of a pottery operation in Savannah. Letters written by the Georgia Trustee

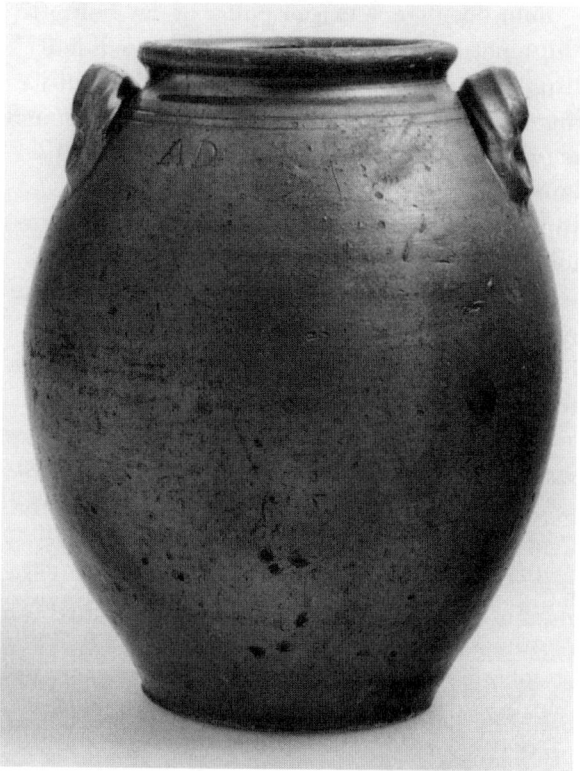

1.4 Lead-glazed earthenware jar stamped AD, possibly made by Andrew Duche in Savannah, Ga. The forked crossbar of the "A" is found on stoneware associated with Andrew's father, Anthony, in Philadelphia. H 13″. Courtesy of the Museum of Early Southern Decorative Arts, Winston-Salem, N.C., with thanks to Brad Rauschenberg.

officers describe Duche's experiments with "fine clay" in Savannah. Although Duche claimed in 1738 to be "the first Man in Europe, Africa or America, that ever found the true material and manner of making porcelain or China ware," it is unclear from written accounts of his work if he ever produced true hard-paste porcelain.[21] Future archaeological investigations at the site of Duche's Savannah pottery may reveal what types of ware he produced there. Duche is the earliest documented potter in South Carolina and Georgia and may have been the first American potter to experiment with native kaolin clays.[22]

John Bartlam, a master potter in the Staffordshire pottery factory of Josiah Wedgwood, left England in 1762 with the intention of establishing a pottery factory in South Carolina. Although described as being insolvent, Bartlam had obtained the support of the mercantile firm of Robertson, Jamison and Company based in Norfolk, Charleston, and the West Indies. The firm was evidently aware of South Carolina's growing reputation for fine clay and recognized the economic advantages of establishing a pottery close to the raw materials required.[23]

By March 1765 Bartlam was producing earthenware pottery at a small settlement called Cainhoy on the Wando River a few miles from Charleston.[24] The operation employed at least four journeymen potters as well as two slaves. Two wagons were used to transport clay to the site and finished ware overland, although most of the pottery was taken to markets in Charleston by canoe. The size of the Cainhoy pottery is indicated by the presence of "five hundred dozen" earthenware vessels at the site in May 1768.[25]

Bartlam's factory at Cainhoy was in serious financial difficulty by 1768. In a newspaper advertisement published the following year Bartlam stated that he had "for a long time labored under great disadvantages, occasioned by sickness of himself & journeymen in establishing his MANUFACTORY OF EARTHEN WARE." Bartlam was searching for another location for his pottery. He stated that "if I can meet with proper encouragement, I will remove the manufactory to or near Charles-Town, if a convenient spot can be got near to a landing or river."[26]

In January 1770 a committee of the General Assembly examined samples of Bartlam's work that he now claimed to be of "marketable quality." The committee found the ware to be "of a degree of perfection worthy of Public Notice" and cited the "large and constant demand" for these goods.[27] The committee also pointed out that local markets for the ware might be supplied 30 per-

cent cheaper than the prices then being charged. The assembly voted to subsidize Bartlam two hundred pounds that year and later supplemented the grant with another one hundred pounds the following year.

An announcement appeared in the Charleston newspaper in October 1770 stating that "a China Manufactory and Pottery is soon to be opened in this town." Also at this time, a number of potters arrived from England to work in Bartlam's Charleston pottery factory, and Bartlam solicited samples of clay from plantations in the interior. A wide variety of creamware vessels were produced at the factory located on Meeting Street. Bartlam boasted that he produced "what is called Queen's Ware, equal to any imported."[28] Most of this consisted of tableware, and much of the surviving ware from the site was decorated, another indication that Bartlam was attempting to produce ware that would rival that of the Staffordshire potteries.

Since Bartlam's backers had hired agents to recruit workmen from England his operations were in direct competition with British pottery manufactures supplying ware to America. Josiah Wedgwood, in a letter written in 1766 to his patron Sir William Meredith, expressed his concerns regarding the threat Bartlam's pottery posed to the English pottery trade:

Permit me to mention a subject of a public nature which greatly alarms us [the Staffordshire potters]. The bulk of our particular manufactures are, you know, exported to foreign markets, for our home consumption is very trifling in comparison, to what is sent abroad; & the principal of these markets are the Continent and Islands of North America. To the Continent we send an amazing quantity of white stoneware & some of the finer kinds, but for the Islands we cannot make anything to rich and costly. This trade to our Colonies we are apprehensive of losing in a few years, as they have set on foot some Pottworks there already, and have at this time an agent amongst us hiring a number of our hands for establishing new Pottworks in South Carolina; having one of our insolvent Master Potters there to conduct them.

He added: "they have every material there, equal if not superior to our own, for carrying on that manufacture."[29] This situation prompted Wedgwood in 1783 to prepare "An Address to the Workmen in the Pottery on the Subject of Entering into the Service of Foreign Manufacturers" in which he related the hazards that had befallen those who had left to work in Bartlam's factory. These misfortunes ranged from shipwreck and loss of wages to widespread illness and death.[30] A major campaign was launched by the Staffordshire potters to discourage the establishment of such potteries in America.

Bartlam's Charleston pottery failed and was closed by 1772. The withdrawal of financial support by the General Assembly was undoubtedly a key factor leading to the demise of the factory. Another development that probably contributed to the failure was the establishment of the Bonnin and Morris Porcelain Factory in Philadelphia in 1770. A number of Bartlam's workers were probably hired away to the Philadelphia factory, which advertised for potters in the Charleston newspaper.

Soon after the close of his Charleston pottery Bartlam and his remaining workers became associated with Joseph Kershaw. Kershaw, a wealthy businessman intent upon making the town of Camden an important urban center in the backcountry, provided political and financial backing for a pottery enterprise. Camden had grown out of Fredericksburg Township, settled in 1751 by Irish Quakers who established plantations along the Wateree River. Bartlam produced ware at a new factory located near Logtown, a small settlement of log residences north of the village of Camden, and sold his ware to Kershaw, who in turn distributed it throughout the surrounding area. A traveler to the area in 1776 commented on the "exceeding good Pans etc. which a Man who had set up there found great demand for." Camden was dependent upon flour milling and trading, with pottery manufacture and the tobacco

trade being important secondary activities. The pottery, mills, wharf, and Kershaw's home were connected to the Indian Trail by the village's secondary roads. Bartlam continued to produce pottery during the Revolution and purchased property of his own in Camden. He died in 1781, leaving an estate valued at less than ten pounds and a number of outstanding debts. Six saucers and four teacups were the only items in his possession that suggested a connection with pottery manufacture.[31] Bartlam's death brought to a close the early period of pottery manufacture in South Carolina. With the discovery of ample supplies of kaolin clays in Cornwall in 1768 the shipment of Carolina clay to England ended. By this time, however, South Carolina's reputation for fine clay had become well established. Although early attempts to establish a pottery factory in the state were ultimately unsuccessful, they helped establish South Carolina's reputation for fine pottery clays and attracted a number of potters to the area from Europe and the Atlantic seaboard.

The migration of earthenware potters out of South Carolina impacted pottery production in other areas of the South. For example, one of Bartlam's English workmen, William Ellis, later introduced molded creamware and stoneware techniques to the Moravian earthenware potters at Salem, North Carolina. The Moravians produced German-style slip-decorated lead-glazed earthenware similar to that of the Pennsylvania Germans and experimented with creamware, stoneware, and faience. Despite the fact that their settlements at Bethabara and Salem (present-day Winston-Salem, North Carolina) were located in an unsettled, dangerous frontier region, the Moravians were "master potters whose quality and scope of workmanship was virtually unparalleled in the entire country during the period."[32] They were the most dominant craftsmen in the Piedmont in the latter half of the eighteenth century and established the first long-term pottery center in the South.

British porcelain manufacturer Richard Champion emigrated to South Carolina in December 1784 and settled in Kershaw County on property that his brother-in-law, John Lloyd, had purchased for him. Champion, who had been in partnership with William Cookworthy in Bristol, purchased patent rights to the use of Cornwall china clay from Cookworthy in 1773 and took over the Bristol porcelain manufactory in 1774. He was immediately opposed by the Staffordshire potters. By 1775 Wedgwood had managed to circumvent Champion's patent. Political and business losses followed, and in 1784 Champion emigrated to South Carolina. Although Champion apparently never produced pottery in America, he may have been attracted to South Carolina because of the availability of local kaolin resources in the area.

Other potters settled in South Carolina in the eighteenth century. For example, William McGill reported to the York County clerk's office in 1856 that "in 1781 his father who was a potter resided in about one fourth of a mile of Hill and Hayne's Iron Works in said District."[33] Hill and Hayne's Iron Works was located on Allison's Creek two miles from the Catawba River.

A few potters of German descent settled in colonial South Carolina. In 1742 a German potter named John Hershinger resided in the township of Saxe Gotha. Located on the south side of the Congaree River below the present-day city of Columbia, Saxe Gotha was established as part of the Township Plan, formulated by the Carolina colony in 1730 to encourage settlement in the backcountry. German and German-speaking Swiss immigrants moved into Saxe Gotha and later, as land became more scarce, into the area between the Broad and Saluda rivers. By 1759 approximately eighteen hundred Germans lived in the area, including parts of present-day Richland, Lexington, and Newberry counties. Although no surviving ware produced by these German immigrants has been identified, most likely, as in the case of the Pennsylvania Germans and

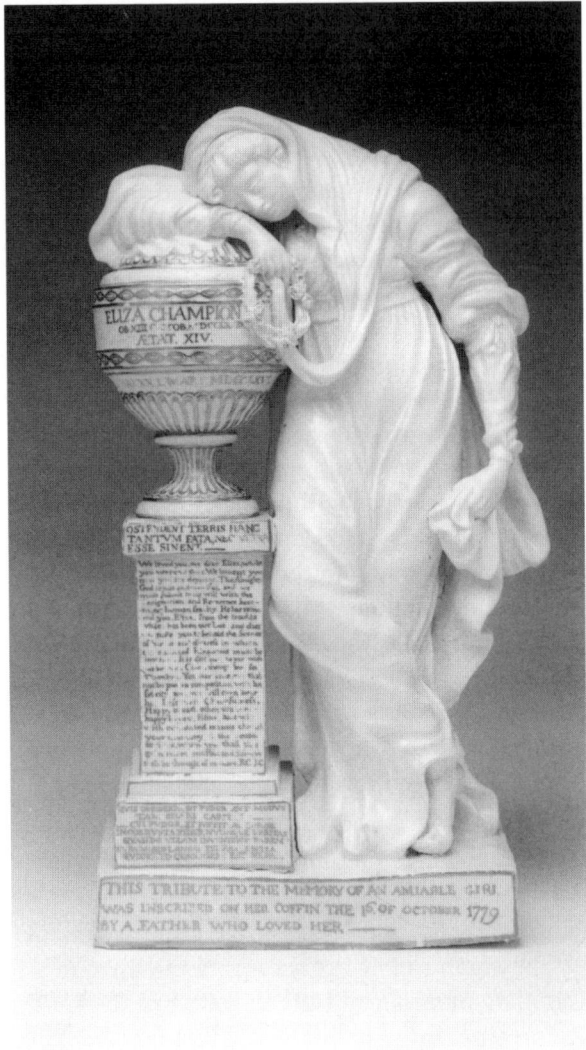

1.5   *Andromache Weeping Over the Ashes of Hector.* Hard-paste porcelain, 1779, Richard Champion, Bristol, England. This figure, taken from an engraving by Thomas Burke, 1772, after a painting by Angelica Kauffmann, was the last dated piece made at Richard Champion's porcelain factory at Bristol, England. Also known as *Dear Eliza*, the figure is dedicated to Champion's daughter, Eliza, who died in 1779. In 1976 the Mint Museum of Art purchased *Dear Eliza* from Mr. and Mrs. C. M. Edmunds of Sumter, S.C., direct descendants of Richard Champion. Gift of the Woman's Auxiliary and the Delhom Service League, Mint Museum of Art, Charlotte, N.C.

Moravians, they retained much of their native culture. This cultural heritage, including the production of earthenware pottery, was carried to South Carolina as these potters migrated into the Carolina backcountry.

Adam Effurt, another German potter who settled in the backcountry of South Carolina, obtained state grants for over a thousand acres of property in the Camden District between 1784 and 1787. By 1791 Effurt owned land in the Ninety Six District, property that became part of the Edgefield District when South Carolina's legislative districts were reorganized in 1800. Effurt acquired 112 acres of Edgefield property on Cloud's Creek in 1812 and appeared in the 1820 Edgefield census with a number of potters—James Kirbee, Emanuel Leopard, John Presley, and William Durham—who were involved in stoneware manufacture in the area. When Effurt died in June 1822, an inventory of his estate included pipemolds, red lead, and manganese. Red lead was used in earthenware glazes and manganese served as a coloring agent for these glazes. This period marked a turning point in South Carolina pottery production.

Worldwide Influences on the American Stoneware Tradition

In order to understand the origins and significance of alkaline-glazed stoneware, it is necessary to have a basic understanding of the various types of pottery. Pottery is the shaping of clay into some preferred form and its firing to a functional hardness. The term "pottery" encompasses a great variety of ware, with crude earthenware at one end, fine earthenware and stoneware constituting an intermediate range, and porcelain at the upper end of the scale. Classification of ceramic ware is based upon the type or composition of material used in production of the ware, the texture or density of the clay body when fired, and the temperature at which the ware is fired.[34] Variations within these three major classifications of ware are based mainly upon the materials used in their production.

Earthenware, unlike stoneware and porcelain, is unvitrified. Only the outer surface of the clay particles becomes soft or molten at the low earthenware firing temperatures, but the surfaces of the particles of the clay body fuse together during the cooling process. Coarse-grained clays containing considerable quantities of iron and other impurities are used in the production of common earthenware. The resulting reddish-colored earthenware bodies are sometimes referred to as redware. Potters coated the porous earthenware with a lead glaze to make it watertight. Manganese, copper, or iron was sometimes added to lead glazes as a colorant. Terra-cotta, faience, and majolica, as well as other coarser ware and refractory materials, fall under the category of earthenware.

Both stoneware and porcelain are vitrified, making them impervious to liquids. Vitrification occurs when the clay particles melt and coalesce completely during firing. Stoneware has a vitreous texture resembling that of porcelain, but while kaolin-rich clays are used in the manufacture of porcelain, more plastic and somewhat less pure clays are used in stoneware production. Stoneware bodies generally fire to a buff, gray, or tan unless they contain a large amount of iron, in which case they will appear much darker. The main difference between stoneware and porcelain is the translucency of the latter, although porcelains vary in their degree of translucency.

Folk potters typically glazed their stoneware before firing or, in the case of salt-glazed stoneware, glazed them during firing. This single firing process was more economical for utilitarian potters. Finer earthenware and porcelain, on the other hand, were usually made into a bisque or biscuit by an initial firing at relatively low temperatures. Then they were glazed and fired a second time to mature the glaze. Most country earthenware was fired only once. Early potters dusted lead ore onto the damp ware before firing.

The first true stoneware was produced by the Chinese in the second or third century prior to the Han period (approximately 500 B.C.). Potters in the Near East were technically superior to the Chinese but since they still used simple updraft kilns were incapable of producing high temperature ware. The Chinese developed a downdraft kiln consisting of a group of beehive-shaped chambers connected by an opening at the base with saggers to deflect flame and gases away from the ware. These kilns were made of refractory materials and insulated with a coating of clay and mud. The use of a downdraft made possible higher firing temperatures than had ever before been achieved. Early Chinese vitrified ware demonstrates a knowledge of construction and firing of kilns, knowledge of refractory clay and knowledge of glaze ingredients.

By the Han dynasty the Chinese had produced a "protoporcelain" or vitrified pottery. Technical developments achieved during this period led to the refinement of white translucent porcelain during the T'ang period, beginning in A.D. 618. A proliferation of ware types followed, including stoneware with feldspathic glazes (ash glazes had been used previously), dense, high-fired stoneware with low relief carving, vitreous white stoneware, and white, translucent porcelain. Chinese stoneware and porcelain production reached a peak period of development during the Sung dynasty (A.D. 960–1223) with the refinement of technique and style. During the Ming and Ching dynasties (1368–1644) foreign influences triggered radical developments in Chinese ceramic production as Chinese porcelain was exported throughout Europe. European demand for the Chinese export ware prompted the growth of large-scale factories specializing in the production of white porcelain with blue underglaze

painting. The arrival of Chinese porcelain in Europe had a profound impact upon the ceramic traditions that developed there during the seventeenth and eighteenth centuries.

European stoneware was first developed in the Rhine River Valley of Germany in the fifteenth century, having evolved from the medieval Pingsdorf and Schinveldt sintered, or hard-burned, earthenware. Probably by accident, German potters found that if salt was introduced into the kiln during the height of firing, it reacted with the stoneware body, producing a glassy, irregular surface impermeable to liquids. Improvements made by German potters in the design and structure of pottery kilns during the period made possible the development of salt-glazed stoneware on a large scale.[35]

European pottery was an expression of the needs and taste of the peasantry as opposed to the refined ware of the Orient. Whereas the significance of Chinese pottery is best viewed in its use by the nobility in the tea ceremony, utilitarian ware such as the German jugs, steins, and tankards best exemplify the early European pottery tradition. This early emphasis on utility also characterized the development of American pottery traditions of the eighteenth and nineteenth centuries.

The Germans were also the first Europeans to produce hard-paste porcelain. In 1690 a Saxon nobleman and scientist, Ehrenfried von Tschirnhausen, established important facts that led to the manufacture of European porcelain. Through his "sun furnace" experiments Tschirnhausen discovered that some minerals melt at higher temperatures, an important factor in the use of fluxing materials. Tschirnhausen met alchemist Johann Bottger in 1701, and together they conducted a porcelain research project during which they built a high-firing kiln. They produced the first European porcelain in 1708 and two years later established a porcelain factory under royal patronage.[36]

British pottery developed relatively slowly. "Cistercian ware," an earthenware made by sixteenth-century monks, had a coarse-grained body with a heavy lead glaze colored with manganese or iron oxide. Slip-ware, earthenware decorated with slip or liquid clays applied with a fine quill, often over a white-slip ground, was manufactured in Staffordshire in the seventeenth century by the Toft brothers and others. In 1671 John Dwight of Fulham (near London) applied for a patent that granted him exclusive right to the manufacture of salt-glazed stoneware in England.[37] The salt-glazed stoneware tradition soon spread throughout England. Staffordshire was already an important pottery center for the production of lead-glazed, slip-decorated earthenware. During the first half of the eighteenth century a variety of very white salt-glazed stoneware forms were developed there, including mugs, teapots, platters, and figurines.[38]

Staffordshire potter Josiah Wedgwood made important contributions to the English ceramics tradition. From 1769 to 1780 letters written between Wedgwood and his partner, Thomas Bentley, include extensive information about Wedgwood's famous ceramic experiments.[39] Through extensive experimentation he developed a variety of clay bodies, some of them vitrified (for example, Jasper ware and Basalt ware). He is best known for the development of creamware, a cream-colored earthenware that provided a perfect background for hand-painted or transfer-printed designs. He later developed pearlware, with cobalt oxide added to the glaze, in response to the demand for a whiter ware. This durable earthenware was cheaper than salt-glazed stoneware and largely replaced stoneware for domestic use.

Lead-glazed earthenware was the principal type of pottery used in colonial America. Major centers of earthenware production were established in New England and eastern Pennsylvania. In the second half of the seventeenth century

New England potters were producing British-style earthenware decorated with tooled horizontal bands, coloring oxides daubed or brushed onto the ware, and clay slip trailed on from a slip cup and covered with a clear lead glaze. The Pennsylvania Germans and Moravians of North Carolina manufactured traditional slipware, that of the former sometimes sgraffito-decorated through a white slip onto a red body with splashes of copper green. Many other colonial potters produced common earthenware for local use.

Lead oxide combines with clay at a relatively low temperature, thereby producing a smooth, glassy coating over areas to which it is applied. This provides a stable base for the earthenware glazes that will not crack or crackle upon cooling. The lead glaze, however, presents potential dangers because poisonous lead compounds can leach out into food or liquids placed in lead-glazed vessels, especially if the ingredients are acidic. By the late eighteenth century the toxic properties of the lead glaze became widely known in the towns and cities of the northeastern and mid-Atlantic states, although people in the more isolated areas of the backcountry continued to use lead-glazed earthenware on a daily basis.[40] By the turn of the nineteenth century many potters sought a substitute for lead-glazed earthenware. A pamphlet by John Bordley entitled *Essays and Notes on Husbandry and Rural Affairs*, published in Philadelphia in 1801, includes a description of the hazards of lead-glazed earthenware and a proposed solution to the problem:

The earthen ware made in America, *is glazed with lead:* and the glazing composition is laid on very savingly, thin and slight: so that it is not only worn away by vegetables and every thing acidulous, but is apt to peale off and be swallowed with meat, greens, and drinks. It is pure *lead,* and consequently a strong *poison.* The effect of lead on the health of glaziers and house painters, is daily seen. A journeyman or working painter may live, continually dying, six or eight years as a large allowance. The master who sees that the work is done, and

works but little, lives longer. All are groaning and pin-
ing, under colicks, gripes, cramps, rheumatisms, aches
and pains, who continue to snuff up and inhale the
vapours of lead for some time; or who gradually swal-
low small portions of it with their milk, greens, cider
and drinks, diffused from the glazing made of *lead.*
The people of New-England, drink much cider, and
use much vinegar, in country families; and there have
been instances of whole families afflicted as above.[41]

Bordley added that "a more perfect, durable and
wholesome earthenware glaze could be made
from wood ash and sand." A Philadelphia potter
approached by Bordley concerning the ash and
sand glaze objected to the use of these materials
because they would require additional labor and
fuel. Nevertheless, Bordley concluded that legis-
lators should promote a change from lead to sand
for glazing earthenware. He went on to point out
that stoneware was preferable to earthenware,
and that domestic stoneware was in great demand
in America due to the high shipping rates placed
on the bulky utilitarian stoneware then being
exported from Europe.

American potters in the North did not take
Bordley's advice. Rather than developing a stoneware with an ash and sand glaze, potters in the
North and upper South gradually adopted salt-
glazed stoneware. In Europe the salt-glazed
stoneware tradition had flourished following its
introduction to England in the seventeenth century. Salt glaze was used for jugs and crocks in
England and Germany. The subsequent export
of large quantities of German and English salt-
glazed stoneware to America discouraged local
production of the ware during the early colonial
period, but by the eighteenth century a domestic salt-glazed stoneware industry had begun to
emerge in the mid-Atlantic region.

Recent archaeological research suggests that
the first American pottery may have been produced in the South. In the *Travels* of Captain
John Smith there is a reference to furnaces for
glass and pottery at Jamestown in operation as

early as 1611. Additional evidence of early southern pottery production has been reported by
Norman Barka, who excavated a pottery kiln
site located in Yorktown, Virginia, dating from
approximately 1720 to 1745. During the excavation of the site archaeologists recovered a delft
cup with blue floral decoration on a white background dated 1720 and incised with the initials
AG. This is perhaps the earliest dated example
of American-made pottery in existence. A wide
variety of earthenware and salt-glazed stoneware
pottery was produced at the Yorktown site. A rectangular updraft kiln with two chambers was used
to fire salt-glazed stoneware, and possibly earthenware as well. The Yorktown pottery was much
more developed and productive than researchers
expected it to be. Barka pointed out that these
findings "may lead to eventual re-evaluation not
only of mercantilism but also of the industrial
development of the colonial South."[42]

Traditional stoneware operations, like the
earthenware potteries that preceded them, were
generally small and unsophisticated and required
little capital investment. Many of these rural potters worked at the trade part-time, side by side
with farming. Family members supplied the bulk
of the labor with occasional assistance by an ap-
prentice or journeyman.[43]

Stoneware production in the North was centered around New York and New Jersey because
of their close proximity to stoneware clay beds.
Also, both had ready access to the coastal trade
and could market their product widely. One of the
earliest known pieces of American stoneware, a
jar dated 1722, was made in New Jersey by Joseph
Thiekson. Philadelphian Anthony Duche (father
of Andrew Duche) is credited with producing the
first American cobalt-decorated gray stoneware in
the 1730s. Two distinct pottery manufactures, the
Remmey and Crolius pottery and the Corselius
pottery, are shown on a map prepared in 1813 by
David Grim depicting the Manhattan area as he
believed it appeared in 1742–44. New York pot-

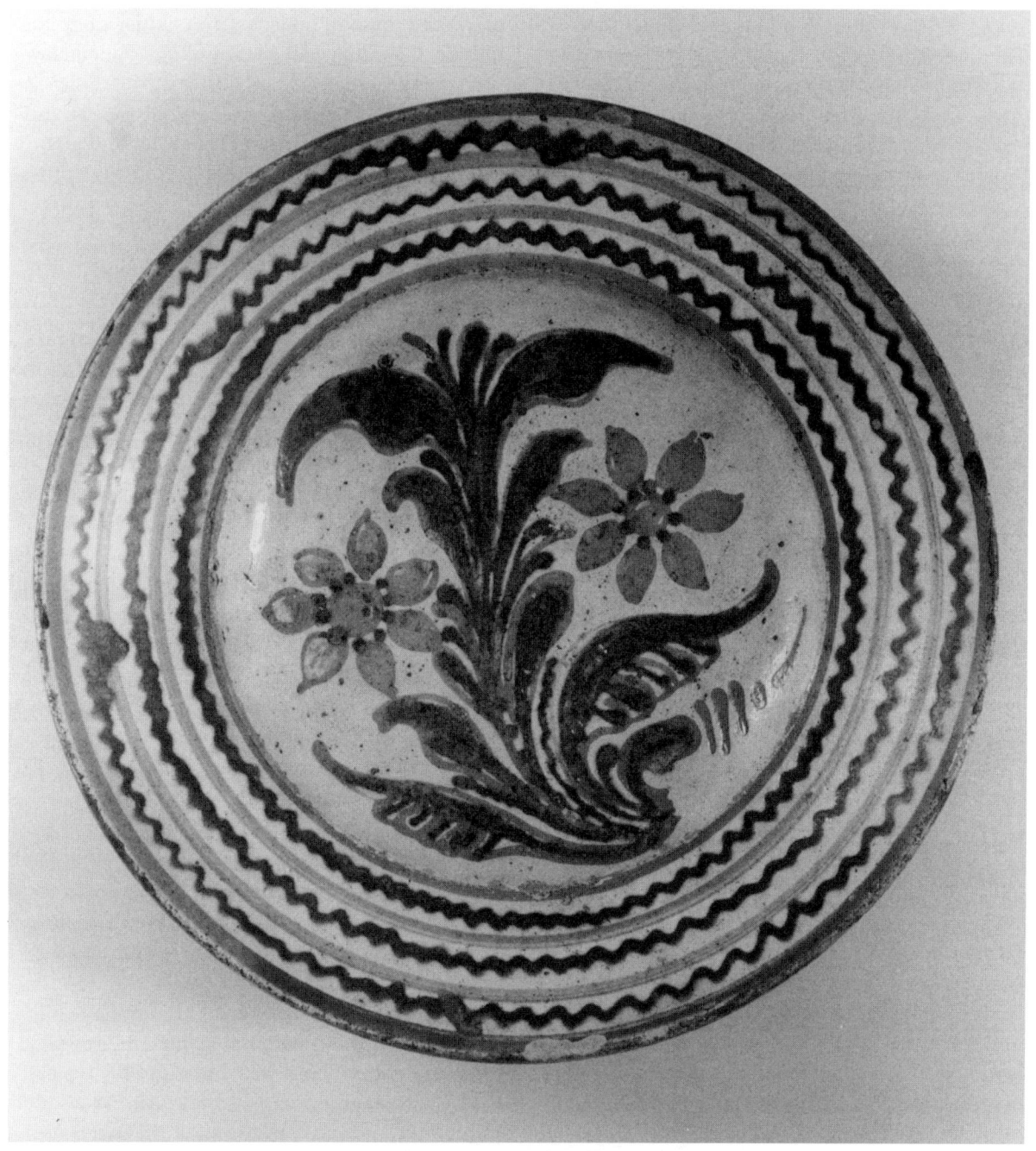

1.6 Lead-glazed slip-decorated earthenware plate, second half of the
eighteenth century, attributed to Gottfried Aust, Forsyth County, Salem,
N.C. H 2⅞″, C 45″. Copper oxide (green) and iron (red) slip over a white
engobe. Mark: ᴏᴍ (at base). Courtesy of the Museum of Early Southern
Decorative Arts, Winston-Salem, N.C., with thanks to Brad Rauschenberg.

tery scholar William Ketchum has noted that "the Remmey and Crolius families always seemed to have their shops at the same or adjacent locations. Thus, the first directory reference to these craftsmen, in 1789, lists 'John Crolius stone potter Augustus Street N. the Powder House' and 'John Remmey—stoneware manufacturer—Augustus Street.'" Ketchum concludes that Crolius and Remmey occupied one of the potteries shown on Grim's map and that the other kiln was operated by earthenware potter John Campbell. The Remmey family continued to produce stoneware in New York until 1831, and the Crolius pottery dynasty survived until 1850.[44]

Clay from New Jersey was transported to New England in the early nineteenth century for use in the pottery shops of the North. Good stoneware clays were also discovered in the Ohio Valley and Middle West. By the nineteenth century "blue and gray" stoneware was being produced throughout the Northeast. Salt-glazed stoneware gradually began to replace earthenware for food storage and preservation, although some potters continued to make the coarse earthenware pottery for local use.

The Emergence of the Southern Alkaline-Glazed Stoneware Tradition

During the same period in the lower South, where salt was a more valuable commodity, potters developed alkaline-glazed stoneware. Alkaline glaze was relatively inexpensive because it was composed of all local ingredients. Based upon Bordley's basic formula of wood ash and sand, the alkaline glaze included a much greater variation of ingredients than the salt glaze. The alkaline substance, in the form of wood ash or lime, acted as a flux and thus lowered the melting point of the glaze. An added silica source such as

clay, sand, quartz, feldspar, iron cinders, or glass produced a glassy glaze texture, and added clay served as a binder.

Aside from these two basic glaze types, an infinite degree of variation in glaze color and texture may be found among alkaline-glazed ware produced in various regions of the South, in different pottery centers, and even by one potter or family. A number of factors determined the glaze color and texture. The presence of certain minerals in the clay body and glaze ingredients, the temperature at which the ware was fired, and the presence or absence of oxygen in the kiln during the firing process all influenced the final appearance of the glaze. The main determinant of glaze color is the amount of iron present in the clay body and glaze mixture. Some body clay is usually added to the glaze to make it adhere more readily to the raw pot during the shrinkage that takes place during drying and firing. White clays having little or no iron produce light straw or greenish (celadon) colors. If the body clay is dark and fires to a ruddy red or deep gray, the clay naturally contains a greater amount of iron. The glaze mixture, incorporating some of the same body clay, will have a deeper color. Iron was sometimes added by the potter to darken the color of the glaze. Coloring agents were usually made from natural ochres, such as limonite, hematite, or "iron sand." The addition of coloring agents was a popular practice in Georgia and South Carolina throughout the nineteenth century and into the twentieth.[45]

The firing range varied not only from one kiln load to the next but within a single kiln as well, given the uneven heat distribution of the typical southern rectangular crossdraft kilns. For example, ware placed closer to the firebox received a much greater amount of heat than that placed at the far end of the kiln. In some extreme cases a pot was fully matured or overfired on one side and underfired on the other. Underfired ware tends to have a rough and opaque glaze because the glaze has not fully matured, whereas a patchy, uneven texture with clouds or streaks may be indicative of overfiring.

Alkaline glaze was first developed by the Chinese during the Han dynasty (206 B.C.–A.D. 220). The gray-green or brown ash glazes were used on the stoneware that had been developed two or three centuries earlier. These "protoporcelains" are almost identical to the alkaline-glazed stoneware of the southern United States in body and glaze composition. When fired in a reducing atmosphere, the glazes, composed mainly of wood ash and clay, produced light green to olive colors. A darker brown color resulted from an oxidized or partially reduced kiln atmosphere and a high percentage of iron in the glaze materials. The Chinese potters greatly refined their alkaline glazes and later used them on both stoneware and porcelain.

Although the Chinese alkaline glazes are similar to those developed by southern stoneware potters, there is no direct European connection that would explain how the glaze came to be used in the South. Several intriguing possibilities have been suggested, however, as to how southern folk potters first learned of the alkaline glaze and came to use it in stoneware production.

American ceramics scholar Georgeanna Greer has suggested an indirect connection with the Orient via England through eighteenth-century potters who sought to duplicate the Chinese porcelain. William Cookworthy, a Quaker druggist who produced "the first true hard paste porcelain manufactured in England," had read the letters of Pere d'Entrecolles, published in England and France during the 1730s, which included a detailed description of the Chinese methods of porcelain manufacture. Cookworthy had by 1758 perfected a glaze made "from the ground moorstone [feldspathic rock] with some of the china earth [kaolin], some lime and fern

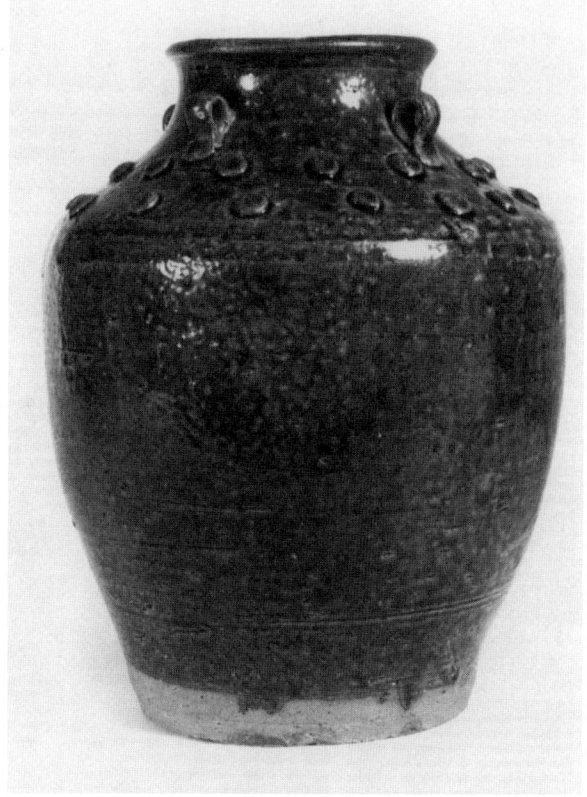

1.7 Alkaline-glazed stoneware jar, ca. 1700, China, Ming Dynasty. H 8¾″, C 22⅛″. Collection of John A. Burrison.

ash," thereby introducing to England the use of plant ash and lime as a flux for high temperature ware.[46]

Cookworthy's partner, Richard Champion, who came to South Carolina in 1784, may have communicated his knowledge of the glaze to potters in the Camden area. It is unlikely, however, that Champion actually introduced the alkaline glaze to South Carolina, since there is no evidence that he ever produced pottery in America.

Folklorist John Burrison has suggested a more direct approach to the alkaline-glaze question. Burrison contends that, like the English porcelain manufacturers, one of the early southern potters may have read the d'Entrecolles letters

1.8 Issue of the *South Carolina Gazette* in which excerpts from Jean-Baptiste du Halde's book *The General History of China* were published. Potters in South Carolina may have learned of the alkaline glaze by reading passages from the book describing the operation of Chinese porcelain factories. Courtesy of the Charleston Library Society, Charleston, S.C.

in his search for improvements in local pottery manufacture. "Key figures in such a process may well have been potting members of the Landrum family, which by 1773 had moved, by way of Virginia and North Carolina, into the Edgefield District of western South Carolina."[47] Abner Landrum, an Edgefield physician, newspaper publisher, land speculator, and founder of the Pottersville Stoneware Manufactory, seems to be the most likely candidate for the introduction of the alkaline glaze to the South. Landrum was a well-educated, highly successful businessman and a member of the South Carolina elite.[48]

In support of this theory, John Michael Vlach

has noted that during the late eighteenth and early nineteenth centuries the Chinese import trade prompted a certain preoccupation with oriental goods on the part of the South Carolina elite. This trend, known as chinoiserie or "Chinese taste," according to Vlach, "was manifested initially in furniture. Eventually it was seen also in silver, wallpaper, textiles and garden and house design."[49] Passages from Jean-Baptiste du Halde's *The General History of China*, in which the d'Entrecolles letters appeared, were published in the *South Carolina Gazette* as early as 1744, and by 1777 this book was the standard reference on Chinese customs. Abner Landrum probably had read du Halde and may well have had a copy of the work in his personal library. Landrumsville or Pottersville, a community founded by Abner Landrum, was the focal point of pottery activity in the Edgefield District during the first quarter of the nineteenth century. In 1826 Robert Mills described Pottersville as a "village altogether supported by the manufacture of stoneware, carried on by this gentleman [Abner Landrum]; and which by his discoveries is made much stronger, better, and cheaper than any European or American ware of the same kind."[50] Furthermore, Landrum named three of his sons—Wedgwood, Palissey, and Manises—after important names in Old World pottery. Archaeological investigations suggest that Abner Landrum and his brother, John Landrum, carried out early experiments with the clays in the Edgefield area.[51]

High-fired, unglazed sherds recovered from the John Landrum pottery site seem to indicate the use of a two-stage firing process for some ware. Greer suggests three possibilities as to the nature of this experimentation. Japanese potters use a two-step firing process on porcelain, an initial high bisque firing and a second glaze firing. Perhaps a potter at the John Landrum site, for example Abner or John Landrum, followed this practice in an effort to produce porcelain. On the other hand, the Landrums may have been earthenware potters in North Carolina before migrating to Edgefield. They may have been attempting to produce stoneware using high-grade earthenware techniques, that is, an initial bisque firing and a second glaze firing. Finally, it is possible that another potter worked at the site before the Landrums. Given the possibility that the unglazed sherds found at the site represented the work of an early potter, it could be feasible to presume that this potter was attempting to produce stoneware or porcelain.

Evidence of Abner Landrum's interest in and knowledge of porcelain manufacture is found in a petition that he made to the state legislature in 1846 for funding to establish a porcelain factory. Landrum had sold his Pottersville factory in

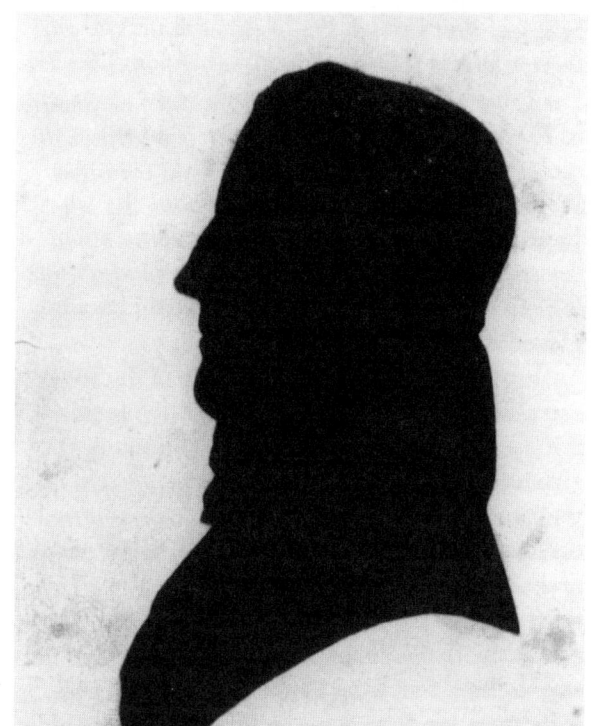

1.9 Silhouette of Abner Landrum, Edgefield newspaper editor, land speculator, and founder of the village of Pottersville. Landrum is credited with the development of alkaline-glazed stoneware in Edgefield. Courtesy of Maria Stork.

1828. Conflicts that he had encountered in Edge-field because of his political views as a Unionist prompted a move to Columbia, South Carolina. In the "sandhills" north of Columbia Landrum established a new pottery. Also in Columbia, Landrum served as editor of an antinullification newspaper, the *Columbia Free Press and Hive,* and as state printer. In his petition to the legisla-ture Landrum stated that "the difficulty attending this [porcelain] manufacture and the importance attached to it as a public concern in France may be inferred from the fact that three distinguished chemists, Lauraquis, Darcet and Legay were engaged for four years . . . in that country before they succeeded in procuring a good Porcelain and there it was not till the Government offered to several pottery makers improvement of their business that French Porcelain attained the per-fection that it has acquired in other countries."[52] Landrum's familiarity with current developments in French porcelain manufacture is a further in-dication of his detailed knowledge of ceramics production. This information supports the sup-position that Landrum, through reading about the techniques of Chinese porcelain production, independently developed the Edgefield alkaline-glazed stoneware.

Another important manifestation of the south-ern alkaline-glazed stoneware tradition involved the use of the "groundhog" kiln. The southern groundhog kiln may be an American version of the English Newcastle kiln, a rectangular struc-ture ranging from eleven to thirty-five feet long and eight to twelve feet high, with an arched roof, a fireplace at the front, and a doorway and chim-ney at the opposite end. A flash wall, constructed two to three feet from the front, protected the ware from the flames of the firebox and provided for better heat distribution. The Newcastle kiln and its German counterpart, the Cassel kiln, were used by European potters for brick production (Figure 1.10). A forerunner of the Newcastle kiln was used for tin-glazed earthenware produc-

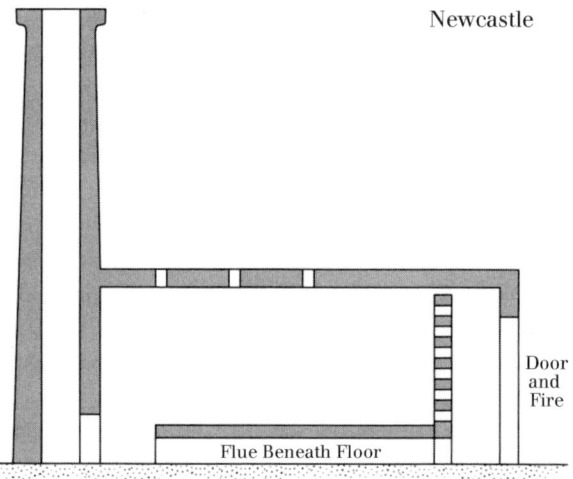

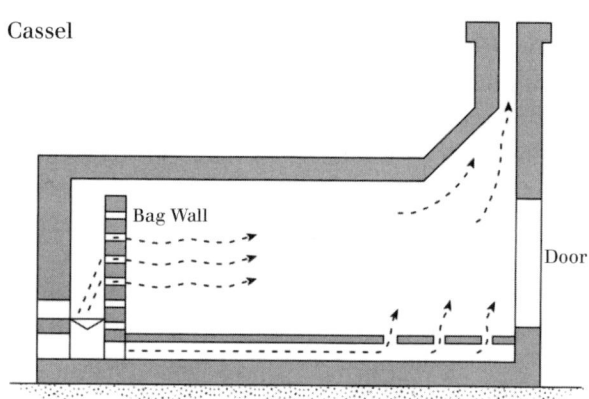

1.10   The Newcastle and Cassel kilns. From Rhodes, *Kilns,* 44–45.

tion at London and Bristol in the seventeenth and eighteenth centuries. By the mid-nineteenth century the Newcastle kiln was being used in northern England for stoneware production.

The groundhog kiln, with its simple design, is easily constructed, and the low horizontal shape is well adapted to the setting or placement of utilitarian stoneware (Figure 1.11).[53] Variations in temperature from the front to the back of the kiln resulting from the placement of the heat source at one end meant that the potter had lim-ited control during firing. Folk potters turned this problem to their advantage by developing a system of positioning ware in the kiln according to size and the melting point of the glazes. For example, the general practice in the Catawba Valley of North Carolina was to set harder cinder-glazed ware near the firebox, glass-glazed ware above, and unglazed earthenware above these, further from the firebox and thus in the coolest areas of the kiln.[54] The position of the firebox could discolor the ware placed near the front of the kiln or produce deposits of fly ash on the surface of the ware. The presence or absence of oxygen in the kiln during the firing process was another factor that affected the glaze color. These imperfections in the glazes, and the various patternings and textures of the ware surfaces that resulted from their placement and the firing conditions within the kiln, are characteristics of alkaline-glazed stoneware that enhance the appeal of this unique folk pottery.

Other equipment employed by alkaline-glazed stoneware potters included the pug mill or "mud mill" used to grind or process the clay prior to "turning"; the glaze mill or querne for processing the alkaline glaze; and the treadle wheel, or "kick wheel," on which the pottery vessels were fashioned. The pug mill consisted of a barrel or tub with a set of blades, or pegs, projecting from an axle. As a mule or waterwheel rotated the axle, the turning "pins" ground the raw clay into fine particles, removing air bubbles and bringing the clay to the proper consistency for turning. The hand-operated glaze mill consisted of a large base stone with a concave upper surface into which a smaller disk-shaped "runner" rested. The glaze, poured into a hole in the runner, was ground between the two stone faces as the mill was rotated. The treadle wheel consisted of a low horizontal bar linked to a vertical crankshaft that the potter peddled with a back and forth motion as he stood or leaned against a support. A heavy flywheel at the bottom of the shaft provided momentum, while the clay was shaped on a smaller turning wheel, or "headblock," connected at the top. A

wooden "crib" enclosed the headblock and supported the ball opener and the height gauge. The ball opener, a hinged wooden lever related to the "jolly" or "jigger" arm used in the factories of the North, was used to open the clay ball and to gauge the vessel base to the proper thickness to avoid cracking. The height gauge, an adjustable pointer clamped between two vertical sticks, could be positioned horizontally to set the height for different volumes of ware, thereby maintaining uniformity of size. With these basic tools the folk potter produced a standard range of stoneware forms.[55]

The actual process of "turning" or throwing is impossible to describe adequately in words due to the hidden complexities and individualized nature of the art. Also, techniques of production vary according to the type and size of the vessel being produced. Most pots, however, were created from a basic cylinder and involved a set of fairly standardized procedures. First, the potter weighed out the proper amount of clay according to the size of the vessel that he wanted to produce. He used a given number of pounds of clay per gallon capacity of the pot to be turned. Next, he wedged and kneaded the clay on a wedging bench. He cut the clay in half on a wire suspended at an angle from the front of the wedging bench to the wall of the shop and then slammed the two pieces together. This process was repeated several times before working or kneading the clay on the bench. When the clay reached the proper consistency for turning, the potter formed it into a ball by slapping it down and rotating it on the bench. Now the clay was ready to be turned.

The first task of turning involved centering the clay ball on the wheel. Once the ball was centered, the potter opened the top of the ball and pulled up a rough cylinder. Churns and storage jars were usually turned in two or three parts, whereas large-capacity vessels such as the storage jars by slave potter Dave of the Edgefield District were thrown and then gradually built up through

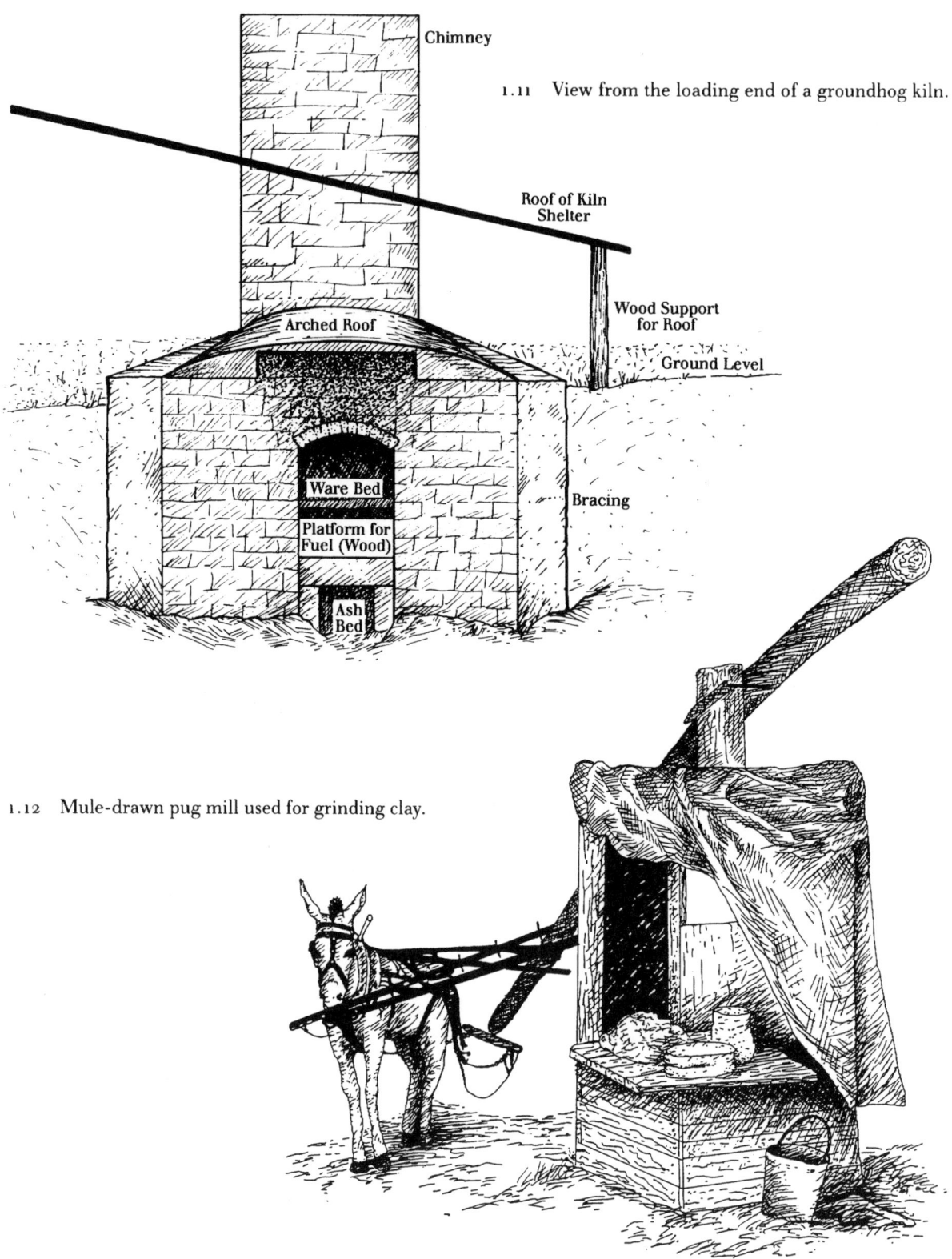

Chimney

1.11   View from the loading end of a groundhog kiln.

Roof of Kiln
Shelter

Arched Roof

Wood Support
for Roof

Ground Level

Ware Bed

Bracing

Platform for
Fuel (Wood)

Ash
Bed

1.12   Mule-drawn pug mill used for grinding clay.

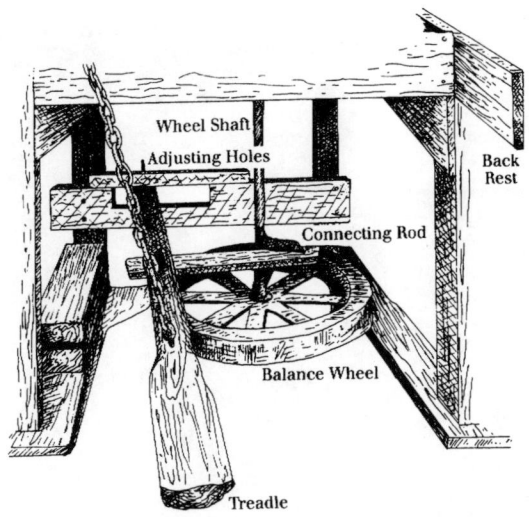

Wheel Shaft

Adjusting Holes

Back Rest

Connecting Rod

Balance Wheel

Treadle

1.13 Treadle wheel.

the use of coils. Once the clay had been pulled up, if he intended to turn the vessel in two parts, the potter sliced off a "cap" and set it aside. Next, he lowered the "ball-opener" until it rested on the splashboard. Then, steadying the clay with one hand while pushing the arm out, he opened the cylinder to the proper diameter and formed a bottom of uniform thickness. He then pulled up the walls of the jar and trimmed the vessel with a rectangular-shaped rib or "chip." At this point, if he was turning the vessel in two parts, the potter formed a wide rim with his chip and placed the unfinished cap on top of it. Then, slowly rotating the wheel, he joined the two units together. If he was fashioning a large-capacity jar he gradually added coils of clay to the rim, slowly turning the wheel as he smoothed the coils into place. Potters who turned tall, large-capacity vessels sometimes had an assistant operate the wheel while they finished the upper portion of the jar. This may have been the procedure followed for a pair of forty-gallon jars signed by Edgefield District slave potters Dave and Baddler. Once the jar was completed the potter used his chip to trim the upper portion and adjusted the height to conform with the height gauge.

Next, he added the handles that he had pulled from a lump of moist clay. There were two basic types of handles: horizontally applied ear or lug handles for jars and bowls, and vertical strap handles for jugs and pitchers. Edgefield District potters also used strap handles on small preserve jars and stew pots. Another variation used by upcountry South Carolina potters was that of applying a single strap handle and an opposing lug handle to churns. Most early Edgefield District potters used strap handles that were rounded in cross section. One exception to this rule was Edgefield potter Thomas Chandler. Chandler used a thinner, ribbed handle that is roughly rectangular in cross section.

The potter's final task was to mark the pot. South Carolina potters used a variety of marks on their ware. These identified the maker, factory, date of manufacture, and gallon capacity. The practice of marking ware dates to as early as the second decade of the nineteenth century. North Carolina folk pottery scholar Charles ("Terry") Zug III notes that "the most obvious motive [for marking ware] is advertising. Because of the dense concentrations of potters, ware was often wagoned long distances to find a market. Thus, future orders for a sturdy, reliable product might depend on the buyer or middleman recalling that stamped name or initials."[56] Some potters, such as Thomas Chandler of the Edgefield District and Robert Boyle of Cherokee County, used the maker's mark as a type of warranty. Chandler actually marked his ware "Warranted" and advertised in the local newspaper that he would "warrant" his ware to be good. Boyle also guaranteed his ware, making a practice of replacing free of charge any defective pot bearing his initials.

Stoneware has been called the typical pottery of the South.[57] Similarly, alkaline-glazed stoneware is a distinctive regional type produced only in the lower South. North Carolina and eastern Tennessee are for all practical purposes the dividing line between salt-glazed and alkaline-glazed

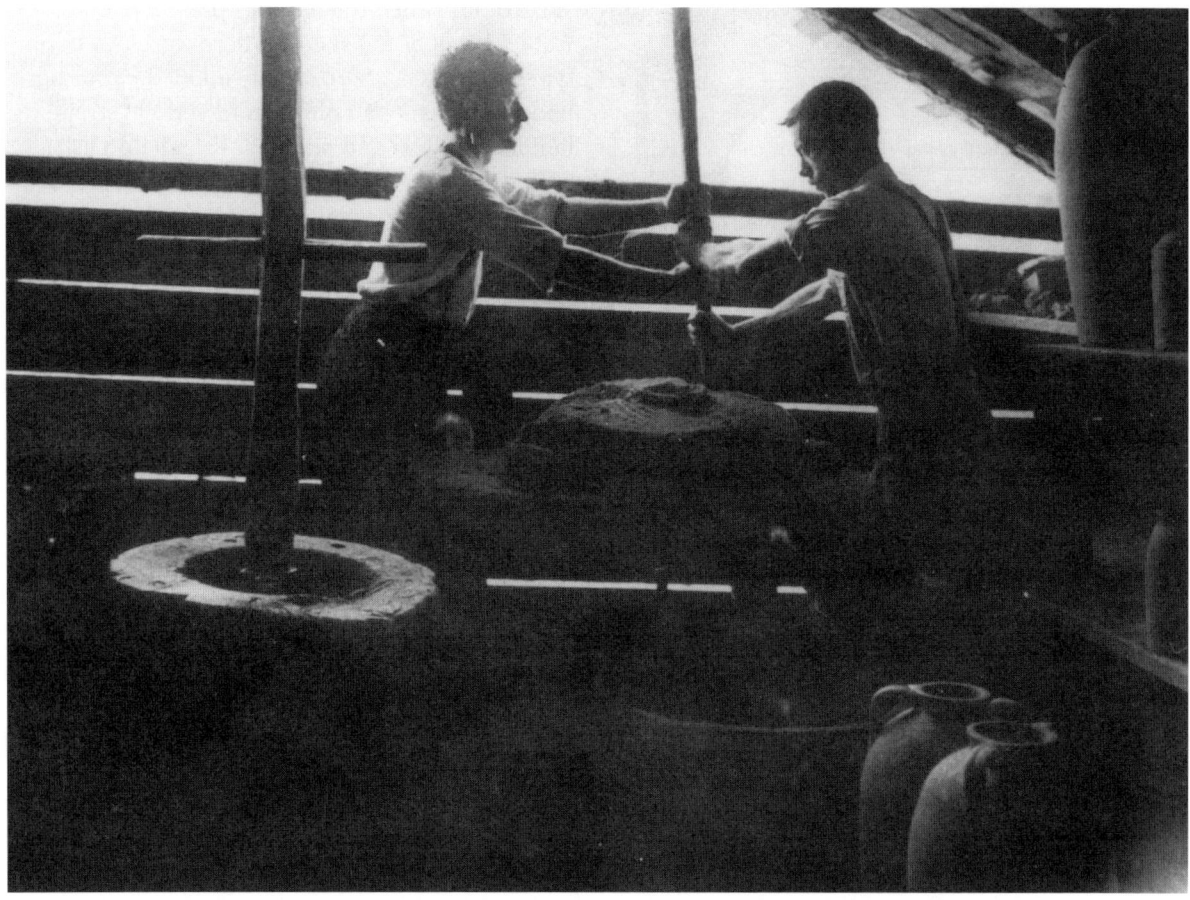

1.14   Two South Carolina potters grinding glaze in a stone mill. A maul suspended from
a springpole at left was used to pulverize glass for the glaze. Photograph by Margaret W. Morley,
courtesy of the North Carolina Division of Archives and History, Raleigh, N.C.

stoneware production in the southeast. Potters in southern ports such as Mobile, Alabama, as well as potters in the upland South, used the salt glaze.[58] The southern salt-glaze tradition in North Carolina, Virginia, Tennessee, Alabama, and Mississippi exhibits major changes from the northern tradition in technology, vessel form, and use of decoration.

The Edgefield District of South Carolina was the cultural hearth of the alkaline-glazed stoneware tradition. Potters of English descent arrived in South Carolina during the latter part of the eighteenth century via the Great Philadelphia Wagon Road, moving southward through Pennsylvania, Maryland, Virginia, and North Carolina. By the early 1800s the descendants of these first generation South Carolina potters had developed a new type of stoneware made from local ingredients and designed for the needs of the local populace. The following chapter chronicles the development of the alkaline-glazed stoneware tradition in South Carolina and the impact of this tradition upon stoneware production throughout the lower South.

CHAPTER TWO

The Edgefield District Stoneware Factories: Origins of a Regional Folk Pottery Tradition

The old Edgefield District of South Carolina was situated between two distinct geological regions, the Piedmont Plateau, or upcountry, and the Sandhills, or lowcountry, a band of rolling hills separating the Piedmont from the lower Coastal Plain.[1] Located in west-central South Carolina, the Edgefield District was bound by Georgia and the Savannah River to the west, and Abbeville District to the north. To the east, separated by the Saluda River, Edgefield was bound by Newberry District. To the south lay Barnwell, Orangeburg, and Lexington districts.

The upcountry, encompassing the Piedmont region of the state, was characterized by heavy red clay soils, lower temperatures, and a shorter growing season because of its proximity to the Blue Ridge Mountains, while the lowcountry, comprising the tidewater and sandhills areas of the state, was identified with the southern plantation aristocracy. Although the Edgefield District was considered part of the upcountry, the sandhills usually associated with the lowcountry extended into the lower part of the district. Historian Vernon Burton has observed that "since the aristocratic elements of the state imputed unattractive connotations to the designation 'upcountry,' many in Edgefield preferred to call part of the district the 'midlands,' identifying 'cultur-

ally' with districts like Camden and Cheraw and the state capital, Columbia."[2]

The inclusion of the district within the geological boundary (known as the Fall Line) between the Piedmont or upcountry and the Coastal Plain or lowcountry created a unique geographical situation in the area. The Fall Line is named for the falls and rapids that form where the more resistant crystalline rock of the Piedmont converges upon the more easily erodible sedimentary limestone of the Coastal Plain. Edgefield potters often established stoneware factories on the banks of these streams and creeks where stoneware clay deposits were exposed by the erosional forces of the water. Essential products used in the production of stoneware—clay, wood, and water—were available in abundance in these riverine areas.

The Savannah River was the most important waterway in the area and provided access to commercial networks throughout the region. Hamburg (present-day North Augusta), on the South Carolina side of the river, was the major port in the Edgefield District. The Sapona River, including Steven's Creek and Hard Labor Creek, in the western part of the district, was a rapid stream that entered the Savannah eight miles above Hamburg after joining the waters of the Seeraw, or Cuffietown Creek, in the northwest section of the district. Turkey Creek flowed northwest into Stephen's Creek after receiving Little Steven's, Mountain, and Log creeks northeast of the town of Edgefield and Beaverdam Creek to the north. The Seerhanna, or Horn's Creek, which flowed into Steven's Creek west of Edgefield, was the only waterway in the district other than the Savannah that held potential for navigation. Other small principle streams in the district included Wilson's, Henley's, Little Saluda, and Rocky creeks, which flowed into the Saluda River to the east; Shaw's Creek, joining with the Edisto to the south; and Cussaboe or Horse Creek, which flowed westward into the Savannah.[3] Potteries were established near Beaverdam, Log, and Mountain creeks, on a tributary of Horse Creek, and on the banks of Shaw's Creek.

Edgefield County was first formed in 1785 out of the Ninety Six District by an act of the General Assembly. The Edgefield District was formed from the original Edgefield County. Edgefield was an operative judicial district from about 1800 to 1868 and included present-day Edgefield and parts of Aiken, Saluda, McCormick, and Greenwood counties. This period roughly coincides with the early developmental and peak periods of stoneware production in the area. Consequently, the most active phase of the alkaline-glazed stoneware tradition in South Carolina has come to be identified with the Edgefield District.[4]

The first Europeans to settle in the Edgefield area were Indian traders, who were active in the region beginning in the seventeenth century. Most of this territory had been in the possession of the Cherokee Indians, and the southern part, lying along the Savannah River, was used by other groups, such as the Creeks, as hunting grounds. Continual conflicts with these aboriginal groups discouraged permanent settlement in the region during the first half of the eighteenth century. The Yemassee War prompted the colonial South Carolina Assembly in 1717 to construct four key forts: Fort Moore (near present-day Augusta, Georgia); Congaree Fort (near the juncture of

Congaree Creek and Congaree River); Palachacolas Fort (on the Savannah River); and Beaufort Fort (on Port Royal Sound). Fort Moore provided a measure of protection to the newly founded settlements in the Savannah River area. However, the Indian conflicts had caused much of the English frontier to be evacuated and depopulated, and concern about neighboring Indians persisted.

New Windsor was formed in 1735 by the Carolina colony as part of the Township Plan, formulated to encourage settlement of the backcountry regions. Through the Township Plan eight tracts of approximately twenty thousand acres each were established at points along the major rivers through the interior, on the Waccamaw River (Kingston), Pee Dee River (Queensborough), Black River (Williamsburg), Wateree River (Fredericksburg), Saluda River (Saxe Gotha), Congaree River (Amelia), Edisto River (Orangeburg), and Savannah (New Windsor).[5] The first permanent settlement in the Edgefield area occurred at New Windsor in approximately 1748, but this thinly settled township did not thrive, perhaps because of its close proximity to Augusta. Historian David Ramsay wrote that as late as "the year 1755 the country from the Waxhaws on the Catawba across to Augusta on the Savannah River did not contain twenty-five families." [6]

From 1756 to 1766 a great wave of immigration occurred into the region (see Figure 2.1). Immigrants included English, Scots-Irish, Welsh, German, Dutch, and French, with the English-speaking settlers being predominant. The major route followed by these settlers was along the Great Philadelphia Wagon Road that extended from Pennsylvania through Maryland and into Virginia, North Carolina, and South Carolina. These people who moved westward into the frontier of Pennsylvania and southward into the Shenandoah Valley of Virginia became the pioneers and frontiersmen who settled the back-

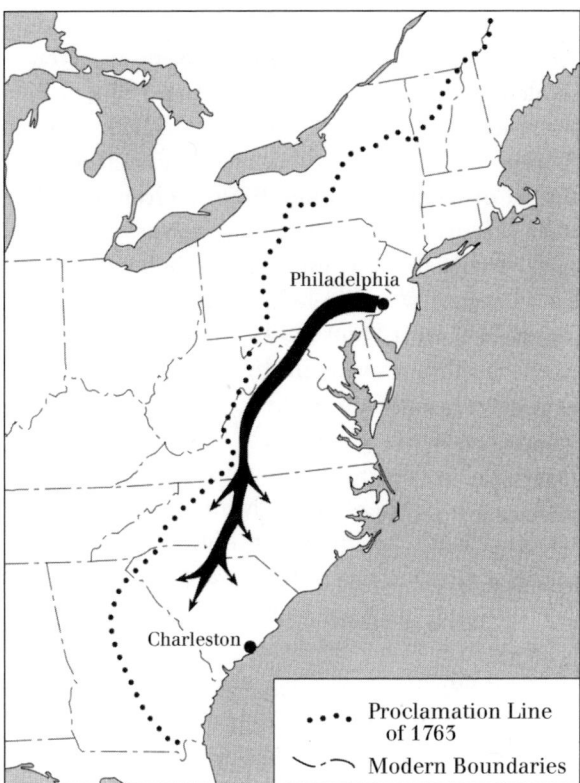

2.1 Map of the eastern United States illustrating the migration route followed by Scots-Irish immigrants who settled in South Carolina during the mid-eighteenth century.

District as "cotton, grain of every description, and wool."[9] Corn, rice, indigo, tobacco, cotton, and sweet potatoes were grown on the plantations and farms of the area. In 1850 the value of produce from Edgefield market gardens was ranked the third highest in the state, and Edgefield led the state in the value of homemade manufactures, an index of self-sufficiency.[10] The cultivation of cotton became increasingly important after the 1840s. South Carolina historian Lewis P. Jones summed up the transition from diversified farming enterprises to large-scale plantation agriculture: "With the spread of cotton, frontier entrepreneurs could gradually move from small operations to large plantations by the acquisition of more red land and more black labor to make more white cotton—and soon there was a new gentry of 'cotton aristocrats' who had had most unaristocratic grandpas."[11]

The expansion of the plantation system in upcountry South Carolina attracted planters from the southern part of the state to the area. An announcement of the sale of lots in Edgefield that appeared in the *Carolina Gazette* in September 1800 was aimed at South Carolina lowcountry planters intent on expanding their agricultural enterprises.

WILL BE SOLD

On TUESDAY, the 28th of October next, being the second day of the District Court of Edgefield, at that place,

A number of LOTS of LAND,

In that Village: a plan of which will be exhibited, and the conditions made known, on the day of sale.

The situation is high, pleasant and healthy, with several springs of most excellent water; twenty-three miles north of Augusta. This place will afford a very pleasant and safe retreat from the low country, in the warm and sickly season.

Arthur Simkins [justice of the peace].[12]

Edgefield was the most important town in the district, having been made the county seat in 1791 and incorporated in 1830. Referred to as Edge-

country of colonial America.[7] Consequently, as Robert Mills noted in 1826, unlike other areas of the state "Edgefield was settled principally, and indeed almost altogether, by emigrants from Virginia and North Carolina."[8]

Throughout the eighteenth and nineteenth centuries the Edgefield District was predominantly rural in character. Agriculture was a diversified activity in the upcountry during the first half of the nineteenth century. Cotton did not become a major cash crop in the region until the invention of the cotton gin by Eli Whitney in 1793. In his textbook *A Geography of South Carolina*, published in 1832, Thomas P. Lockwood listed the agricultural products of the Edgefield

field Village, Edgefield Court House, or simply "the Court House," Edgefield was the political, judicial, and social hub of the area. Lockwood noted that Edgefield "stands on elevated ground affording from the south a very beautiful prospect" and that "its houses are neat and spacious [and] with the usual public buildings it contains a very handsome meeting-house, and one printing office [probably the office of the *Edgefield Hive* newspaper]." This community, with a population of four hundred, had a library, an Agricultural Society, and several good schools, including the Baptist Theological Seminary. Lockwood added that "within one mile of Edgefield is Landrum's Pottery, forming a village of about 150 inhabitants. . . . There is another similar Pottery on the Cussaboe [Horse] Creek. Here is also a large Cotton Factory for coarse fabrics on a large scale."[13] The village of "Landrum's Pottery," also known as Pottersville or Landrumsville, was established by Abner Landrum. Although another contemporary, Robert Mills, described Pottersville as "altogether supported by the manufacture of stoneware," the village apparently supported a variety of tradesmen, including blacksmiths, coach makers, wagon drivers, millers, and wheelwrights.[14] Pottersville was the first large-scale stoneware operation established in the Edgefield District. John Landrum, Abner Landrum's brother, operated the pottery and cotton factory located on the Cussaboe (later known as Horse Creek). Abner and John Landrum and a third brother, Amos, were pioneers of stoneware production in Edgefield.

The communities of Hamburg and Augusta became major commercial centers due to their strategic location on the Savannah River. Augusta was the central cotton market for upper South Carolina and Georgia. With a population of 12,493 in 1860, Augusta was the only urban center in the area around Edgefield County during most of the nineteenth century.[15] In the 1830s and 1840s Hamburg (present-day North Augusta), located on the east bank of the Savannah River, rivaled Augusta in the marketing of cotton and the distribution of trade from the upstate regions. Charleston merchants financed the construction of the South Carolina Railroad from Charleston to Hamburg in order to take advantage of the highly profitable Savannah River valley trade, and a twenty-six-mile-long plank road from Edgefield Court House to Hamburg was built to handle traffic from the north.[16] Although most of the pottery produced in the Edgefield area was transported by wagon and sold to planters and merchants in nearby communities, some stoneware manufacturers took advantage of the South Carolina Railroad, the longest in the world at the time, for distribution of their ware to wider markets throughout South Carolina and into eastern Georgia.

The following newspaper advertisement, which appeared in the *Edgefield Hive* in March 1830, foretold the impact that the railroad was to have on the fledgling pottery industry in the area.

There has been left with us a Porcelain Milk Pot, manufactured in Philadelphia, from a specimen of white clay, from the Chalk Hills, as they are called, in Edgefield District in this state. We understand that the supply of this clay is inexhaustible. As the Rail Road is expected to pass immediately through these lands, this clay may one day become an article of inconsiderable value to the proprietors of the soil, as well as of profit to the Rail Road Company.[17]

The introduction of the railroads prompted the creation of towns all along the lines (see Figure 2.2). For example, the antebellum town of Aiken, located seventeen miles from Hamburg, began as a railroad station on the line between the Barnwell and Edgefield districts. During the 1830s and 1840s Aiken prospered and became a small marketplace, and in the latter part of the century it became a nationally famous resort

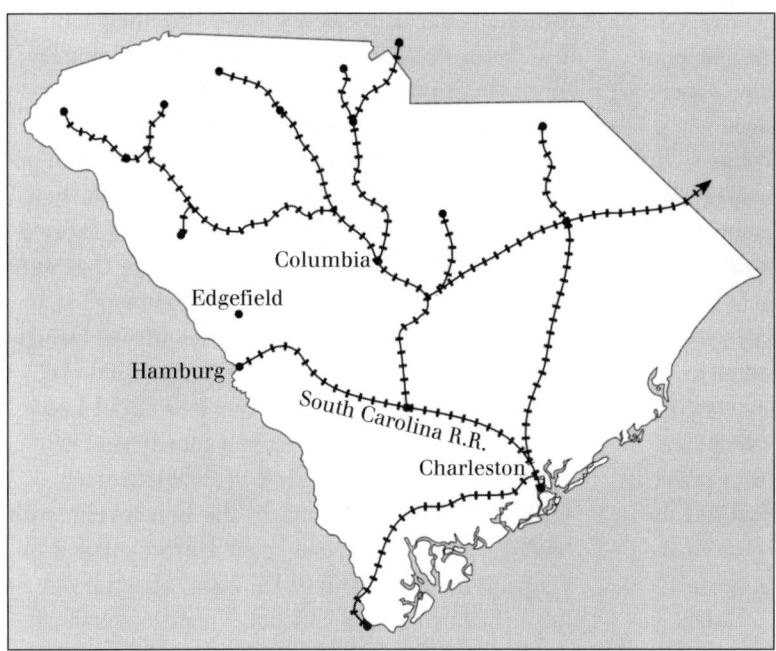

2.2 Map of South Carolina showing the location of railroads in 1860. Edgefield District stoneware manufacturers shipped their ware by rail throughout the state and into Georgia.

town, providing a haven for prosperous northerners during the winter months. At least one early stoneware pottery was established within the present city limits of Aiken near the original railroad line.

Pottery factories were established in other Edgefield-area towns that emerged during Reconstruction. Ware produced at a stoneware factory operated by John Seigler and located in the Shaw's Creek community in present-day northern Aiken County is stamped J.W.S. & CO. / PINE HOUSE / SC, and ware produced at the same factory by John Seigler's son is stamped G.P. SEIGLER / TRENTON / S.C. The Pine House, an area landmark dating from the Revolutionary War, was located on the Edgefield-Aiken wagon road. The village of Trenton, located seven miles south of Edgefield and twenty-six miles from Augusta and Hamburg, grew up around the Pine House due to its proximity along the Charlotte-Columbia-Augusta Railroad line. In 1870 the name of the

earlier post office at Pine House was changed to Trenton. Therefore, ware produced at the Seigler pottery and marked PINE HOUSE was evidently made before 1870, while ware from the factory marked TRENTON dates from the last quarter of the nineteenth century.[18]

The 1860 Edgefield census listed seventy-four "factories," including a paper mill at Bath and two cotton textile plants at Graniteville and Vaucluse. Located about twenty and twenty-five miles from Hamburg and Augusta along Horse Creek, these textile factories were two of the oldest and most successful in the South. Vaucluse, mentioned in Lockwood's 1832 geography of South Carolina, was the older of the two; Graniteville, established in 1849, was operated by William Gregg, one of the South's most celebrated industrialists. With a total of 399 male and female workers, these two textile factories employed nearly half of the total laborers in the state engaged in textile production. Another important industry, lumber saw-milling, with twenty-six businesses, employed 113 men and one woman in 1860. Most Edgefield District factories were smaller businesses with few employees.

Edgefield also contained two gold mines that produced small quantities of ore. When he died in 1891, Dr. John Landrum, son of stoneware factory owner Rev. John Landrum, owned the property on which one of these mines was located. Landrum had inherited the property from his father-in-law, James Smyley. Referred to in his will as the "gold mine tract," the property consisted of about forty-one acres, according to a survey made in 1876, and was located in present-day Edgefield County. Dr. Landrum willed the "gold mine tract" and the mineral rights to the gold located on the property to his daughters, Marian Kate Mims and A. Pamela Holland. According to Mrs. Matthew Hansford Mims, whose husband is a descendant of Marian Kate Mims, the mine was worked by slaves. Since the gold recovered from the mine was in powder form, a time-consuming water processing procedure was necessary in order to extract it. After the Civil War, when slaves were no longer available to carry out this labor-intensive process, the mine became unprofitable. Another Edgefield District gold mine, the Dorn mine, located in present-day McCormick County, was owned by Cyrus McCormick.[19]

Early Edgefield Stoneware Factories

Throughout the South kinship played a key role in the establishment and continuation of the stoneware tradition. Patterns of obligation, social bonding, and business association were reinforced through kinship relations. In Edgefield, kinship and intermarriage among families often strengthened more formal business partnerships. The transfer of the skills and knowledge of the pottery craft from one generation to the next was primarily accomplished within extended families. Sons often worked in their fathers' pottery shops beginning at an early age, and in many instances men who married the daughters of stoneware factory owners became involved in pottery production through associations with their fathers-in-law. Families of potters often formed alliances through ancestry or marriage that were maintained through several generations.[20]

In the Edgefield District the Landrum family was the most important of these so-called clay clans or pottery dynasties. The Edgefield Landrums were descended from a family that is believed to have emigrated to America from Aberdeenshire, Scotland, in the late seventeenth century. John Landrum came from Scotland to Virginia in 1688. One of his sons, also named John (born in Essex County, Virginia, in about 1700) moved to Chatham County, North Carolina, in the mid-eighteenth century. There he purchased 640 acres of land on Mill Creek near the Rocky River area. John Landrum and his sons—John, Charles, Reuben, Samuel, Benjamin, and Joseph—were living in present-day west-central Chatham County in the third quarter of the eighteenth century. The Landrums lived in Chatham County for about twenty years and their presence is evident from nineteenth-century maps of this area that identify present-day Mill Creek as Landrum Creek. Documents relating to the Regulator Movement indicate that two of the Chatham County Landrums, Charles and Reuben, were associated with Peter Craven and Philip Hartzo, patriarchs of two important North Carolina potter families.[21] Although no conclusive evidence has been found to indicate that the Landrums produced pottery in North Carolina, the following letter to the Charleston Museum written by O. B. Anderson of Ridge Realty Company, and accompanying research notes on the Pottersville factory, written by Agatha Abney Woodson, then president of the Edgefield Historical Society, suggests that this is the case.

Ridge Realty Company
Incorporated
Johnston and Edgefield
South Carolina
Edgefield, S.C.

September 2, 1927
The Charleston Museum,
Charleston, S.C.

Gentlemen—

Referring to our correspondence in regard to the Pottery which operated within a mile of Edgefield for about one hundred years, closing about 1868, I beg to enclose a copy of article written by Mrs. A. A. Woodson, Edgefield, S.C.

Please look up what Mills has to say about this pottery in his book, printed in the early part of the last century, and you will get the connection. It was not known then as the Miles Mill Pottery, but the Miles Mill people bought the machinery and moved it to Miles Mill, about twenty miles away, in Aiken County.

After reading the account, please look into the matter; and in the meantime I will endeavor to secure some valuable specimens. As a new railroad is being built through this property, it is hoped that it will again be in operation.

Very truly,
O. B. Anderson

Notes in regard to the old pottery which was once near the village of Edgefield, S.C.

Before and during the Revolutionary war there was a large pottery near the town of Salisbury, North Carolina. There are still remains of this old work which was said to have made pottery which vied with the Wedgwood potteries in England. As a matter of fact, clays were sent from that locality to be used in the Wedgwood potteries in England where the most beautiful ware in the world is still made.

Several men living in and near Salisbury came down to Edgefield, South Carolina just after the Revolutionary war and settled at a place called Landrumsville. These men were skilled workers from the Salisbury potteries, and the leaders among them were the Landrum brothers. Abner Landrum settled at Landrumsville or Pottersville (which is one mile of where now Edgefield now stands), as that locality was then called.

His brother settled down near Augusta in 1817. There is a record of a pottery owned by Rev. John Landrum. This was about four miles from the Pine House near where Trenton now is and just above Hatcher's pond, on the north fork of Horse Creek.

At Landrumville (one mile north of where Edgefield now is) was established a pottery and in this old pottery was manufactured some very beautiful specimens of the clay worker's art. There is in Edgefield now a beautiful sugar dish which was made there. It is in the possession of Mrs. Emily Strother Dunivant and was a gift to Grandmother Strother. In this old pottery was made all of the ordinary pots and vessels used by our pioneer fathers, and some of these vessels were large heavy plates of a light and dark color. There is now to be seen the large mixing basin in which the potters used to mix the clay [glaze], and the inside is as smooth as glass.

This Edgefield clay is pecularily adapted to the manufacture of both coarse and fine pottery. The white kaolin was used in those old days, some of it having been brought from what is now Aiken County, and is supposed to have been used in making dishes.

Evidently the potters who came from Salisbury found this clay here well adapted for their purposes, for they did not leave Edgefield, but continued to make vessels until all of the old people were dead and until after the war between the States when the plant was sold and moved to Hamburg [probably a reference to the Hahn or Baynham pottery], and they are still in operation as the Georgia Carolina potteries and making flower jars and other vessels.

In 1825 according to Mills Statistics there was a neat little town of about 17 houses and 150 people at Landrumsville one mile north of where Edgefield now stands and surrounding the pottery. The factory in which the work and firing and polishing [glazing] the pieces was done was a large building and the foundations of which is still to be seen. There was a warehouse and other conveniences. On an old map printed in 1817 is the site of the pottery on one side of the old Cambridge road and Landrumsville on the other.[22]

The town of Salisbury, North Carolina, to which Mrs. Woodson was referring, is located in present-day Rowan County. A number of potters were

active in Rowan County during the late eighteenth and early nineteenth centuries.[23]

Samuel Landrum married Nancy Sellers in
Chatham County, North Carolina, in 1763. They
moved to the Ninety Six District of South Carolina in the third quarter of the eighteenth century
following the birth of their first son, John. In 1786
Samuel Landrum acquired a state plat for 224
acres of land on Turkey Creek in Ninety Six District. The road from Augusta to Island Ford on
the Saluda River ran through this property, which
was located just east of the village of Edgefield in
what later became the Edgefield District. In 1792
Samuel acquired a second state plat for 207 acres
in Ninety Six District. Thomas Sellers, perhaps
an in-law who had also moved to South Carolina from Chatham County, appeared in the 1792
plat as the owner of adjoining property. Abner
Landrum, a son of Samuel Landrum, was named
administrator of his father's estate in 1818 when
Samuel died without a will. Harvey Drake agreed
to provide security for Samuel's debts in lieu
of an inventory of the estate, thereby releasing
John C. Lewis, who had formerly acted as security for Abner Landrum. This early association
between Harvey Drake and the Landrum family
is of interest since Drake later became involved in
stoneware manufacture in Edgefield. Samuel and
Nancy Landrum had five sons—John, Reuben,
George, Abner, and Amos. Three of these—John,
Abner, and Amos Landrum—were instrumental
in the establishment of the Edgefield alkaline-
glazed stoneware tradition in South Carolina (see
Appendix 1).

Three major areas of stoneware activity
emerged within the Edgefield District in the
first half of the nineteenth century. Pottersville,
a small community established by Abner Landrum just east of the town of Edgefield, was an
important center of pottery production in the district throughout the first half of the nineteenth
century. The property on which Abner Landrum
founded Pottersville probably was part of the

original Turkey Creek tract granted to Samuel
Landrum in 1786. During the 1820s and 1830s
John and Amos Landrum and related families established pottery factories throughout the
Horse Creek valley in the southern section of
the district. A series of stoneware factories that
were established on Shaw's Creek, just east of
the John Landrum pottery, are considered to
be within the Horse Creek–area pottery center.
Some of the Horse Creek–area potteries were
continued into the second half of the nineteenth
century, and some new pottery factories were
established in the area during the latter part of
the century. A third pottery center was established in the Kirksey's Crossroads section above
Edgefield by potters who, although associated
with the Landrum family, do not appear to have
been directly related to the Landrums. Some
of the journeymen potters who worked in the
Edgefield District stoneware factories moved
between these pottery centers, so related vessel
styles may be found at pottery factories throughout the district. Edgefield ware can sometimes be
identified with a particular potter but most often
is recognized on the basis of particular attributes
or techniques associated with a specific pottery
factory located within the district. The Edgefield
District stoneware industry that emerged in the
early decades of the nineteenth century in these
three pottery centers—the village of Pottersville,
Horse Creek valley, and Kirksey's Crossroads—is
discussed below.

Pottersville Stoneware Manufactory

A pottery located a mile and a half northeast of
the Edgefield Court House in the community of
"Landrumsville" is indicated on Robert Mills's
1825 map of the Edgefield District. In his *Statistics of South Carolina*, published in 1826, Mills
described the village of Pottersville, which he

named Landrumsville in honor of its founder, Abner Landrum. According to Mills, Landrum had developed a type of stoneware that was "stronger, better and cheaper than any European or American ware of the same kind."[24] Another record of this newly developed stoneware is found in an advertisement that appeared in an 1819 issue of the *Camden Gazette*. A local merchant offered "370 pieces of the Edgefield made stone ware. . . . The first of the kind (and superior in quality to any) ever offered here for sale."[25]

In the early nineteenth century Abner Landrum acquired property in Edgefield, which he divided into lots and sold to create the village of Pottersville. Pottersville was the first stoneware factory in the Edgefield District run as a full-time business. Most southern potteries were part-time, seasonal, family owned and operated enterprises established by local farmers as a means of supplementing their incomes between the planting and harvesting seasons. The stoneware factories established in Edgefield during the first half of the nineteenth century were unique in that they were run as businesses by owner-investors who relied on journeyman potters and African-American slaves as laborers. The entrepreneurial attitude toward stoneware production that prevailed in Edgefield profoundly influenced the development of the alkaline-glazed stoneware tradition in the area.

The 1820 Digest of Accounts of Manufacturing Establishments in the United States, recorded for the Edgefield District, listed a pottery in the Edgefield District employing five men and two children. A fair amount of capital, $8,800, had been invested in the operation. Four wheels were the only equipment listed, but the enumeration of raw materials—clay and lead—may indicate that lead-glazed earthenware was produced at this early Edgefield pottery. Unfortunately, the owner of this operation is not named. A brief note, "proprietors about enlarging this establishment," is of interest since the pottery was already

of a larger scale than most nineteenth-century southern potteries. This information may be a reference to the Pottersville factory, yet it is possible that the manufacturing census detailed a pottery operation other than Abner Landrum's Pottersville factory. Earthenware potter Adam Effurt, for example, appeared in the 1820 Edgefield census, and his estate records, filed in the Edgefield probate office, provide evidence of his continuing involvement in earthenware manufacture. However, Effurt died in 1822, and it is doubtful that he could have been actively involved in such a large-scale enterprise in 1820. Abner Landrum's brother John also owned a pottery factory in the district in the 1820s that appears to have been as old, if not older, than the Pottersville factory. Nevertheless, Robert Mills's contemporary description of Abner Landrum's Pottersville stoneware factory seems to correspond well with the limited information presented in the census. If the 1820 census information refers to the Pottersville factory, it suggests that the Landrums were earthenware potters who, through experimentation with local clays and locally produced glaze formulas, developed alkaline-glazed stoneware. An archaeological survey of the Pottersville site, however, has revealed no conclusive evidence of earthenware production there.[26]

Early ware produced at the Pottersville factory typically has light gray-green or yellow-green glazes, whereas darker olive-green to brown-black glaze colors characterize later Edgefield ware (Figure 2.4). The early Pottersville ware tends to be shorter and squatter than later ware, although ware produced throughout the area in the first half of the nineteenth century is generally ovoid in form. Crescent-shaped lug handles were applied horizontally at the upper shoulder of storage jars. A number of stoneware fragments have been recovered from the Pottersville site that are associated with the early period of production. The glaze color and features found on these sherds correspond to dated Edgefield vessels that

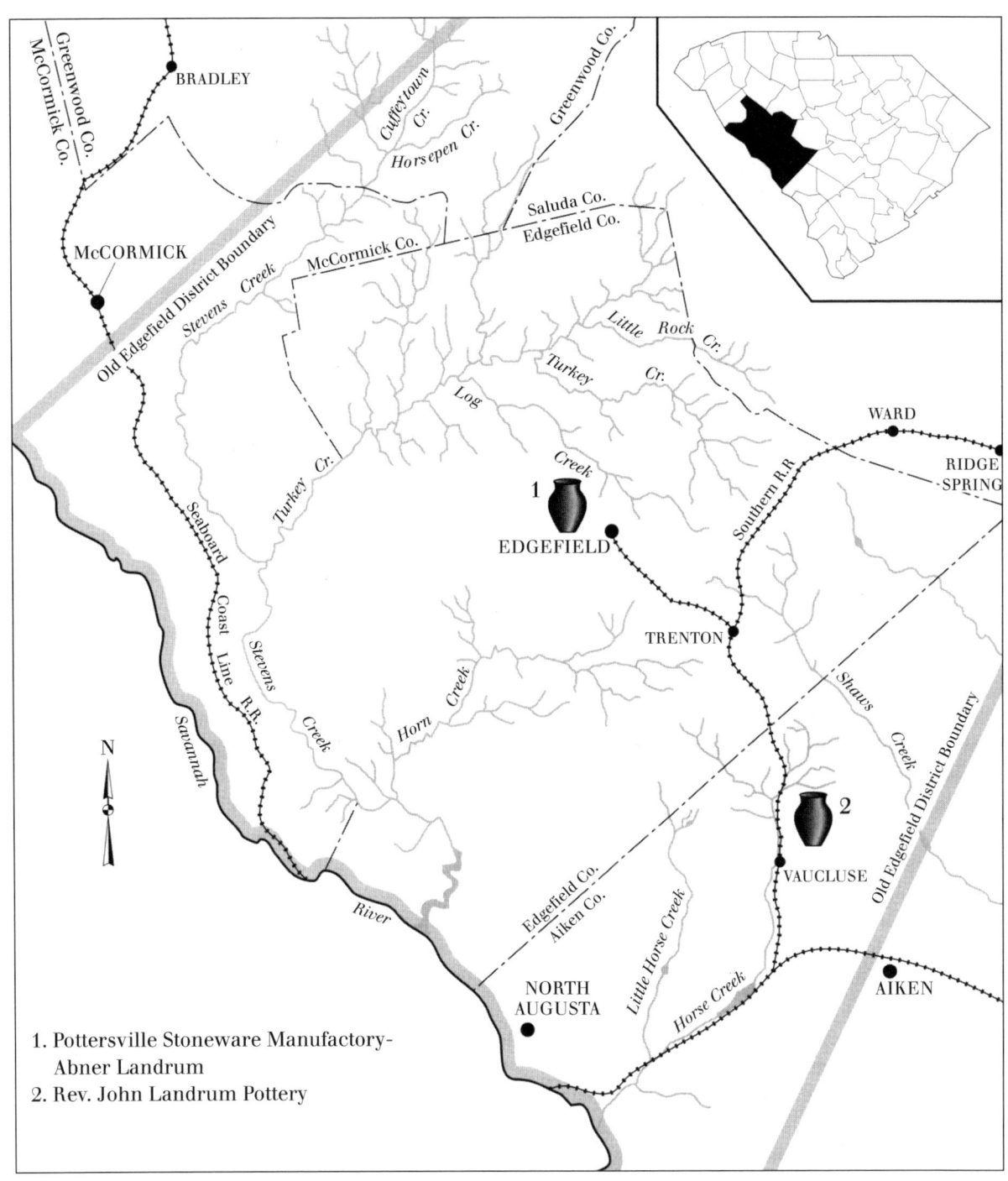

2.3 Map of the present-day area encompassing the old Edgefield District showing locations of stoneware pottery sites established prior to 1820.

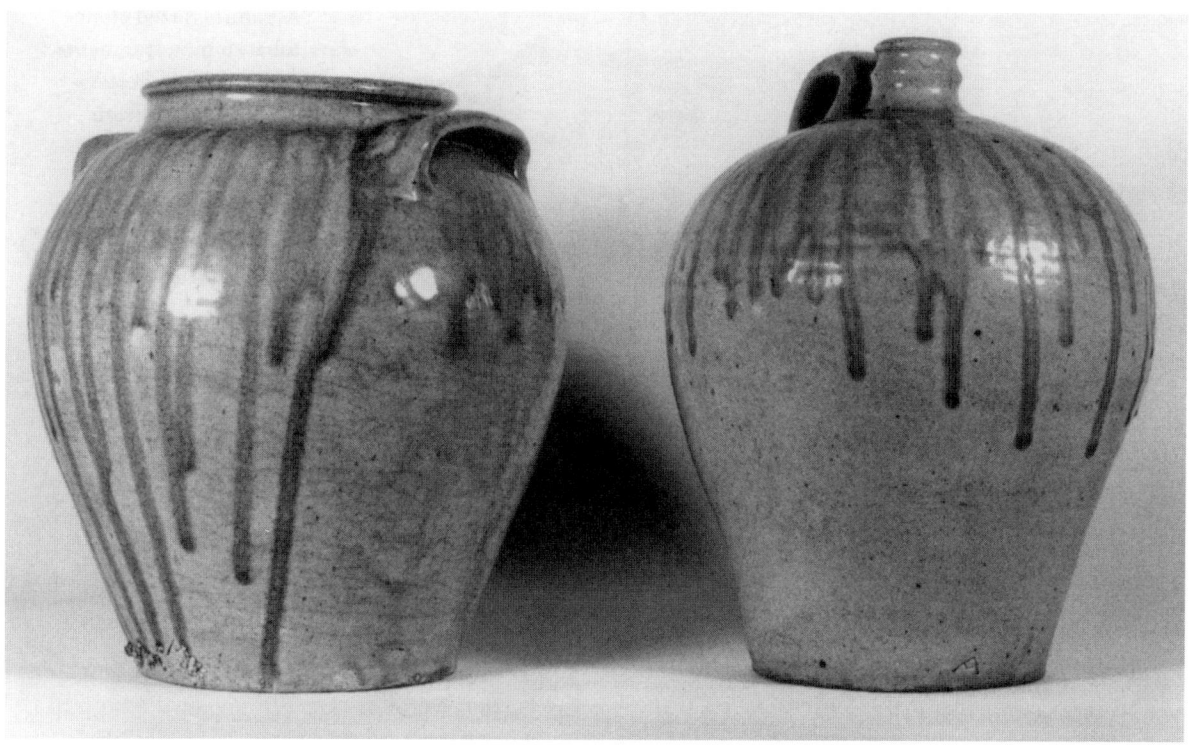

2.4 Alkaline-glazed stoneware preserve jar and jug, ca. 1810–30, attributed to the Pottersville Stoneware Manufactory, Edgefield District, S.C. Preserve jar: H 11½″, C 33″. Jug: H 13″, C 30¾″. The light glaze colors and impressed marks at the lower body identify these as Pottersville ware. Collections of Mr. and Mrs. Levon C. Register, and Terry and Steve Ferrell.

have been identified in public and private collections. Many of these sherds have stamps, consisting of letters or other marks that appear to have been impressed with metal type. These stamps are typically placed at the foot of the vessel just above the base. Since Abner Landrum was a newspaper publisher, use of these stamps may coincide with the period of his ownership of the factory. Several fragments of alkaline-glazed stoneware tobacco pipes were also recovered from the site, including one that was fused to a portion of a kiln waster (Figure 2.5).

An 1827 agreement in which Abner Landrum sold Harvey and Reuben Drake the rights to timber located on his property preceded the eventual transfer of the factory to the Drakes. According to the agreement, one-half of the "oak wood" and an unspecified quantity of hickory and black jack were to be for the use of the "furnace and shops." Apparently, the furnace and shops that Landrum referred to were the pottery shops and stoneware kiln of the Pottersville Stoneware Manufactory. The oak, hickory, and black jack probably were used as fuel for the stoneware kiln and for heating the shops in winter. The Landrum-Drake agreement indicates the use of both hardwoods (oak, hickory, and black jack) and softwoods (pine) at Pottersville, so either type of wood may have been used to fire the kiln. Landrum placed a higher value on pine than on hardwoods. He gave the

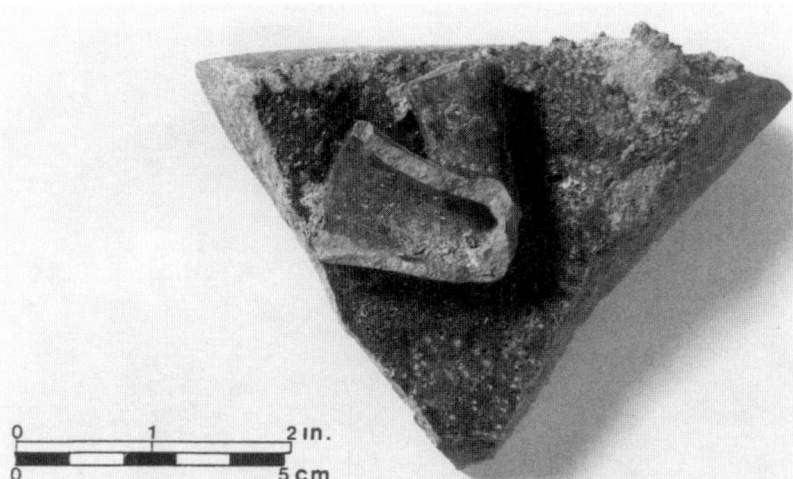

2.5 Alkaline-glazed stoneware tobacco pipe fragments recovered from the Pottersville site (38ED11). From Castille, Baldwin, and Steen, *Archaeological Survey of Alkaline-Glazed Pottery Kiln Sites in Old Edgefield District, South Carolina*, 49.

Drakes the option of using hardwoods exclusively at a cost of forty dollars per year, or pine timber for sixty dollars per year. He also stipulated in the agreement that if the Drakes decided to reduce the scale of operations at the factory to less than twenty-four blasts (firings) per year, he would agree to reduce the price of pine timber accordingly. For example, if the Drakes made only twelve blasts per year, he would charge thirty dollars per year for the pine timber.[27] At a rate of twenty-four kiln loads of ware per year, or about two firings per month, Pottersville was a full-time operation.

The Pottersville timber rights agreement was the initial step in the eventual transfer of the Pottersville factory to Harvey and Reuben Drake. Landrum sold his Pottersville property to the Drakes in November 1828. In the following years the factory was run by several partnerships of investor-owners (a summary of the ownerships through which the Pottersville factory was transferred is presented in Appendix 2). Harvey Drake died in 1832, and shortly thereafter Collin Rhodes purchased one-half interest in the factory. The name of the business was then changed to the Drake and Rhodes Factory.[28] On 1 January 1836

Nathaniel Ramey purchased one-third interest in the business, creating the firm of Drake, Rhodes and Company. Only one vessel produced during the Drake, Rhodes, and Ramey partnership has been identified. It is a large, ovoid, double loop-handled syrup jug with a light, straw-colored alkaline glaze. The jug is signed in script in what appears to be an iron-bearing slip "Drake, Rhodes & Co. / Improved Stoneware / Edgefield Ct.H. S.C. / 183[6]" (Figure 2.6). This is the earliest known Edgefield vessel with an applied slip treatment.

Rhodes and Ramey continued to hold interests in the Pottersville factory during the years that followed, while several other local businessmen also invested in the enterprise. Robert Mathis acquired Reuben Drake's interest in the Pottersville factory in September 1836, and the partnership of Ramey, Rhodes and Company was formed, thereby ending the Drake, Rhodes and Company partnership.[29] Two years later, in June 1838, the Ramey, Rhodes and Company partnership was dissolved when Jasper Gibbs, a former agent for the Vaucluse Manufacturing Company, replaced Robert Mathis as the third partner, creating the firm of Rhodes, Ramey and Gibbs.[30] Sometime

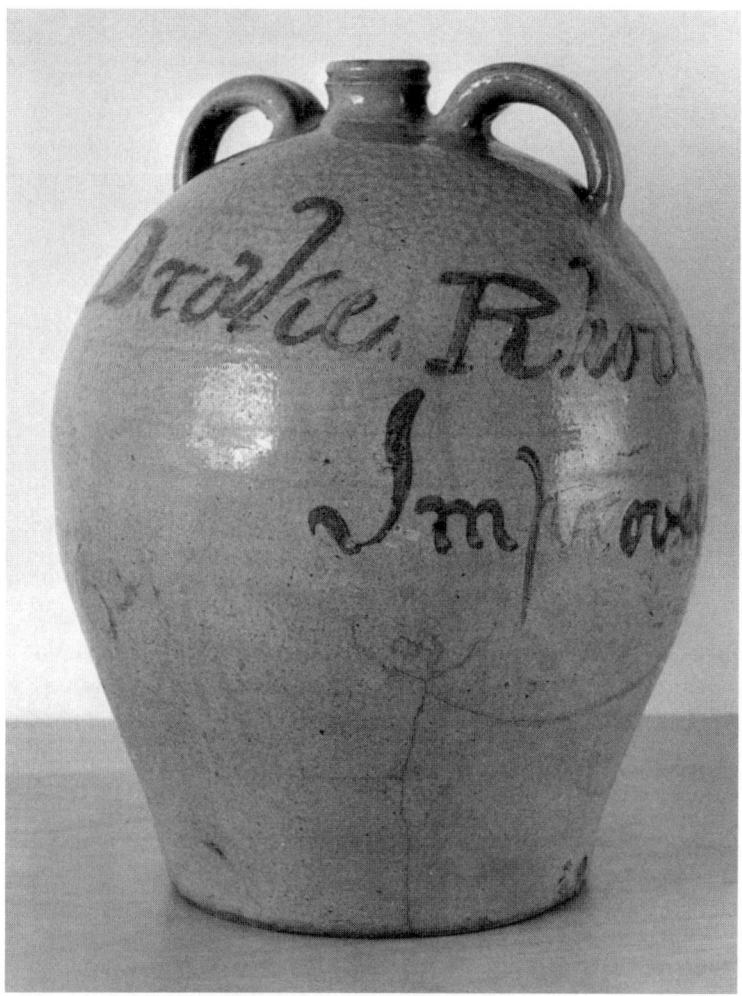

2.6 Alkaline-glazed stoneware syrup jug, 1836, Pottersville Stoneware Manufactory, Edgefield District, S.C. H 17½″, C 44¼″. Signed in iron-based slip: Drake, Rhodes & Co. / Improved stone / ware / Edgefield Ct.H. S.C. / 183[6]. Courtesy of the Museum of Early Southern Decorative Arts, Winston-Salem, N.C.

between June 1838 and January 1839 John Hughes acquired Collin Rhodes's interest in the factory, creating the firm of N. Ramey and Company. Collin Rhodes and John Hughes filed an indenture in January 1839 in which Hughes transferred his interest in the factory to Rhodes with the provision that Hughes be allowed to retain possession of the property on the condition that he make payments to Rhodes on three notes due in 1840, 1841, and 1842.[31] Several alkaline-glazed stoneware jars from the Gibbs, Ramey, and Hughes ownership of the factory have survived. These tan-brown ovoid jars are stamped in

small type at the upper shoulder "N. Ramey & Co" (Figure 2.7).

The years 1839 and 1840 marked a decline in financial support for the Pottersville factory. Jasper Gibbs sold his equity in the factory in October 1839, thereby dissolving the Rhodes, Ramey, and Gibbs partnership.[32] In April of the following year Nathaniel Ramey and John Hughes mutually dissolved their partnership, and Ramey deeded his interest in the factory to Jasper Gibbs and his brother, brickmaker James W. Gibbs. At this time the factory was advertised for sale by mutual consent of the owners for division

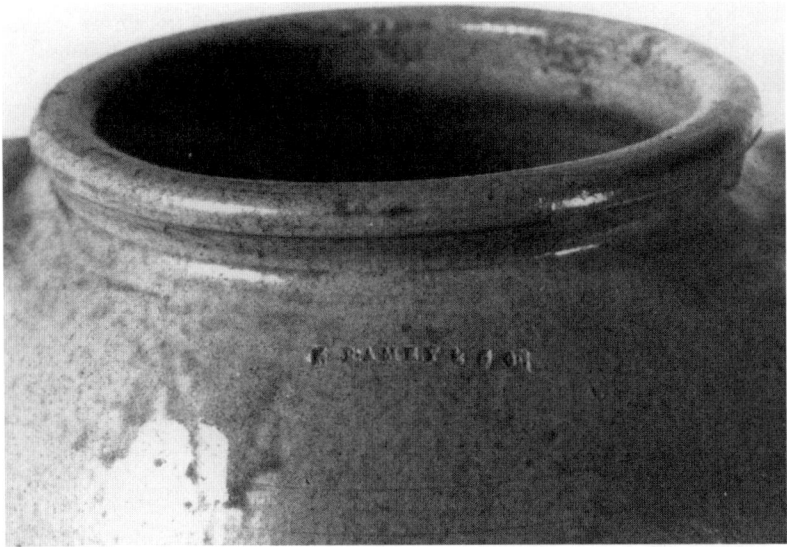

2.7   Closeup of maker's mark, alkaline-glazed stoneware storage jar, 1839, Pottersville Stoneware Manufactory, Edgefield District, S.C. Stamped: N. Ramey & Co. Collection of Mr. and Mrs. Gary S. Thompson, Jr.

and was divided into smaller shares as the number of investors increased. By 1842 six investors held an interest in the factory. J. D. Nance mortgaged his "undivided Sixth of Seventeen and a half acres of Land on which the furnace and Shops [were] situated, called the manufacturing Lott, [and] Clay & chalk privileges" to Jasper Gibbs in 1842.[33] In February 1843 J. Gibbs and Company advertised "our entire Pottersville property, both real and personal, consisting of four Negroes, viz, three Turners and one wagoner, thirteen mules, one saddle horse, three strong six-mule wagons and harness, one first rate two-horse wagon, one set Blacksmith tools, stock of stoneware, brick and tyle, fodder, and hay; stock of goods, consisting of Homespuns, sugar and coffee. Iron, Leather, shoes, white lead, etc. on a credit till 1st January, 1844."[34] Gibbs placed the following notice in the *Edgefield Advertiser* newspaper in April 1843.

NOTICE

I intend shortly to move to Mississippi, and to leave my brother and Mr. J. D. Nance, to act as Agents in winding up all my unsettled business at Pottersville.

After reasonable indulgence to those who are indebted to me, costs will be added.[35]

A few years earlier Reuben Drake had purchased a tract of land in present-day Bienville Parish, Louisiana, from his brother-in-law Martin Canfield. This land constituted the entire site of the community of Mt. Lebanon, Louisiana. Drake arrived in Bienville Parish between 1835 and 1837 with a colony of seven South Carolina families. He had a general store and purchased a considerable amount of property there. In 1850 he was living in Natchitoches Parish where he owned a large saltworks. He is listed as a "manufacturer" in the census for that year. Jasper Gibbs was married to Drake's daughter. The Gibbs family migrated to Bienville Parish at about the same time as Drake and settled at Gibsland. Collin Rhodes also moved to Bienville Parish and purchased land there in 1854. No evidence has been found that any of these men were involved in stoneware manufacture in Louisiana.[36]

Francis W. Pickens, later governor of South Carolina, owned a stoneware and brick factory in Edgefield District in 1850 employing four men. Pickens had $1,400 invested in the factory, which was valued at $1,250. According to private researchers Joe L. Holcombe and Fred E. Holcombe, Pickens acquired the Pottersville factory sometime between 1844 and 1850.[37] Little is known about the ware produced during Pickens's ownership of the Pottersville factory, but the operation evidently declined during his ownership.

The Pottersville stoneware factory was a proving ground for the early Edgefield stoneware potters. Two of Pottersville's investor-owners, Collin Rhodes and Robert Mathis, later established another large-scale stoneware operation in the district. Some of the journeymen who started out at Pottersville later worked at other Edgefield-area stoneware factories. More impor-

tant, many early Edgefield journeymen potters who started out at Pottersville migrated to other southern states, where they continued to produce alkaline-glazed stoneware and thus diffused the alkaline-glazed stoneware tradition throughout the lower South.

Horse Creek Valley

John Landrum, the eldest of the three Landrums involved in stoneware manufacture in Edgefield, founded a pottery on Horse Creek during the same period in which Abner Landrum established the Pottersville factory. "Abdel Stot & Wife" sold 988 acres of property on Big Horse Creek to John Landrum in 1795.[38] "Rev. J[oh]n Landrum's Pottery" is shown on Robert Mills's 1817 *Atlas* map of the Edgefield District south of Edgefield Village on a tributary of Big Horse Creek.

Heavy, thick-walled ovoid forms characterize most of the ware produced at the John Landrum site. Jugs typically have rolled neck-rims and thick rolled and flattened loop handles attached well below the neck. Storage vessels produced at the John Landrum site are solidly built, often having extremely heavy bottoms (Figure 2.9). Bases may have wire marks where the vessels were cut from the wheel or they may be smooth.

Recent archaeological investigations at the John Landrum site indicate that a great deal of experimentation with local clays was carried out here. For example, the recovery of high-fired unglazed stoneware fragments at the site in a wide variety of thin-walled forms suggests a possible transition from earthenware to stoneware production by the Landrums. This supposition is further supported by the presence of clay objects at the site that have been identified as kiln supports and separators. Kiln furniture was rarely used by alkaline-glazed stoneware potters since they typically did not stack their ware in the kiln.[39] Alka-

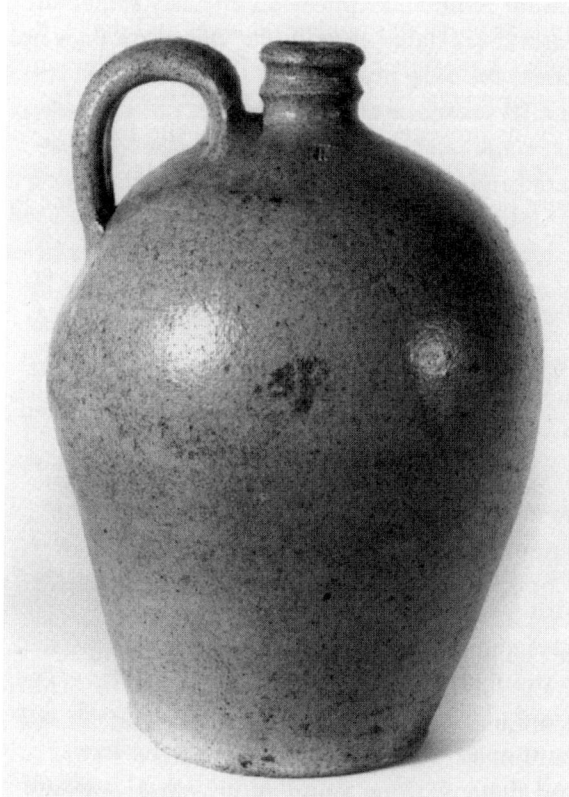

2.8 Alkaline-glazed stoneware jug, ca. 1850, possibly made at the Pottersville Stoneware Manufactory, Edgefield District, S.C., under the ownership of Francis W. Pickens. H 10½″, C 24⅝″. Stamped: P (two stamps below neck and three at midbody). Collection of Charles Comolli.

line glaze tends to run when it is fired, so vessels that were stacked in the kiln were often fused together during firing. In order to minimize this problem the potter usually placed alkaline-glazed ware in a single layer, or in "single shot" fashion, on a sand- or flint-covered kiln floor before firing. Southern earthenware potters, on the other hand, are known to have utilized kiln furniture such as shelves and shelf supports in the firing of ware.[40] Light gray-green and yellow-green alkaline-glazed stoneware fragments, similar to the early Pottersville ware, were also found at the John Landrum site. Early dated Edgefield ware

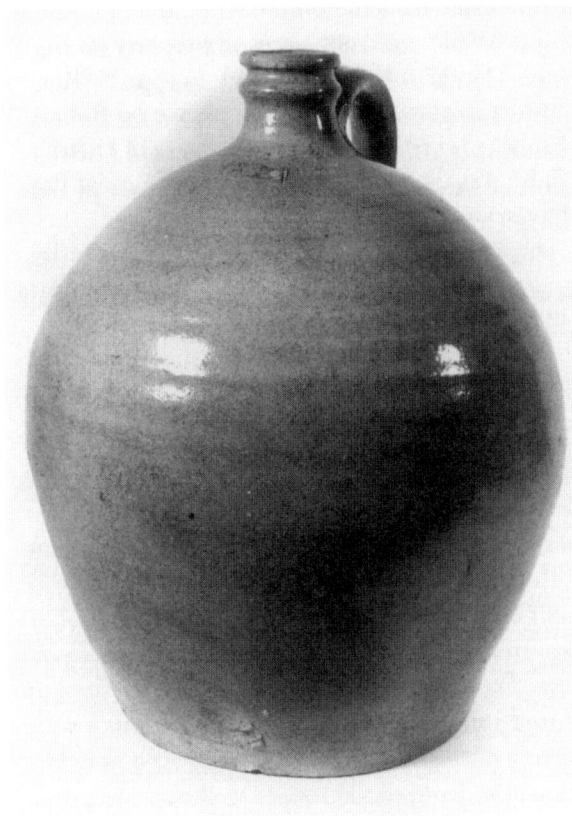

2.9   Alkaline-glazed stoneware jug, 1821, attributed to the Reverend John Landrum Pottery, Horse Creek Valley, Edgefield District, S.C. H 14⅛″, C 37⅜″. Incised, upper body opposite handle: "1821" and set of three incised marks. Collection of Tony and Marie Shank.

(with incised dates ranging from 1821 to 1825) have similarly colored glazes. Other glaze types produced at the John Landrum site include a rich opaque brown glaze, a transparent brown glaze, and an opaque reddish-brown glaze.

A number of maker's marks were used on ware produced at the John Landrum site. The most commonly used mark was a stamped x, often seen with L- or T-shaped terminals. Some variants on this include a mark that appears to be an x with one leg missing, and two examples of an x formed from four separate marks. Singular and paired slash marks also appear on ware from the site, sometimes accompanied by circular punctates. Similar punctates appear on an early Edgefield preserve jar dated 1821. Since this mark does not appear on ware produced at the Pottersville factory, its presence at the Landrum site suggests that some of the earliest alkaline-glazed stoneware produced in the district may be attributed to the John Landrum pottery. The slash marks used on ware produced at the Landrum site have been interpreted as a system of capacity markings by some researchers, but this theory is problematic since no pattern related to capacity of the vessel on which a given mark appears can be discerned in some cases.

Single, double, and triple triangular punctates measuring approximately three millimeters in length are also found on ware recovered from the John Landrum site. A small ovoid preserve jar with a band of closely spaced triangular punctates applied below the rim may be attributed to the John Landrum pottery (Figure 2.10). The triangular marks, measuring approximately .05 centimeters each in width, are similar in size and shape to those found at the John Landrum site. This thin-walled, symmetrical jar has a light gray-green, glassy, transparent glaze, measures about 9½ inches tall, and is complete with a domed knob-handled lid that fits over a plain everted rim. Small, thin-walled preserve jars were rarely produced in Edgefield, but fragments of

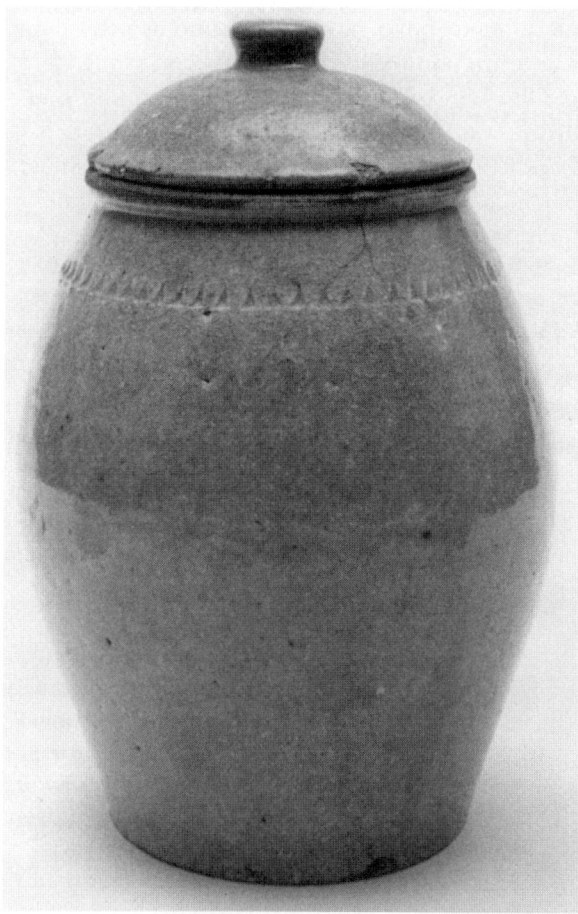

2.10   Alkaline-glazed stoneware preserve jar, ca. 1810–30, attributed to the Reverend John Landrum Pottery, Horse Creek Valley, Edgefield District, S.C. H 9½″, C 20⅛″. Band of evenly spaced triangular impressed marks at upper shoulder. Collection of Paul and Sally Hawkins.

similar thin-walled forms and ware with light gray-green glazes were recovered from the John Landrum site. Other marks found on ware at the Landrum site include a stamped "3" (probably a capacity marking), a B (stamped sideways with the straight side facing up), and what appears to be a backward s. Marks are usually located just above the base at the foot of the vessel, especially in the case of the triangular and slash marks.

Some marks (particularly x marks) are found at the lower handle attachment of jugs.[41]

A pair of slash marks similar to those found on sherds at the John Landrum site also appear on an early Edgefield storage jar signed by Dave, a celebrated Edgefield slave potter (Figure 2.11). The marks are incised at the foot of the pot just above the base. This jar, the earliest known vessel by Dave, is dated "July 12, 1834" and bears a verse in incised script: "Put every bit all between / surely this jar will hold 14." Dave signed and dated many of the vessels that he made and further individualized much of his ware with verses—rhymed couplets—incised at the upper shoulder just below the neck-rim. Dave may have trained as a turner at the John Landrum pottery or at Pottersville. He was associated with Abner Landrum in Pottersville, and his later owner, Lewis Miles, was the son-in-law of John Landrum.

Lewis Miles was listed as a "stoneware mfgr [manufacturer]" in the 1850 Edgefield census and as a "stoneware maker" in 1860. Although the location of Miles's early pottery factory has not been positively identified, a portion of a tract of land owned by Miles is shown on a plat of property surveyed for Collin Rhodes in 1848. The tract, identified as L. J. Miles's and S. Day's property, was located east of Shaw's Creek and was bound by the creek on the west and by two tracts of land owned by F. Posey and Martin Posey on the east. Another tract of land owned by Miles, located on Horse Creek and Wolf Branch and bound by lands of John Landrum, B. F. Landrum, and John Randall, is shown on an 1847 plat of 650 acres surveyed for the Reverend John Landrum.[42]

When John Landrum died in 1846 Miles evidently acquired some of his father-in-law's Horse Creek property. An executor's sale of the estate took place in February 1847 and included "all of [John Landrum's] personal property, consisting of 18 likely Negroes, among whom are two good

Wagonners, an excellent Stone Ware Turner, and a good Cook, one Horse, Mules, Cattle and Hogs. Also, Household and Kitchen Furniture, a Piano Forte, one Carriage, Wagon and Carts, one Still, a Bark Mill, and lot of Tan Bark, Leather, Raw Hides and Hides in tan, set of Blacksmith's Tools, Corn, Fodder, Peas, Stone Ware, Bacon, and various other articles." [43]

In an 1847 advertisement Miles announced that he was "living on Horse Creek, at the Saw Mill formerly owned by Rev. John Landrum, decd., 12 miles from Edgefield C.H. [Court House]." [44] The remains of a mill, presumably the sawmill

mentioned above, have been found near the John Landrum pottery site.

John Landrum's son, Benjamin Franklin Landrum, was also a stoneware manufacturer. B. F. Landrum and Lewis Miles appeared as business partners in an 1840 Edgefield judgment. Both men signed a promissory note agreeing to pay Rosela Blalock $125 for the hire of a slave boy for a year. This document indicates that Lewis Miles and B. F. Landrum jointly operated a business. B. F. Landrum's grandson Frank Landrum and granddaughter Rebecca Steele verified this partnership. According to Frank Landrum, Lewis

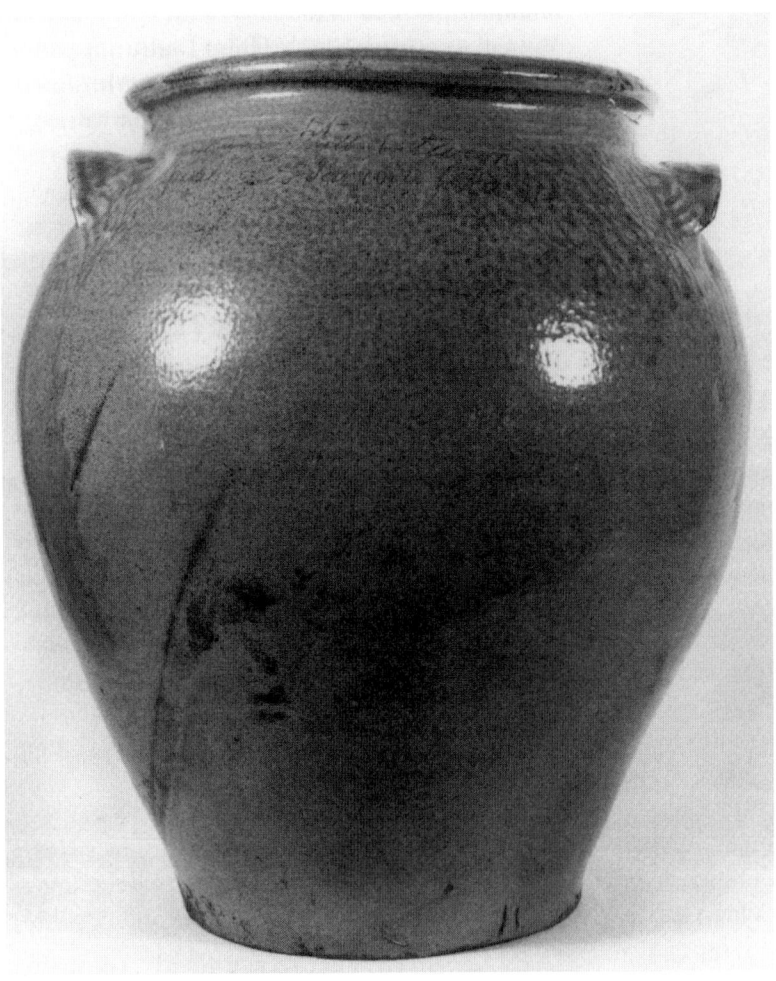

2.11 Alkaline-glazed stoneware storage jar, 1834, Dave (slave potter), attributed to the Reverend John Landrum Pottery, Horse Creek Valley, Edgefield District, S.C. H 19¼", C 4' 7⅞". Incised in script at upper shoulder on opposite sides: July 12, 1834, put every bit all between / surely this jar will hold 14. Horizontal row of fourteen punctates underlined by a wavy line to right of date and two evenly spaced slash marks at lower body. Collection of the South Carolina State Museum, Columbia.

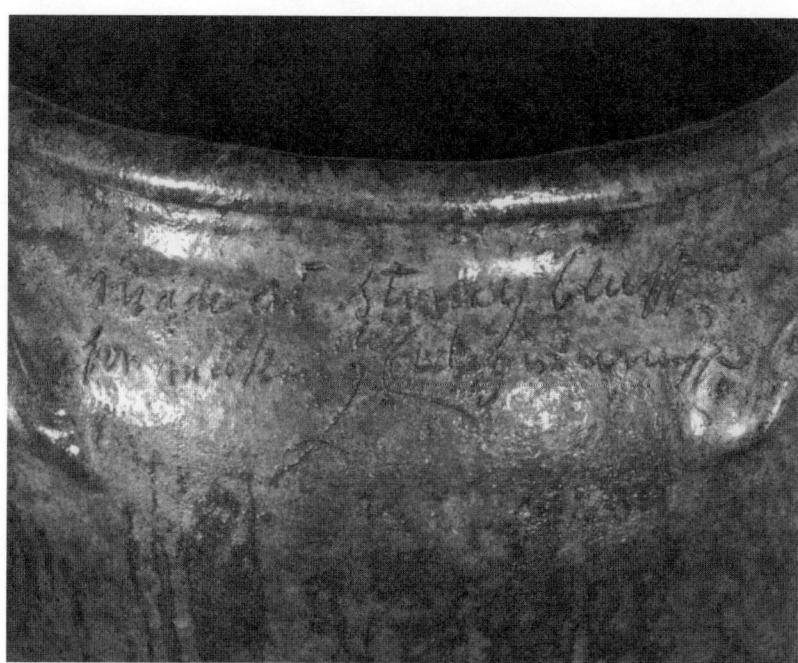

2.12 Alkaline-glazed stoneware storage jar, 1859, Dave and Baddler (slave potters), Lewis Miles Pottery, Horse Creek Valley, Edgefield District, S.C. H 2′ 4¾″, C 6′ 7¼″. Detail of incised verse: Made at Stoney Bluff / for Making lard Enuff. Maker's mark and date incised in script, May 13, 1859. Collection of the Charleston Museum, Charleston, S.C.

Miles married the Reverend John Landrum's daughter Mary and worked with his father-in-law in the pottery. After John Landrum's death, his son B. F. Landrum and son-in-law Lewis Miles continued the pottery together. Rebecca Steele recalled that her father had told of riding on a covered wagon to Charleston, Columbia, and Augusta carrying Landrum and Miles pottery to market. She added that Landrum and Miles later had a disagreement prompting them to start separate factories.[45] The Landrum-Miles partnership was dissolved sometime before 1850, because by that date Lewis Miles and B. F. Landrum appear in the Edgefield industrial census as owners of separate stoneware factories.

Lewis Miles's stoneware factory was valued at four thousand dollars in 1850 and employed seven male and two female laborers. A signed storage jar by Dave dated 13 May 1859 is inscribed: "Made at Stoney Bluff / for Making lard Enuff" (Figure 2.12). The location of Miles's Stoney Bluff plantation is unknown, but it was undoubtedly in the Horse Creek area. The ware that Dave produced at Lewis Miles's factory bears the maker's mark "Lm" in incised script (Figure 2.13).

In 1862 Miles announced the opening of his "NEW FLOURING MILLS . . . on the Beaver Dam, 1 ½ miles from his residence, 4 miles Southeast of Pine House, and 4 miles from Mr. Julius Day's."[46] An 1867 advertisement in which Miles outlined the full range of his business interests seems to indicate that he may have relocated his pottery and other businesses to a new area at this time. The advertisement reads as follows:

DOMESTIC TRADE

All of my Manufacturing Interest is now concentrated in one place. My Grain Mill, Saw Mill, as well as the Tannery and Stone Ware Factory are in complete operation.

I have on hand and for sale a quantity of Flour, Lumber, Leather, Jugs, Jars, etc. Any of these articles I will give in exchange for Raw Hides.

My motto is to build up business at home, and establish at least, a Commercial Independence.

Lewis J. Miles[47]

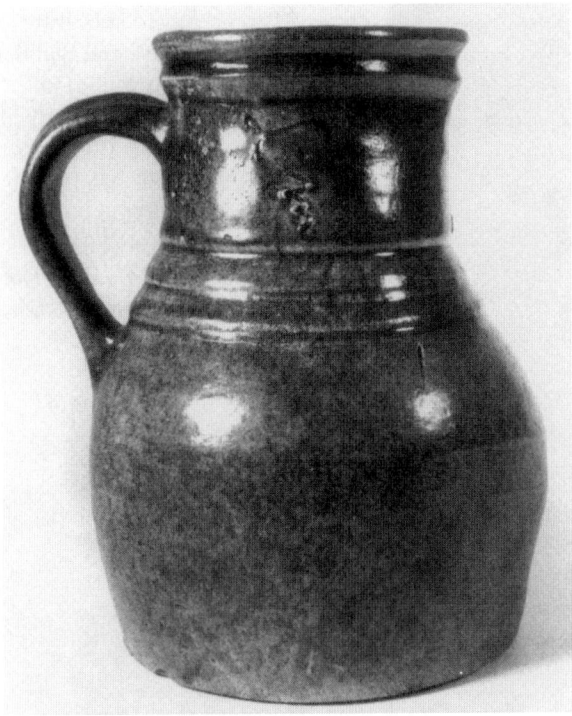

2.13   Alkaline-glazed stoneware pitcher, ca. 1840–50, attributed to Dave (slave potter), Lewis Miles Pottery, Horse Creek Valley, Edgefield District, S.C. H 9⅞", C 24". Incised in script: Lm. Collection of Tony and Marie Shank.

Apparently, Miles had acquired John Landrum's tannery and saw mill along with the property that he purchased from the estate in 1847. He probably also purchased the property on which the John Landrum pottery was located and equipment associated with the operation.

By 1867 Miles's businesses were probably located in an area of Edgefield later known as Miles Mill, in the present-day community of Sunnybrook. This site is situated along the Aiken-Edgefield county line. John Miles, Lewis's son, took over the pottery and mills when his father died. Miles's mill and pottery were located near the Charleston, Columbia, and Augusta Railroad line. Mrs. Irene Gingrey, John Landrum's great-granddaughter, told the following story of how

Miles Mill got on the map. "He [Lewis Miles] ordered some freight and it was supposed to have gotten off at Miles' Mills, and [Miles' Mill] wasn't named so the freight [was to go on] to Graniteville, and he stopped the train. He wouldn't let it go to Graniteville, and he padlocked it to the railroad track. That was what was told me, and that's where Miles' Mill came in. It was named after [Lewis Miles] . . . until he boarded the train and got whatever was on there for him."

Benjamin Franklin Landrum owned a stoneware and brick factory valued at four thousand dollars in 1850 and employing seven male and two female workers. Some of the ware produced at the B. F. Landrum factory was stamped with circular impressed marks with a raised cross or x inside (Figure 2.14). Examples of vessels from the site have been found with a single mark and groups of four or five marks clustered together. Glazes on vessels produced at the B. F. Landrum factory range in color from tan or straw-colored to olive, olive brown, or brown-black. Storage jars typically have two opposing half-circular wheel-thrown handles. Some churns or preserve jars

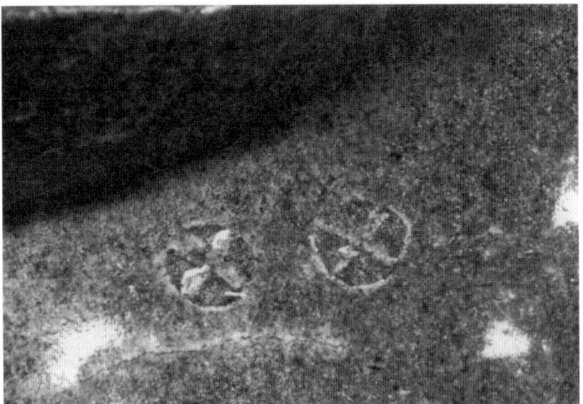

2.14   Detail of impressed circular stamps at upper shoulder of stoneware vessel fragment recovered from the Benjamin F. Landrum site (38AK498). From Castille, Baldwin, and Steen, *Archaeological Survey of Alkaline-Glazed Pottery Kiln Sites in Old Edgefield District, South Carolina.*

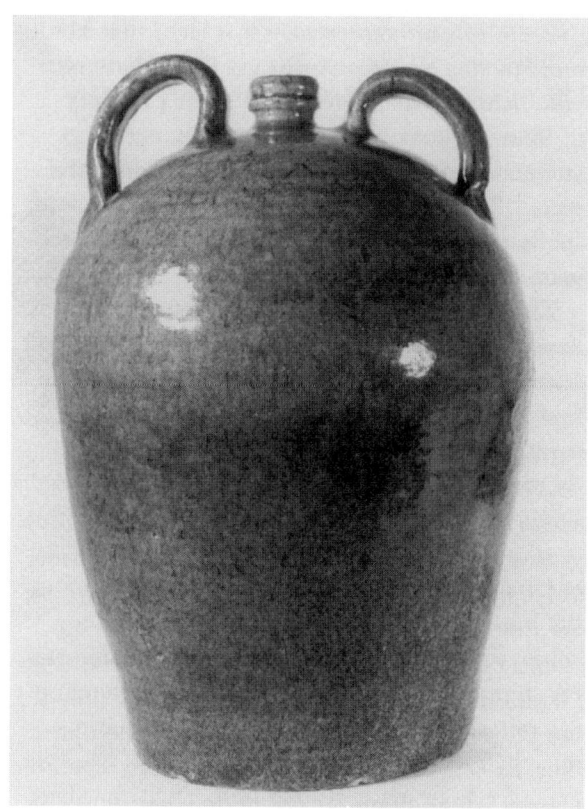

2.15 Alkaline-glazed stoneware syrup jug, ca. 1850, Benjamin F. Landrum Factory, Horse Creek Valley, Edgefield District, S.C. H 17½″, C 38½″. Incised in script: B. F. Landrum. Collection of Terry and Steve Ferrell.

produced at the B. F. Landrum factory have lid ledges inside the mouth and indented, banded collars.

At least three stoneware shops were established on Shaw's Creek in the south-central section of Edgefield District just east of the Horse Creek valley. In the Shaw's Creek area of Edgefield the entrepreneurial attitude of the Edgefield factory owners prompted innovative approaches to production and distribution of stoneware. The earliest stoneware factory in the area appears to have been established by Amos Landrum, brother of Abner and John.

Amos Landrum owned a lot in the village of

Pottersville and land on Turkey Creek. He lived in Pottersville and was probably turning ware there in the early decades of the nineteenth century. Amos and John Landrum also jointly owned property on Shaw's Creek. In an 1835 indenture Amos Landrum sold part of his Shaw's Creek property to Reuben Drake and Jasper Gibbs, co-owners of the Pottersville Stoneware Manufactory. The property transfer included a slave, Buster, who was named as a turner in the agreement.[48] Amos Landrum's son-in-law, Collin Rhodes, held interests in two stoneware factories established on Shaw's Creek prior to 1850.

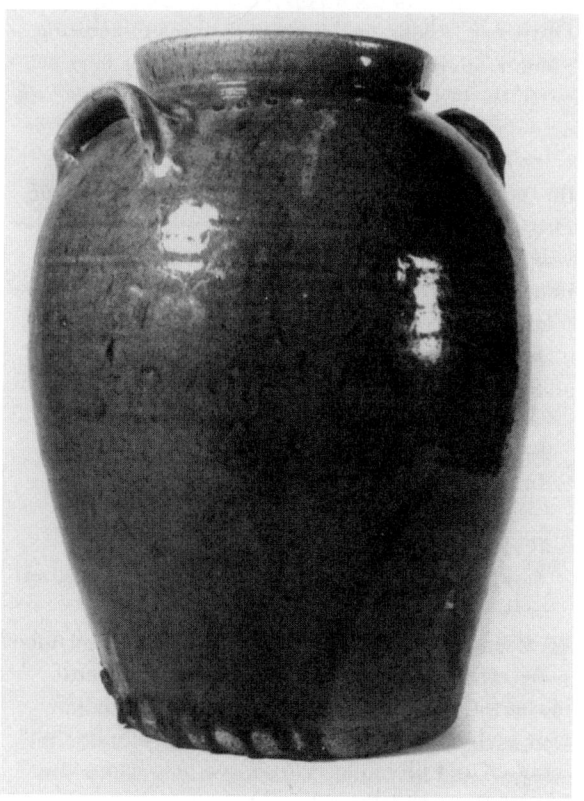

2.16 Alkaline-glazed stoneware storage jar, ca. 1850, Benjamin F. Landrum Factory, Horse Creek Valley, Edgefield District, S.C. H 15⅛″, C 37″. Row of four circular impressed stamps with raised cross or "X" at upper shoulder. Collection of the Charleston Museum, Charleston, S.C.

Collin Rhodes and his partner Robert Mathis announced the opening of the Phoenix Factory on Shaw's Creek in an 1840 issue of the *Edgefield Advertiser.*

Phoenix Stone Ware Factory

TO MERCHANTS AND THE PUBLIC
IN GENERAL

The Subscribers having been engaged in the manufacturing of Stone Ware at Pottersville, in Edgefield, S.C. for many years and from long experience, and former owners of that establishment, have located themselves at the Phoenix Factory, Shaw's Creek, twelve miles from Edgefield C. House on the main Road leading from Newberry, Union, and the upper Districts to Aiken, for the purpose of manufacturing Stone Ware in all its various branches. They have procured the best of workmen and are constantly making up, and have a large stock on hand. Their assortment is the most complete ever before offered for sale in this market to which they would call the attention of Druggists, Merchants and Planters, and all those who wish to purchase any thing in their line. Among the many articles of which their stock is composed, are the following viz:

Jars of all sizes from ½ gallon to 20 gallons.

Jugs of all sizes do. ¼ do. 20 do.

Churns of all sizes 2 do. 5 do.

Bowls or pans of all sizes, from ½ do. to 5 do.

Butter Pots of all sizes from ½ do. to 3 do. with covers.

Pitchers of all sizes from ¼ do., to 3 do.

And lids neatly made for jars and churns if desired.

Stew Pots of various sizes, &c. &c.

All of the above is inferior to none made in the United States. Orders addressed to us at Edgefield Court House S.C. will be promptly attended to, and delivered to the Merchant's door, any distance under one hundred and fifty miles. Charleston merchants can have their ware delivered at the depot, in Aiken, at 12½ cents per gallon. The Price at the Factory is 12½ cents per gallon.

MATHIS & RHODES
April 1, 1840 [49]

From this announcement it is clear that Mathis and Rhodes, former co-owners of the Pottersville factory, established the Phoenix Factory at Shaw's Creek in an effort to gain access to surrounding markets in Newberry, Union, and Aiken. They employed experienced workmen at the factory who produced a wide range of stoneware forms.

The Phoenix Factory is said to have been named for the *Phoenix*, a steam locomotive built from parts of the *Best Friend of Charleston*, the first American steam locomotive designed for regular passenger and freight service on the South Carolina Railroad. The *Best Friend* was financed by lowcountry businessmen in an effort to counteract a decline in trade through the city of Charleston. The Piedmont was fast becoming the most productive area of the state, and up-country cotton was routinely carried to Augusta for shipment to Savannah. With the opening of the railroad, planters could transport their produce by rail to markets within the state. The *Best Friend*, which made its debut on Christmas Day in 1830, was accidentally destroyed after only a few months of operation. On 17 June 1831 a fireman, unfamiliar with the workings of the steam locomotive and annoyed with the hissing of the escaping steam, sat on the safety valve, causing an explosion that scattered parts of the locomotive all over the countryside. The locomotive that replaced the *Best Friend*, called the *West Point*, was named for the foundry where it was built. The *West Point* made its first run on 15 July 1831. The *Phoenix*, built with parts (wheels, cylinders, gears) from the *Best Friend* that had been recovered from the wreckage, went into operation on 18 October 1832. [50]

By 1833 the South Carolina Railroad extended 136 miles from Charleston to Hamburg. [51] The owners of the Phoenix Factory evidently depended upon the railroad for the distribution of their ware throughout South Carolina. Their advertisement indicates that they had their ware transported by rail from Aiken to merchants in Charleston. But the *Phoenix* may have held even greater significance for the proprietors of the Phoenix Factory. The symbolism of the phoenix comes from Greek legend. The phoenix, a legendary bird, is said to have lived five hundred years, burned to ashes, and rose from the ashes to live again. Just as the *Phoenix* was built from parts recovered from the *Best Friend of Charleston*, the Phoenix Factory was built from property that had formerly comprised the Pottersville stoneware factory. Mathis and Rhodes evidently purchased some of the Pottersville property, relocated to Shaw's Creek, and established the Phoenix Factory from capital, equipment, and labor that they had recovered from the sale of the Pottersville factory.

Two of the highly skilled turners who worked at the Phoenix Factory were Thomas Chandler and Isaac Durham. Durham had turned ware at the Pottersville factory and came from a family of potters. Chandler, Edgefield's premier potter, was born in Drummondtown in Accomac County, Virginia, in 1810.[52] Isaac Durham, Collin Rhodes, and Thomas Chandler were living near each other in the Shaw's Creek area in 1840.[53] Robert Mathis was also living nearby. Mathis and Rhodes were owner-investors who probably never actually produced any ware. Surviving examples of the work of Thomas Chandler indicate that he was the principal turner at the Phoenix Factory. Chandler signed two storage jars below the handle in incised script, one with his name, "Thomas Chandler," and the other with the maker's mark "Phoenix Factory" (Figure 2.17). The signed Phoenix Factory jar is a tall, ovoid vessel with a light yellow-green underfired glaze, a rolled rim, and four opposing slab handles attached at the upper shoulder below the neck. The piece is decorated between each set of handle attachments with an iron-based slip loop and floral pattern.

The Phoenix Factory was the first Edgefield

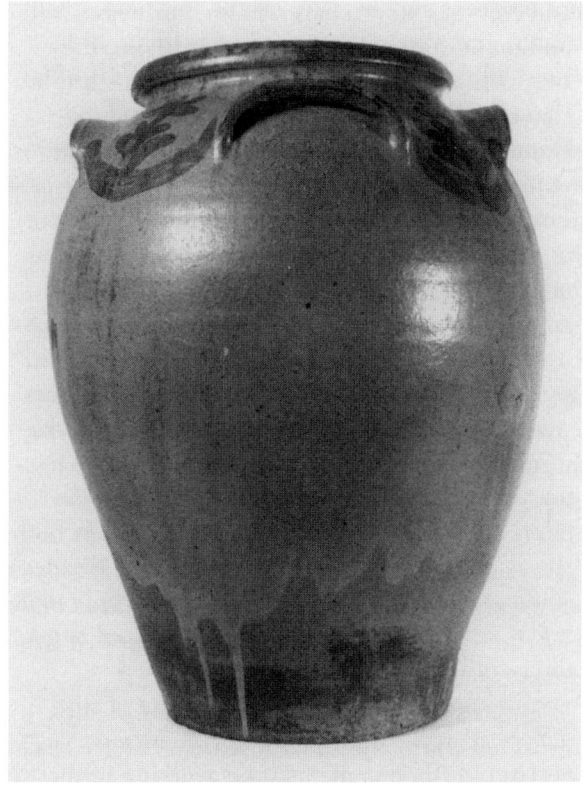

2.17   Slip-decorated alkaline-glazed stoneware storage jar, ca. 1840, Phoenix Factory, Shaw's Creek, Edgefield District, S.C. H 19¼", C 21½". Incised in script: Phoenix Factory. Collection of Terry and Steve Ferrell.

stoneware factory where slip decoration was widely used. Slips consisted of a solution of clay mixed with water to the consistency of heavy cream. This solution was brushed or trailed onto the dried ware with a slip cup. Cream-colored kaolin slip and brown-black iron-based slip were often combined, and sometimes used separately, on ware produced at the Phoenix Factory.

In May 1840 Collin Rhodes advertised for sale "Three first rate Negroes," including a twenty-seven-year-old man, whom he described as a good wagoner, and his "entire interest in stoneware on hand." Also in the ad he stated that "any person desirous of buying and letting the mules and Negroes stay to carry on the business, I will remain and attend to the same for them, if desired." In an 1840 advertisement Collin's brother Coleman Rhodes announced that he had purchased an interest in the Phoenix Factory consisting of "Negroes, Mules, Wagons, Harness and stock of ware . . . for the purpose of Manufacturing Stoneware." During the same year Coleman married Harriet Swearingen. Harriet Swearingen was probably an in-law of the Reverend John Landrum's daughter, Elizabeth C. Swearingen.[54] By 1846 Rhodes had established a second stoneware shop, C. Rhodes Factory, on the site of the former Phoenix Factory. The Collin Rhodes Factory was a large-scale operation involving the efforts of a number of workmen, most likely both slaves and journeymen laborers. In 1850 Rhodes's stoneware and brick factory employed three male and three female laborers and was valued at two thousand dollars.

Rhodes's factory featured a full line of slip-decorated ware, and some researchers have suggested that the female laborers working in the factory in 1850 were employed as decorators. A higher monthly wage of $45 for females ($15 each), in comparison to an average wage of $30 for males ($10 each) at the Rhodes factory, is cited as evidence, since greater value presumably was placed upon the skills of the decorator. Two women were also employed at Lewis Miles's factory in 1850, but no decorated ware is known to have been produced there. The women at Miles's factory were paid an average of only $12 per month ($6 each), while the men were paid about $70 per month ($10 each). Since no decorated ware was produced at Miles's factory, perhaps the women who worked there were relegated to more menial tasks that were not as highly valued, or perhaps they did not work as many hours as the men. Furthermore, no women were employed at the Thomas Chandler factory in 1850, although virtually all of Chandler's ware was slip decorated. This suggests that tasks performed by men

and women varied from one Edgefield stoneware factory to the next. The census does not indicate whether the women employed in these stoneware factories were slaves, freed blacks, or whites. More evidence is needed to determine conclusively whether women were employed as decorators at the Edgefield stoneware factories.

By 1860 women were employed at all but one of the Edgefield stoneware factories, although their presence was never as great as that of the men. Ten male and four female laborers were employed at Lewis Miles's factory that year, and two males and one female at both the B. F. Landrum and John Seigler factories. The only Edgefield stoneware factory without female laborers in 1860 was owned by W. D. Roundtree. The Roundtree factory was located at Kirksey's Crossroads near the former site of the Thomas Chandler factory.

Kirksey's Crossroads Area

Kirksey's Crossroads, located in northern Edgefield District at the juncture of three major roads running north to south through the area, was named for John Kirksey, who owned a tavern situated at the crossroads. Three stoneware factories were established in the Kirksey's Crossroads area in the first half of the nineteenth century—the Turner, Trapp-Chandler, and Thomas Chandler factories. The earliest direct reference to a stoneware factory in the area is an 1840 advertisement in which John Presley offered the following property for sale:

the Plantation on which he now resides, about eighteen miles above Edgefield C. House and one and a half miles southwest of Mr. Williams' Steam Saw Mill. Also his stone ware manufactory with excellent furnace and everything necessary to carry on the Stone ware business, all in good order.[55]

Presley appeared as a defendant in an 1841 notice of a court action involving the sale of property

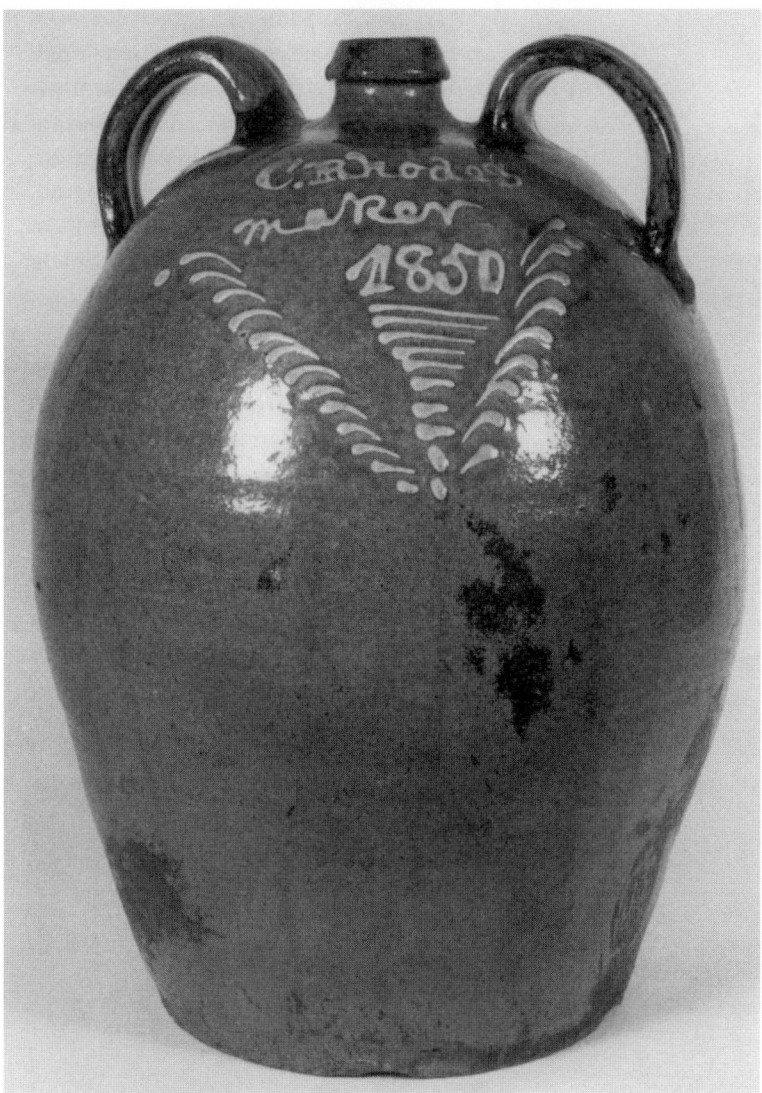

2.18 Slip-decorated alkaline-glazed stoneware syrup jug, ca. 1850, Collin Rhodes Factory, Shaw's Creek, Edgefield District, S.C. H 17⅜", C 41¼". Signed in slip: C. Rhodes / Maker / 1850. Collection of Dr. and Mrs. Charles M. Webb.

at a pottery factory located on the Martintown Road. Esau Brooks and John Trapp were also named in the notice. The Martintown Road was located north of Edgefield in the Kirksey's Crossroads area, so the pottery mentioned in the 1841 notice is undoubtedly the same factory advertised for sale by Presley in 1840. Jordan Holloway and John Lake, executors of an estate, brought the complaint against Brooks, Presley, and Trapp, apparently debtors in the case, but it is unclear

whose estate the executors represented. The defendants, Brooks, Presley, and Trapp, may have been co-owners of the Martintown Road pottery.

In 1843 John Trapp paid John Durham two hundred dollars for a tract of land containing about twelve acres "laying on both sides of the Martin Town road . . . being a small tract on which there is now a stone factory."[56] Most likely, this stoneware factory, the stoneware factory named in the 1840 Presley ad, and the pottery

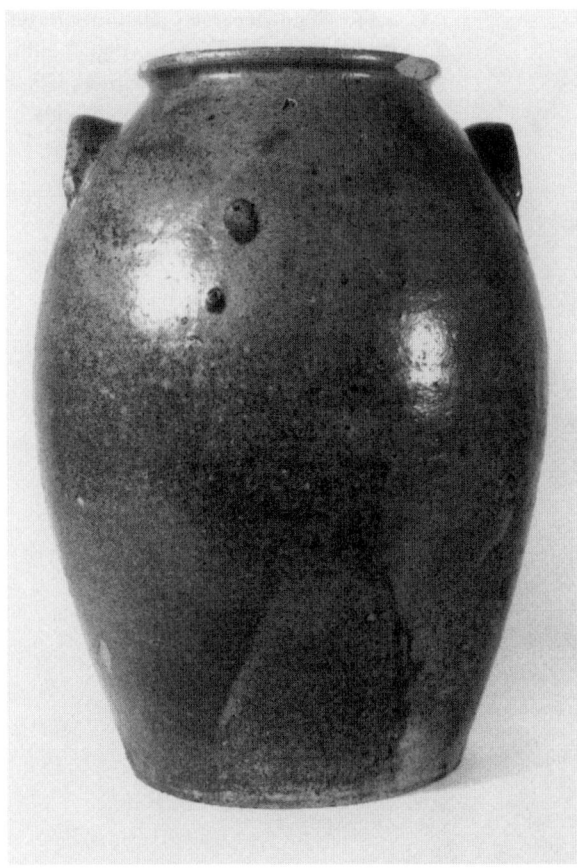

2.19 Alkaline-glazed stoneware storage jar, ca. 1840, attributed to the John Presley Factory, Kirksey's Crossroads, Edgefield District, S.C. H 15¾″, C 37⅝″. Stamped: P. Collection of Terry and Steve Ferrell.

mill, a pottery, and as many as eighteen slaves. Trapp moved to the Kirksey's Crossroads area in 1829 from Fairfield, South Carolina, and was ordained as a minister at Mountain Creek Baptist Church in 1833. His church had over five hundred members in 1850, "including the colored."[57] Trapp was a circuit preacher until his death in 1876. In August 1842, March 1847, and June 1847 Trapp preached at Horn's Creek Baptist Church. The Reverend John Landrum served as pastor of Horn's Creek church from 1809 until 1824 and was a member of the church until his death in 1847. His son, Benjamin Franklin Landrum, also a pottery manufacturer, was listed in the church records as a member of the church as late as 1859, so Trapp may have maintained an association with the Landrum family.[58] Trapp appears to have been an owner-investor in the Trapp-Chandler

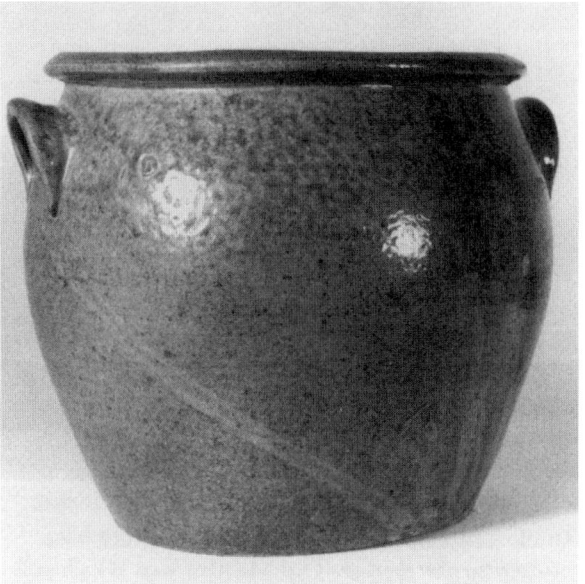

2.20 Alkaline-glazed stoneware jar, ca. 1840–43, attributed to the John Durham Factory, Kirksey's Crossroads, Edgefield District, S.C. H 9½″, C 33⅝″. Stamped: D. Stoneware fragments with this maker's mark were recovered from the Trapp-Chandler site (38GN343) at Kirksey's Crossroads. Collection of Terry and Steve Ferrell.

factory mentioned in the 1841 court notice were the same. If this is the case, then the Martintown Road pottery, like the Pottersville factory, must have passed through several investor-owners from 1840 to 1843. The site of the stoneware factory that John Trapp purchased from John Durham in 1843 has been positively identified. Known today as the Trapp-Chandler site, it is located just south of Kirksey's Crossroads in present-day Greenwood County on a tract of land known as Matthew's Field.

John Trapp was a successful businessman who owned over twelve hundred acres of land, a saw-

factory rather than an active potter. The only evidence of his ever having produced pottery is a very crudely thrown cup incised in script, "John Trapp First Turning 18—," that was recovered from the Trapp-Chandler site during the 1983 excavation of the site by Keith Landreth.[59]

Records pertaining to a lawsuit filed against Trapp in 1850 by Jordan Holloway, Trapp's partner in a sawmill business, contain information regarding a partnership between Trapp and Chandler. According to the records, they purchased 1,090 feet of rough-edge poplar from the sawmill in 1848, and 900 feet in 1849.[60] This wood may have been used to fire pottery produced at the factory.

Thomas Chandler evidently operated the Trapp-Chandler pottery factory and acted as the principal turner. Chandler may have become involved in the Martintown Road factory through his association with the Durham family. In 1838 Chandler married John Durham's daughter Margaret.[61] By this time John Durham may have owned the Martintown Road stoneware factory that John Trapp later purchased. Another member of the Durham clan, Isaac, who appeared in an 1843 land conveyance as owner of a tract of land located adjacent to John Trapp's Kirksey's Crossroads property, may have also been a turner at the Trapp-Chandler factory. It is unclear precisely when Thomas Chandler became involved in stoneware manufacture at Trapp's stoneware factory, but a number of pottery fragments recovered from the site bear the stamped maker's mark TRAPP & CHANDLER. A storage jar in the collection of Stephen and Terry Ferrell incised in script "Chandler Maker / 1844." (front, upper body, between handles) and "Mr. B. Harland" (opposite, between handles) may be representative of Chandler's earliest work at the Trapp-Chandler factory and of early experiments with the local clays (Figure 2.21). This atypical Chandler storage jar has two opposing lug handles placed high on the shoulder, just below the neck. The vessel

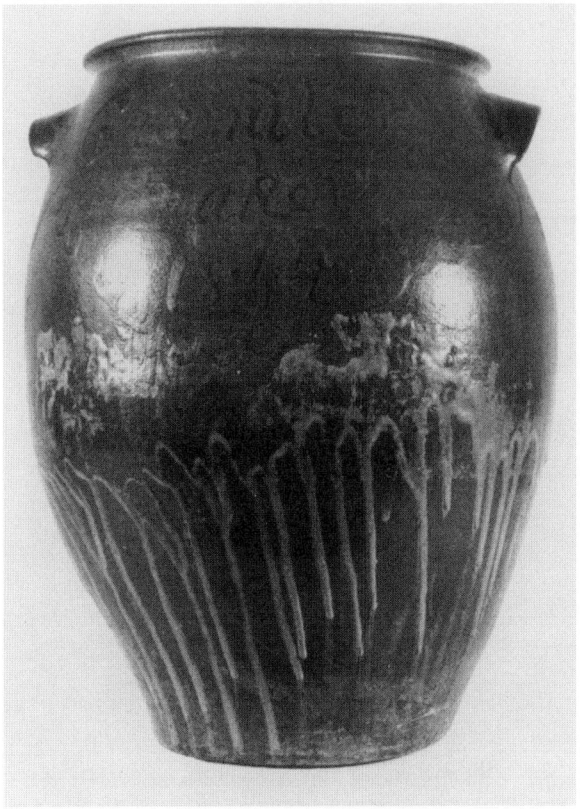

2.21 Slip-decorated alkaline-glazed stoneware preserve jar, 1844, Thomas Chandler, attributed to the Trapp-Chandler Factory, Kirksey's Crossroads, Edgefield District, S.C. H 17¾", C 44⅞". Incised in script: Chandler Maker / 1844; Mr. B. Harland (opposite). Collection of Terry and Steve Ferrell.

has a full, ovoid form, tapering inward toward the base, and a brown-black to dark brown alkaline glaze. Below the incised maker's mark is an iron-bearing slip loop and swag decorative motif. While most Chandler storage jars have a wide shoulder at the midpoint between the base and rim, this jar has a high, wide shoulder located just below the rim. Another atypical feature of this vessel is the dark, streaky glaze. Most of Chandler's ware has smooth, light gray-green to blue-green glazes.

Vessels produced at the Trapp-Chandler factory include pan-form bowls, jugs, storage jars,

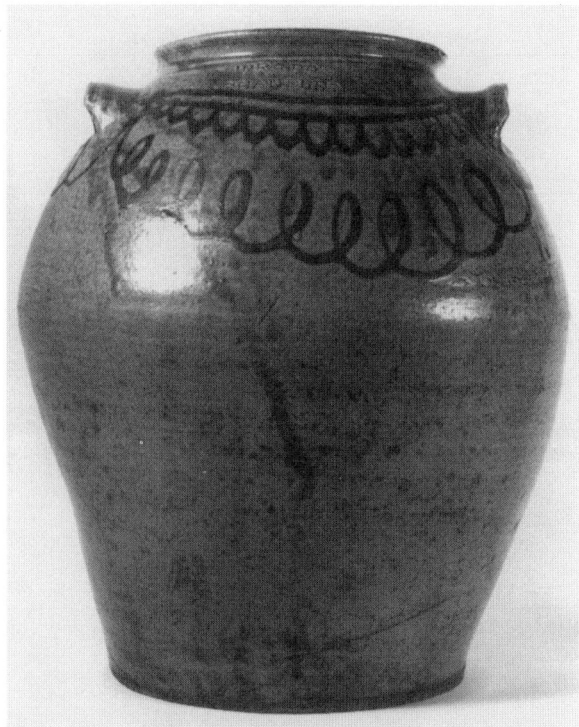

2.22 Slip-decorated alkaline-glazed stoneware storage jar, ca. 1845, Trapp-Chandler Factory, Kirksey's Crossroads, Edgefield District, S.C. H 14⅞″, C 42⅜″. Stamped: TRAPP & / CHANDLER. Collection of Georgeanna H. Greer.

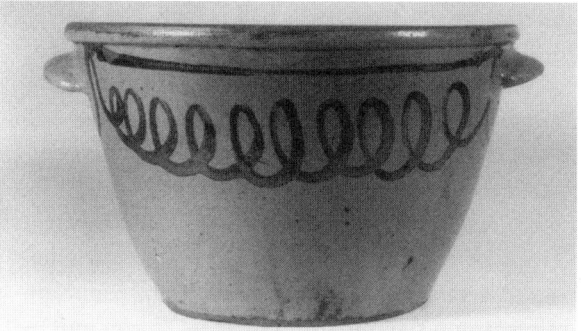

2.23 Slip-decorated alkaline-glazed stoneware bowl, ca. 1845, Thomas Chandler, attributed to the Trapp-Chandler Factory, Kirksey's Crossroads, Edgefield District, S.C. H 7¼″, C 37½″. Collection of Donnie F. Garrett.

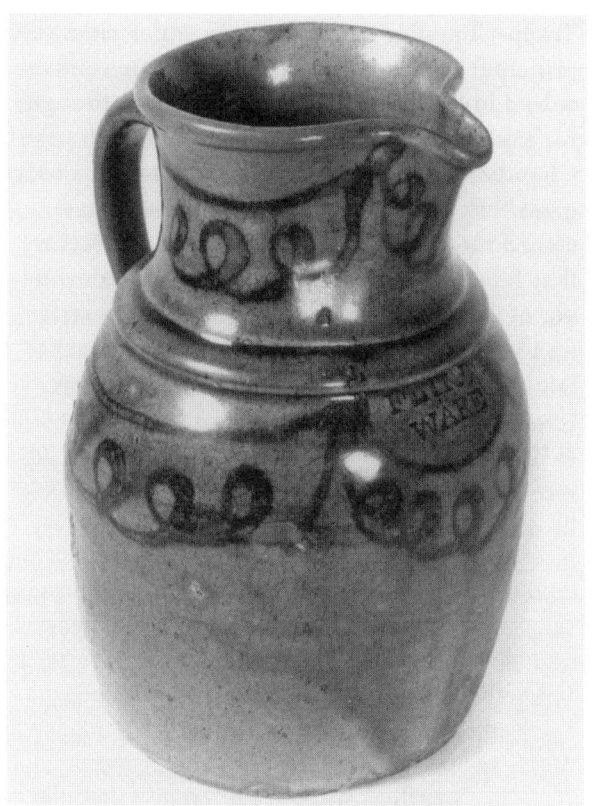

2.24 Slip-decorated alkaline-glazed stoneware pitcher, ca. 1845, Thomas Chandler, Trapp-Chandler Factory, Kirksey's Crossroads, Edgefield District, S.C. H 10½″, C 23¼″. Stamped: FLINTWARE. Collection of Tony and Marie Shank.

churns, chamber pots, and cups (see Figures 2.22 and 2.23). All of the ware produced at the site is alkaline-glazed. Glaze colors range from tan and pale blue-greens, or celadons, to olive greens. Blue clouding or glaze patches found on some stoneware fragments recovered from the site indicate the unintentional inclusion of rutile (titanium dioxide) in the clay body of the ware. Rutile is a naturally occurring mineral found in some Edgefield-area stoneware clays. Vessels with Chandler's mark have a smooth, even-textured glaze, probably produced by the addition of feldspar and lime to the glaze ingredients. Feldspar is a source of silica and therefore produces a glassier glaze. The addition of lime to the glaze ingredients may also account for the smoother, more even glaze texture. Some ware produced at the Trapp-Chandler site is marked FLINT WARE, probably in reference to the addition of quartz (known as "flint" by nineteenth-century potters) in the form of feldspar to the glaze ingredients. Over twenty-three pounds of mineral identified as feldspar were recovered from a test unit at the Trapp-Chandler site in 1978, a further indication of the use of this material in the production of stoneware at the site.[62]

Other than the TRAPP & CHANDLER and FLINT WARE marks, some Trapp-Chandler vessels are stamped or impressed at the neck just below the rim, or at the rim, with incised or stamped symbols. The marks consist of the following: I, sideways I, V, upside down V, E, backward E, U, and W. The symbols are often grouped, appearing similar to Roman numerals. The significance of these symbols is not known.

The Trapp-Chandler factory closed in 1849. In 1850 Chandler established a stoneware and brick factory of his own at Kirksey's Crossroads. Chandler announced the opening of his factory in the *Edgefield Advertiser*.

STONE WARE!

The subscriber believeing that a good article of this useful and necessary Ware is much needed, has come to the conclusion to make and keep on hand a splendid article, which he will not only recommend, but will warrant to be good.

He, therefore, most respectfully solicits the patronage of those who deal in and use this kind of Ware, knowing that they will be satisfied with his Ware and prices.

All orders directed to me at Kirksey's X Roads, Edgefield District, South Carolina, will meet with prompt attention.

My jugs are marked "Chandler Maker—Warranted."

T. M. Chandler[63]

Many examples of ware marked "Chandler Warranted" have been recovered from the site of this factory (Figure 2.25).

Chandler employed eleven slave and journeyman potters in 1850 at a cost of $165 per month.

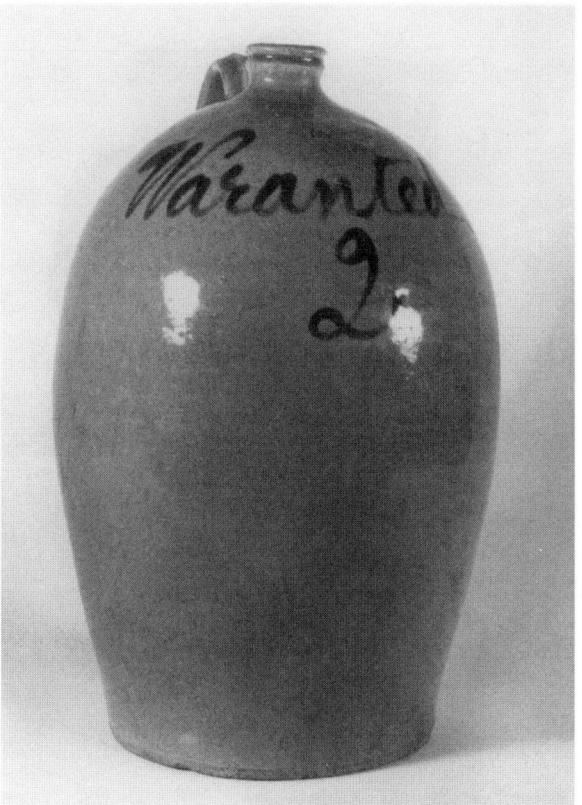

2.25 Alkaline-glazed stoneware jug, ca. 1850, Thomas Chandler, Thomas Chandler Factory, Kirksey's Crossroads, Edgefield District, S.C. H 13¾″, C 29″. Stamped: Chandler Maker. Signed in iron-based slip: Waranted / 2. Collection of Georgeanna H. Greer.

His factory was valued at $2,500 that year, and he had $1,500 invested in the business. Chandler produced a wide assortment of stoneware forms—milk pans, pitchers, chamber pots, jugs, and storage jars—ranging in size from one-half gallon to ten gallons. Pitchers were tall, ovoid baluster-shaped vessels (Figure 2.26). The chamber pot was short, squat, and bulbous in form with a flaring rim and a single loop handle. Storage jars produced by Chandler were also bulbous and typically had two opposing wide and up-curved lug handles, whereas churns were more cylindrical in form. Syrup jugs were typically tall ovoid forms with square or rounded collared necks, as

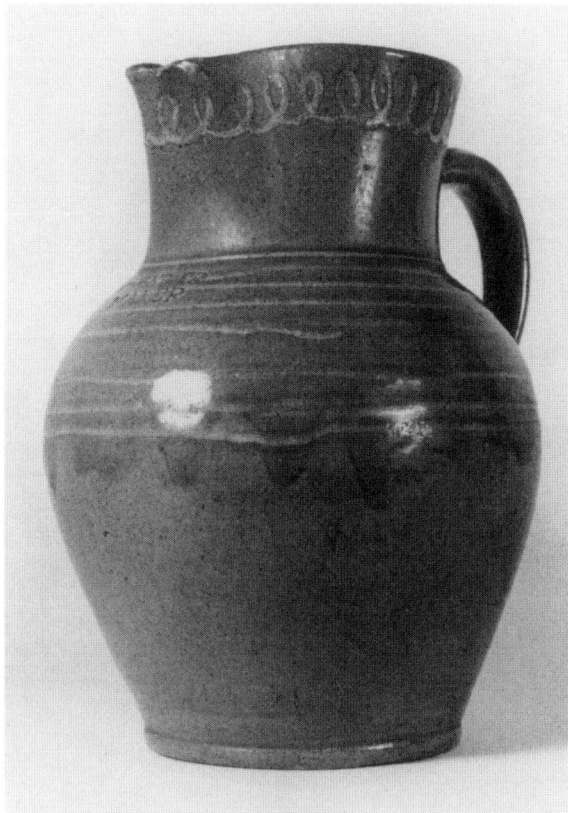

2.26　Slip-decorated alkaline-glazed stoneware pitcher, ca. 1850, Thomas Chandler, Thomas Chandler Factory, Edgefield District, S.C. H 10¼″, C 24½″. Stamped: CHANDLER MAKER. Collection of Tony and Marie Shank.

opposed to the double collars typically found on ware produced at other Edgefield factories, and had double loop handles attached at the shoulder well below the neck. Smaller whiskey jugs were cylindrical with rounded shoulders.

In an analysis of vessel fragments recovered from the Thomas Chandler site Landreth noted that over 72 percent (4,207) of the sherds recovered from the site were decorated in finely trailed kaolin-slip designs unlike those found at the Trapp-Chandler factory. Three maker's marks—CHANDLER, CHANDLER / MAKER, and CHANDLER / WARRANTED—appear on the Thomas Chandler factory ware. Variations in these marks

include the use of the lower case letters *er* in the CHANDLER mark (with the lowercase letters being the same height as the other letters), and in the case of the CHANDLER / WARRANTED mark, CHANDLER is stamped into the ware, and WAR-RANTED is either stamped (sometimes upside down) or written in script in iron-based slip.[64]

An 1849 Georgia newspaper notice indicates that slaves hauled ware produced at Kirksey's Crossroads into neighboring states. According to the notice, a slave named Pearl who claimed to be a trader in jugs and jars had passed through Ray-town, Taliaferro County, Georgia, that year "and had with him two Waggons, and loads of [stone-ware]—the teams driven by two lads." According to the notice, Pearl, who was wanted for passing counterfeit money, claimed to have been in the Kirksey's Crossroads area during the previous summer.[65]

In September 1850 Thomas Chandler's son drowned in a pond (perhaps an abandoned clay pit) located near "the old pottery" and about two hundred yards from Chandler's house. Two witnesses, Stewart Durham and Francis Devlin (var. Devillin), offered testimony regarding the circumstances of the death in a coroner's in-quisition. Devillin, who was listed as a potter in the 1850 Edgefield census, was living near Chandler.[66] Stewart Durham, most likely a mem-ber of the John Durham family, and Devillin were probably journeyman potters in Chandler's stoneware factory.

The Thomas Chandler factory was in operation for less than two years. In 1852 Chandler filed a deed in which he placed his property in trust for his wife and children. Apparently, he was in ill health and wanted to provide for his family in the event of his death. Chandler and his family moved to Buncombe County, North Carolina, a few months after the trust deed was filed. He died two years later at the age of forty-four.

A man named Turner established a third stone-ware factory at Kirksey's Crossroads in about

1840. This factory, which was continued well into the second half of the nineteenth century, is discussed further in the following chapters.

Aiken Stoneware Pottery

A pottery located in Barnwell District, just south of the Edgefield-Barnwell District boundary on the outskirts of the city of Aiken, may have been one of the earliest stoneware potteries established in South Carolina. Although the potter who worked at this site has not been positively identified, several families associated with pottery manufacture in Edgefield appear in late eighteenth- and early nineteenth-century Barnwell District records.[67]

An extensive surface collection of artifacts carried out at the Aiken site by J. Walter Joseph, Jr., has revealed important clues to the significance of this early nineteenth-century stoneware site (see Figure 2.27). Stoneware fragments of pipkin forms were recovered from the site. The pipkin is a small cooking pot with a single handle. Pipkins were used much like modern saucepans. The pipkin form consists of a flat base, slightly raised in the center and a curving bag-shaped wall with the pot being wider at the base than the rim. Pipkins often have three feet. They have a slightly everted rim with a gently rounded lip and a hollow tubular handle attached at right angles to the body wall. This form was noted by Barka in both salt-glazed stoneware and lead-glazed earthenware at the Yorktown Pottery site, which dated from about 1720 to 1745. The pipkin was a common seventeenth- and eighteenth-century earthenware form.[68]

The presence of vessel forms at the Aiken site typically associated with earthenware manufacture but here rendered in alkaline-glazed stoneware suggests the application of earlier earthenware technology to the production of stoneware. Other stoneware forms recovered from the Aiken site include plates, chamber pots, pan-form bowls, and small preserve jars with nested, knob-handled lids. Some plate fragments recovered from the site have kiln supports fused to the interior surface. Since this type of kiln furniture was rarely used by southern alkaline-glazed stoneware potters but was commonly used in the production of earthenware, the presence of these supports may be further evidence of the use of earthenware techniques at the site.

Teapot sherds (spouts with strainers and body fragments) were also recovered from the Aiken site. These may indicate that the site was established in the early decades of the nineteenth century. Early Georgia potters associated with the Landrums produced alkaline-glazed stoneware "coffee boilers," which are similar to the teapot yet taller and more elongated than the rounded

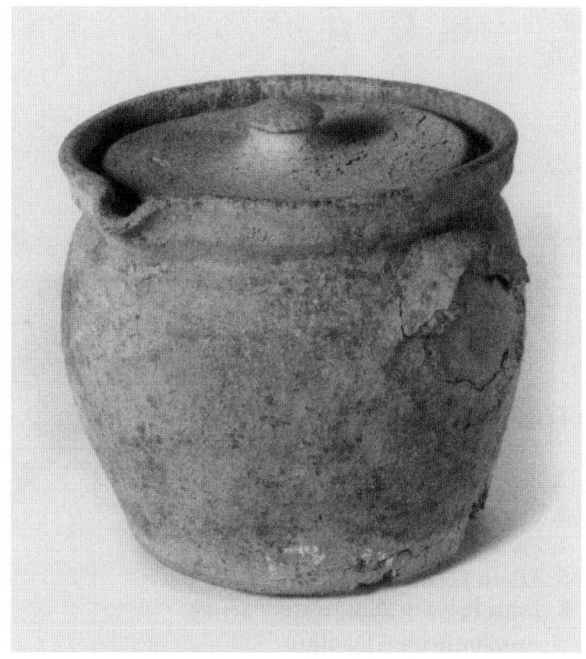

2.27 Alkaline-glazed stoneware pipkin, ca. 1810–30, Hitchcock Woods site (38AK172), Aiken County, S.C. H 4½", C 5¾". Collection of the Aiken County Historical Museum, Aiken, S.C.

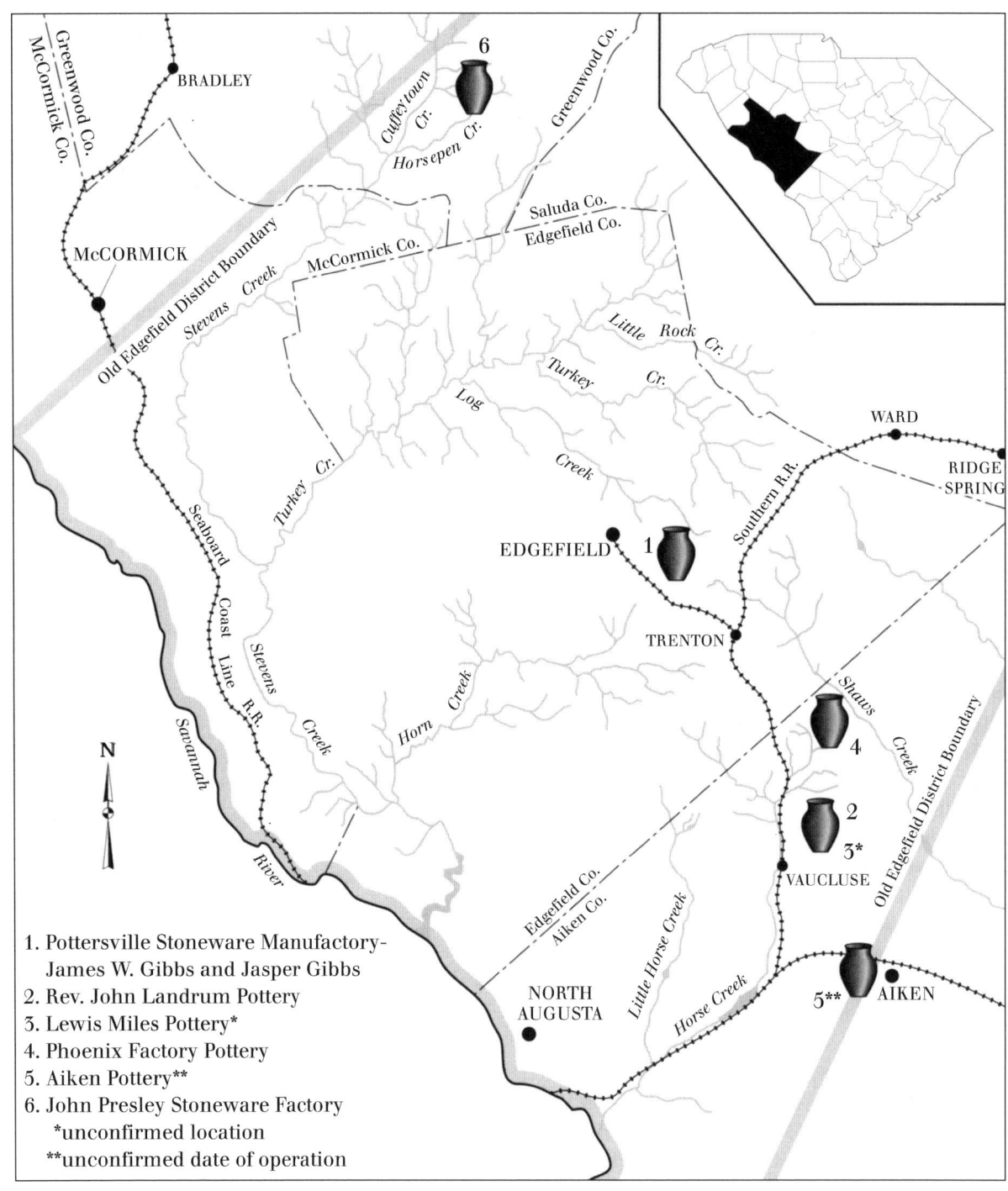

1. Pottersville Stoneware Manufactory–
   James W. Gibbs and Jasper Gibbs
2. Rev. John Landrum Pottery
3. Lewis Miles Pottery*
4. Phoenix Factory Pottery
5. Aiken Pottery**
6. John Presley Stoneware Factory
     *unconfirmed location
     **unconfirmed date of operation

2.28 Map of the present-day area encompassing the old Edgefield District showing locations of stoneware pottery sites in operation in 1840.

or squat teapot form.[69] Although archaeologists have dated the Aiken site to post-1820 on the basis of a single artifact recovered there, ceramics scholar Georgeanna Greer believes that the site was established earlier in the first or second decade of the nineteenth century.

A great variety of alkaline glazes were produced at the Aiken site, ranging in color from light yellow-green to almost black, and a wide range of glaze colors was typically found on a single sherd. The clays used at this site appear to have been poorly suited for stoneware production because many sherds exhibit cracking caused by excessive shrinkage during firing. Archaeologists have concluded that "this site appears to represent a brief experiment rather than a long-term, full scale production effort."[70]

By 1840 six stoneware factories were in operation in the Edgefield District. With the exception of the Aiken site, all of these early potteries were located within three major areas of Edgefield pottery activity: Pottersville, the Horse Creek Valley, and Kirksey's Crossroads. These areas continued to be major centers for pottery activity in the district during the following decades (see Figures 2.28 and 2.29).

Edgefield Influence on the Southern Stoneware Tradition

Many journeyman potters who trained in the Edgefield District during the first half of the nineteenth century migrated to states throughout the lower South where they continued to produce alkaline-glazed stoneware. Greer has traced the migrations of stoneware potters from Edgefield into Georgia, Alabama, Mississippi, and Texas.[71] These migration routes follow geological formations with ample deposits of stoneware clays. One of these zones, known to geologists as the Tuscaloosa Formation, passes through southern Georgia and Alabama. The western fringe of this geologic region extends into eastern and central Texas, where it is known as the Wilcox Group. Southern stoneware potters sought out the deposits of rich stoneware clays that were exposed in riverine areas along these geologic boundaries. Edgefield-trained potters also carried the alkaline-glazed stoneware tradition into western North Carolina and central and northern South Carolina.

The alkaline-glazed stoneware tradition was introduced into Georgia in the second decade of the nineteenth century by potters associated with the Landrum family. The most significant connection was between Abner Landrum and Washington County, Georgia, potters Cyrus Cogburn and Abraham Massey. In 1814 Massey witnessed an Edgefield deed in which Abner Landrum acquired property that he later divided into lots and sold to create the village of Pottersville. Three stoneware manufacturers—Cyrus Cogburn, Abraham Massey, and Isaac Kirkland— witnessed another 1814 deed in which John Landrum purchased a lot on Horse Creek.[72] Massey and Cogburn had introduced the recently developed alkaline glaze to Washington County, Georgia, by 1820. They both appeared as "stone ware manufacturers" in the Washington County manufacturing census for that year: "Abraham Massey. Jugs, Jars, Coffee boilers, etc. $2000 [annual market value of products]. Cyrus Cogburn. Jugs, Jars, & etc. $3000." The marshall's assistant closed his enumeration with this note: "There is on the Little Ogechee river the firm of a Stone-ware Manufactory, the men who are engaged in the business informed me that their ware was equal to any in the Southern States, tho' as yet they were only able to carry it on in a small way."[73] This claim was repeated by alkaline-glazed stoneware manufacturers throughout Edgefield. Coffeepots with tubular spouts, perhaps similar to the coffee boilers produced by Massey, have been recovered from two Edgefield District stoneware factory sites, suggesting that

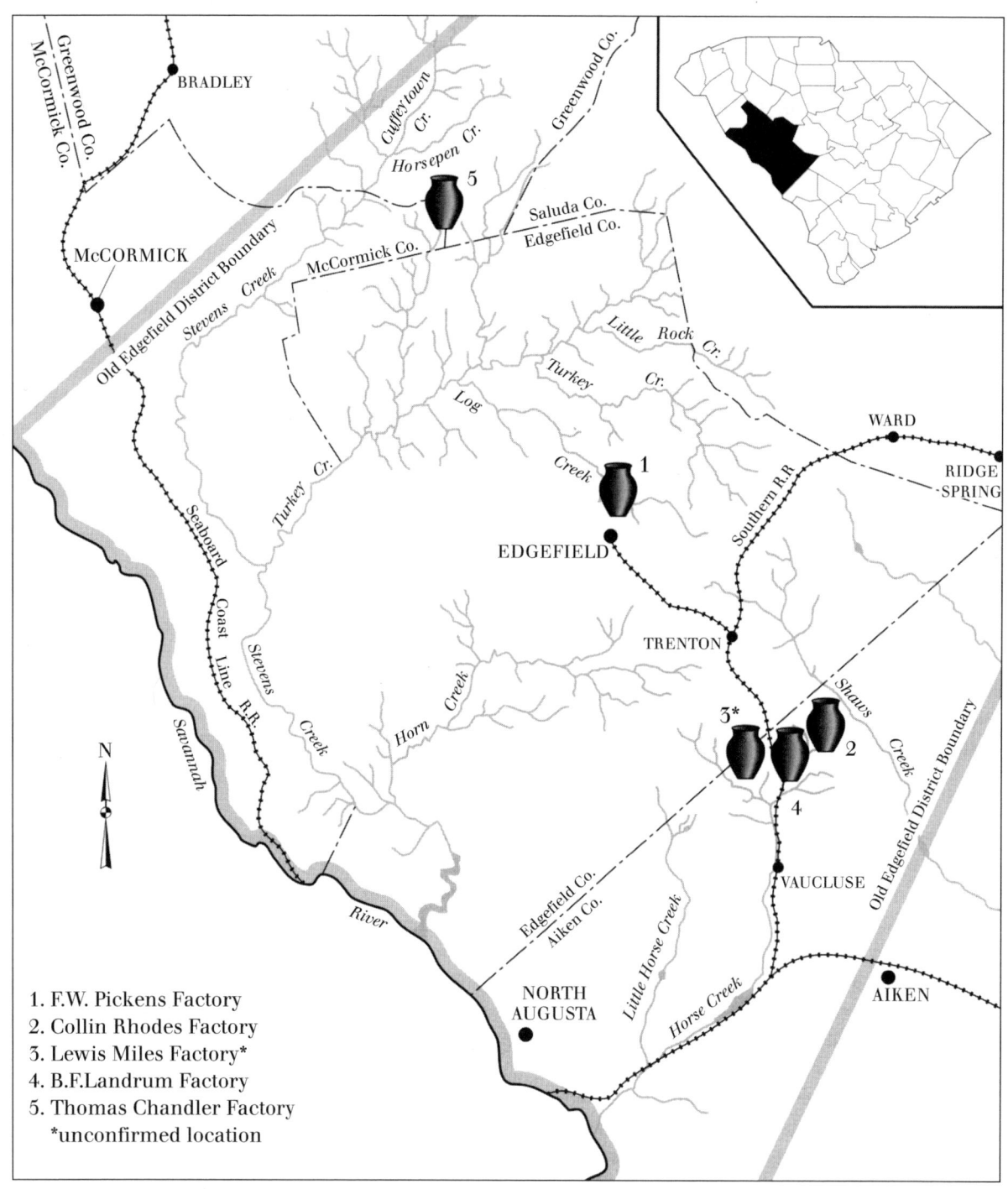

1. F.W. Pickens Factory
2. Collin Rhodes Factory
3. Lewis Miles Factory*
4. B.F.Landrum Factory
5. Thomas Chandler Factory
   *unconfirmed location

2.29   Map of the present-day area encompassing the old Edgefield District showing locations of stoneware pottery sites in operation in 1850.

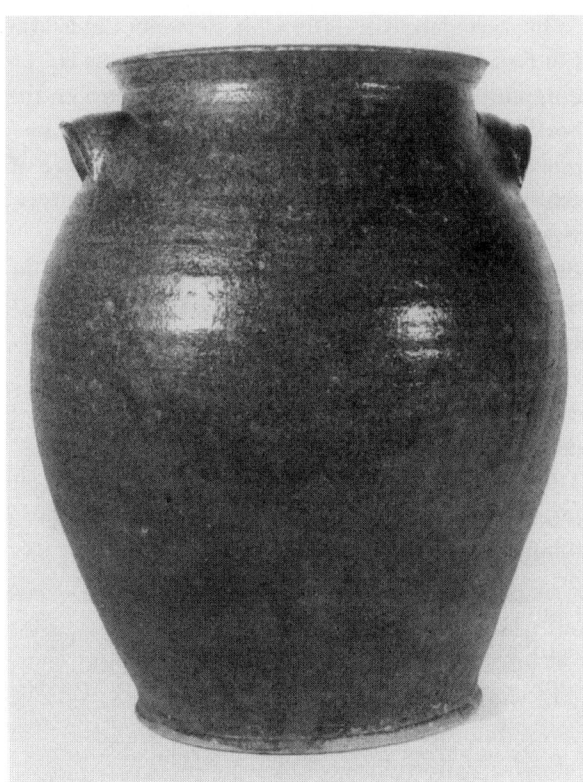

2.30 Alkaline-glazed stoneware storage jar, ca. 1820, attributed to Abraham Massey, Washington County, Ga. H 14½″, C 37⅝″. Incised marks: M (front, between handles) and "5" (below handle). Collection of John A. Burrison.

Massey may have worked at either the Pottersville or John Landrum factory before moving to Georgia.[74] In 1818 Cogburn was paying taxes in Washington County, and by 1825 he owned three hundred acres of pineland on the (Little) Ogeechee, near a tract owned by Abraham Massey. He was paying taxes for land in Upson County in 1827–28 and was in Talbot County by 1830. Cogburn appeared in census records in Macon County, Alabama, in 1840 and in Rusk County, Texas, in 1850, where he and his sons continued to produce alkaline-glazed stoneware.[75]

Other Georgia potters trained in the Edgefield stoneware factories. Tenuous connections have been established between the Landrum family

and members of the Ferguson clay clan. In an 1828 Edgefield probate court confession James Ferguson and Richard Christmas promised to pay Abner Landrum $128 plus interest "for value Rec.d."[76] Charles H. Ferguson migrated from Edgefield to Walton County, Georgia, in about 1827. By 1846 he had established a shop in Jackson (now Barrow) County near present Statham. A complex network of pottery families was established as men were drawn into the craft through marriage into the Ferguson clan. By the turn of the century all the Georgia potters of the DeLay, Archer, Dial, Robertson, and Hewell families were interrelated through the Fergusons.[77]

Members of another important clay clan

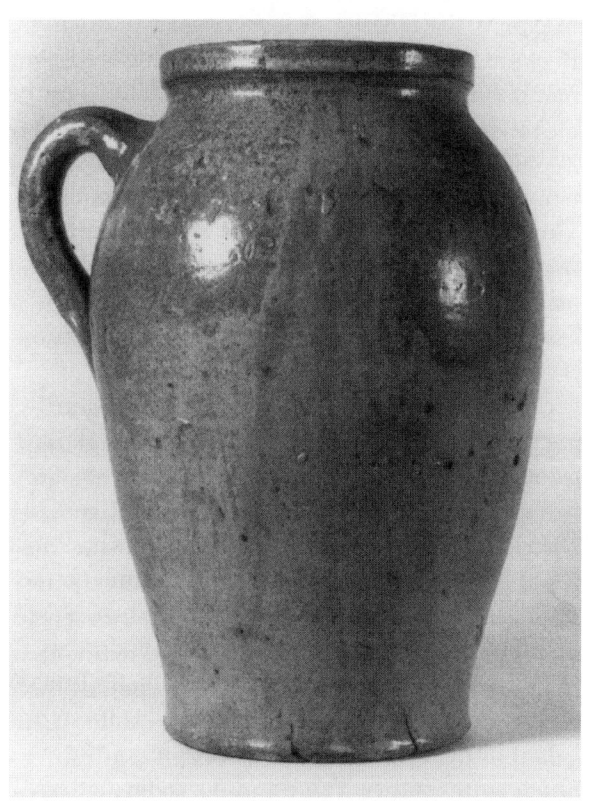

2.31 Alkaline-glazed stoneware preserve jar, ca. 1850, attributed to Cyrus or T. I. Cogburn, Rusk County, Tex. H 12″, C 25¾″. Incised maker's mark: 2 (right of handle). Collection of Georgeanna H. Greer.

passed through Edgefield on their way to Crawford County, Georgia. The Becham family was potting in eastern Crawford County by 1850, their ancestors having come from England to Virginia and, later, to Granville County, North Carolina, the Edgefield District of South Carolina, and Washington County, Georgia.[78] It is unclear whether the Bechams learned the pottery craft through contact with their neighbors, the Longs in Crawford County, or by a previous generation in England, the Edgefield District, or Washington County, Georgia, but there is some evidence of a connection with Edgefield families involved in stoneware production. In 1786 John Becham, Jr., acquired a state grant for 612 acres of land on Gilders Creek and Peters Creek in Ninety Six District. A few years later Thomas Beckum (var. Becham) sold a three-hundred-acre plantation on Horn's Creek in Edgefield County to Aquilla Miles, father of Edgefield stoneware manufacturer Lewis Miles.[79] This property was bound by two tracts of land formerly owned by Thomas Presley and a member of the Hatcher family. The Presley and Hatcher families were associated with the Landrums, and both families were involved in Edgefield stoneware manufacture.

One of the most perplexing problems regarding the development of southern alkaline-glazed stoneware involves the relationship between the two earliest alkaline-glaze centers: the Edgefield District of South Carolina and the Catawba Valley of North Carolina. The North Carolina pottery tradition is apparently the older of the two. German potters moved into the western Piedmont of North Carolina during the second half of the eighteenth century, and the craft was well established in the area by the early decades of the nineteenth century. The Catawba Valley potters continued to produce earthenware well into the nineteenth century. Meanwhile, Abner Landrum was perfecting a "stronger, better" stoneware that soon became the standard in Edgefield.

The problem of relationship between the Edgefield and Catawba Valley pottery traditions is compounded by the sharp divergence between the two. The principal families involved in alkaline-glazed stoneware production in Edgefield were of British descent, while the Catawba Valley potters were of German extraction. Also, in the Edgefield District the plantation system made possible a larger scale of stoneware production than that found in the Catawba Valley. Edgefield stoneware factory owners were wealthy entrepreneurs who employed hired turners and skilled slave artisans in their operations. In contrast, Catawba Valley potters owned modest farms and operated potteries in order to supplement their farming incomes. They owned few slaves, and there is no evidence that black potters worked in the Catawba Valley.

In addition to these socioeconomic contrasts, there were fundamental differences in the raw materials used by potters in the two areas. Catawba Valley clays, unlike the relatively pure kaolin-rich clays of the Edgefield District, were saturated with iron and other impurities. Consequently, the Catawba Valley ware exhibits dark colors and highly variable textures. Slip decoration was never used in the Catawba Valley, although some potters (primarily the Seagle and Hartzo [var. Hartzog] families) employed a technique of placing glass on the mouths, necks, handles, and ends of ware before firing in the kiln. The glass melted when fired, creating a pattern of thick, contrasting drips along the length of the pot.[80]

The Weaver family may provide a possible link between these two early pottery centers. Catawba Valley potter Ernest Auburn Hilton credited Jacob Weaver with the founding of the North Carolina Jugtown pottery center in Catawba and Lincoln counties. Hilton cited Weaver's "secret color formula for pottery" but did not know if he had learned to make pottery in Catawba County or elsewhere.[81] Several Weavers appear in early

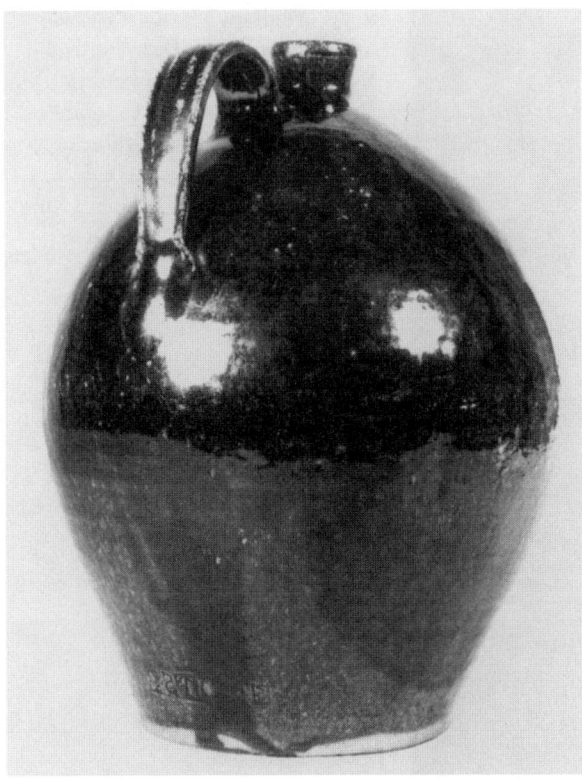

2.32   Alkaline-glazed stoneware jug, ca. 1850, Edward Stone, Buncombe County, N.C. H 12⅛″, C 30⅝″. Stamped: ESTONE (backward S and N). Collection of Doug and Jane Penland.

nineteenth-century Edgefield District census records. For example, a John Weaver appears in the 1800 Edgefield census, a Jonathan Weaver in the 1820 census, and a J. R. Wever in 1840. Also, an Ed Weaver appears in the 1840 York District census on the same page as North Carolina potter George W. Hance. This information suggests that members of the Weaver family may have carried the alkaline glaze from the Edgefield District to the Catawba Valley of North Carolina.

A possible relationship between members of the Landrum family of Chatham County, North Carolina, and patriarchs of two important North Carolina clay clans, the Hartzos and Cravens, has already been discussed. However, no direct links have been found between the Edgefield District and Catawba Valley alkaline-glazed stoneware traditions.

A direct connection has been established between the Edgefield District and the alkaline-glazed stoneware traditions of Buncombe County, North Carolina. Potter Edward Stone appeared as a defendant in an 1841 court action in which "one lot of Jugs, Jars, etc." was sold "at the Pottery on the Martintown Road."[82] Apparently, the property was being sold in order to settle debts incurred by the owners of the factory. A related announcement involving the sale of fifteen hundred gallons of ware belonging to Esau Brooks at the Martintown Road pottery, and naming "Jordan Holloway and John Lake, Ex'ters [Executors] vs. Esau Brooks, John Presley and John Trapp," had appeared only a few days earlier.[83] The court action apparently referred to a pottery located in the Kirksey's Crossroads area of Edgefield. In 1840 John Presley advertised the sale of his plantation and stoneware factory located about eighteen miles above Edgefield, presumably near Kirksey's Crossroads. John Durham owned a pottery located on the Martintown Road that he sold to John Trapp in 1843. John Presley apparently sold his pottery to John Durham, and Durham later sold the stoneware factory to John Trapp. Esau Brooks and Edward Stone were probably journeyman turners at the factory.

The great-grandson of William Penland, founder of a pottery in Buncombe County, North Carolina, claimed that Penland went into business with E. W. (Edward) Stone in South Carolina in 1836 to learn the stoneware trade and that Stone learned the trade from Thomas Chandler. A contradictory account, published in 1930, holds that William Penland founded a pottery in Candler (located in Buncombe County, North Carolina) in 1831 and that Edward Stone was the second turner employed by Penland. Stone apparently arrived in Buncombe County in about 1843 or 1844. Three other South Carolina potters—Isaac Matthews, Francis Devillin, and

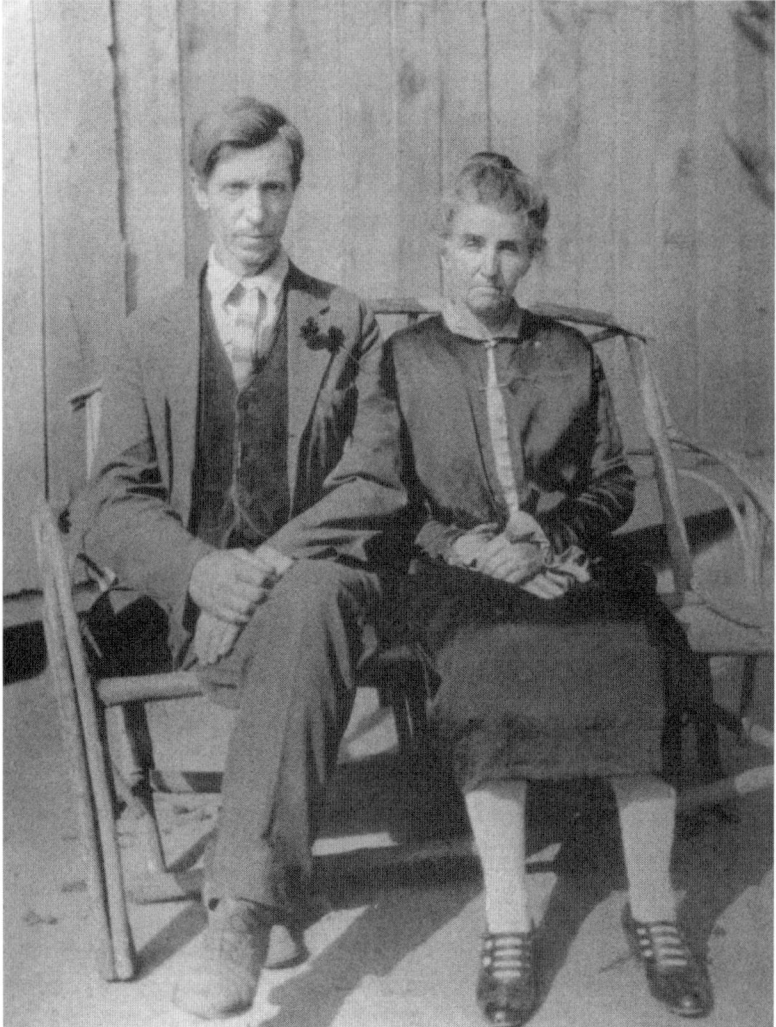

2.33   William Marion Penland and Emma Stone, Candler, N.C. Potter William M. Penland of Buncombe County, N.C., married Emma Stone, daughter of Edgefield-trained potter Edward Stone. Courtesy of Doug and Jane Penland.

William Rhodes—apparently also worked at the Stone-Penland shop.[84] Devillin, who appeared as a witness in a September 1850 inquisition into the drowning of Thomas Chandler's young son, a few months later was living in Buncombe County. R. W. Matthews, possibly a relative of Isaac Matthews, was living in Edgefield near Isaac Durham, Thomas Chandler, and Collin Rhodes in 1840 and most likely was a turner at the Phoenix Factory. Also in 1840, two men between the ages of twenty and thirty were living in the household of Collin Rhodes. William Rhodes, perhaps the brother of Collin, may have been one of these two men.[85]

The Edgefield potters probably arrived in Buncombe County via the Saluda Gap Road. This was the first main route of travel from the Piedmont of South Carolina to the Blue Ridge Mountains of North Carolina. The Saluda Gap Road, completed after 1825, was part of the state road from Charleston to Columbia and Greenville. The Buncombe Turnpike Company was chartered in 1824, the first tollgate was opened in 1827, and the turnpike was completed in 1828. This route served the communities of Flat Rock and Fletcher, located between the Gap and Asheville, which served as summer retreats for lowcountry planters.[86]

Early ware produced at the Stone-Penland pottery is further evidence of these associations between potters in Buncombe County, North Carolina, and Edgefield. A syrup jug produced by Edward Stone's son, J. H. Stone, bears striking similarities to ware produced by Thomas Chandler in Edgefield. The tall, thin-walled, symmetrically ovoid form of this jug and the two loop handles attached well below the neck and at the upper shoulder of the vessel are characteristics identified with ware produced by Chandler (see Figure 2.34).

Another early North Carolina pottery center with ties to South Carolina was located in Union County on the South Carolina border immediately to the southeast of Charlotte near the crossroads hamlet of Altan. The Union County pottery tradition was established shortly before the mid-nineteenth century by settlers from South Carolina. George W. Hance, the earliest recorded South Carolina potter in the county, appears in the 1850 census.[87] A George W. Hance was listed in the Union District, South Carolina, census in 1830, and a G. W. Hance was living in York County in 1840. These records may indicate that Hance was associated with Edgefield-trained potter Thomas W. Owensby. Owensby, who appeared in the 1810 Edgefield census, later migrated to northern Union District (present-day Cherokee County) where he established a pottery shop. Hance apparently migrated from Union District to York County on the North Carolina border, just west of Union County, North Carolina. It is not known whether Hance established a pottery shop in York County or if he worked at an already established shop, but it seems likely that he potted there since suitable clays for stoneware produc-

tion were available in the area. Other potters are known to have settled in York County. Martin A. Helton of the North Carolina Hilton clan established a pottery in the York County community of Sharon in about 1900, and another potter, Daniel Forbes, was in Kings Mountain Township, northwestern York County in 1900. Interestingly, also during the early 1900s potter William Franklin Outen, brother-in-law of potter James C. ("Jug Jim") Broom of Union County, North Carolina, established a pottery in Lancaster, South Carolina, south of Union County, and at Catawba Junction in southeastern York County to the west (see also Chapter 4).

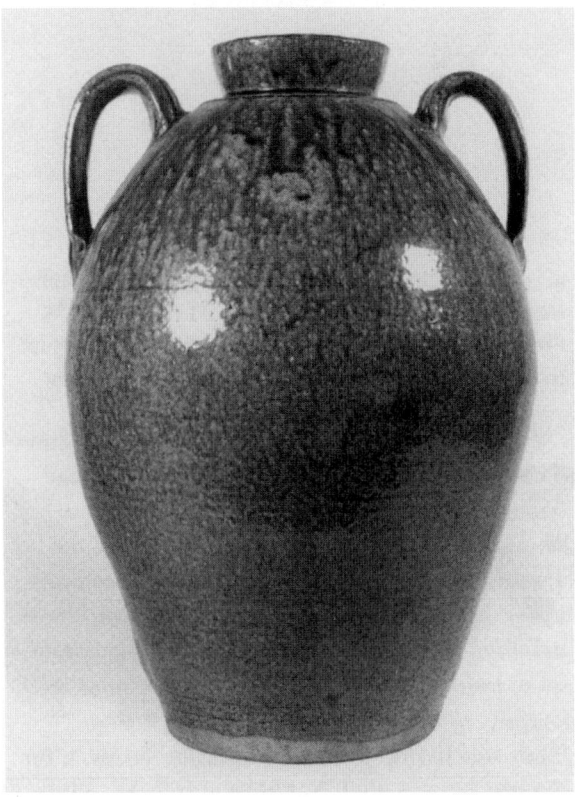

2.34 Alkaline-glazed stoneware storage jar, ca. 1870, James Henry Stone, Buncombe County, N.C. H 18⅞″, C 42¾″. Stamped: JHSTONE (backward *N*). Collection of Doug and Jane Penland.

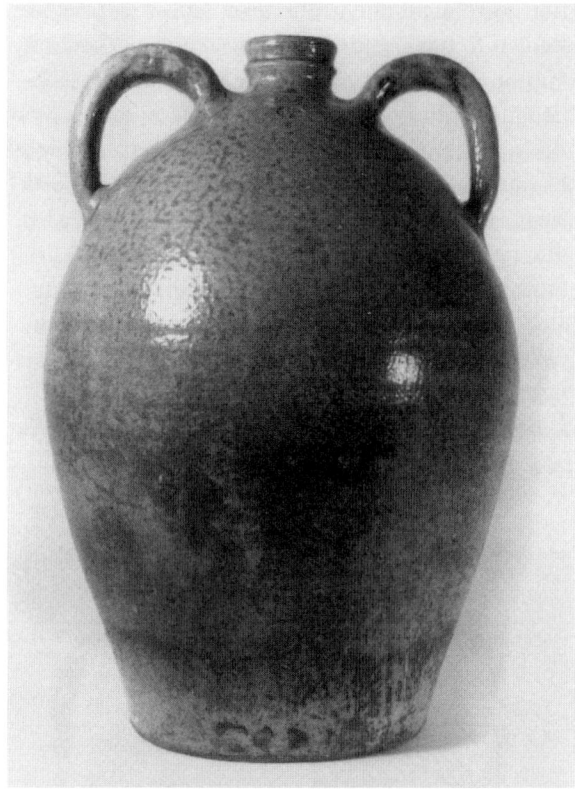

site located near Nash's residence in the Mims Chapel area of Marion County (Figure 2.35). Two vessels with Nash's mark have been identified that are similar in form and features to Edgefield ware. The Nash pottery was apparently shortlived because by 1860 Nash was heavily involved in an iron foundry business.[89]

Manuel and Thomas Leopard were residents of Edgefield in 1810. Members of the Leopard family began to migrate out of Edgefield in the third decade of the nineteenth century. Two brothers, John and Holland Leopard, were in Fayette County, Georgia, in 1830, but it is not known if they ran a pottery there. By 1840 they had moved to Randolph County, Alabama. In 1850 Holland Leopard was potting in Winston County, Mississippi, and John had established

2.35 Alkaline-glazed stoneware jug, ca. 1850, Jefferson S. Nash, Marion County, Tex. H 16½″, C 37¾″. Stamped: J. S. NASH. Circular impressed stamp below maker's mark. Collection of Georgeanna H. Greer.

Edgefield-trained potters carried the alkaline-glazed stoneware tradition into other areas of Georgia, and into Alabama, Mississippi and Texas. In January 1849 Jefferson S. Nash, executor of the estate of Jasper Gibbs, placed a notice in the *Edgefield Advertiser* advising those indebted to the Gibbs estate to "make payment on or before the first day of February next, as I expect to leave for Texas about that time."[88] Nash was living in Marion County, Texas, a few months later, near J. N. Gibbs and P. M. Gibbs of South Carolina. Although Texas census schedules give no indication of Nash having owned a pottery, stoneware fragments marked J. S. NASH have been recovered from the remains of a pottery

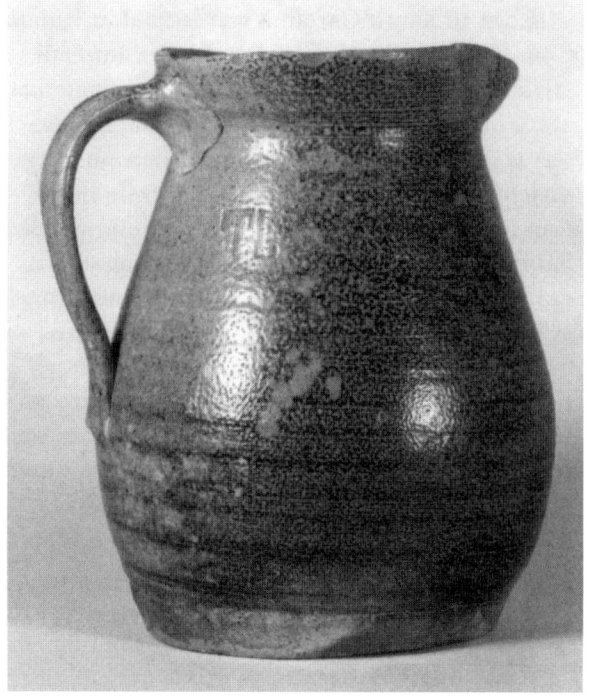

2.36 Salt-glazed stoneware pitcher, ca. 1890–1900, Thad Leopard, Winston County, Miss. H 7¼″, C 18⅞″. Stamped: TL. Collection of the Mississippi State Historical Museum, Jackson, Miss.

a shop in Rusk County, Texas. John and Robert Leopard of South Carolina, probably also brothers, were listed as jugmakers in the 1860 Rusk County census, and in 1870 John listed himself as a potter. Another brother, Hilary Leopard, also worked in John Leopard's Rusk County pottery. The relationships among Robert, Hilary, and John Leopard have not been positively established, but an Emanuel Leopard appeared in the 1800 and 1810 Edgefield District census records. Emanuel, or Manuel, believed to be the father of the Leopards who migrated out of Edgefield, had seven males under the age of twenty-one living in his household in 1810. These were probably the members of the Leopard family who migrated into Georgia, Alabama, and Texas in the following decades.[90] Another potter with an Edgefield background, B. F. Kirkland, was living near John Leopard in Rusk County, Texas, in 1880. Kirkland probably also worked in Leopard's shop. Members of the Kirkland family produced alkaline-glazed stoneware in Randolph County, Alabama, in the mid-nineteenth century as well.

The Kirbees were another family of potters who started out in the Edgefield District. Lewis Kirbee and Lewis Miles witnessed an 1841 Edgefield District deed in which Amos Landrum transferred a tract of land on Shaw's Creek to his brother John.[91] James Kirbee was living in Edgefield in 1810 and 1820. By 1830 he had migrated out of Edgefield into Elbert County, Georgia, on the Georgia–South Carolina border. Kirbee continued to move westward and by 1840 was in Harris County, Georgia, on the Georgia-Alabama border. Two households of Kirbee potters were listed in the 1850 census in Montgomery County, Texas. Lewis Kirbee, age twenty-nine, was listed as a stoneware manufacturer, while James and M. J. (Jefferson) Kirbee were listed as potters. James Kirbee, age sixty, was living in the household of M. J. Kirbee. All of these men were born in South Carolina.[92] The Kirbees evidently trained in the Edgefield stoneware factories,

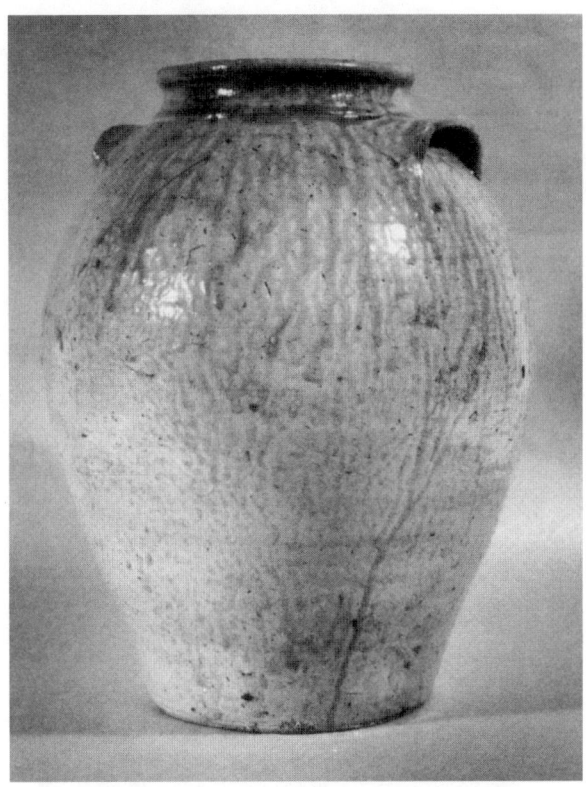

2.37 Alkaline-glazed stoneware jar, ca. 1850, Kirbee Pottery, Montgomery County, Tex. H 17″, C 36¾″. Collection of the Sam Houston Memorial Museum Complex, Huntsville, Tex. Photograph by David Wight.

where they learned how to produce alkaline-glazed stoneware. They migrated to Georgia, where they may have continued to produce stoneware as journeyman potters, and later, to Texas, where they were able to establish their own small factory.

Both salt-glazed and alkaline-glazed stoneware were produced at the John M. Wilson site (41-GU-6) in Guadalupe County, Texas. Joey Brackner, who excavated the site in 1981, noted a number of "Edgefield characteristics and Southernisms" that he had observed upon superficial examination of the waster pile at site 41-GU-6.[93] These included Edgefield-type handle attachments on jugs, from side to shoulder rather

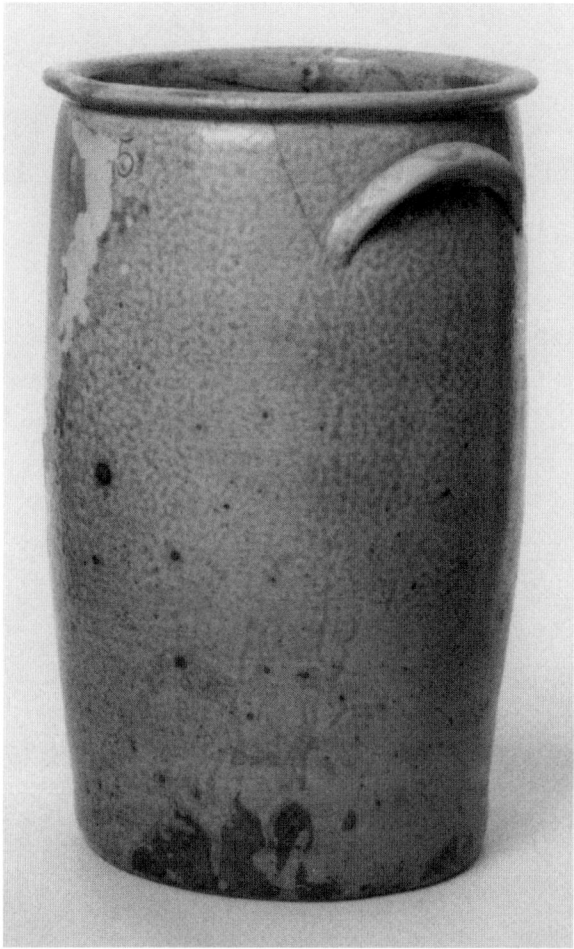

2.38   Alkaline-glazed stoneware storage jar, ca. 1857–
69, John M. Wilson Pottery, Guadalupe County, Tex.
H 16½″, C 31⅛″. This wide-mouthed cylindrical jar is a
special form, probably designed for curing sauerkraut.
Collection of Georgeanna H. Greer.

in both coloration and decoration. These Edgefield characteristics most likely represent a direct
transferral of the alkaline-glazed stoneware tradition from Edgefield to Texas. M. J. Durham
and freed black potter John Chandler arrived
in Guadalupe County from South Carolina in
1864 or 1865. Chandler turned ware at the Wilson pottery, and Durham acted as sales agent for
the operation. In 1869 Durham and Chandler
purchased the factory. Durham may have been
related to Edgefield potters John and Isaac Durham. Thomas Chandler married John Durham's
daughter, so John Chandler may have learned the
potter's trade in Edgefield as the slave of Thomas
Chandler.[94]

From these examples of the movements of a
few pottery families a greater pattern of migration emerges. The migrations of potters from
Virginia and North Carolina into the Edgefield
District suggest an early connection to the Piedmont culture area. As outlined by Wilbur Zelinsky and others, the Edgefield District represents a
cultural hearth, a locus from which the tradition
of alkaline-glazed stoneware was diffused.[95] The
early pattern of migration or diffusion was into
adjacent areas of the South, initially into Washington County, Georgia. As the cultural domain
of the tradition increased, the sphere of influence
was extended into Alabama, Mississippi, and
eastern Texas, and into the uplands of western
North Carolina.

Many of the potters who were involved in
alkaline-glazed stoneware production in the
Edgefield District of South Carolina in the first
quarter of the nineteenth century sought greater
opportunity to the west. Potters who worked as
journeymen in the Edgefield factories were able
to establish their own shops on the western frontier. The greater availability of rich farmland and
good stoneware clays to the west prompted many
potters to leave Edgefield for essentially the same
reasons their forebears had first come to the area.

than from the side to the neck; horizontally attached slab handles; the flat-topped tie-down
rim, with an edge protruding outward from the
vessel to facilitate sealing with a cloth top tied
beneath the rims; location of gallon capacity
numbers above the vessel shoulder; a basic ovoid
form; and the presence of a small vessel fragment at the site with a white slip-trailed arc and
an alkaline overglaze, similar to Edgefield ware

Edgefield Influence on the Stoneware Tradition in South Carolina

Stoneware potteries with Edgefield connections were established in central and northwestern South Carolina in the first half of the nineteenth century. Abner Landrum moved to Columbia, South Carolina, in 1831 and by 1850 had established a stoneware shop on his property in the sandhills located east of the city in the Richland District. Potter Thomas Owensby, who had trained in Edgefield, carried the alkaline-glazed stoneware tradition into the Union District (present-day Cherokee County) in the first half of the nineteenth century. His descendants carried on the tradition in the Cherokee Ford area until the 1940s. Stoneware produced at these early nineteenth-century Richland and Union district potteries are illustrative of associations with the Edgefield stoneware tradition, yet they exhibit distinctions based upon local resources and techniques.

Abner Landrum's Unionist views became increasingly unpopular in Edgefield during the second decade of the nineteenth century as polarization occurred among Nullifiers and Unionists. As editor of the *Edgefield Hive* newspaper, Landrum believed that he had a moral obligation to defend his pro-Union stance. He printed numerous articles in defense of the Union and in repudiation of the views of men such as Thomas Cooper, who warned that the tariff was transferring southern wealth to the North.

Many South Carolina planters objected to trade protectionism brought about by the high tariff that had been enacted by Congress in 1816. The tariff allowed the new manufacturers of the North to obtain higher prices for their goods and put them in control of the domestic market while southerners dependent upon overseas markets feared that "tariffs would inevitably destroy foreign demands for rice and cotton" if foreign nations retaliated against American exporters in retribution for the tariffs.[96] The slave conspiracy inspired by Denmark Vesey in 1822, coupled with the depressed southern economy, contributed to a general mood of fear and insecurity in the region. Some South Carolinians who opposed the tariff proposed nullification of the law. When John C. Calhoun spoke out publicly in favor of nullification in July 1831 an increasingly radical pronullification element was unleashed, and the stage was set for a confrontation.

Landrum left Edgefield in 1831 when he was offered an opportunity to serve as editor of the *Columbia Free Press and Hive*, a newspaper described as "the organ of the Union cause." Landrum declared that one of the articles of his confession of faith in establishing the *Columbia Free Press and Hive* was that "the famous doctrine of Nullification has neither the sanction of JEFFERSON nor MADISON, but is the watch-word of a party which would effect by stratagem what they dare not attempt in open day, *the dissolution of the Union.*"[97] Landrum expressed his disdain of the nullification movement in an editorial that appeared in the *Columbia Free Press and Hive*:

> Whether nullification be a demoniacal spirit or an exhilarating gas, it may be impossible to determine; but the disease it produces is established by the clearest principles of nosology; it belongs to the class Neurosis, order Vesania, and genus Amentia. It is chiefly confined to the brain, producing slight fever with extreme thirst for blood, and occasional prostration of appetite for Kentucky hogs and mules and Yankee manufactures, and a perfect loathing of wooden nutmegs. But should it continue a fixed Neurosis, an adequate enlargement of our already spacious lunatic asylum may be all that is requisite.[98]

In 1832 the Nullifiers prevailed and the South Carolina legislature called a special convention that declared the federal tariff null and void. Other southern states denounced the Nullification Ordinance and President Andrew Jackson prepared to rally the Unionists to arms against the Nullifiers. At an 1833 State's Rights Party Convention the Nullifiers delayed putting their Nullification Ordinance into effect, thereby allowing time for Congress to act on the issue. Calhoun resigned the vice presidency, accepted a senate seat, and went to Washington to work out a tariff compromise. The crisis was abated when Congress adopted a new, gradually declining tariff. Both sides claimed victory, bringing to a close the first skirmish in a political conflict that would eventually lead to the Civil War.

It is unclear how long the *Columbia Free Press and Hive* was published, but according to one local account Landrum retired in about 1837 to his sandhills estate where he spent his last years as a potter and planter.[99] Landrum's 1846 application to the state legislature for funds to establish a porcelain factory indicates his continued interest and involvement in pottery

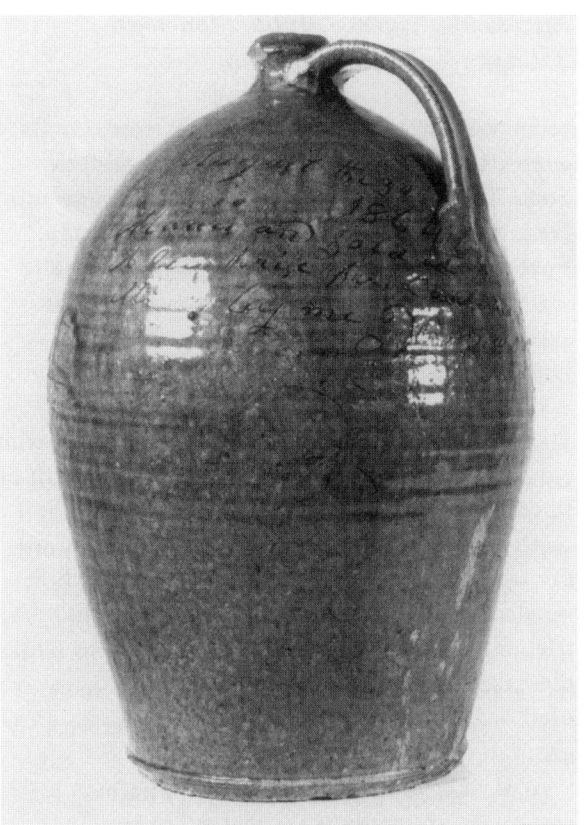

2.40   Alkaline-glazed stoneware jug, 1864, Thomas Owensby, Union District, S.C. H 13⅞″, C 30″. Incised in script: August the 30 / 1864 / Maid an Sold at / A low price fore Confedrent / Money by me / Thomas Ownbey. Collection of Georgeanna H. Greer.

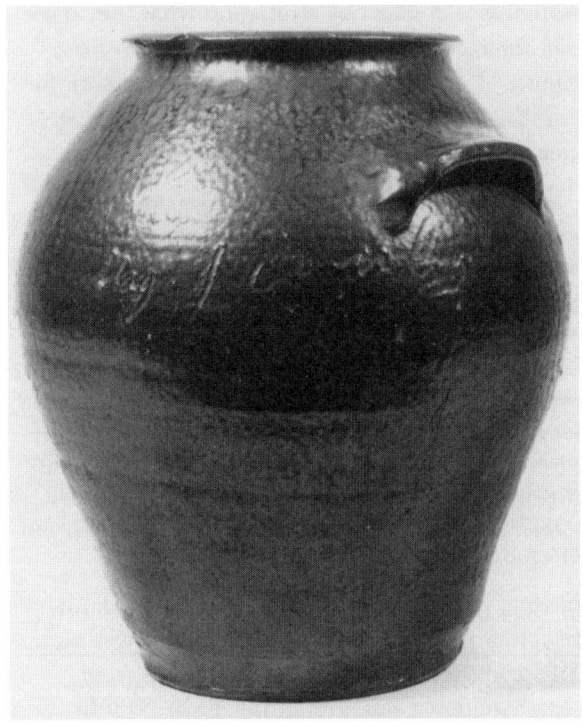

2.39   Alkaline-glazed stoneware jar, ca. 1850, Thomas Owensby, Union District, S.C. H 10¾″, C 30⅞″. Incised script: Maj. T Owenby / T E. Collection of Terry and Steve Ferrell.

manufacture. The application was denied, but Landrum continued his experiments in pottery production. The first Richland District census of manufactures, conducted in 1850, included information regarding a pottery owned by Abner Landrum. The operation was valued at twelve hundred dollars and employed four males at a cost of twenty-four dollars per month. The factory produced about twelve thousand gallons of "Pot & Jug Ware" per year. Landrum also made firebrick at the Columbia-area pottery.

Thomas Owensby was living in the Edgefield District in 1810, where he probably worked as a journeyman at the Pottersville or John Landrum stoneware factory. T. W. (Thomas William) Ownsby (var. Owensby), age fifty-six, is listed as a potter in the 1850 Spartanburg District census. Owensby operated a pottery shop in the Corinth community of Union District (present-day Cherokee County). Potters William and Jesse Whelchel, age twenty-three and thirty-six, were living near Owensby in 1850. According to Thomas W. Owensby's great-grandson, Rochelle Boyle, Owensby was married to Mary Whelchel, daughter of Francis Whelchel, Jr., of the Union District. William and Jesse Whelchel then were apparently in-laws of T. W. Owensby and worked in his pottery shop. Another Thomas Owensby, age twenty-seven, listed as a jugmaker in the 1850 Union District census, was the son of T. W. Owensby. A jugmaker named Francis Parker, age twenty-nine, who was living near Thomas Owensby, Jr., in the Union District in 1850, was also related to the Owensby family. Mary Owensby's sister, Polly, was married to Frank Parker, so Francis Parker was also an in-law of T. W. Owensby. The Owensby pottery was located near the present county lines separating Spartanburg, Cherokee, and Union counties, so even though T. W. Owensby and the Whelchels were living in the Spartanburg District, and Thomas Owensby, Jr., and Francis Parker, in the Union District in 1850, all of these men were potting at T. W. Owensby's shop. T. W. Owensby had another son, Joel, who also worked at his father's pottery. Joel, at age forty, appeared as a potter in the 1860 Spartanburg County census. He had six children in his household, including a son, Thomas Jr. Joel Owensby later moved to Shelby County, North Carolina.

The ovoid jugs and storage jars produced at the Owensby pottery were similar to ware produced in Edgefield and throughout the South during the first half of the nineteenth century (see Figure 2.39). Other typical Edgefield characteristics that appear on early Union County ware include horizontally applied slab handles on storage jars, jug handles applied below the neck

and at the shoulder rather than from shoulder to neck, and gently rounded tie-down rims designed to receive cloth seals. One signed and dated jug, attributed to Thomas Owensby, Jr., does not fit this pattern, however (Figure 2.40). Even though the ovoid form of this piece is reminiscent of the Edgefield ware, the single loop handle attached at the neck rather than below and the inverted cone collar are divergent. These features are not typically associated with antebellum Edgefield stoneware production, although they are found on alkaline-glazed stoneware produced in North Carolina and Georgia.

A four-handled alkaline-glazed stoneware storage jar in the collection of the Museum of Early Southern Decorative Arts in Winston-Salem, North Carolina, is signed "Hiram Gibbs / Union Dist. / S. Cr. / Presented 1836" (Figure 2.41).

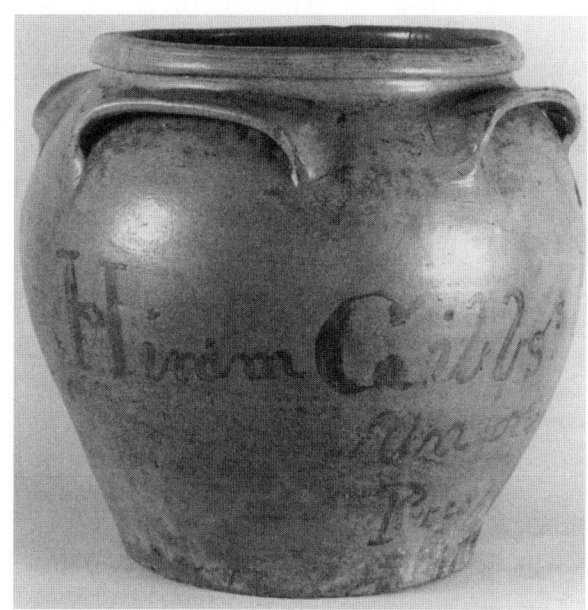

2.41 Alkaline-glazed stoneware storage jar, ca. 1836, attributed to the Pottersville Stoneware Manufactory, Edgefield District, S.C. H 18½″, C 20¾″. Signed in iron-based slip: Hiram Gibbs / Union Dist. / S Cr. / Presented 1836. Courtesy of the Museum of Early Southern Decorative Arts, Winston-Salem, N.C., with thanks to Brad Rauschenberg.

This jar is almost identical to the storage jars turned by the slave potter Dave in Edgefield and was most likely produced in Edgefield for Gibbs's Union District plantation. In 1838 Jasper Gibbs placed in the *Edgefield Advertiser* newspaper a notice in which he offered to "lease or sell a valuable PLANTATION recently purchased from his father, situated in Union District, 8 miles west of the Ct. House, half a mile north of the Stage road, and 2 miles from Murphy's Mills on Tiger River." [100] This reference to the Gibbs plantation on Tiger (var. Tyger) River is significant. A major center of alkaline-glazed stoneware production emerged during the mid-nineteenth century in the Tyger River area along the present boundary between Greenville and Spartanburg counties. Collin Rhodes, Nathaniel Ramey, and Jasper Gibbs co-owned the Pottersville Stoneware Manufactory from June 1838 until January 1839. Even though the Hiram Gibbs storage jar was evidently not produced in Union District, the inscription appearing on it indicates another early Edgefield-Union District connection and provides an early link between the Edgefield and Tyger river alkaline-glaze traditions.

The pottery established by Abner Landrum in Richland District and the Owensby pottery in the Union District (present-day Cherokee County) are the only known South Carolina stoneware potteries with direct connections to the Edgefield District. Another major South Carolina pottery center known as Jugtown, located in the Tyger River area of Greenville and Spartanburg counties, was established in the second half of the nineteenth century.

The stoneware industry that flourished in the Edgefield District of South Carolina was unprecedented in the South. Edgefield stoneware factories, unlike most stoneware potteries of the region, were large-scale operations employing journeyman potters and African-American slaves. Much of the ware manufactured in Edgefield during the height of stoneware production in the area, from 1840 to 1850, was slip decorated. Decorated stoneware was rare in other areas of the South. The unusually large scale of stoneware production in Edgefield and the widespread use of slip decoration on ware produced in the area is directly related to the businesslike approach of the Edgefield factory owners. Many of these men were investor-owners, rather than potters, who viewed the stoneware factories as business enterprises. This entrepreneurial attitude promoted a competitive spirit among the stoneware factory owners. Edgefield stoneware manufacturers advertised their ware widely and used maker's marks or trademarks by which their stoneware could be distinguished from other ware produced in the area. Factory owners made use of statewide transportation networks, most notably the railroads, in an effort to gain larger markets for their ware. Antebellum Edgefield ware set the standard for stoneware production throughout the region during the period. The most important consequence of these large-scale production efforts in Edgefield was the migration of Edgefield-trained potters out of the district. Journeyman potters set out for the West in search of land and opportunity. These men carried with them the newly developed alkaline-glazed stoneware tradition, eventually diffusing it throughout the lower South.

CHAPTER THREE

The African-American Presence in the Edgefield District Stoneware Tradition

In 1962 Ivor Noel Hume described a type of unglazed, low-fired plain earthenware that he had found at Williamsburg and that had been found by archaeologists at several early colonial sites on the southern Atlantic coast. He called the pottery Colono-Indian ware because it was similar to both prehistoric and historic (nineteenth-century) Indian ware in Virginia. Although Noel Hume thought that the ware had been made by Indians, he surmised that it must have been used by African-American slaves, since glazed ware would have been available to all but the poorest colonists.[1]

More recent research by anthropologist Leland Ferguson suggests that this ware is more closely associated with non-Indians than with Indians, and that it was produced and used by African-Americans. Ferguson points out that African people had a long tradition of manufacturing low-fired coiled and hand-modeled earthenware, and that the forms and techniques of manufacture of Colono-Indian ware are similar to those found in Africa. He adds that, although there is no direct historical reference to pottery production by African-Americans in South Carolina before the Revolution, there is evidence of pottery activity in a slave context from the Lesser Antilles, including Barbados, and the islands of Antigua and Nevis. African-Americanist scholars have noted that many of the early planters from

Barbados later settled in South Carolina.[2] Ferguson argues that since the makers and users of the ware must be determined on a site by site basis, the suffix "Indian" should be dropped.[3] Some of this "Colono-ware," then, was apparently made and used on eighteenth-century plantations by African-Americans (see Figure 3.1).

These conclusions may be particularly significant in light of the role that African-Americans played in development of the stoneware tradition in South Carolina. African-American slaves were involved in stoneware production in South Carolina throughout the nineteenth century. Slaves in the Edgefield District of South Carolina produced distinctive pottery forms that have been traced to Africa and the West Indies.

The presence of African-American slaves in the Edgefield District stoneware factories was perhaps the single most important influence on stoneware production in the area. Edgefield slaves who adopted the European-derived ceramics technology and materials made unique contributions to the alkaline-glazed stoneware tradition in the South. Distinctive styles of pottery, characterized by divergent vessel forms, unusual decorative techniques, and in one rare instance, highly individualistic and personalized maker's marks, were produced by slaves and freed blacks in Edgefield.

Slaves constituted a significant portion of the

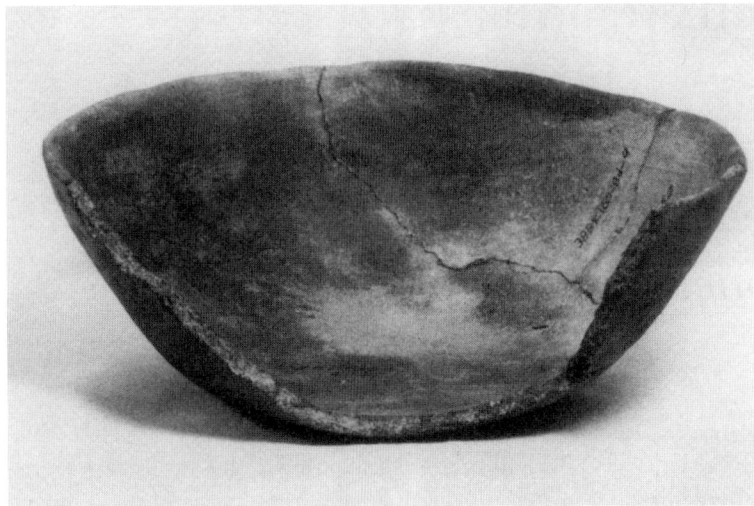

3.1 Colono-ware bowl fragment from the Spiers Landing site (38BK160), Berkeley County, S.C. Excavated by Carolina Archaeological Services, Inc. Photograph by Emily Short. Courtesy of Leland Ferguson.

labor force in nineteenth-century Edgefield industry. From 1800 to 1820 the number of slaves in Edgefield increased four times while the white population decreased. This fluctuation of the white and slave populations signaled the emergence of an increasingly wealthy white planter class. Edgefield's wealth came from agriculture, and slaves were employed mainly as plantation laborers. During the same period the local pottery industry, which employed a significant amount of slave labor, was established to satisfy the needs of plantations for food storage and preservation.

The Plantation Food System

A variety of vessel types and sizes was produced for the tasks of food storage, preservation, and serving on the plantation. Twenty-, thirty-, and even forty-gallon storage jars were produced in Edgefield, sizes that were rare in other areas of the South. These large-capacity storage jars were designed to meet the requirements of the plantation food system. Rendered lard and salted meat were packed into the stoneware jars during the slaughtering season and stored for use throughout the year. Some Edgefield slave turners specialized in the production of these large-capacity jars. The potter typically applied two horizontal lug handles to jars of up to fifteen gallons, and four evenly spaced lug handles to twenty- to forty-gallon jars. When full, the jars were extremely heavy and were probably placed in a smokehouse, shed, or pantry, thereby providing easy access for periodic retrieval of the foods stored within.

Another common stoneware form, the syrup jug, with two opposing loop handles, was designed to hold cane syrup, the principal sweetener on nineteenth-century southern farms and plantations.[4] Syrup continued to be important in rural areas of the lower South well into the twentieth century. Anne Bell, a former slave of Fairfield County plantation owner John Glazier Rabb, provided a detailed description of the plantation larder in her account of the arrival of Union troops on the plantation. "Befo' they went they took everything. They took de meat and 'visions out de smoke-house and de 'lasses, sugar, flour, and meal out de house. Killed de pigs and cows, burnt de ginhouse and cotton, and took off de live stock, geese, chickens and turkeys."[5]

The plantation food system promoted a sense of community. This attitude is reflected in the recollections of a former slave from Berry Cochran's plantation. "Marster put out a side uv meat and a *barrul o'meal and all ub us would go and git* our rations for de week. Eve'ybody, had er garden patch an' plenty greens and taters and all dat kinder thing."[6] According to Edgefield historian Vernon Burton, "Allotments of food were made on an individual basis; each slave laborer generally received three pounds of bacon or pork and a peck of meal for the week."[7] The amount of food that each slave received appears to have varied according to the size of the plantation, the amount of concern felt by the master or overseer for the welfare of the slaves, the location of the plantation, the size of the slave family, the presence of children, the ability of slaves to produce food themselves, the time available to procure wild foods, and the amount of food slaves could barter, purchase, or steal. Sometimes the rations were issued to a cook who prepared meals for the slaves at a central kitchen. However, Casper Rumple, a former slave from Edgefield, recalled that adult slaves were responsible "for their own cooking."[8] Adults' eating routines often differed from those of children. Francis Pickens enforced an elaborate diet routine and instructed his overseers "that no child shall want food for a moment. See that the woman who cooks for them does justice to all."[9] Slave men and women maintained year-round gardens. Matilda Brooks, a former slave of Governor Francis Pickens, recalled a diet consisting "largely of potatoes, corn bread, syrup, greens, peas, and occasionally ham, fowl, and other meats or poultry. Their chief beverage was coffee made from parched corn."[10]

Hunting and fishing provided additional variety and nutrition to the slave diet. A former slave of Judge Andrew Pickens Butler recalled that "we used to hunt 'possums, rabbits, squirrels, wild turkeys, doves, and partridges, and set traps for partridges and set box gums for rabbits." Another former slave, Peggy Grigsby, stated that "the men folks hunted much; doves, partridges, wild turkeys, deer, squirrels, and rabbits. Sometimes

dey caught rabbits in wooden boxes, called 'rabbit gums.' "[11] Slaves sometimes raided the smokehouse, "stealing" chicken, pork, and potatoes. This widespread use of small mammals and wild birds at interior slave sites suggests more active hunting at interior sites than was required in coastal settings.[12]

Archaeologists have been able to clearly illustrate that the core slave diet of corn, pork, and beef was supplemented by other foods. Slave populations on plantations of various sizes throughout the sea islands of Georgia, Florida, and North and South Carolina, as well as in other environmental zones, exploited many environmental niches with a variety of technological methods. Archaeological analysis of animal bones recovered from tenant/sharecropper houses occupied after 1860 on the Millwood Plantation (located in Abbeville County, South Carolina, and Elbert County, Georgia) revealed both wild and domestic species. Hogs outnumbered cattle in the collection, with domestic animals comprising 45 percent of the individuals identified. Wild resources consisted primarily of opossum, rabbit, squirrel, and fish.[13]

Most coastal rice and cotton plantations operated on the task system rather than the gang system, owing to the labor-intensive requirements of the major cash crops grown there; upcountry plantation overseers typically relied on the gang system. Under the gang system a team of slaves worked together for a specified period of time, usually from dawn to dusk. Under the task system slaves were assigned a specific task or individual plots of land to tend. When this task was completed to the satisfaction of the overseer, the slave was finished for the day. Tasks were divided into heavy, moderate, and light categories, and slaves were classified according to the amount of tasks they performed. Presumably, under the task system slaves might finish work by midday, with time left to devote to gardening, stock-raising, fishing, hunting, or other activities. Even under the task system, however, the workday could be fifteen to sixteen hours long during the peak harvest season. Under the gang system the overseer usually set aside some free time for the slaves. Each slave cabin in Edgefield had a garden patch, and residents of cabins were allowed time off from plantation chores in order to tend gardens. A former slave of James Henry Hammond recalled that "we always had a half holiday on Saturday."[14]

During working hours slaves were employed in a variety of agricultural, domestic, and industrial enterprises. Although the majority of slaves were field hands, some slaves were trained in a wide range of skilled occupations.

Edgefield Slave Potters

Pottery manufacture was one of a number of skilled trades practiced by slaves in South Carolina. Historian Carl Bridenbaugh noted that "in the Carolinas the overwhelming majority of artisans were Negro slaves."[15] Slave occupations included carpentry, blacksmithing and other ironwork, milling, tanning, weaving, cloth making, and sewing. As in Africa, craftsmen were held in great respect in preindustrial America because of the expense of importing goods from Europe.

Southern society was patriarchal. Planters referred to slave leaders as "head men," and the "driver," or leader, was considered the "most important negro on the plantation."[16] This male authority system provided for the sharing of influence between the slave head man or leader and the white master. Likewise, pottery manufacture was a male-dominated activity in nineteenth-century Edgefield. "Turner" was the most commonly listed occupation for slaves who labored in the Edgefield pottery factories, although slaves were undoubtedly involved in every aspect of stoneware production, from digging, hauling, and preparing the clay to turning and firing the ware and wagoning it to market. Slave families,

however, were not named in court records pertaining to the stoneware factories. Women and children would have performed more menial tasks, while men were trained in all aspects of the pottery craft and, most important, in the role of turner. The slave turner was a skilled artisan and therefore was highly valued by the slaveholder. A few Edgefield slave turners were afforded special privileges because of their favored status.

The 1850 census provides information regarding the ownership of slaves by Edgefield stoneware manufacturers. Edgefield stoneware factory owner Lewis Miles owned fourteen slaves that year. Another stoneware maker, B. F. Landrum, owned six male and two female slaves in 1850. Collin Rhodes's slaveholdings in 1850 included thirty-five blacks and mulattoes ranging in age from forty-six years to three months, the largest number of any Edgefield stoneware factory owner.

Slaves were often mentioned in court records and newspaper advertisements involving the Edgefield stoneware factories. Seven slaves—Daniel, Sam, George, Abram, Old Harry, Young Harry, and Old Tom—were named in records pertaining to the Pottersville factory. Daniel was listed as a turner, and Old Tom as a wagoner.[17] Abram may have also worked at the John Landrum pottery. A bill of sale for a "negro boy, Abram," from Samuel Landrum to John Landrum was recorded in Edgefield on 5 December 1795.[18] In an 1840 advertisement announcing the sale of his land and stoneware manufactory, John Presley listed "three or four Negroes" along with livestock and other equipment associated with the factory. "Three Negro men, two of whom are Turners," were mentioned in an 1840 sale of the Pottersville Manufactory, and an 1843 listing of the Pottersville property included "four Negroes, viz three Turners and one Wagoner." An 1847 executor's sale of the John Landrum estate offered "18 likely Negroes," one of them "an excellent Stone Ware Turner."[19]

In an 1852 deed Thomas Chandler had the following property placed in a trust for his wife, Margaret Chandler, and their children: "four negro slaves of names & ages as follows: Simon about fifty years old, Easter about forty six years old, John about eighteen years old, and Ned about eighteen years old, and three waggons now in my possession, one of which is a four horse road waggon and the other two are two horse waggons, and eight mules and one mare, all of which are now in my possession."[20] Although white journeyman potters are known to have worked at the stoneware factories operated by Chandler, this document suggests that Chandler also relied upon slaves as laborers in his pottery. John, one of the slaves named in the 1852 deed, may have later turned alkaline-glazed stoneware at the John M. Wilson pottery in Guadalupe County, Texas.[21]

Thomas Davies and Anson Peeler employed over fifty slaves in their Palmetto Fire Brick Works during 1862 and 1863. Some of these laborers were hired as part of a team, while others were employed as individuals. Their salaries ranged from five to one hundred dollars per month.[22] The operation, later known as the Bath Fire Brick Works, was established as a fire-brick factory, but by 1863 alkaline-glazed stoneware jars, jugs, milk pans, and chamber pots were being produced there.

Slave Women in the Edgefield Stoneware Factories

Farms with at least twenty slaves (plantations) were the home of 60.3 percent of Edgefield slaves in 1850 and 64.2 percent in 1860. About one-third of the slave population was made up of children too young to work. Men and women generally worked at different tasks, but both were expected to perform hard physical labor.

An 1848 coroner's inquisition provides direct evidence of the presence of slave women in the Edgefield pottery shops. The case involved the death of a female slave, Ann, who was a laborer in the Benjamin Franklin Landrum factory. Landrum testified that he had whipped Ann and tied her up when she refused to do the work assigned to her. Then, according to the report, he had "left the dec[ease]d and two other negroes at his shop at [the] stone ware factory to go to breakfast." Landrum claimed that when he returned about forty-five minutes later one of the slaves he had left at the shop told him that Ann had hung herself and that she was dead. Then, he said, he "went into the shop and found the negroes loosing the rope from around her neck." From the position that he claimed to have found her in, he surmised that Ann had wrapped the end of the rope around her neck twice and squatted or leaned upon it to choke herself to death. He added that he had tied her up because she had "threatened to runaway [and] was of turbulent disposition." John L. Atkinson testified that Landrum came to him and his son William and told them "that his negro woman Ann had hung herself." They inspected the body (which had been laid out in the kitchen) for marks and bruises, and Landrum took them "to the shop where it was said she hung herself and shewed witness where dec[ease]d had thrown herself down in the furnice and had loosened a brick and where she had hung herself."[23] They then helped Landrum bury the body because the coroner had gone to Columbia. Two other men, John Whitlock and John Green, provided supporting testimony in the case, testifying as to the bad disposition of the deceased slave.[24] The testimony presented in connection with the death of B. F. Landrum's slave, Ann, establishes that slave women were employed as laborers in the Edgefield stoneware factories.

The documentary evidence suggests that although female slaves as well as males were employed as laborers in the Edgefield stoneware factories, the involvement of women in pottery production was typically limited to more menial tasks. The status of slave men and women varied according to the amount of skill and training their occupation required. Turners were usually afforded greater status and recognition than other laborers in the Edgefield stoneware factories.

Dave

Edgefield's most famous slave potter was a man called Dave. An 1863 *Edgefield Advertiser* editorial promoting the healthful properties of buttermilk is the only known direct documentary reference to this remarkable potter. The article consists of a dialogue between an elderly black man named Dave and the editor of the newspaper. The editor refers to Dave as "Dave Pottery" but suggests that many readers will remember him as "the grandiloquent old darkey once connected with a paper known as the *Edgefield Hive*."[25] This information is particularly significant since stoneware manufacturer Abner Landrum was editor and publisher of the *Hive* newspaper before moving to Columbia in 1831. Dave was literate, and since it became illegal to teach slaves to read and write in South Carolina

in 1837, some scholars have suggested that Dave may have acquired his skills as a turner while assisting Landrum on the newspaper. A Dave jar dated 18 April 1859 bears the verse "hive is eighteen; hundred + fifty nine / unto you all I fill [feel] in, cline[d?]." Perhaps a reference to himself as "hive," or to the newspaper, this verse may be further evidence of Dave's early association with Abner Landrum.

The most important evidence of Dave's extraordinary abilities is his ware. Dave was a prolific potter. Many of the storage jars and jugs that he produced survive in public and private collections. Approximately twenty of these vessels are inscribed with original poetry, and at least fifty additional Dave vessels have been identified by a signature, maker's mark, date, or other inscription. (A list of the verses inscribed on ware produced by Dave is presented in Appendix 3.) The storage jars turned by Dave are bulbous in form as is most antebellum Edgefield ware. Unlike other ware produced in the area during the period, Dave's jars are widest at the top. They are wide-mouthed forms with thick, rolled rims and high, broad shoulders. Contemporary potters who have examined Dave's thick-walled, large-capacity storage jars are amazed at the

3.2   Alkaline-glazed stoneware storage jar, 1840, Dave (slave potter), Lewis Miles Factory, Horse Creek Valley, Edgefield District, S.C. H 15⅛″, C 41⅝″. Incised script: 31st July 1840 (front, upper shoulder between handles); Dave belongs to Mr. Miles / wher the oven bakes & the pot biles (opposite). Collection of the Charleston Museum, Charleston, S.C.

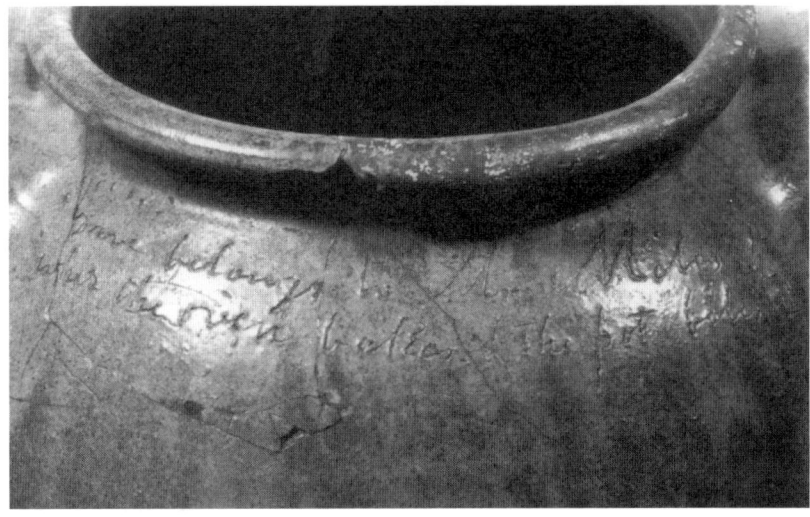

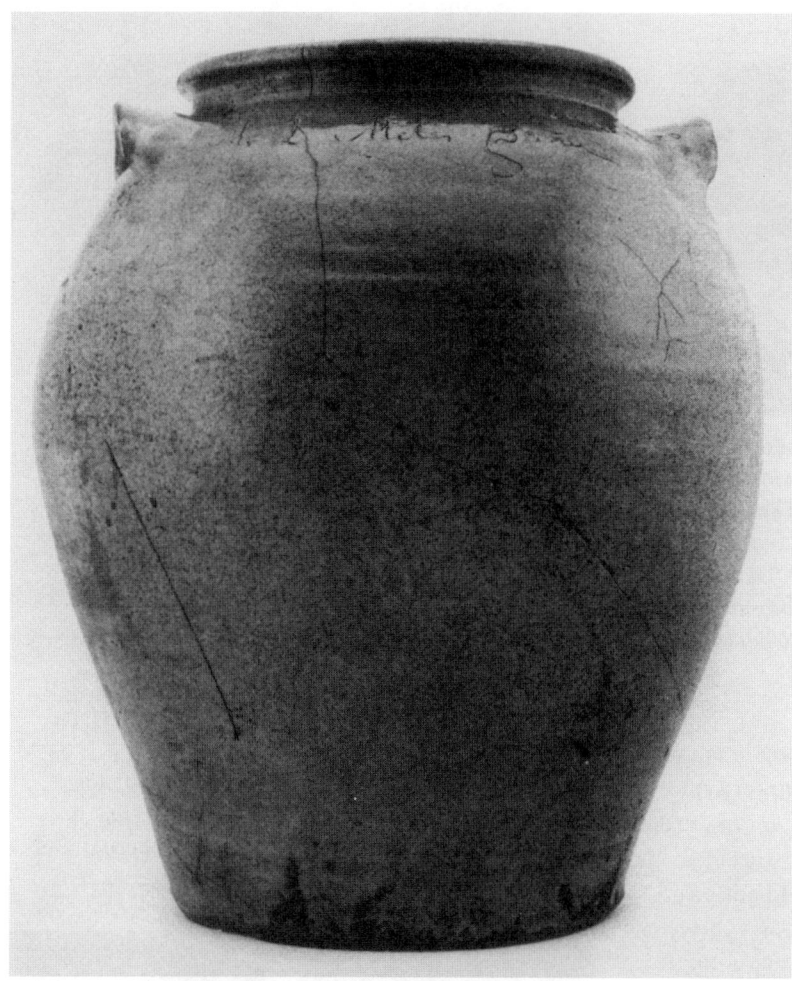

3.3   Alkaline-glazed stoneware storage jar, 1840, Dave (slave potter), Lewis Miles Factory, Horse Creek Valley, Edgefield District, S.C. H 14½″, C 40½″. Incised script: 27th June 1840 / Mr. L. Miles Dave (front, upper shoulder between handles); Give me silver or either gold; / though they are dangerous; to our soul (opposite). Collection of Dr. and Mrs. George V. Rosenberg.

great strength and skill that was required to produce vessels of such size. This technical skill, coupled with the unique poetic compositions that he inscribed on many pieces of his ware, have distinguished Dave as the most outstanding African-American potter of his time.

In the third decade of the nineteenth century Dave began to inscribe the storage jars that he turned with maker's marks, dates of manufacture, signatures, and poems. By 1840 he was turning ware at the Lewis Miles stoneware factory. A storage jar dated 31 July 1840 reads "Dave belongs to Mr. Miles / wher[e] the oven bakes & the pot biles" (Figure 3.2). Another jar, made the same year, is signed "Mr. L. Miles Dave" (Figure 3.3). Dave inscribed the maker's mark "Lm" in script, the initials of stoneware factory owner Lewis Miles, on most of his signed and dated ware (see Figure 3.4). A pair of forty-gallon storage jars dated 13 May 1859 and signed by Dave and another slave named Baddler are the largest and most spectacular slave-made vessels known (see Figure 3.5). The incised verse "Made at Stoney Bluff / for Making lard Enuff" appearing on one of these jars, refers to Lewis Miles's Stoney Bluff plantation. These marks and the correlation of dates that appear on Dave's pots indicate that Miles acquired Dave after Abner Landrum

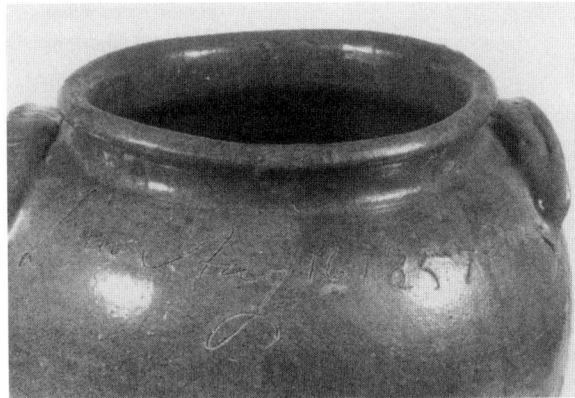

3.4 Detail of maker's mark. Incised script: Lm Aug 16 1857 / Dave. Alkaline-glazed stoneware storage jar, 1857, Dave (slave potter), Lewis Miles Factory, Horse Creek Valley, Edgefield District, S.C. The factory mark "Lm" identifies the Lewis Miles Factory as the place of manufacture and the date "Aug 16 1857" indicates when the vessel was made. Collection of Mr. and Mrs. Larry R. Carlson.

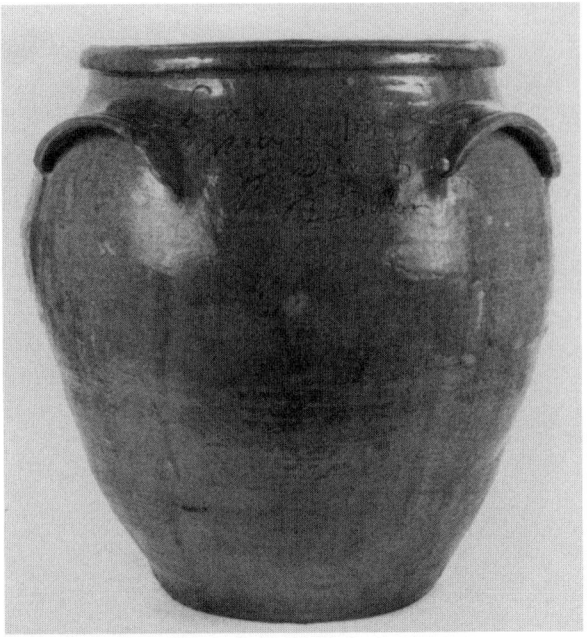

3.5 Alkaline-glazed stoneware jar, 1859, Dave and Baddler (slave potters), Lewis Miles Factory, Horse Creek Valley, Edgefield District, S.C. H 25¾″, C 81¼″. Incised script: Lm May 13, 1859 / Dave & Baddler (front, upper shoulder between handles); Great & Noble jar, / hold sheep, goat and bear (opposite). Collection of the Charleston Museum, Charleston, S.C.

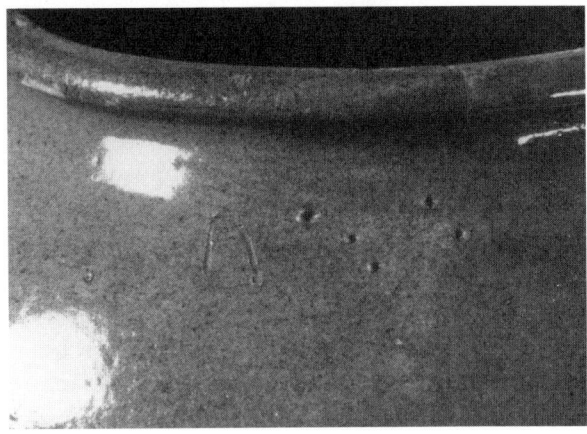

3.6 Detail of incised marks, alkaline-glazed stoneware storage jar, ca. 1850, attributed to Lewis Miles Factory, Horse Creek Valley, Edgefield District, S.C. Collection of the Charleston Museum, Charleston, S.C.

moved to Columbia. Dave undoubtedly acquired his skill as a turner through an apprenticeship at the Pottersville and/or John Landrum potteries.

Dave applied other marks to his ware. For example, some signed Dave vessels bear circular impressions, punctates, slash marks, and/or horseshoe-shaped marks, either grouped together in a pattern or with one type of mark applied in a series (see Figure 3.6). Some scholars have suggested that these are a system of capacity markings used by illiterate slaves on Edgefield-area plantations. Although in some instances this interpretation appears to be correct, no systematic application of the marks is apparent on some of the ware. The marks then may have served other functions as well—for example, as maker's marks to identify the work of a particular potter or of the pottery factory where the ware was produced. Whatever their significance, it is clear that in Edgefield these marks were typically used by slave potters and are most often associated with the Lewis Miles factory.

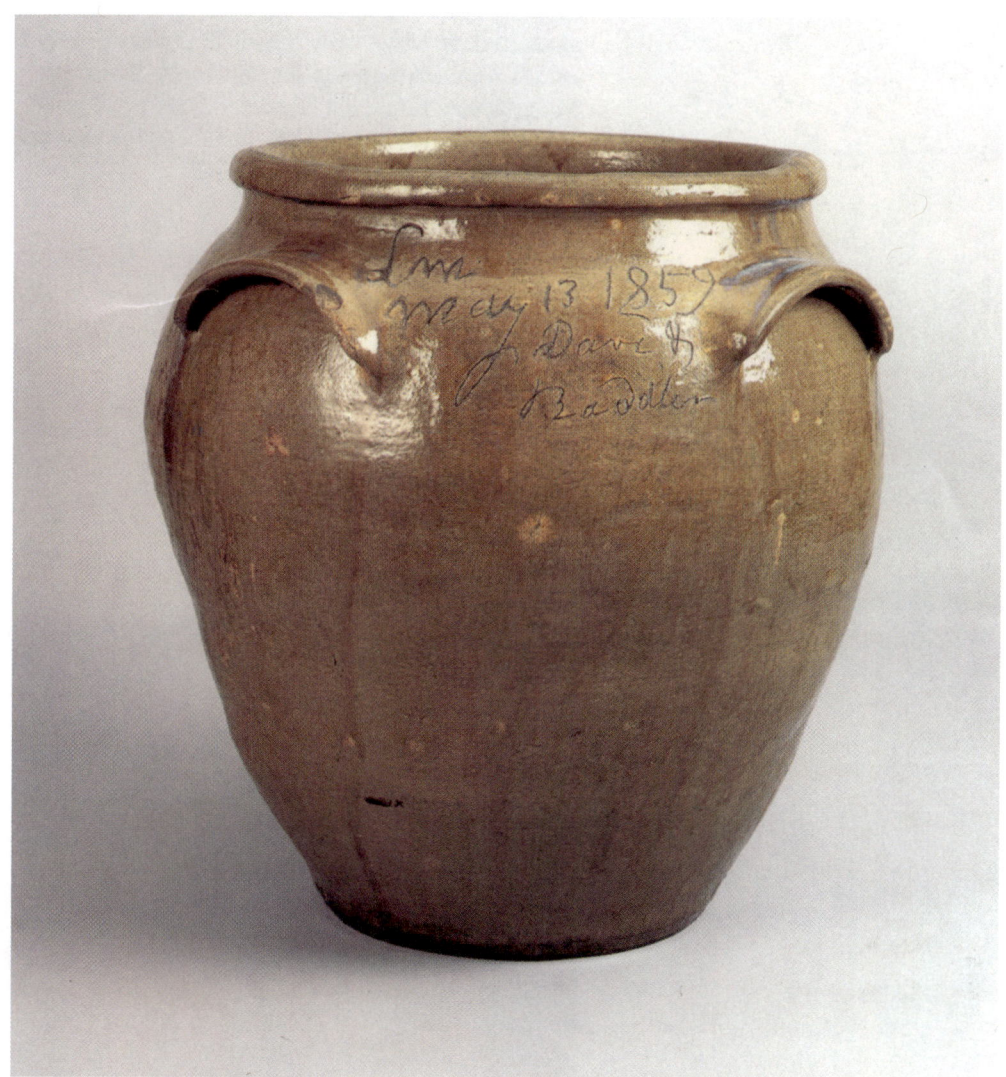

Alkaline-glazed stoneware jar, 1859, Dave and Baddler, Lewis Miles Factory, Horse Creek Valley, Edgefield District, S.C. H 25¾″, C 81¼″. Incised script: "Lm May 13, 1859 / Dave & / Baddler" (front, upper shoulder between handles) and "Great and Noble jar, / hold sheep, goat and bear" (opposite). Collection of the Charleston Museum, Charleston, S.C.

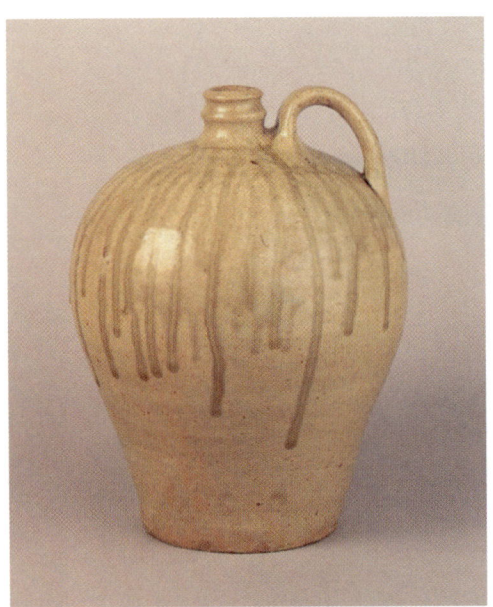

Alkaline-glazed stoneware jug with light, drippy glaze characteristic of the early Edgefield District pottery factories, ca. 1810–30, attributed to the Pottersville Stoneware Manufactory, Edgefield District, S.C. H 13″, C 30¾″. Incised at lower body above base: "A" (with a forked crossbar). Collection of Terry and Steve Ferrell.

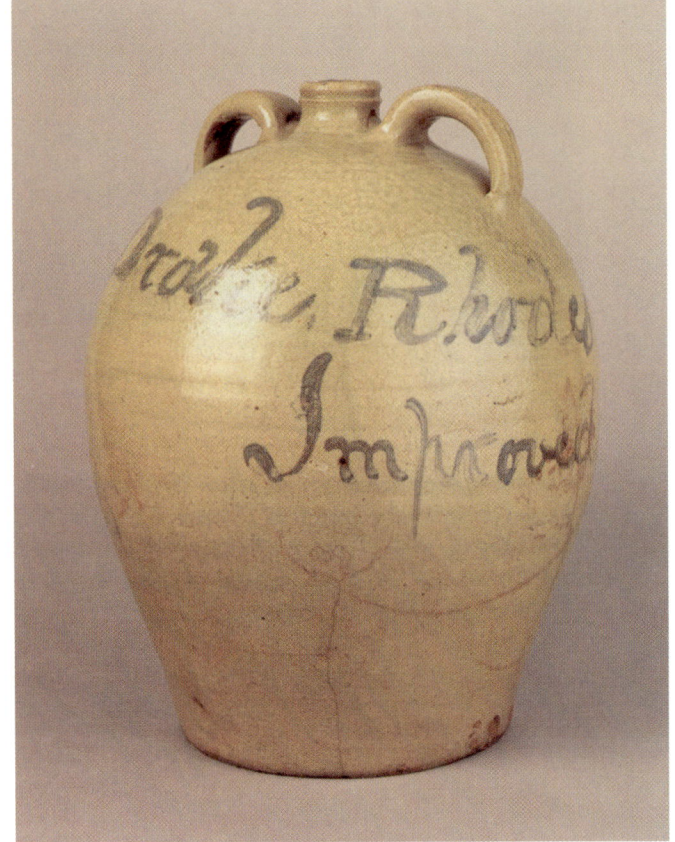

Alkaline-glazed stoneware syrup jug, 1836, Pottersville Stoneware Manufactory, Edgefield District, S.C. H 17½″, C 44¼″. Signed in slip: "Drake, Rhodes & Co. / Improved stone / ware / Edgefield Ct.H. S.C. / 1836." Courtesy of the Museum of Early Southern Decorative Arts, Winston-Salem, N.C.

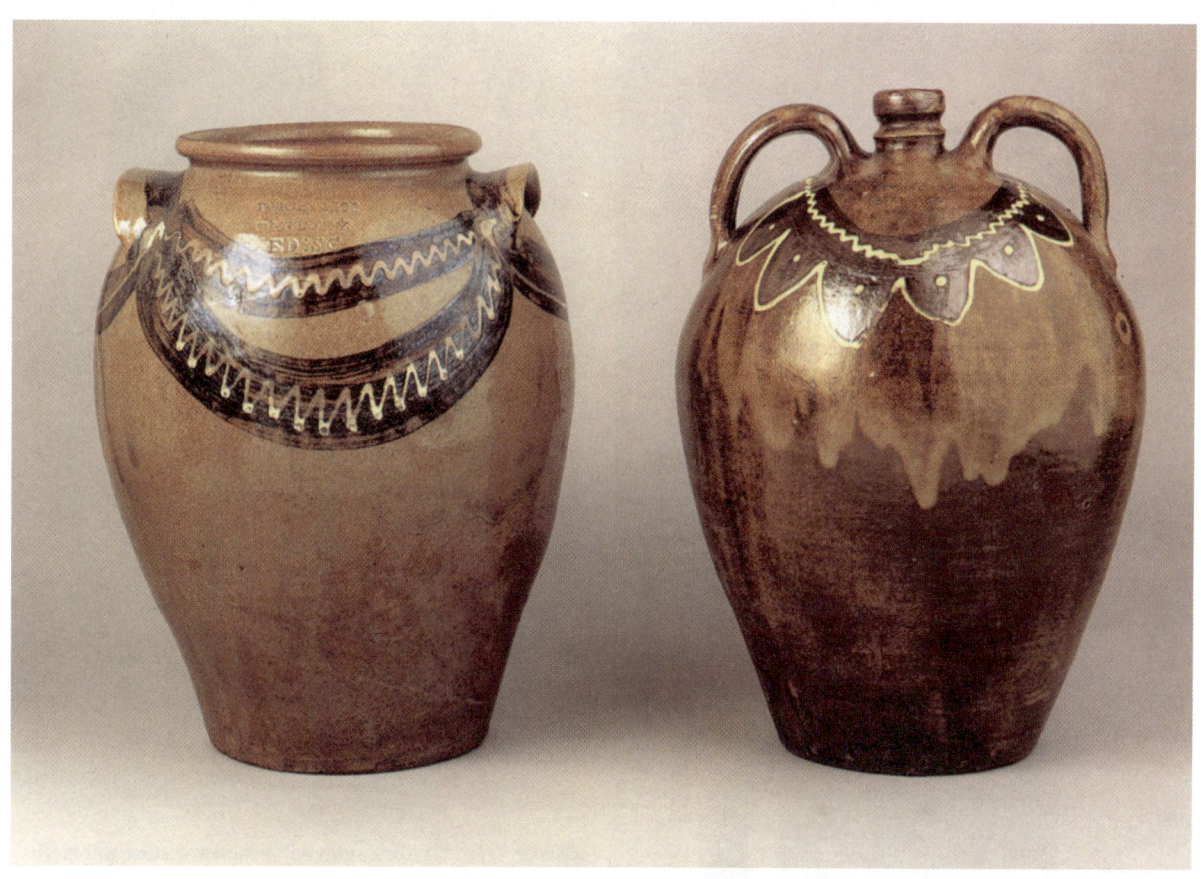

Alkaline-glazed stoneware storage jar and jug with kaolin and iron slip decoration, ca. 1840, Phoenix Factory, Edgefield District, S.C. Jar: H 16¾″, C 39½″. Jug: H 16¾″, C 37¾″. Both have stamped factory mark: "PHOENIX / FACTORY / ED:SC." Storage jar: Collection of Guy Kennedy. Jug: Courtesy of the Museum of Early Southern Decorative Arts, Winston-Salem, N.C.

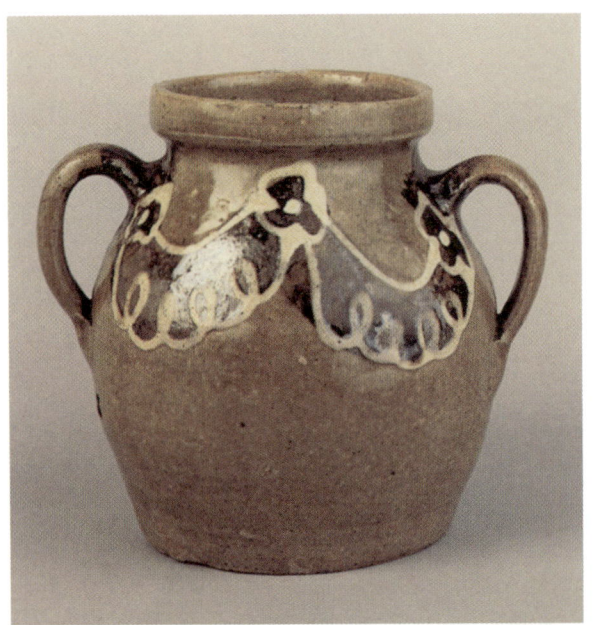

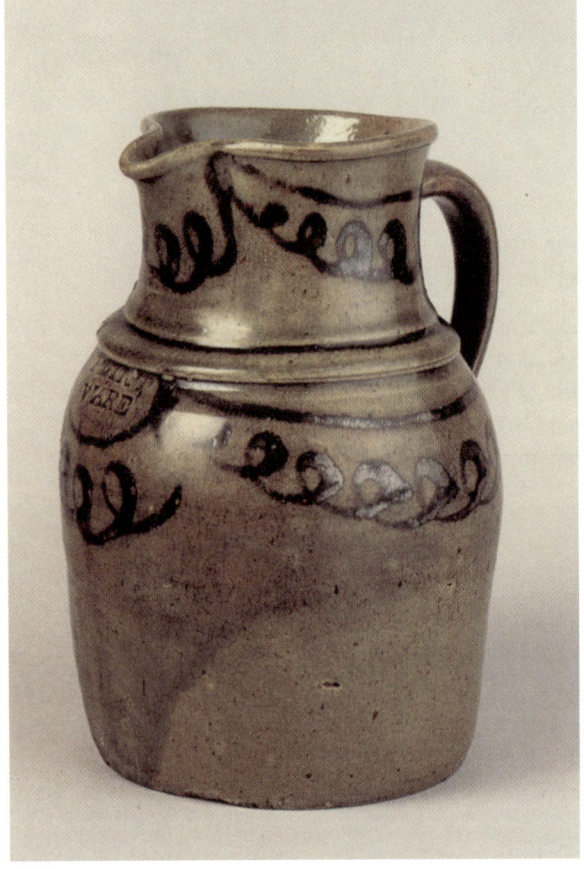

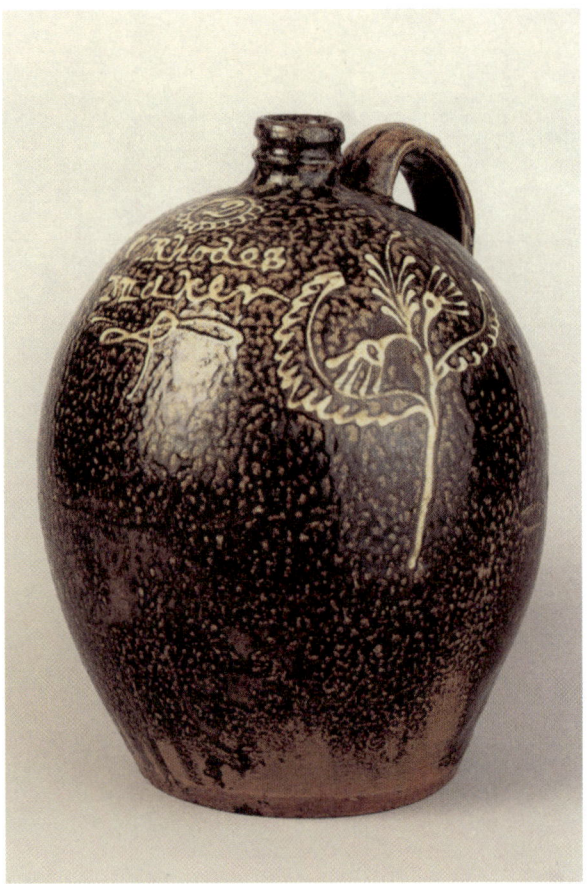

Above, left: Alkaline-glazed stoneware stew pot with loop and swag design in kaolin and iron slip, ca. 1840–50, attributed to the Phoenix Factory or Collin Rhodes Factory, Shaw's Creek, Edgefield District, S.C. H 6⅜″, C 18¾″. Collection of Tony and Marie Shank.

Above, right: Slip-decorated jug with brown-black ash-based alkaline glaze, ca. 1850, Collin Rhodes Factory, Shaw's Creek, Edgefield District, S.C. H 13″, C 32½″. Gallon capacity and maker's marks applied in kaolin slip script at upper shoulder opposite handle: "2" (inside kaolin slip medallion) and "C Rhodes / Maker." Collection of Terry and Steve Ferrell.

Slip-decorated alkaline-glazed stoneware pitcher, ca. 1845, Thomas Chandler, Trapp-Chandler Factory, Kirksey's Crossroads, Edgefield District, S.C. H 10½″, C 23¼″. Stamped: "FLINT WARE." Collection of Tony and Marie Shank.

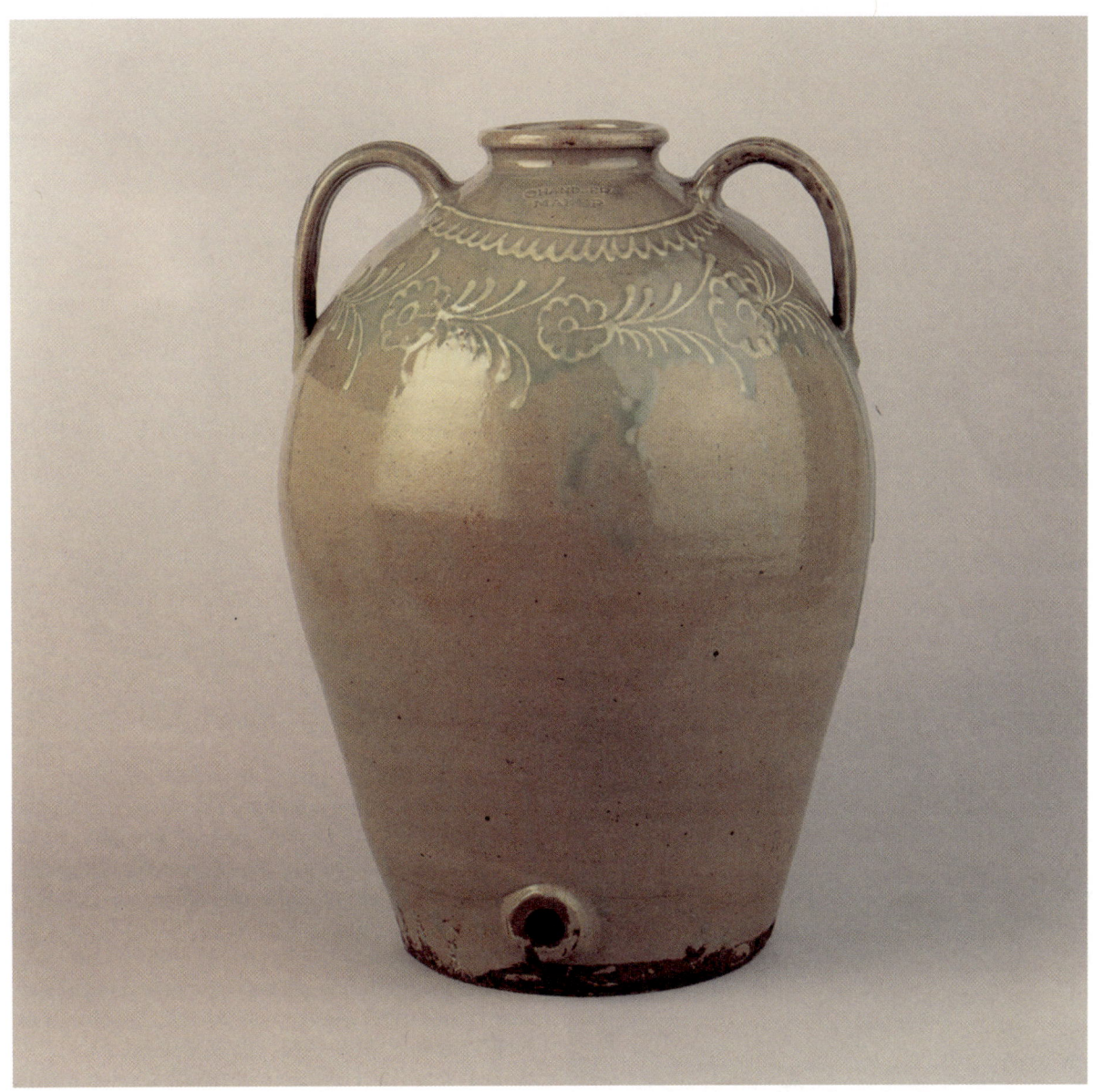

Wide-mouthed slip-decorated alkaline-glazed stoneware cooler with kaolin slip loop and swag motif and floral spray, ca. 1850, Thomas Chandler, Thomas Chandler Factory, Kirksey's Crossroads, Edgefield District, S.C. H 19⅞″, C 46¾″. Stamped: "CHANDLER / MAKER" (front, upper shoulder between handles). Stoneware vessels from the Thomas Chandler Factory are characterized by highly symmetrical forms, standardized kaolin slip decorative treatments, and highly refined lime-based alkaline glazes. Collection of Terry and Steve Ferrell.

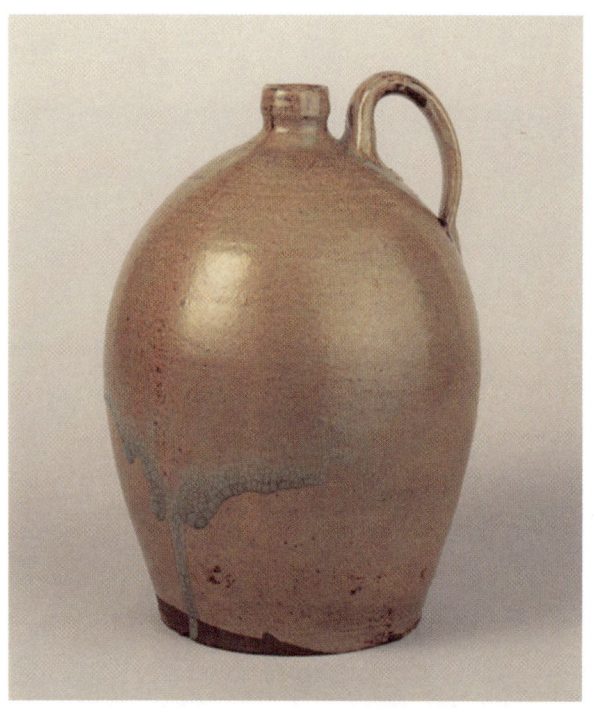

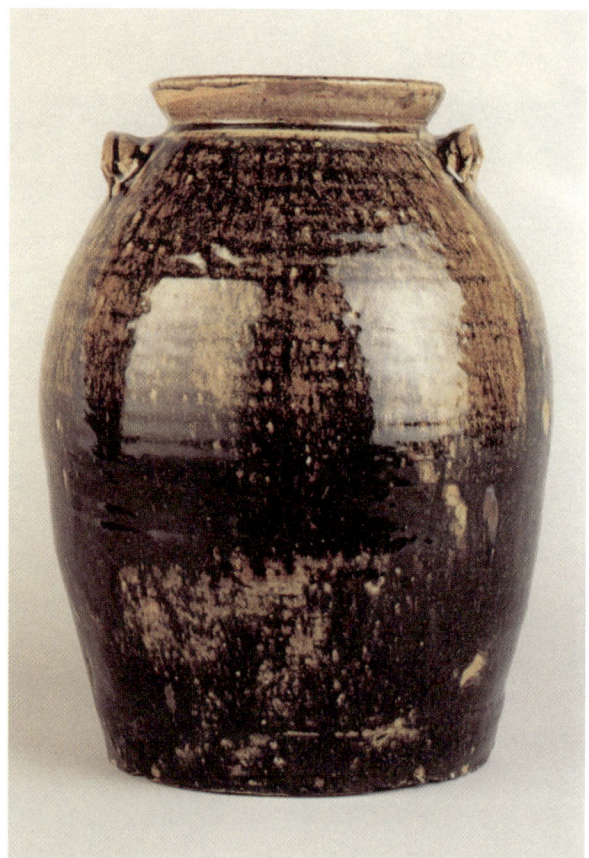

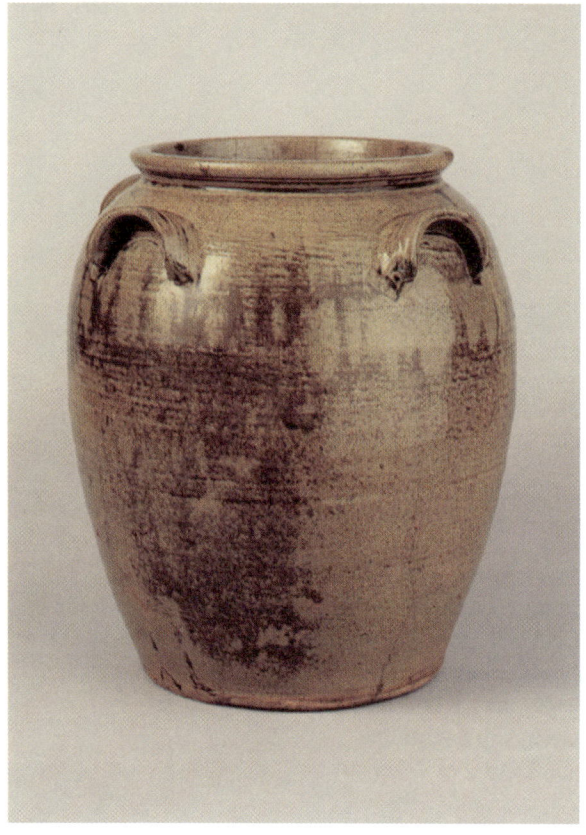

Above, left: Alkaline-glazed stoneware jug, 1872, Jesse P. Bodie Pottery, Kirksey's Crossroads, Edgefield County, S.C. H 13″, C 28¼″. Incised date and gallon capacity mark: "1872 / 2." Stamped maker's mark: "J. P. Bodie / Maker." Collection of Terry and Steve Ferrell.

Above, right: Alkaline-glazed stoneware storage jar with "paint rock" glaze, ca. 1880–1900, attributed to Jack Thurman, Miles Mill, Aiken County, S.C. H 16¼″, C 40⅛″. Collection of the Charleston Museum, Charleston, S.C.

Alkaline-glazed stoneware storage jar with four lug handles, ca. 1880, W. F. Hahn Pottery, Aiken County, S.C. H 14⅞″, C 40⅜″. Stamped gallon capacity and maker's mark: "5 / W F HAHN / TRENTON / SC." Collection of Terry and Steve Ferrell.

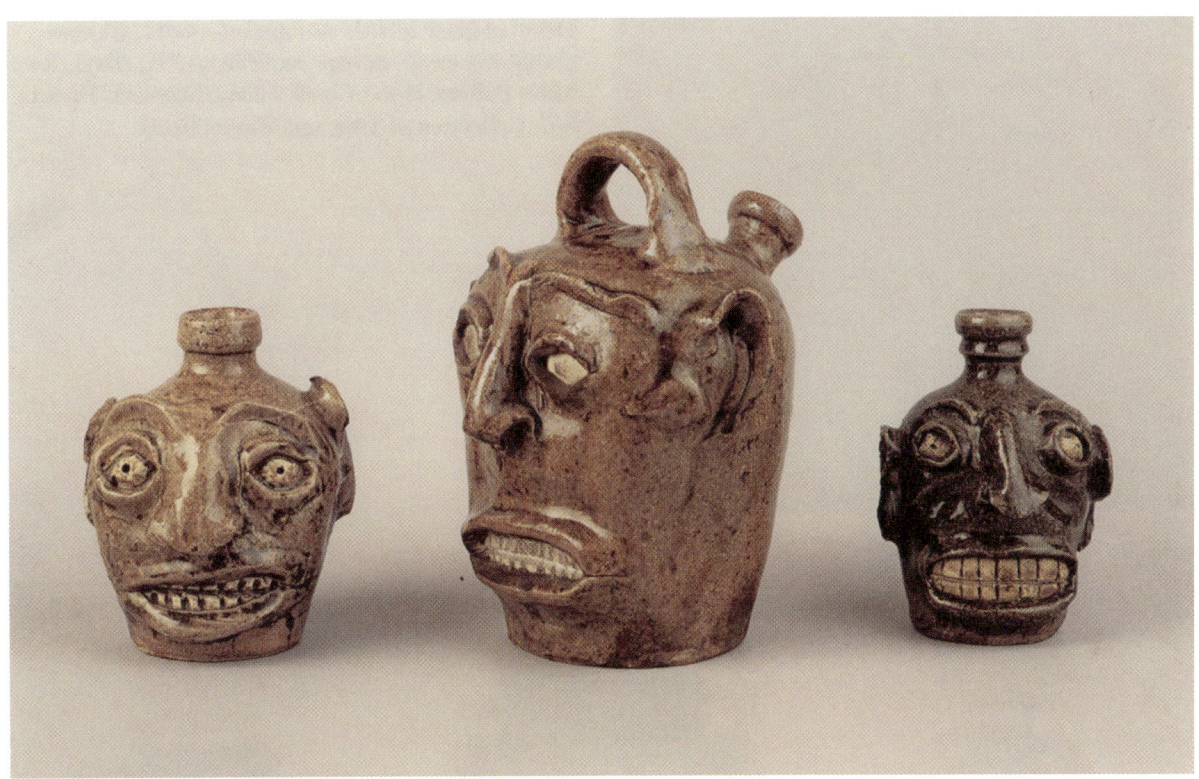

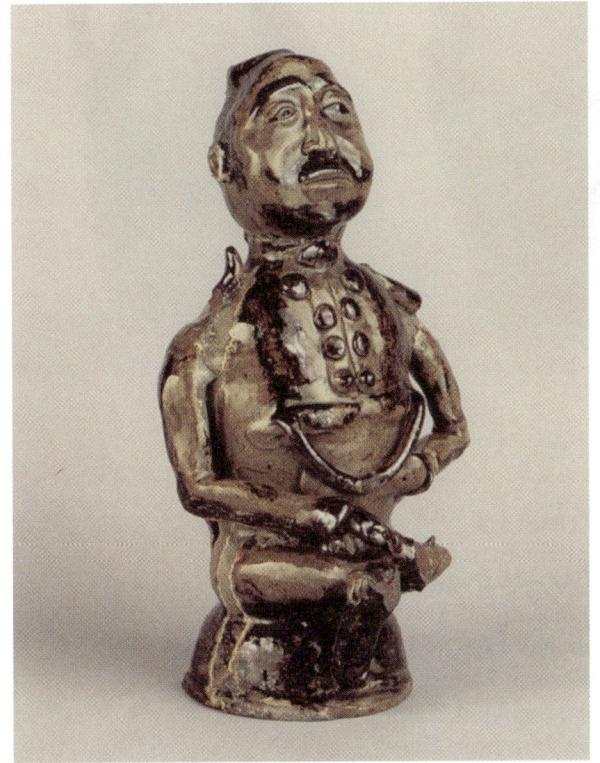

Alkaline-glazed stoneware face vessels, ca. 1860–80, attributed to African-American potters, Edgefield District, S.C. *Left:* H 5¾″, C 5⅞″. *Center:* H 9″, C 22″. *Right:* H 5½″, C 12⅜″. Collection of Tony and Marie Shank.

Alkaline-glazed stoneware figural bottle, ca. 1860–70, attributed to African-American potter Jim Lee, Roundtree and Bodie Pottery, Kirksey's Crossroads, Edgefield District, S.C. H 12¼″, C 16¾″. Collection of the Charleston Museum, Charleston, S.C.

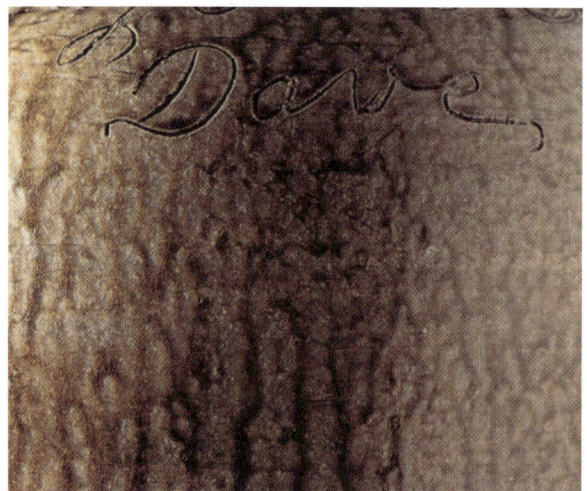

Detail of glaze texture and maker's mark, alkaline-glazed stoneware storage jar, May 3, 1862, Dave, Lewis Miles Pottery, Horse Creek Valley, Edgefield District, S.C. Collection of Tony and Marie Shank.

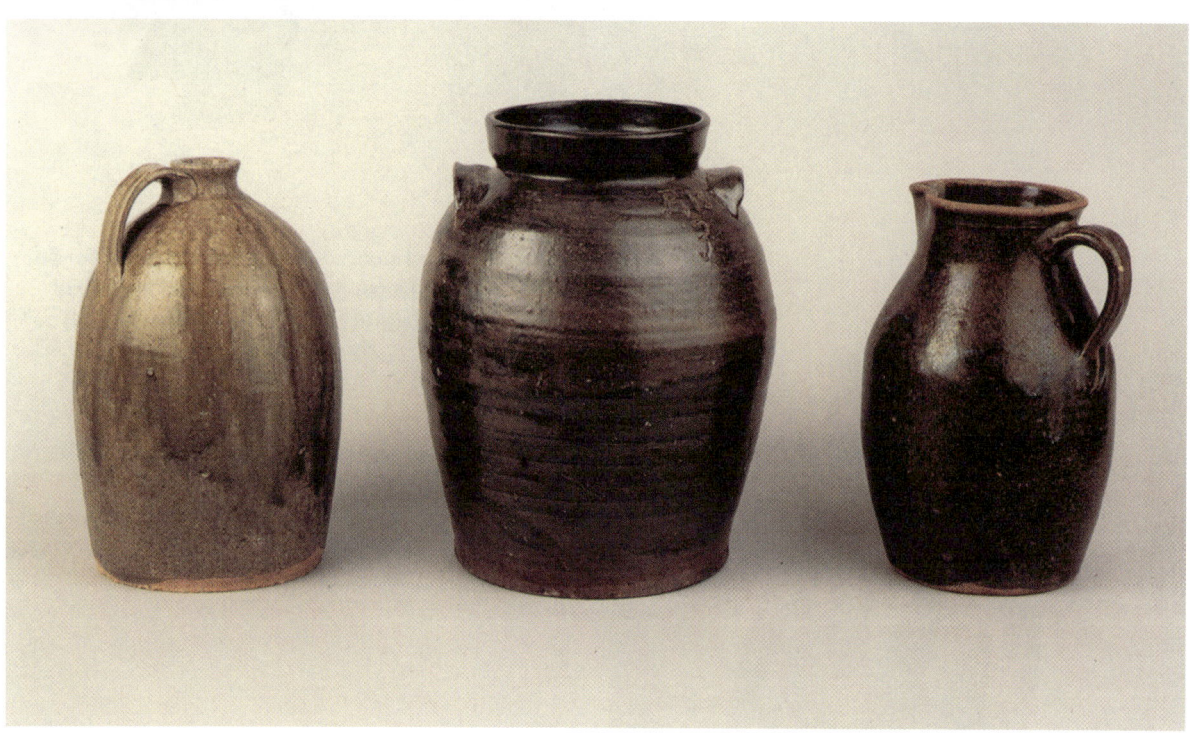

Upcountry South Carolina alkaline-glazed stoneware vessels, *Left:* Jug with kaolin-rich olive green alkaline glaze, ca. 1880, David Carr Henson, Spartanburg County, S.C. H: 11¼″, C 23¼″. *Center:* Storage jar with iron-rich cinder glaze, ca. 1930, Boyle Pottery, Cherokee County, S.C. H: 12¼″, C 31½″. *Right:* Pitcher with blue clouding at glaze drips resulting from naturally occurring rutile present in clay, ca. 1910–1940, Clayton Jug Factory, Holly Springs community, Spartanburg County, S.C. H 10½″, C 22″. Jug: Collection of Billy Henson. Storage jar and pitcher: Collection of McKissick Museum, The University of South Carolina, Columbia.

Edgefield Sculpted Vessels

In addition to utilitarian stoneware, Edgefield slave potters produced a distinct style of ceramic sculpture. Known variously as "grotesques," "voodoo jugs," or "monkey jugs," they consisted of a wheel-thrown vessel, usually of ovoid form, onto which facial features were applied in modeled clay. Jugs, pitchers, lidded jars, cups, and water carriers were produced with this type of treatment.

Thomas Davies, owner of a pottery established in Edgefield District at Bath (located between present-day Aiken, South Carolina, and Augusta, Georgia) in 1862, remarked in an interview with ceramics historian Edwin Atlee Barber that the slaves were allowed time on their own, which they spent "in making homely designs in coarse pottery. Among these were some weird-looking water jugs, roughly modeled in the front in the form of a grotesque human face evidently intended to portray the African features."[26] Barber also noted that the slaves inserted white porcelain clay for eyes and teeth, a technique that he deemed "ingenious" and reminiscent of "aboriginal art as formerly practiced by the ancestors of the makers in the Dark Continent."[27] A small stoneware face cup found on a waster pile at the site of the Davies pottery confirms this account (Figure 3.8).[28]

Two similarly sculpted vessels in the collection of the Charleston Museum are attributed to Miles Mill (see Figure 3.9). However, no archaeological evidence has been found to indicate that face vessels were produced at the Miles Mill site. Even if this attribution is correct, it seems unlikely that the form was first developed at Miles Mill because the historical record indicates that the first pottery located at the site dates to about 1867. Since the Davies and Miles Mill potteries were in operation during roughly the same period, slaves may have been exchanged between the two operations, either through sale or hiring

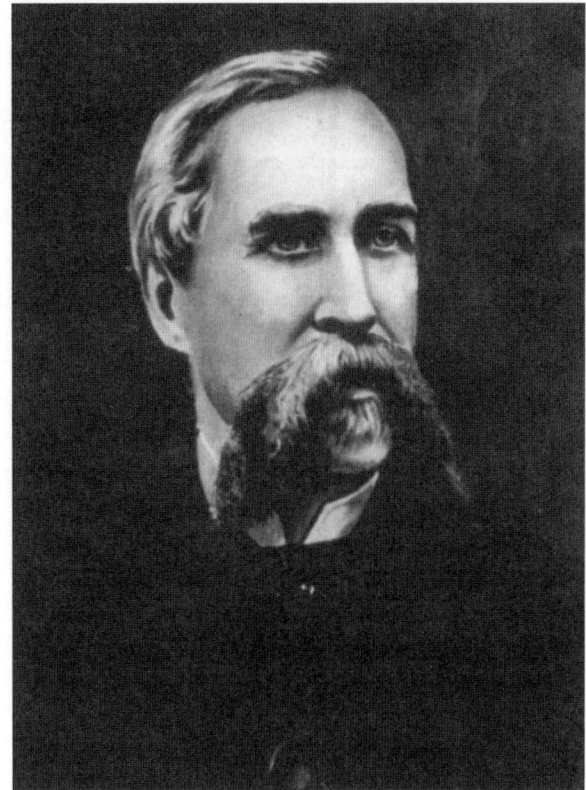

3.7 Portrait of Colonel Thomas Davies. Courtesy of the Blue Ridge Institute, Ferrum College, Ferrum, Va., with thanks to Roddy Moore.

out.[29] The commonality of forms could then be explained as an outcome of shared skills and borrowing of techniques of manufacture. Another face vessel has been discovered that is signed in incised script "Joe Kirksey" (Figure 3.10). This piece has a flattened face, unglazed kaolin eyes and teeth, a strap handle attached horizontally across the top, and a rear pouring spout. The style and features of the "Kirksey" and Miles Mill vessels may indicate that they are later versions.

Davies indicated that face vessels appeared on the scene rather suddenly in 1862. However, the sophistication of the design and elaborate techniques required to produce the ware indicate that this vessel type was developed over a period of several years. Stoneware clay and porcelain have

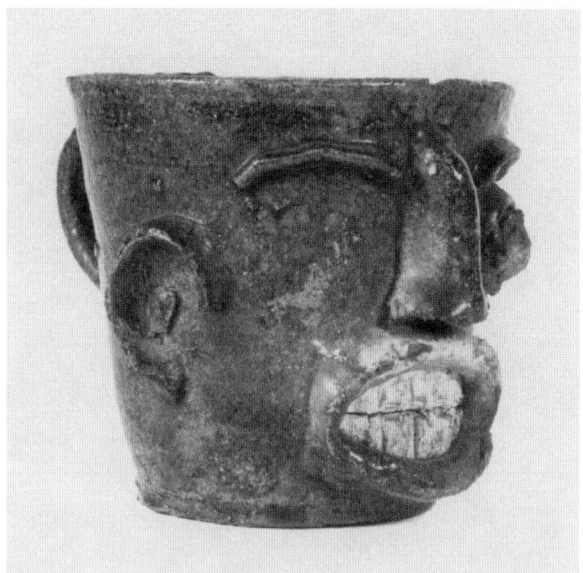

3.8   Alkaline-glazed stoneware face cup with applied clay features, ca. 1862, Thomas Davies Pottery, Bath, Edgefield District, S.C. H 3⅞″, C 14⅝″. Collection of the Augusta-Richmond County Museum, Augusta, Ga.

different shrinkage rates, so if the kaolin insert is not bulky enough, it will shrink up and fall out of its socket when fired. Since the slave potters were working with highly unpredictable groundhog kilns, a period of trial and error would have been required to calculate the right combination of duration and position for firing. Finally, some scholars have pointed to an evolution of form as indicative of various stages through which the face vessel was developed. Scholar Robert Farris Thompson has identified certain features or groups of features with a particular "master" potter. For example, he credits one substyle, in which the potter incised the kaolin teeth with slanted rather than vertical strokes, to the "Master of the Diagonal Teeth." Folklorist John Michael Vlach maintains that these variations in style and technique suggest an evolution of form that may have taken twenty-five years to complete. According to Vlach, "the most refined of those pots feature a three-color format with variations in texture as

well: white matte finished eyes and teeth, shiny green or brown vessel body, and eye rims and lips of either a buff or reddish brown color that were left unglazed."[30] To Vlach, this evolution in form demonstrates that face vessels were produced by African-American slaves in the Edgefield area well before 1862.

Several possibilities have been proposed regarding the inspiration for the Edgefield face vessels. African-Americanist scholars have compared the stoneware vessels to African wood carvings made by the Kongo people from the coastal areas of central Africa. They point to the fact that most of South Carolina's slave population was imported from lands controlled by the Kongo and closely related peoples.[31] Both the Bakongo wood

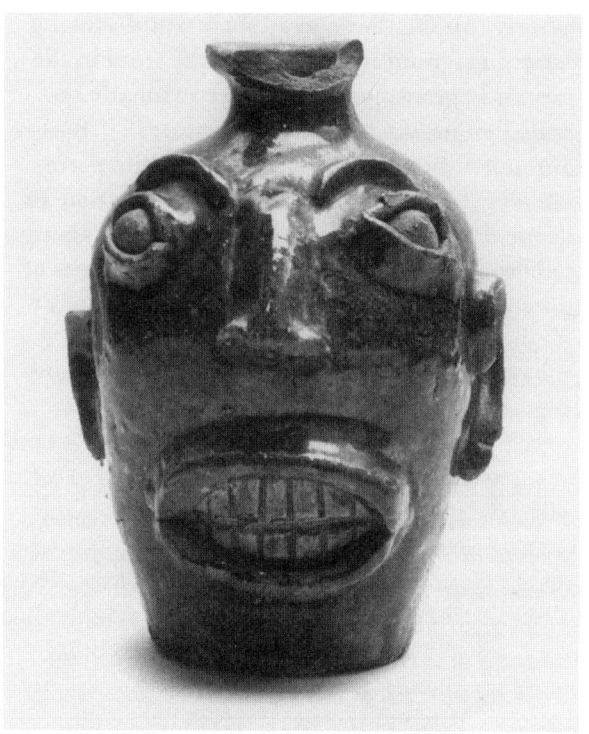

3.9   Alkaline-glazed stoneware face jug with applied clay features, ca. 1880, attributed to slaves at Miles Mill Pottery, Aiken County, S.C. H 6″, C 13⅜″. Collection of the Charleston Museum, Charleston, S.C.

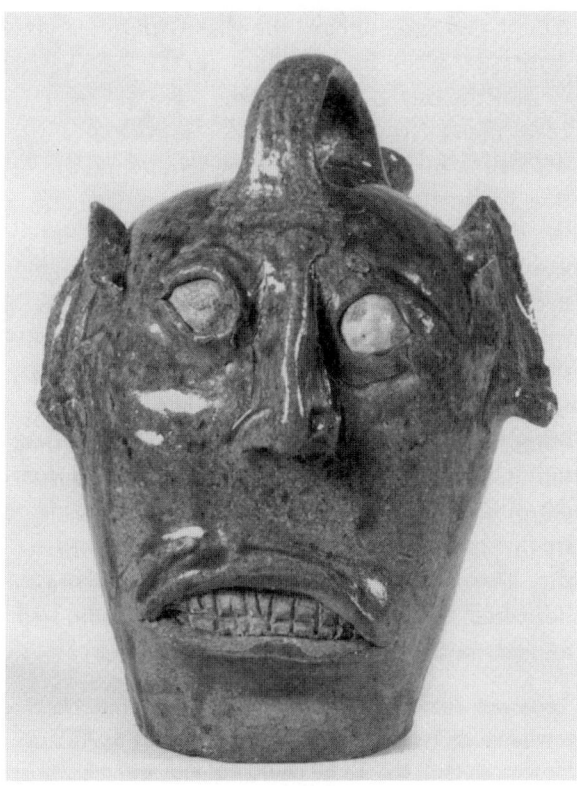

3.10 Alkaline-glazed stoneware face jug with applied clay features, ca. 1860–80, Edgefield District, S.C. H 9″, C 19¾″. Incised script: Joe Kirksey. Collection High Museum of Art, Atlanta, Ga.; purchased with funds from the Decorative Arts Endowment, 1987.20.

ground." Similarly carved walking sticks with lizards and snakes were noted at Brownville, west of Savannah. At Frogtown and Currytown wood carvers produced full-length human figures and busts mounted on blocks of wood. Clay sculptures produced on Wilmington Island during the same period may have represented an extension of the woodcarving tradition: "The African men used to all the time make little clay images. Sometimes they like men and sometimes they like animals. Once they made a big one. They put a spear in his hand and walk around him and say he was the chief."[32] Thus the production of ceramic face vessels in Edgefield by African-American slaves may have represented a transferral of African woodcarving techniques.

The decoration of pottery with faces was common in Great Britain from the Roman era onward, and this treatment was also used throughout the United States. The English Toby jug, first made in Staffordshire in the late eighteenth century and later imitated by American potters, may have also indirectly influenced the Edgefield face vessels. Thompson noted the presence of "Tobyizing" images in Kongo art beginning in the first half of the nineteenth century.[33] Tobys were exported to Africa soon after their invention and were used among the Kongo as models for stone funerary sculpture and grave ornaments. Kongo potters soon developed their own versions of the Toby, sculpted from terra-cotta clay. The Toby, then, may have represented memories of Africa for slaves in the New World.

John Vlach suggests that potters from Bennington, Vermont, brought to the Edgefield District in 1858 to establish a porcelain factory at Kaolin (present-day Bath, South Carolina), may have introduced the Toby form to the area. Tobys were stock items in New England, and Vlach points out that the spouts on two Edgefield pitchers resemble the profile of the Toby's emblematic tricorn hat.[34]

The Kaolin factory, later known as the South-

carvers and the Edgefield potters employed a mixed-media approach in the depiction of facial features. Thompson and Vlach interpret this stylistic parallel as an African survival.

There was a strong woodcarving tradition among former slaves living in coastal Georgia in the 1940s. WPA researchers, remarking on the work of a wood carver called "Stick Daddy" in the settlement of Yamacraw near the Savannah River, asserted that the chief characteristic of his canes (carved with snakes and crocodiles) was "the boldness with which the carved figures, dark-stained and highly polished, stand out against their unfinished natural wood back-

ern Porcelain Manufacturing Company, was located near Davies's pottery in present-day Bath, South Carolina. Anson Peeler, a carpenter and skilled mechanic who had previously been involved in the design and construction of the United States Pottery in Bennington, Vermont, had been brought to South Carolina by William H. Farrar to oversee the construction of the Kaolin porcelain factory. In 1862 Peeler persuaded Davies to establish a firebrick factory on the South Carolina Railroad line at Bath. Davies supplied slaves and capital for the operation, and Peeler was made manager. During the Civil War Davies's Palmetto Fire Brick Works was converted into a stoneware factory for the production of jars, pitchers, and cups to supply Confederate hospitals. Meanwhile, the production of fine china ware was discontinued at the Kaolin factory. In 1862 the factory, under new ownership and renamed the Southern Porcelain Manufacturing Company, was producing porcelain telegraph insulators for the Confederate government and earthenware water pipes for the regional market. The Southern Porcelain Manufacturing Company was destroyed by fire in 1863 or 1864, and the Davies pottery was closed in 1865. Davies later became manager of a kaolin mine where some of his former slaves were probably employed as kaolin miners. The skilled turners, many of whom had been brought to Bath from the Edgefield vicinity, probably hired on with local Edgefield-area stoneware factory owners after the close of the Palmetto Fire Brick Works.[35]

Newly arrived Kongo slaves may have inspired the Edgefield potters to attempt the difficult Toby-style sculptures. Although a federal law prohibiting the slave trade went into effect in the United States in 1808, shipments of slaves were often illegally smuggled into friendly ports in the South. In 1858 one of the last slave cargoes brought to this country landed on the coast of Georgia. This group of Africans, primarily Kikongo-speaking people, was brought to Jekyll Island, Georgia, aboard the ship *Wanderer*. Some were then taken by steamboat up the John's River to Florida and sold, and others were disposed of on the coasts of Georgia and South Carolina. About 170 of the Africans were carried up the Savannah River by steamboat to a landing on the Carolina side of the river, about two miles south of Augusta, Georgia. They were then taken to the Edgefield plantation of a relative of the principal owner of the *Wanderer* where they were sold, mainly to planters in the area.[36] In the early 1900s a few of these native Africans were still living within a few miles of the point where they had debarked from the steamboat. Some of their Carolina-born friends and relatives still recall the presence of these individuals in the community. Floyd White of St. Simons Island, Georgia, described Tom Floyd, one of the slaves who had arrived on the *Wanderer*, in the following passage.

He wuz shawt an tick set. I tinks he was Ibo. He used to whoop an holluh. He say dey do da way in Africa. He wuz doctuh too an he could cut yuh wid a knife an cop [cut or bleed] yuh. I wish he wuz yuh right now tuh cop me. I sho needs it an it make yuh feel lots bettuh. I heah him talk plenty bout Africa but I caahn membuh so much ub it coz uh wuz young boy den. He say he lib in a hut on a ribbuh an dey eat coconut an bread wut grow on a tree. Dey plant yam ebry seben yeah an dey dohn hadduh wuk it. Dey hab peanut an banana. He call it by anudduh name but I caahn membuh it. I seen plenty ub African people an dey all say dey plant duh crop an dey dohn hadduh wuk it. I heah lot ub em tell how dey git obuh yuh. Dey trap em on a boat wid a red flag.[37]

Slaves from the *Wanderer*, therefore, reintroduced African customs, healing methods, and agricultural practices to their fellow slaves in the Georgia sea islands. Some of these newly arrived Africans apparently retained their African beliefs. For example, anthropologist Charles Montgomery offered the following description of Uster Williams, a former slave living in the Richmond County Home near Augusta, who had been a passenger on the *Wanderer*: "His present condition is peculiarly sad. Almost blind, and with little mind left, thinking he has had a 'spell' put on him by 'witchcraft,' he seems to think that someone is going to kill him; yet he retains his memory of African words and customs in a remarkable degree. He says he came from near the 'Bezy' river in Africa."[38]

Lucinda Thurmond, a former servant on the Seigler plantation in Edgefield, remembered four of the African men pictured in Montgomery's 1908 article on the *Wanderer*: "Uncle Ward (Cilucangy, or Ward Lee), Uncle Tucker (Pucka Geata, or Tucker Henderson), Uncle Romeo (Tahro, or Romeo), and Uncle Uster (Mabiala, or Uster Williams)." Tahro, or Romeo, the oldest of those interviewed by Montgomery, built an African-style straw house that Mrs. Thurmond remembered playing in as a child. Mrs. Thurmond also recalled that Tucker once scared her by waving a red pocket hanky and saying "I liked to had ya, I liked to had ya." When asked why she was afraid, she replied that "they said, that's the way they brought 'em over here from Africa."[39] These memories of Africa evidently made a lasting impression upon African-Americans living in the Edgefield area. The retention of African magico-religious practices by the slaves from the *Wanderer* may be particularly significant since the African Tobys were infused with magical power.[40]

A slave named Romeo, possibly the Romeo brought to the Edgefield area on the *Wanderer*, appears in a business ledger kept by Thomas J. Davies as a workman at the Palmetto Fire Brick Works.[41] Romeo appears in three separate entries. In the first, dated 28 May 1863, he is listed as part of a work gang hired out from slaveholder R. O. Starke during the month of May for $90. The gang consists of Romeo and four other slaves— Jim, Dennis, Bob Seles, and Ike. On 13 September of the same year slaveholder W. P. Starke hired out another gang—Romeo, Dennis, Ike, Jim, and Rob—to the factory for $262.50 during

June, July, and August. In the third entry, dated 1 November, R. O. Starke hired out Dennis, Jim, Rob, Silas, Romeo, and Ike during September and October for $180. Although it is unclear what sort of tasks Romeo performed at the factory, his presence there may be the first evidence of direct Kongo influence on the production of face vessels in the Edgefield District.

Other sculpted forms were produced by freed blacks during the postbellum era. A figural bottle in the Charleston Museum is attributed to a black potter named Jim Lee who worked at the Roundtree-Bodie factory at Kirksey's Crossroads in Edgefield District (Figure 3.11). Although the Charleston Museum records indicate that the bottle was made before 1860, the Bodie pottery does not appear in the Edgefield industrial census records until 1870. W. D. Roundtree was listed in the 1860 census of industry as the owner of the stoneware pottery later operated by Bodie. According to local historian Margaret Watson, the site was first established as a stoneware factory in 1840 by a man named Turner. W. D. Roundtree acquired the pottery shortly before the Civil War and later sold it to J. H. Burnett. Burnett sold the property to Bodie around 1870, and Bodie reportedly operated the stoneware factory until about 1884.[42] This account suggests two possibilities. Jim Lee either made the bottle at the Roundtree pottery in about 1860, or he turned the piece at the pottery under Bodie's ownership sometime after 1870.

The Jim Lee bottle is different in design and technique from the Davies and Miles Mill face vessels. This unusual form was reportedly made in the likeness of a local preacher, the Reverend Pickett. The sculptural detailing of the body and costume is reminiscent of the Tobys, and the iron-slip marking, applied to features such as hair, buttons, epaulets, bow tie, collar, and sleeves, is similar to that found on fragments of a ceramic figure recovered from the site of the Phoenix Factory. The Phoenix Factory figure, thought to have been a depiction of an Indian chief, bears a gray-green alkaline glaze similar in color and texture to the glaze formulas developed by Thomas Chandler. This is not surprising since Chandler was one of the principal turners at the Phoenix Factory. Facial features were applied in kaolin and iron slip to both the Phoenix Factory figure and the figural bottle attributed to Jim Lee. Lee also used an unusual decorative technique typically associated with Catawba Valley, North Carolina, folk pottery—that of placing pieces of broken glass on the rim (in this case,

on the shoulders of the figure). The glass fragments liquefied when fired, creating a pattern of thick, contrasting drips along the length of the bottle (Figure 3.12). Since this technique was not commonly used in Edgefield, the piece may be indicative of the interaction between potters in the Kirksey's Crossroads–area of Edgefield and the Catawba Valley of North Carolina.

Edgefield potters continued to produce face vessels well into the twentieth century. For example, a crudely designed face jug in a private collection is inscribed "E G / Aiken /

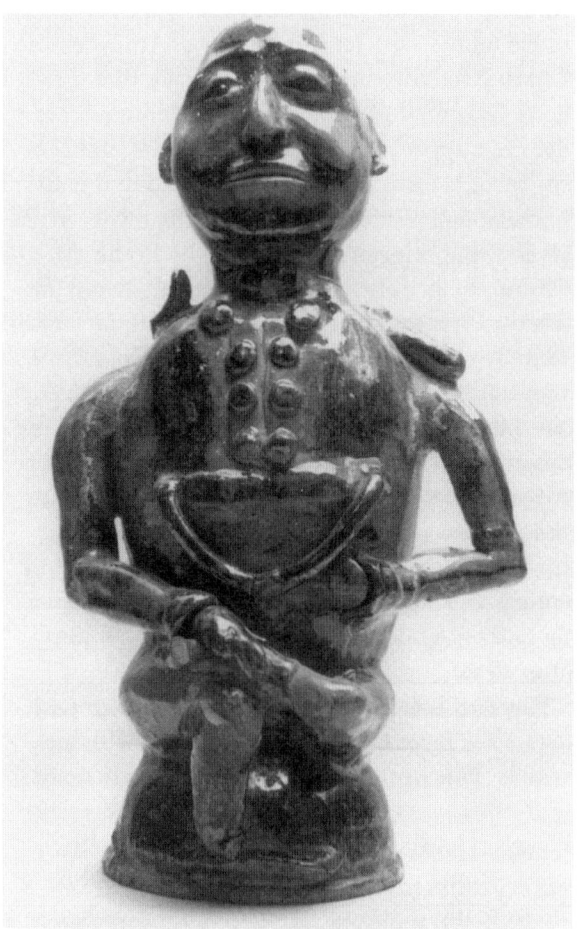

3.11 Alkaline-glazed stoneware figural bottle, ca. 1860–70, attributed to African-American potter Jim Lee, Roundtree and Bodie Pottery, Kirksey's Crossroads, Edgefield District, S.C. H 12¼", C 16¾".

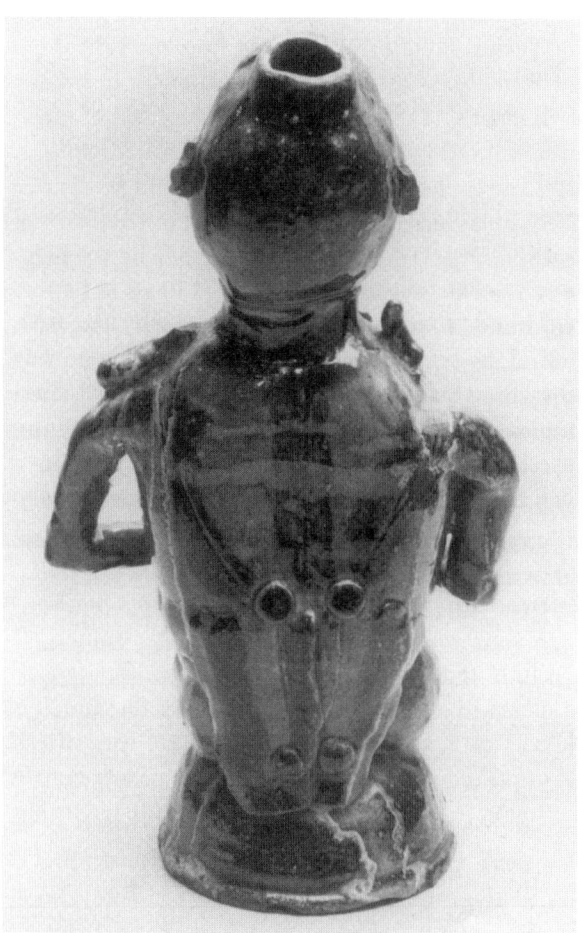

3.12 Reverse view of Figure 3.11. The vertical drips along the length of the bottle were achieved by placing pieces of glass on the rim before firing. Collection of the Charleston Museum, Charleston, S.C.

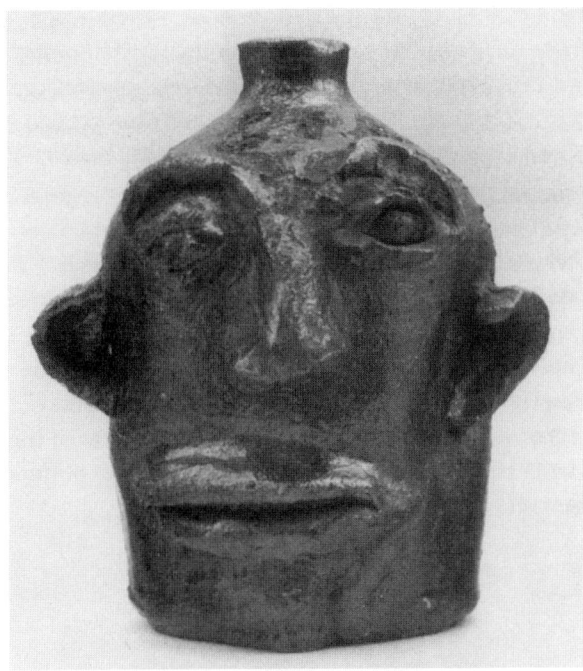

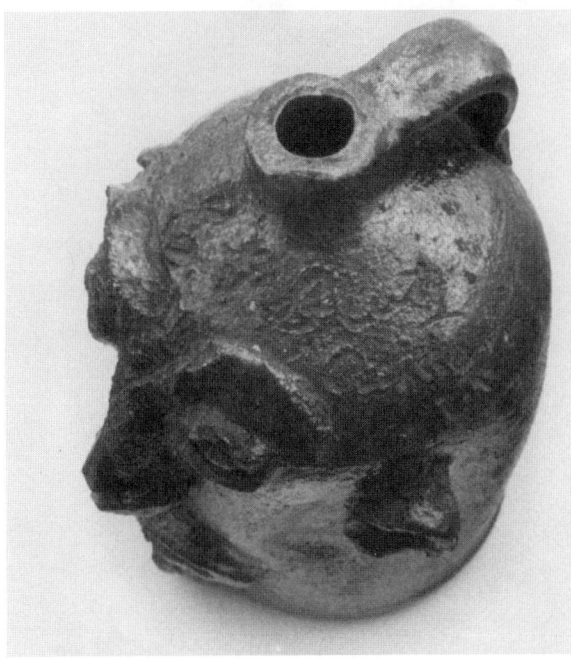

3.13 Alkaline-glazed stoneware face jug with applied clay features, 1917, Aiken County, S.C. H 8″, C 20⅝″. Incised script: E G / Aiken / S.C. / 6-24-17. Courtesy of Roddy and Sally Moore.

S.C. / 6-24-17" (Figure 3.13). American folk art collector Herbert Hemphill reported that an African-American living near Mobile was making stoneware sculpture similar to that made by African-American slaves in Edgefield as late as the decade preceding World War II. John Vlach has suggested a continuation of the aesthetic force of the Edgefield face vessels in the contemporary clay sculptures of James ("Son Ford") Thomas of Leland, Mississippi.[43]

Southern Anglo-American folk potters may have borrowed the earlier African-American face vessel design and technology. For example, until his death in 1967 folk potter Cheever Meaders of White County, Georgia, produced alkaline-glazed stoneware jugs with sculpted facial features and fragments of earthenware dishes inserted for teeth. His son, Lanier Meaders, produces similar face vessels today, as does folk potter Burlon Craig in the Catawba Valley of North Carolina (see Figure 3.14).[44] John Burrison identified "at least seven white pottery families" that have made face vessels in Georgia.[45] Members of one of these families, the Browns, reportedly introduced the face vessel to North Carolina when they established a shop at Arden in 1923.

Sculptor, potter, and historian Michael Hall has proposed an alternative explanation for the appearance of face vessels in America. Hall rejects the presumption that face vessels represent a black folk art form. He contends instead that "face vessels originated in a white world and are linked to the American temperance movement."[46] Through specific examples from Pennsylvania, Ohio, and North Carolina he links their production to the growth and spread of temperance throughout the United States. Although Hall overdoes his thesis that the temperance movement is the key to face vessels, he ranges wide in his evidence, demonstrating the appearance of American face vessels long before the South Carolina versions. Thus, it remains unclear whether Anglo potters borrowed the face vessel

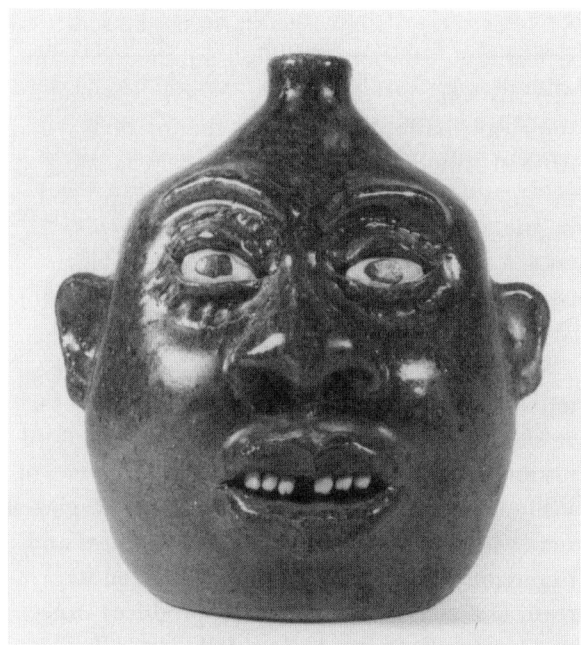

3.14 Alkaline-glazed stoneware face jug, 1979, Lanier Meaders, Cleveland, Ga. H 9⅛″, C 22½″. Incised script: Lanier Meaders (at base). Collection of McKissick Museum, The University of South Carolina, Columbia.

design and technology from African-Americans.

Another type of vessel found in Edgefield that may have been African-inspired is a water carrier known as the "monkey jug." This vessel, made in unglazed earthenware in Africa and the West Indies and in alkaline-glazed stoneware in Edgefield, was ovoid in form with an overarching stirrup handle and a tubular spout attached at an angle (see Figure 3.15). The use of the term "monkey" in connection with these jugs is reportedly a reference to their function and significance rather than to their resemblance to the head of a monkey. Barber noted that porous vessels made for holding water and cooling it by evaporation were called by that name. The use of the term "monkey" to mean a strong thirst dates to as early as the late eighteenth century and is still used by blacks in South Carolina.[47] John Vlach speculates that since the monkey jug was known in the Caribbean, it may have been a remembered African form. In support of this theory he points out that Bakongo potters made earthenware vessels called *m'vungu* that resemble water coolers made throughout the West Indies. John Burrison has suggested that pots with stirrup handles and canted spouts were alien to British folk pottery and maintains that water carriers of this type were unknown in England until about 1900. Georgeanna Greer points out that this form appears in Europe much earlier and that it may be Iberian in origin. Greer adds that the "monkey" form was called a harvest jug in some parts of the United States and was produced by Anglo potters as well as African-Americans.[48]

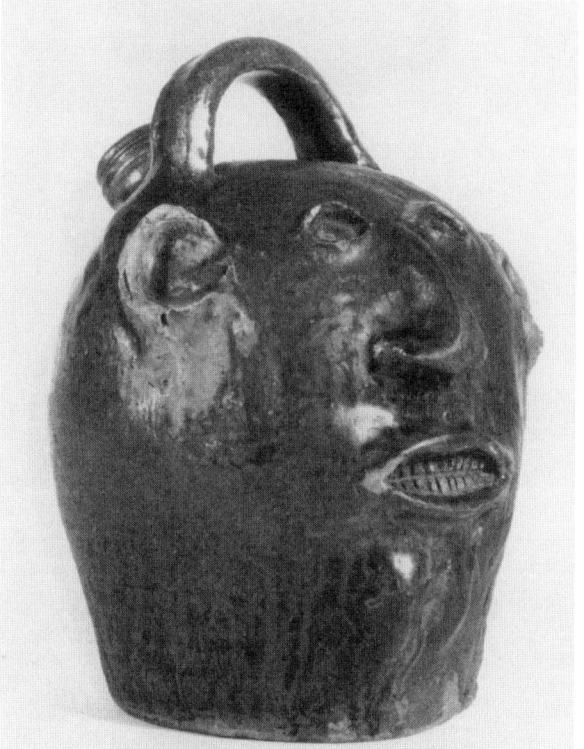

3.15 Alkaline-glazed stoneware "monkey" jug with applied clay features, ca. 1862, attributed to the Thomas Davies Pottery, Bath, Edgefield District, S.C. H 8¼″, C 20½″. Collection of the Augusta-Richmond County Museum, Augusta, Ga.

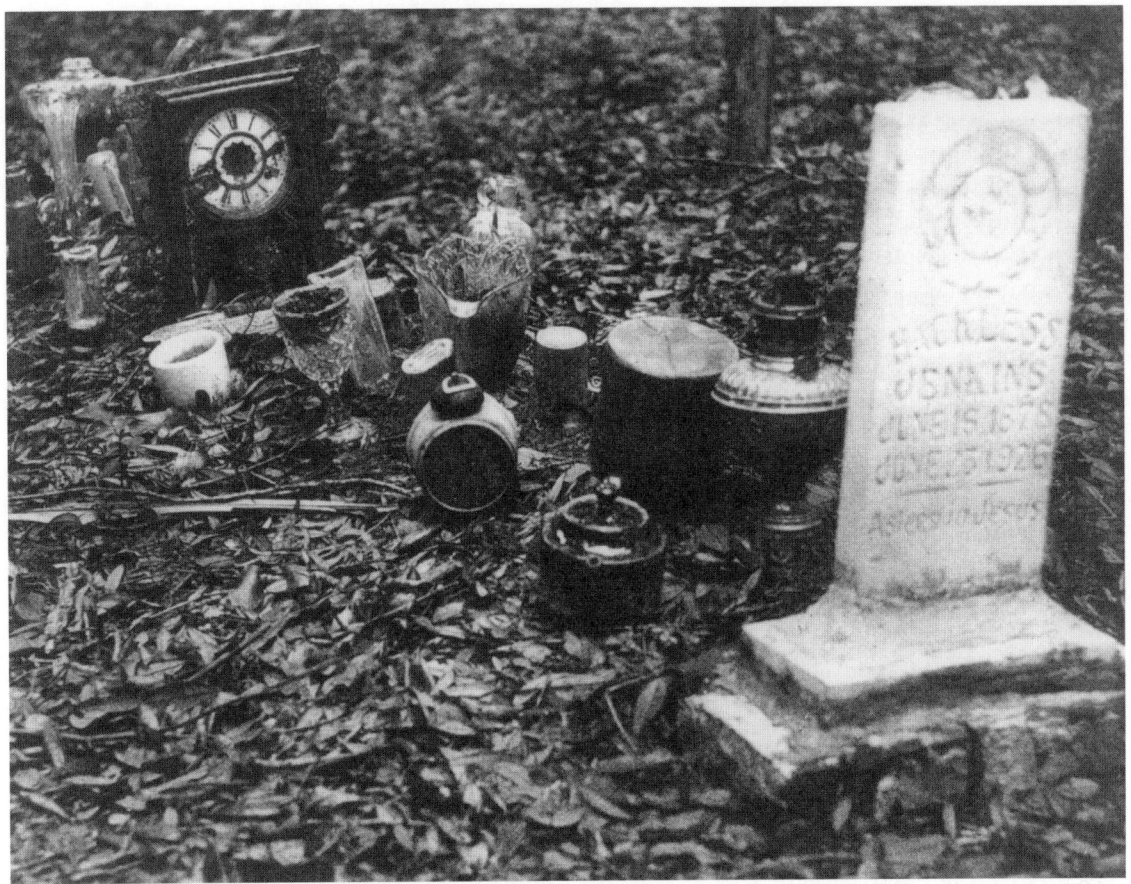

3.16 African-American grave decoration, Sea Islands, Georgia or South Carolina, 1933.
Photograph, collection of the Library of Congress, Washington, D.C.

Robert Farris Thompson has proposed another possible African derivation of the term "monkey"—the Kikongo word for "devil," *mbugi.* Thompson maintains that the Edgefield face vessels, some of them fashioned in the monkey form, may have been derived from a Kongo ceremony in which the chief drank palm wine from a skull-cup (and later from a Toby) to symbolize his power over life and death. Presumably, the Edgefield face vessels, called Afro-Carolinian face vessels by Thompson, were modeled after the African Tobys and therefore were also imbued with mystical powers.[49]

Thompson also noted that American ceramics historian C. Malcolm Watkins had informed him "of a notice of Afro-Carolinian vessels having been found in Afro-Carolinian burial grounds," and that a collection of face vessels in the possession of William Raiford Eve, a descendant of Thomas Davies, had holes "very carefully chipped out of the bottom, as if to break the objects without spoiling them, to prepare them as items of broken crockery, which traditionally covered the graves of Carolinians of African descent" (see Figure 3.16).[50]

In his *Folk Beliefs of the Southern Negro,* Newbell Niles Puckett observed that African-Americans in Mississippi, Georgia, and South Carolina placed broken objects on the graves of friends and relatives in order to appease the spirit of the deceased. He wrote that "in South Carolina, bleached sea shells, broken crockery and glassware, broken pitchers, soap-dishes, lamp chimneys, tureens, coffee-cups, syrup jugs, all sorts of ornamental vases, cigar boxes, gun locks, tomato cans, teapots, flower pots, bits of stucco, plaster images, pieces of carved stone-work from one of the public buildings during the war, glass lamps and tumblers in great number, and forty other kitchen articles are used."[51] WPA fieldworkers in the Georgia sea islands also reported on this custom. In Sandfly, a community located about nine miles southeast of Savannah, workers observed "the practice of placing broken bits of pottery and possessions last used by the dead person on the grave for the purpose of supplying the needs of the spirit." An informant in Brownville, west of Savannah, explained that the things a person used last were placed on the grave "to satisfy the spirit and keep it from following you back to the house," and in Harris Neck, south of Savannah: "You put dishes and bottles and all the pretty pieces what they like on the grave. You always break these things before you put 'em down. You break [them] so that the chain will be broke. You see, the one person is dead and if you don't break the things, then the others in the family will die, too."[52] Since similar burial customs have been practiced in West Africa for hundreds of years, the appearance of the tradition in the United States is generally viewed by African-Americanist scholars as an African cultural survival. Melville J. Herskovits wrote that "whatever else has been lost of aboriginal custom, the attitudes towards the dead as manifested in meticulous rituals cast in the mold of West African patterns, have survived."[53] African-American graves in South Carolina were still being covered with bits of broken crockery, lamps, and toys as late as 1914 and still are today in the sea islands.[54]

This analysis of stoneware vessels produced in Edgefield by African-American potters reveals a process identified by anthropologists as "syncretism," whereby elements of two diverse cultures that are most similar are interwoven, creating a new entity or cultural hybrid. In this instance, African concepts of form and decoration combined with Western ceramic technology and materials (that is, stoneware and porcelain clay, glazes, throwing wheels, and kilns) to create a hybrid artifact that may be viewed as reflective of the African-American response to a hostile and alien environment. Nineteenth-century Edgefield face vessels are often labeled grotesque jugs, but for their black makers and the African-Americans who used them they may have served as ritualistic objects. Although such interpretations have been criticized as speculative and poorly documented, as John Vlach pointed out in his study of African-American art and craft, "if we fail to understand that there is a black history behind black artifacts, we risk missing the essence of Afro-American creativity."[55]

Studies of other early nineteenth-century industries in the South suggest that skilled slave potters may have achieved greater autonomy as a result of their increased value to the slave owner.[56] Skilled slaves were afforded greater freedom of movement among plantations and were allowed free time to cultivate a garden or to earn capital for their personal use. Associations between Edgefield stoneware factories were strengthened and maintained through the practice of hiring out or selling slaves, and the exchange of slaves between potteries formed a larger, interconnected community of slave potters.

African-Americans continued their involvement in Edgefield stoneware production during the second half of the nineteenth century, and at least one freed black, John Chandler, appears to have been among a group of migrant potters who carried the alkaline-glazed stoneware tradition from Edgefield to Texas.

Freed blacks worked at the Seigler, B. F. Landrum, Bodie, and Miles Mill potteries. Most likely, some of these men were former slaves who had been trained in stoneware manufacture during the antebellum period. Two black turners, David Drake and Mark Jones, appear in the 1870 Edgefield County census living near stoneware manufacturer John Miles. Thomas, Brewster, and Mark Jones also worked at the Seigler pottery. Some black potters may have taken the surnames of their former masters. For example, Scott and Moss Miles reportedly worked at the B. F. Landrum pottery, and Edgefield turners Philip and Oliver Miles were living in Shaw's Creek in 1870. A black man named Josh Miles appears in the 1880 Aiken County industrial census as the owner of a "Judge Factory" located on Shaw's Creek and employing six male and female laborers. This was probably a family owned and operated pottery run by members of the Miles family. It is the only documented black-owned stoneware factory in the Edgefield area.

Black potters were also active in the Jugtown area of South Carolina. In her book *The Carolina Mountains*, published in 1913, Margaret Morley wrote about an African-American potter named Rich Williams who was operating a shop located in the Tyger River area near Gowensville, South Carolina (in present-day Greenville County) (see Figure 3.17). Williams produced "jugs, wide-mouthed butter crocks, and pitchers" with a glaze

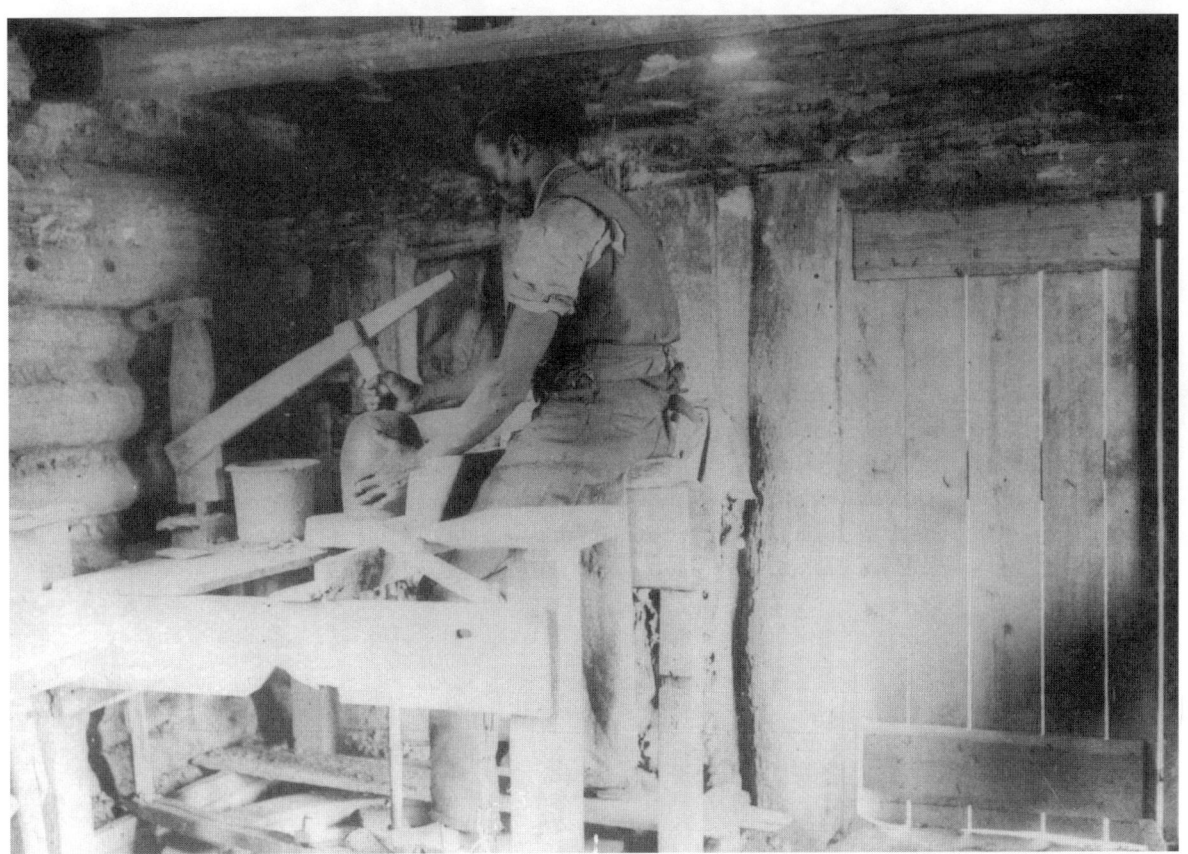

3.17 African-American potter Rich Williams at the wheel. Photograph by Margaret W. Morley, courtesy of the North Carolina Division of Archives and History, Raleigh, N.C.

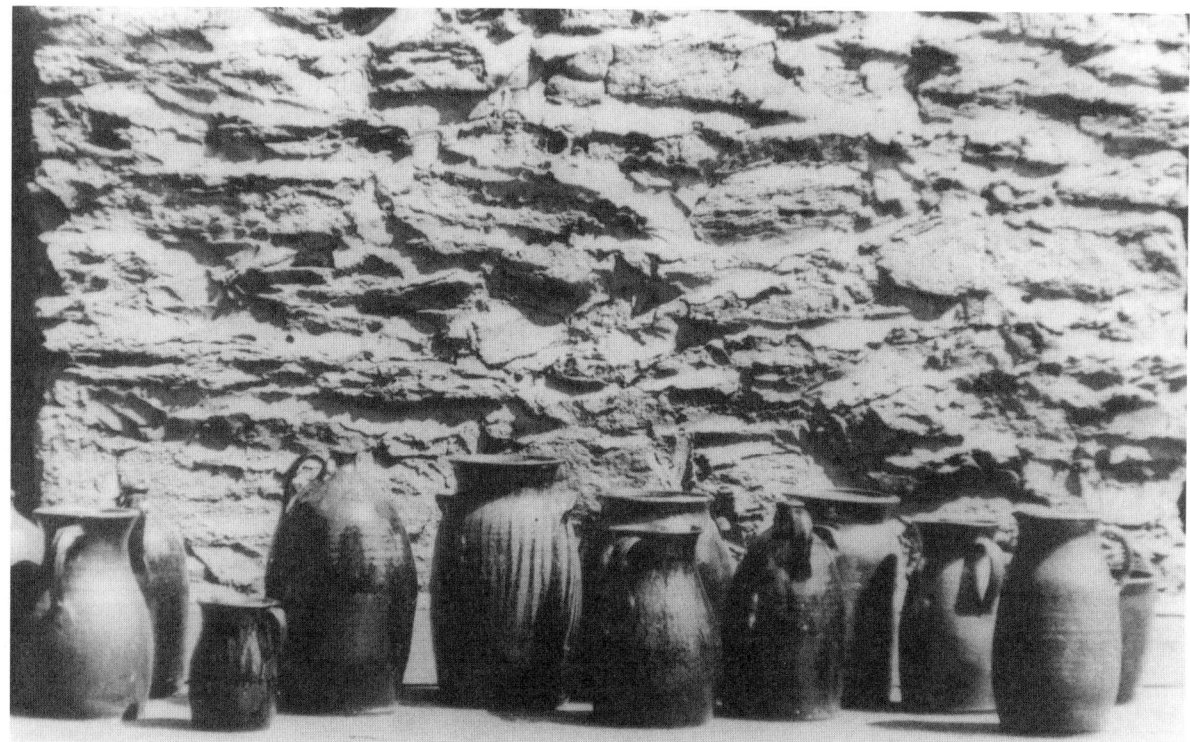

3.18   Alkaline-glazed stoneware vessels by Rich Williams. Photograph by Margaret W. Morley, courtesy of the North Carolina Division of Archives and History, Raleigh, N.C.

made from ash and clay (see Figure 3.18). Morley described Williams's kiln as "a long, low vault of bricks and clay, with a fire hole at one end and an opening at the other."[57] This kiln type was used by alkaline-glazed stoneware potters throughout the South.[58] Although no positive connection has been found between Rich Williams and Edgefield African-American potters, at least one other black man with the surname Williams appeared as a potter in late nineteenth-century Edgefield-area census records.

Clearly, African-Americans made lasting contributions to the southern stoneware tradition. Surviving ware produced in the Edgefield District and throughout the South attest to the skill, creativity, and individuality of African-American potters.

CHAPTER FOUR

Post–Civil War Stoneware Production in South Carolina

Four stoneware factories producing 129,000 gallons of ware and employing sixteen men and six women were operating in the Edgefield District in 1860. Two other potteries, the Southern Porcelain Manufacturing Company and Thomas Davies's Palmetto Fire Brick Works, were also in operation during the period (see Figure 4.1). During the following decade the stoneware industry experienced a sharp decline. A stoneware factory owned by Jesse P. Bodie and employing eight male laborers was the only pottery listed in the 1870 Edgefield industrial census. A second pottery, owned by John Miles, was in operation at Miles Mill (see Figure 4.2). A general pattern of migration out of the region during the period, the disruption of local businesses and industries by the Civil War, and subsequent changes in markets for locally produced goods were some of the factors that contributed to the decline in stoneware production in the Edgefield District during the late nineteenth century.

By 1860 most of the large-scale Edgefield stoneware factories had been closed. Thomas Chandler, one of the area's most prolific potters, moved to North Carolina in 1852. During the same period some of the most prominent Edgefield stoneware factory owners sold out and moved west. For example, Collin Rhodes sold his property on Shaw's Creek in 1853 and moved to Bienville Parish, Louisiana. Many of the potters who migrated westward out of Edgefield during the early part of the century were journeymen who did not have the resources to establish their own pottery shops in Edgefield. Their westward migrations generally preceded the migration of the factory owners and the subsequent decline of the stoneware tradition in the area. The movements of the Edgefield journeyman potters and stoneware factory owners followed a general pattern of heavy migration out of South Carolina from 1830 to 1860. This trend was a reflection of the stagnant economy. Planters and farmers were pushed out of the state by declining fertility and productivity of Carolina soils and pulled out by the cheap lands in Georgia, Alabama, and Mississippi.[1]

The Civil War added to the problems of an already ailing local stoneware industry in Edgefield. The most apparent threat to the community in the years immediately following the conflict was the continuation of violence. In February 1866 John Devereux, U.S. commissioner assigned to the Edgefield District, reported that Edgefield was one of the largest and most unruly districts in the state, and he pointed out that the small force stationed there was "entirely inadequate to exact the proper respect for the United States authorities." He went on to describe the situation in the district in greater detail.

There are two organized Bands of Outlaws, one consisting of eight (8) men and the other of thirteen (13) men, led by an ex-Confederate Major named Coleman, at present, raiding this District and committing with

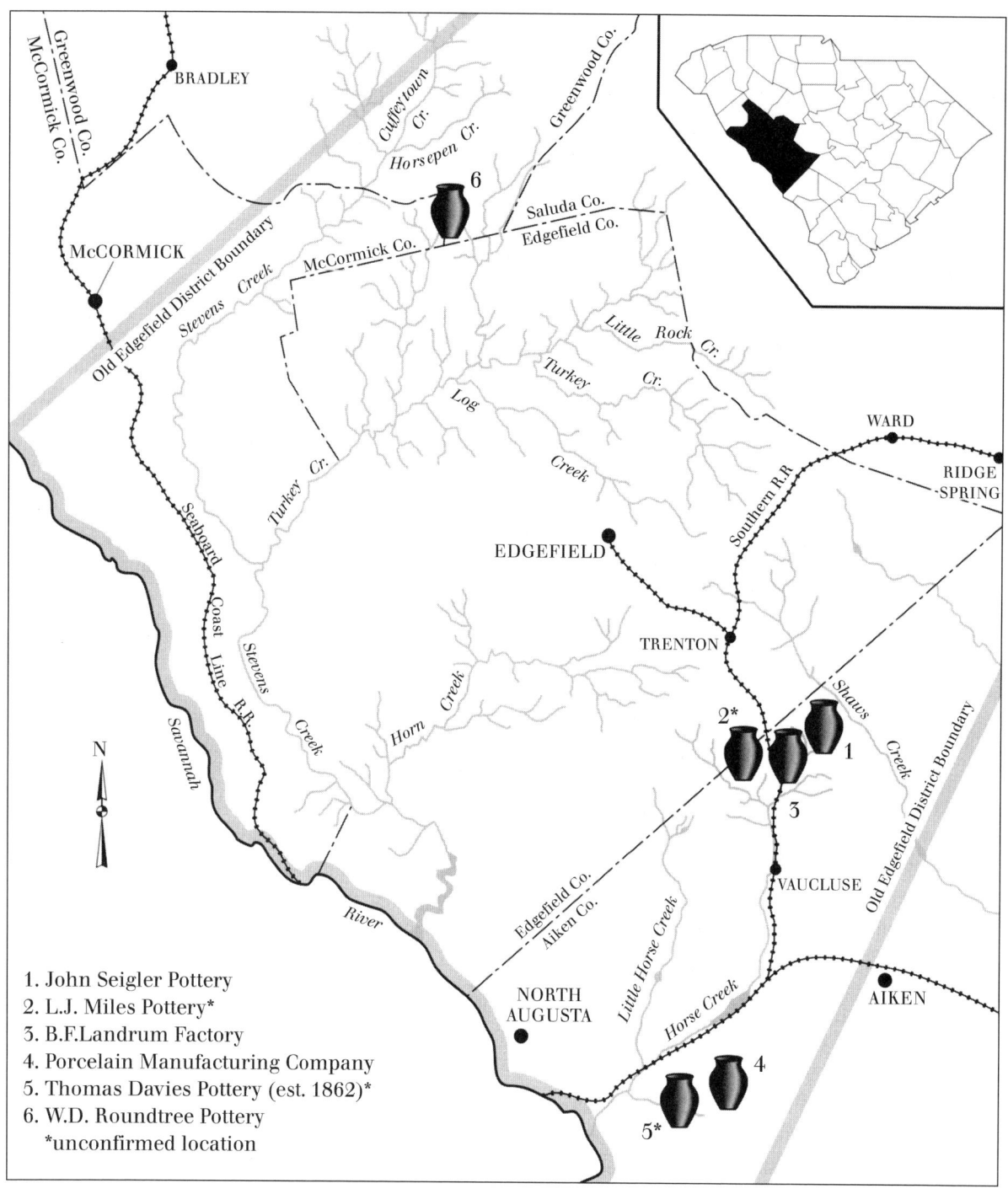

Greenwood Co.
McCormick Co.

BRADLEY

Cuffeytown Cr.

Greenwood Co.

Horsepen Cr.

6

Saluda Co.
Edgefield Co.

McCORMICK

Old Edgefield District Boundary

Stevens Creek

McCormick Co.

Little Rock Cr.

Turkey Cr.

WARD

Log Creek

RIDGE SPRING

Seaboard Coast Line R.R.

Turkey Cr.

Southern R.R

EDGEFIELD

Stevens Creek

TRENTON

Shaws Creek

Savannah

N

Horn Creek

2*

1

3

Old Edgefield District Boundary

River

Edgefield Co.
Aiken Co.

VAUCLUSE

Little Horse Creek

AIKEN

NORTH AUGUSTA

Horse Creek

4

5*

1. John Seigler Pottery
2. L.J. Miles Pottery*
3. B.F.Landrum Factory
4. Porcelain Manufacturing Company
5. Thomas Davies Pottery (est. 1862)*
6. W.D. Roundtree Pottery
   *unconfirmed location

4.1   Map of the present-day area encompassing the old Edgefield District
showing locations of pottery sites in operation by 1860.

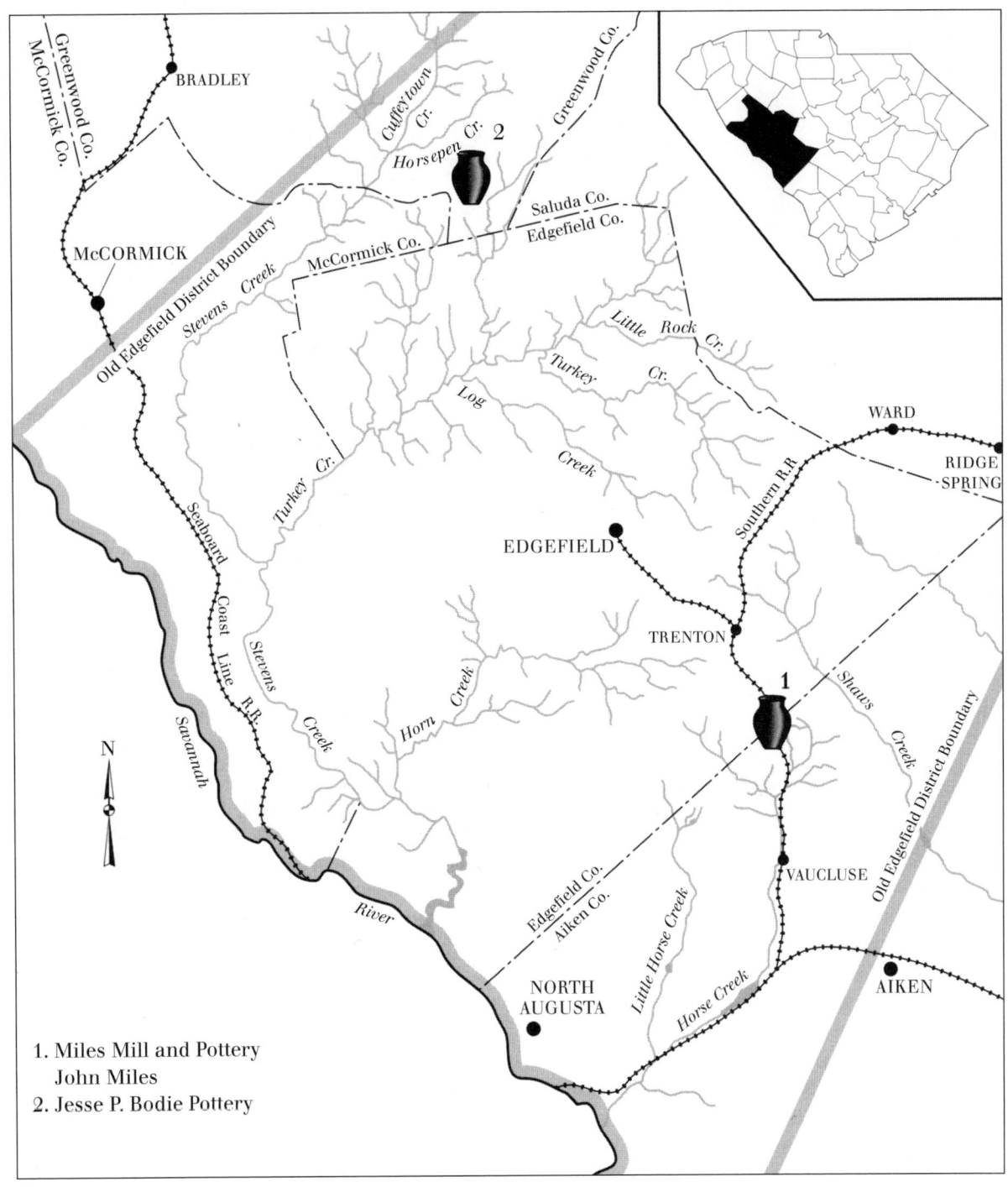

BRADLEY

Greenwood Co.
McCormick Co.

Cuffeytown Cr.

Greenwood Co.

Horsepen Cr. 2

Saluda Co.
Edgefield Co.

McCORMICK

Old Edgefield District Boundary

Stevens Creek

McCormick Co.

Little Rock Cr.

Turkey Cr.

Log

Creek

WARD

RIDGE
SPRING

Turkey Cr.

Seaboard Coast Line R.R.

Southern R.R

EDGEFIELD

TRENTON

Stevens Creek

Horn Creek

Shaws Creek

1

Savannah

N

Old Edgefield District Boundary

VAUCLUSE

Edgefield Co.
Aiken Co.

Little Horse Creek

River

Horse Creek

AIKEN

NORTH
AUGUSTA

1. Miles Mill and Pottery
   John Miles
2. Jesse P. Bodie Pottery

4.2 Map of the present-day area encompassing the old Edgefield District
showing locations of stoneware pottery sites in operation by 1870.

impunity the most fiendish outrages on Union men and negroes. They have murdered a number of negroes, and one white man, without provocation, robbed and driven from their homes several Northern men who have property here. Coleman the leader is a desperate character, he has exhibited, to several persons whom I saw, eight (8) ears cut from colored persons. He carries them in an envelope and shows them as trophies. This man is a native of Edgefield, but the rest of the gang consist of Texans and others from different locations. The property owners as far as I have conversed with them, say they regret these outrages very much and certainly when called upon have turned out to defend the property and lives of Northern———who were threatened, but it is my decided opinion that nothing will restore the supremacy of the laws and render the lives of Union men or Freedmen safe in this part of the country but the hunting down and extermination of these desperadoes by a respectable force of calvary, as they are mounted in the best manner, and belong to the class mis-called gentlemen (in the South) and no doubt are harbored and kept well posted by many of the inhabitants.[2]

Local businesses as well as individuals were apparently targeted for attack by these gangs. Commissioner Devereux also wrote that "Coleman's men, last week came into Hamburg and robbed the hotel keeper in broad daylight."[3]

The entrepreneurial nature of Edgefield stoneware manufacture proved to be particularly detrimental to the industry during the political, social, and economic upheavals that took place during and after the war. Census records indicate a sharp decline in wealth during this period. Forty-one wealthy individuals recorded in the 1860 and 1870 censuses experienced a decline in mean real estate valuation of 75 percent and in personal valuation of 97 percent. Much of this wealth consisted of slaves. Edgefield stoneware manufacturers who had relied heavily on slaves as a stable source of labor in the factories now faced serious reductions in the skilled labor force.

Free African-Americans gained political rights and power, and accompanying wealth and social prestige, following the war. The freedmen also sought family autonomy. They resisted the antebellum gang labor system that had been enacted on the large farms and plantations of the area, demanding instead their own land and family farms. The tenantry system, based on family labor, was the resulting compromise.[4]

Commissioner Devereux, in his February 1866 report on Edgefield, offered the following information regarding the status of freedmen immediately after the war.

As to the dispositions and conditions of the Freedmen of this district, I am able to report favorably as far as I can observe during the short time I have been here. The freed-people are generally at work under reasonably fair contracts, are giving satisfaction to their employers, and are contented themselves. Of course I speak in a general sense, and time, and closer inspection may indicate desirable changes. Many persons are working for their former masters and do not desire to be removed.[5]

Although many former Edgefield slaves apparently continued in their previous jobs, working for their former masters as freedmen after the war, employers were now required by law to enter into formal contracts with the freedmen and to provide fair wages for their labor. For example, a contract was approved in the subdistrict of Aiken in March 1868 between John Landrum (son of stoneware manufacturer Reverend John Landrum) and two families of freedmen. The first family included one full hand, or family head, and four fractional hands (women, children, or the elderly). One full hand and three fractional hands were enumerated in the second contract. The terms of the contracts entitled each family to one third of the crop.[6]

In a report dated 28 March 1866 the Edgefield commissioner observed that "many contracts, approved by the Military Commander before my arrival, do not allow sufficient compensation to the laborer, but in cases where the hands are well used, and the aged and helpless freed-people of the families of the hands are fed and provided for by the Planters, it certainly would not be advantageous to disturb the existing status."[7]

The commissioners described several other problems relating to the freedmen contracts. Freedmen were entitled to a specified portion of the crop that they grew, usually one-third. Once their duties relating to the cultivation of the crop were finished some freedmen took jobs unrelated to the crop in order to supplement the family income. The planters sought to obtain as much labor from the freedmen as possible, in the commissioner's words, "to bring them in their industrial relations as near to the condition of slavery as possible and exact from them unremunerative labor which was never contemplated by the freedmen when making the contract."[8] The planters punished the freedmen for hiring out to other planters by charging them with violating the terms of contract, by forcing them off the plantation, and by depriving them of their share of the crop. Other plantation owners enforced the same penalty for any slight offense or disregard of orders. In effect, Edgefield plantation owners manipulated the freedman contracts to their own advantage and to the detriment of the freedmen. These problems were further aggravated by the fact that civil suits involving more than thirty dollars had to be tried in the district Superior Court where there were often delays of several months before a case was tried. One commissioner reported that many freedmen were leaving the state for Mississippi, Louisiana, and Arkansas, where they could obtain better wages. This movement was encouraged, however, because the commissioners believed that "by providing a scarcity of laborers here, those [freedmen] who remain can obtain better wages, and can get employment with responsible persons."[9] These post–Civil War labor conflicts between planters and freedmen further hindered the recovery of local industries and businesses.

Edgefield, Aiken, and Greenwood Counties

A few antebellum Edgefield stoneware factories continued into the late nineteenth century, and a few new factories were established in the Edgefield area in the second half of the century. While the factory system suffered as a result of the Civil War, the post–Civil War Edgefield factories continued to be very large in comparison to most southern stoneware potteries.

As glass and metal containers became more widely available during the late nineteenth century, stoneware manufacturers were faced with a sharp decline in local demand for their products. In response to this situation many factory owners adopted industrial-style production methods, abandoning the earlier emphasis on individual craftsmanship for a more standardized product. Bulbous or ovoid storage jars and jugs became gradually more cylindrical in form. Cylindrical vessels could be placed closer together in the kiln during firing and in the wagon for transport. The wide variety of alkaline glazes produced in the area early in the century declined as potters began to use imported slip glazes. Slip glazes, consisting simply of clay mixed with water, were much more easily prepared and not caustic to use as were the alkaline glazes.

Benjamin Franklin Landrum Pottery

In the late nineteenth century several of the Edgefield stoneware factories in operation were located in or near Horse Creek valley. For example, John Landrum's son, Benjamin Franklin Landrum, was still operating his pottery on Horse Creek in 1860. Landrum appeared in the 1860 Edgefield census as a stoneware maker. He owned real estate worth thirty thousand dollars and had a personal estate valued at $17,095. According to the 1860 manufacturing census, the B. F. Landrum pottery was producing approxi-

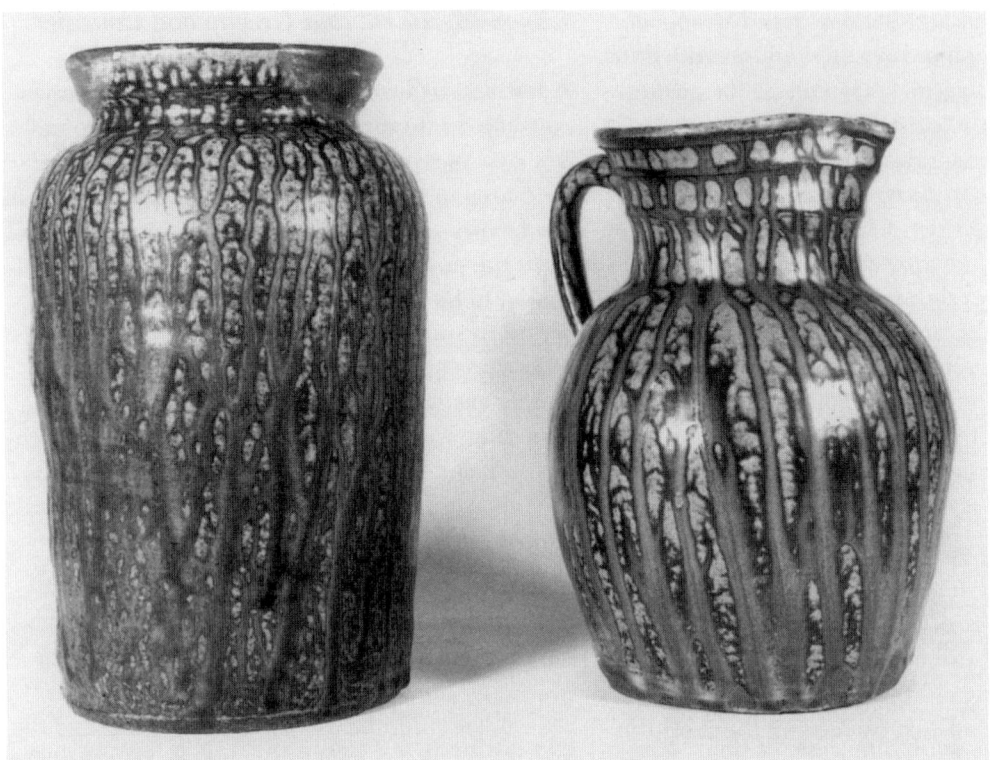

4.3   Alkaline-glazed stoneware preserve jar and pitcher, ca. 1860, attributed to the
Benjamin F. Landrum Pottery, Aiken County, S.C. Pitcher: H 9⅞″, C 22⅝″. Preserve jar:
H 11″, C 22¼″. Collection of the Charleston Museum, Charleston, S.C.

mately forty thousand gallons of stoneware annu-
ally, valued at four thousand dollars. Two males
and one female were employed there. Stoneware
fragments recovered from the B. F. Landrum pottery site are alkaline-glazed, and ware produced
at the site from about 1850 to 1860 retains the
early ovoid forms.

The Ben Landrum pottery, operated by B. F.
Landrum's son, who was also named Benjamin
Franklin Landrum, was listed in the 1880 Aiken
County manufacturing census.[10] Ware produced
at the Ben Landrum factory was valued at five
thousand dollars that year. The factory employed
eight men and three women and was in operation
nine months of the year. A thirty-two-horsepower

water turbine located on Horse Creek provided
power for the Ben Landrum pottery. A variety of
ware types were produced at the factory, including jugs, storage and preserve jars, pitchers, and
spittoons. Surviving ware attributed to the pottery
typically has dark, drippy or runny olive-brown
alkaline glazes (see Figure 4.3). A gradual evolution of form is apparent in B. F. Landrum factory
ware. Early ware from the factory, dating from
about 1850 to 1860, has rounded, gently tapering shoulders. Jugs have double-collared necks.
Late nineteenth-century Ben Landrum ware is
cylindrical in form. Jugs typically have tooled
shoulders with a stacker-type ledge and flared
mouths flattened at the lip.

Three freed blacks, Scott and Moss Miles and Jack Thurman, reportedly worked at the Ben Landrum factory (according to records associated with stoneware vessels collected by the Charleston Museum in the 1920s and 1930s). A black man, "M. [Milage] Williams," who is listed in the 1870 Edgefield census as a stoneware turner in Shaw's Creek Township living near B. F. Landrum, probably also turned ware at the Landrum factory. Two other blacks, Thomas Jones, occupation "in Jug Factory," and Philip Miles, "turner," were also living in Shaw's Creek Township in 1870, and most likely also worked at the factory.[11] Ben Landrum reportedly closed his pottery factory in 1902 because his old turners had died.

Lewis J. Miles Pottery

The Miles Mill factory was also located on Horse Creek. The Lewis Miles pottery produced an average of fifty thousand gallons of stoneware in 1860 valued at five thousand dollars. Miles's factory was a much larger operation than the B. F. Landrum pottery, having employed up to ten male and three female laborers. Also, a four-horsepower water-powered turbine was utilized at Miles's factory, while the B. F. Landrum pottery made use of only a one-horsepower turbine at that time.

Early ware produced at Miles's factory is bulbous or ovoid in form, gradually becoming more cylindrical late in the century. Jugs produced at the factory from about 1830 to 1860 are wide-shouldered with loop handles attached below a thick, double-collared neck, and at the upper shoulder. Olive-brown alkaline glazes were typically applied to ware produced at the Lewis Miles factory. Late nineteenth-century jugs attributed to Miles's factory are roughly pear-shaped with upper handle attachments placed at the neck rather than below.

Miles owned twenty slaves in 1860 and employed many of them in his stoneware factory. Turners at Miles's factory applied distinctive markings to much of the ware that they produced. Sets of incised diagonal lines or slashes and punctate marks, usually appearing in rows or clusters, were applied separately or in combination to ware produced at the factory. These marks, typically located at the upper shoulder of the pots just below the neck, apparently often served as capacity markings.

The slave potter Dave continued to produce stoneware for Lewis Miles until about 1863, and many signed and dated examples of Dave's later work have survived. These vessels exhibit quite a bit of variation in form and glaze type. For example, a churn produced by Dave dated 6 July 1857 is roughly cylindrical in form (Figure 4.4). The vessel also has an unusually dark brown-black alkaline glaze. A storage jar signed by Dave and dated 24 August 1854 bears an atypical thick, dark glassy glaze that appears to be an alkaline glaze containing a large amount of clay and silica. Most of Dave's early ware has thin, dark, mottled olive-brown glazes.

Former Edgefield turner George Fletcher told the following story about Lewis Miles in a 1930 interview:

[Lewis Miles] Died two years after the Civil War. [He was] Fine looking—looked like Gen. ["Stonewall"] Jackson—awful intelligent face, broad white forehead. Supposed to [have] made [the] best ware [in the] country. Darkies peddled it all over Georgia, South Carolina and North Carolina. Jugs for corn liquor and brandy . . . [were] Trade[d] for dried apples, peaches. [Miles's ware was] Sold [in] Augusta. [Miles had a] Reputation for giving to the poor—"if you give a dollar he'd give a hundred." About five years before the Civil War Mr. Miles saw trouble coming and didn't think paper [money] was going to be no count, so every month he had Dave mold a special small-mouthed (not 3 inch) jar [with a mouth measuring less than

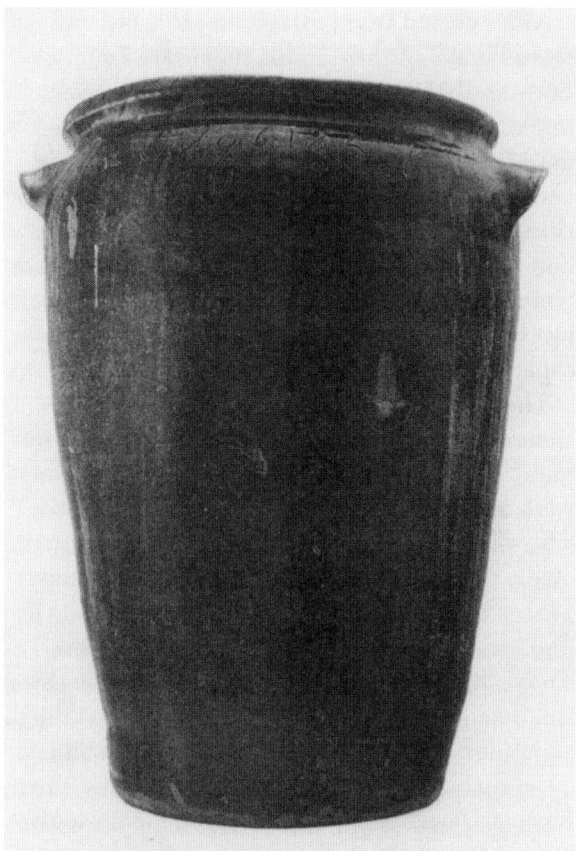

4.4   Alkaline-glazed stoneware storage jar,
1857, attributed to Dave (slave potter), Lewis Miles
Factory, Edgefield District, S.C. H 21⅝″, C 48¼″.
Incised script: Lm July 6 1857 (front, upper shoulder
between handles); for Mr. John Monday (opposite); w
(below handle). Collection of Dr. and Mrs. George V.
Rosenberg.

This colorful story suggests that following the
Civil War Edgefield stoneware factory owners
continued to rely upon African-Americans for the
day-to-day operation of the potteries.

Lewis Miles died in June 1868. Part of Miles's
estate was sold immediately in order to pay
outstanding debts, but his Miles Mill property
remained intact until 1879. Lewis Miles's son,
John, continued his father's pottery factory. The
operation, identified as "Miles Mill and Pottery,"
is shown north of the town of Vaucluse on a tributary of Horse Creek on Isaac Boles's 1871 map
of Edgefield County. Stoneware with an annual
value of $5,200 was produced at John Miles's

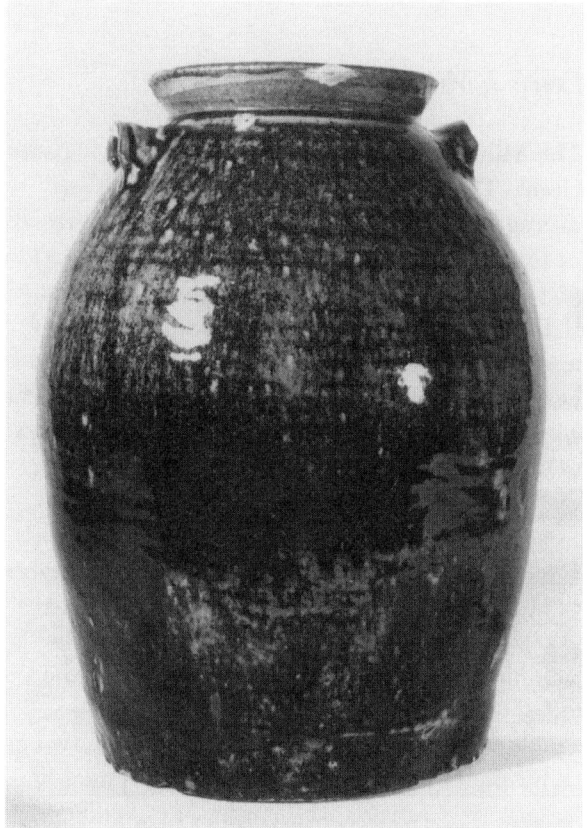

three inches in diameter] which he would fill with gold
and silver and bury. After his death his grandchildren
found several [of these jars]. "Old Man Landrum"
[Ben] found 2 [jars that held] several hundred dollars.
Other grandchildren from Denver came about a year
before Uncle Jack [Thurman] died (1907) and had
Uncle Jack Thurman (took his mother's name after he
was freed but was a Miles) open [Lewis Miles's] grave
to find money. Mr. Flesher saw bones—no money.
Uncle Jack said he could tell it was his old man by his
bald head.[12]

4.5   Alkaline-glazed stoneware storage jar, ca. 1880–
1900, Jack Thurman, Miles Mill, Aiken County,
S.C. H 16¼″, C 40⅛″. Collection of the Charleston
Museum, Charleston, S.C.

pottery in 1880. A thirty-five-horsepower water turbine provided power for the operation. Ten laborers working an average of two-thirds time were employed in the pottery year-round. Some of these laborers were former slaves who had turned ware at Lewis Miles's pottery.

A storage jar in the collection of the Charleston Museum attributed to Miles Mill was turned by freed black potter Jack Thurman (Figure 4.5). This ovoid jar has two opposing horizontally attached lug handles placed high on the upper shoulder, and a glassy, mottled, tan-brown to brown-black alkaline glaze. Thurman, who is listed in the 1880 Aiken County census in Shaw's Creek Township with the occupation "turning judges [jugs]," reportedly also worked at the Ben Landrum pottery.[13] Since pottery production was a seasonal activity, freed blacks may have frequently worked at more than one factory.

Seigler Pottery

John Seigler established a stoneware factory near the former site of the C. Rhodes Factory at Shaw's Creek in the Edgefield District. Rhodes placed the following notice in the *Edgefield Advertiser* in 1851, offering for sale his plantation and pottery.

2,200 Acres Pine Lands For Sale
Being desirous of making a change in my business I will sell at private sale my lands on Shaw's Creek, 13 miles from Edgefield, and 10 from Aiken. On the premises are an abundance of water power, well improved with dwellings and other houses, and also, my Pottery attached. There can now be a bargain had.
C. Rhodes[14]

In 1853 Seigler purchased Collin Rhodes's Shaw's Creek property, and Rhodes moved to Louisiana. Seigler did not actually run the factory himself but hired itinerant potters to operate it for him. Members of the Staubes family apparently managed the pottery for Seigler. John Staubes and Jacob Staubes of Germany, both listed as stoneware makers, were enumerated in the 1860 Edgefield census as living next door to John Seigler. John Staubes, age thirty-nine, and Jacob Staubes, age thirty, most likely were brothers. John's wife, Betsy Staubes, age forty-three, and their children, John J., age twelve, Luther, age nine, and Betsy Jr., age six, were also living in the household. The family had apparently moved to the area recently because everyone in the household was listed as having been born in Germany.[15]

Emma Ergles Williamson, daughter of David Ergles and granddaughter of Frederick Ergles, reported that her grandfather and three other Germans—Jacob Ergle[s], Jonathan Ergles, and Jacob Staubes—had settled in South Carolina in the early nineteenth century. According to Mrs. Williamson, "Jacob Staubes settled near Miles' Mill, above Vaucluse, and was a potter."[16]

In October 1930 E. B. Chamberlain visited the Seigler site and conducted an interview with Carey Dickson, a black man who had formerly worked at the Seigler factory, and with Paul Seigler, grandson of stoneware factory owner John Seigler. Dickson, variously known as Uncle Carey and Carey Posey, claimed that a German potter named Mr. Stobbs (var. Staubes) had worked for Seigler, thus verifying that members of the Staubes family worked at the Seigler site.[17]

Many of the freed blacks who turned at the Seigler factory were probably former slaves who had worked at Collin Rhodes's factory or at other stoneware factories in the area. Carey Dickson recalled that the last potters who worked at the factory were "Mark Jones (later a blind preacher), Brewster Jones, and Oliver Miles."[18] According to Paul Seigler, all of these men were black except Oliver Miles, whom he described as a mulatto whose father was reputed to be one of the Mileses. Thomas Jones, age eighteen, appears in the 1870 Edgefield census in Shaw's Creek Township with the occupation "in Jug Factory."

Jones and two other freed blacks, Alfred Landrum, wagoner, and Phillip Miles, turner, living in the same household, probably also worked at the Seigler factory. Mark Jones, age thirty-five, listed as a turner, was also living in Shaw's Creek Township in 1870. He was enumerated on the same page as stoneware manufacturer John Miles and therefore may have worked at the Seigler and/or Miles Mill pottery factories.[19]

According to Carey Dickson, the products of the Seigler factory were pitchers, jugs, jars, bricks, and pipes. Vessels produced at the factory during the first few years of operation are similar to other Edgefield stoneware produced just prior to the Civil War (see Figure 4.6). About thirty thousand gallons of ware valued at three thousand dollars were produced at the Seigler pottery in 1860, when the factory employed two men and one woman. John Seigler factory ware is stamped J.W.S. / PINE HOUSE, S.C.

John Seigler's son, George P. Seigler, apparently inherited the Shaw's Creek property and pottery in the late nineteenth century. Ware produced during the younger Seigler's ownership of the factory is stamped "G.P. Seigler / TRENTON / S.C.," reflecting a change in the name of the post office from Pine House to Trenton in 1870 (see Figure 4.7).[20] A general trend toward production of more industrial-type ware is evident in surviving vessels and vessel fragments from the Seigler factory. Most of the ware produced at the Seigler factory during the latter part of the century

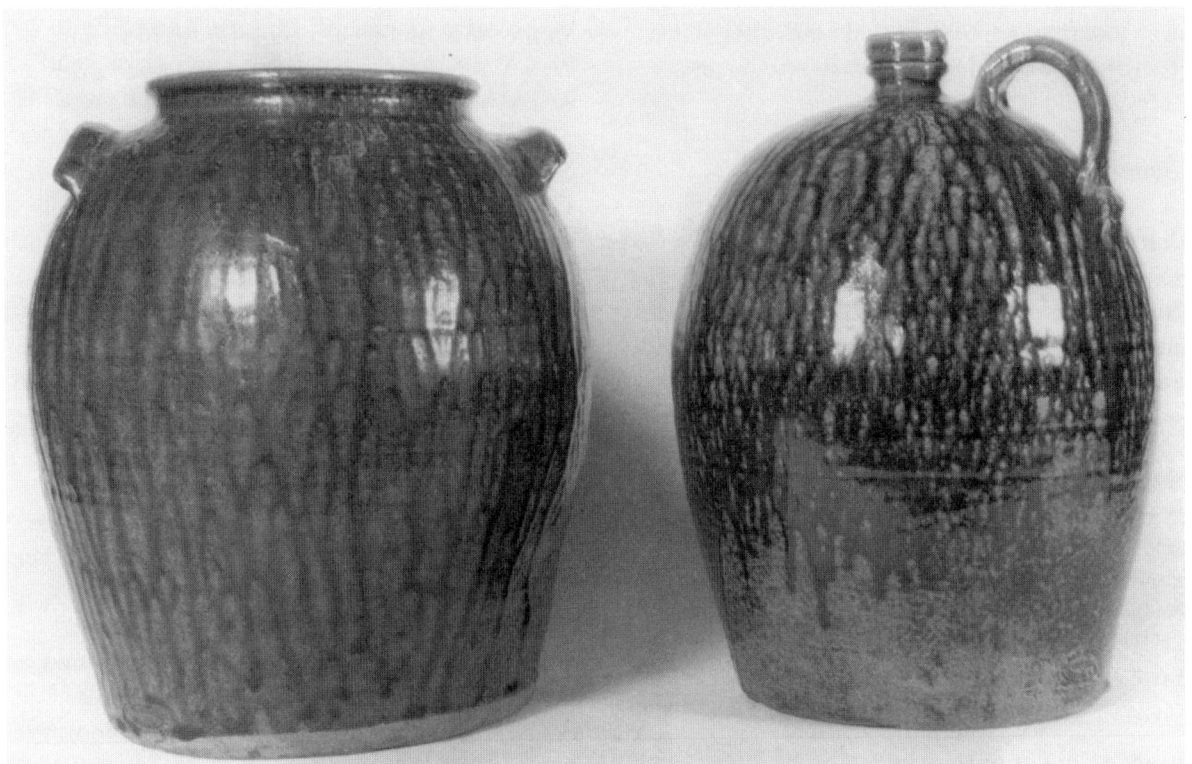

4.6   Alkaline-glazed stoneware storage jar and jug, ca. 1860, John W. Seigler Pottery, Shaw's Creek, Edgefield District, S.C. Storage jar: H 12¾", C 36⅜". Jug: H 15⅝", C 31⅝". Stamped: J. W. Seigler / Trenton, S.C. Collection of the Charleston Museum, Charleston, S.C.

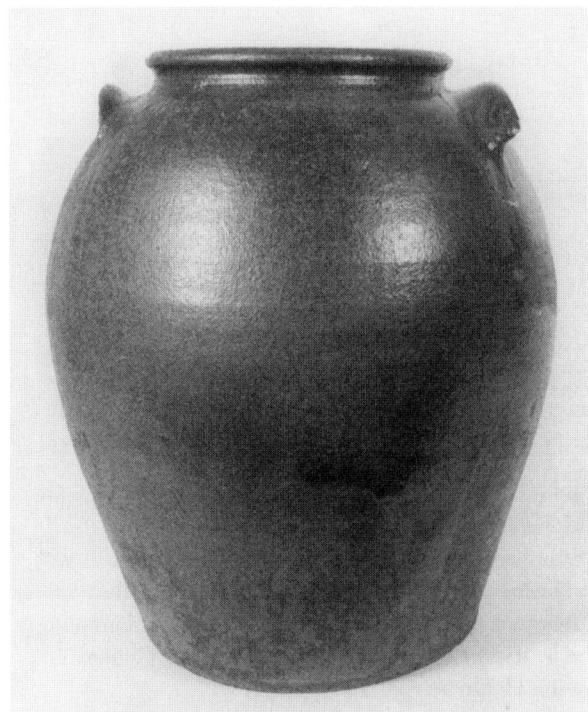

4.7 Alkaline-glazed stoneware storage jar, ca. 1880, George P. Seigler Pottery, Aiken County, S.C. H 14½″, C 39½″. Stamped: G. P. Seigler / TRENTON / S.C. Collection of Dr. and Mrs. Charles M. Webb.

are crudely turned jugs with thin, poorly developed glazes. Although the alkaline glaze was still predominant, a substantial amount of ware with Albany-slip glaze was produced at the site during the 1870s and 1880s. This transition in techniques of production was most likely a response to the greater availability of cheaper mass-produced goods during the late nineteenth century.

Hahn Potteries

Local residents claim that members of the Hahn family also worked at the Seigler factory. Alkaline-glazed stoneware pitchers, churns, and storage jars marked W. F. HAHN / TRENTON / SC have been identified in public and private collections,

but it is unclear whether these were produced at the Seigler pottery or at another site in the Trenton area (see Figures 4.8 and 4.9). No ware with the Hahn stamp has been recovered from the Seigler site.

Two men with the surname Hahn, William Hahn and P. L. Hahn, both listed as potters, were living in Shultz Township, Edgefield County, in 1900. Shultz Township was named for Henry Shultz, an eccentric German who was responsible for the emergence of Hamburg (present-day North Augusta) as a major trading and distribution center during the 1830s and 1840s.[21] P. L. Hahn was renting a home in Shultz Township in 1900, while William Hahn owned his home.

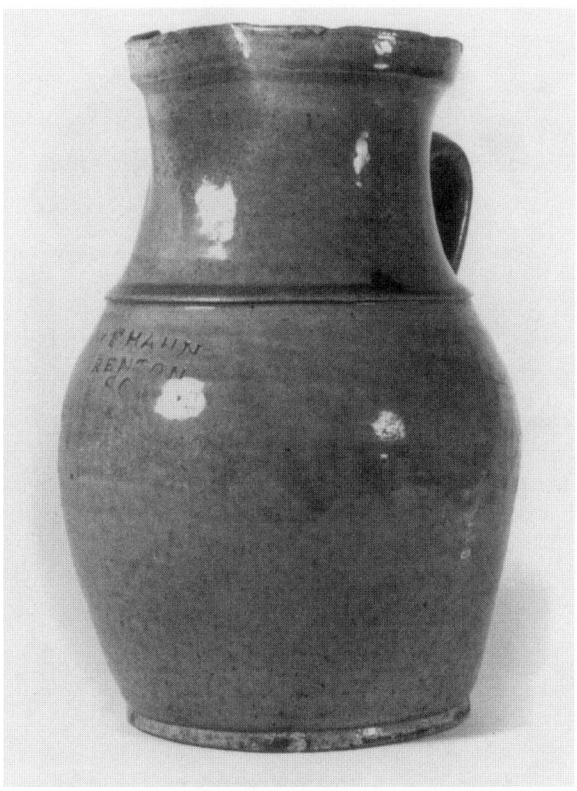

4.8 Alkaline-glazed stoneware pitcher, ca. 1880, W. F. Hahn Pottery, Aiken County, S.C. H 10⅝″, C 24″. Stamped: W. F. HAHN / TRENTON / SC. Collection of the Charleston Museum, Charleston, S.C.

William Hahn appears to have been the owner of a pottery in North Augusta. William's daughter, Elizabeth Hahn, and a black servant, Albert McKenon, were laborers in the pottery. A German potter, George Fletch, who was living near the Hahns, and a black man named Wash Kinard also worked at the Hahn pottery. Albany-slip-glazed fruit jars stamped HAHN POTTERY WKS. / AUGUSTA, GA are attributed to the North Augusta pottery operated by the Hahns (see Figure 4.10).[22]

William Hahn, then, evidently operated two potteries—one in the Trenton area, where he produced alkaline-glazed stoneware, and a later shop in North Augusta producing mainly Albany-slip-glazed ware. Variations in vessel form as well

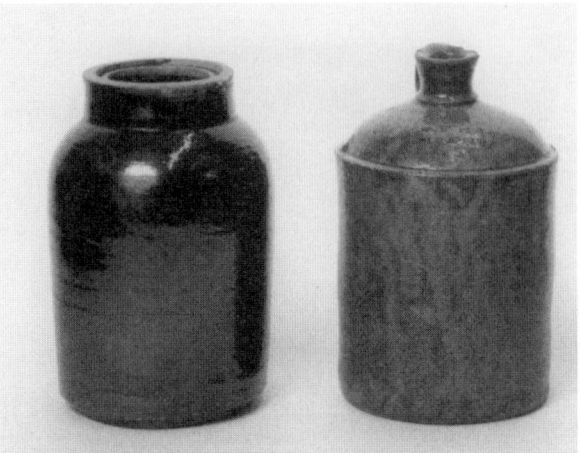

4.10   *Left*: Albany-slip-glazed preserve jar, ca. 1900, Hahn Pottery, North Augusta, S.C. H 8½″, C 18¾″. Stamped: HAHN POTTERY WORKS / AUGUSTA, GA. *Right*: alkaline-glazed stoneware jug, ca. 1890, Hahn Pottery, Trenton, Aiken County, S.C. H 7″, C 59″. Stamped: W. F. HAHN / TRENTON / S.C. Collection of George-anna H. Greer.

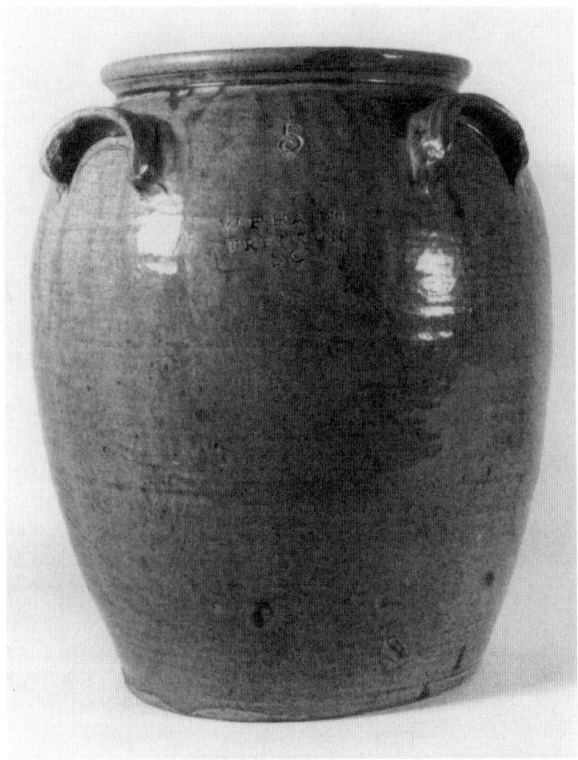

4.9   Alkaline-glazed stoneware storage jar with four lug handles, ca. 1880, W. F. Hahn Pottery, Aiken County, S.C. H 14⅞″, C 40⅜″. Stamped: W F HAHN / TRENTON / SC. Collection of Terry and Steve Ferrell.

as glazes indicate that the Trenton-area pottery was in operation earlier than the North Augusta pottery. The Trenton ware is slightly ovoid with gently rounded shoulders and has glassy alkaline glazes. This ware dates to around 1870 to 1880. The Albany-slip-glazed fruit jars of the North Augusta pottery were produced during the early twentieth century.

Roundtree-Bodie Pottery

In 1860 W. D. Roundtree owned a pottery valued at one thousand dollars that employed two male workers. The Roundtree pottery was located on the Martintown Road near Kirksey's Crossroads in northern Edgefield District (present-day Greenwood County). The site had first been established as a pottery by a man named Turner in about 1840. In April 1919 P. M. Rea interviewed Mrs. James Turner, whose husband was a descendant of Edgefield potter James Turner. Rea recorded the following information about the Turner pottery for the Charleston Museum: "James Turner (earlier generation) had a pottery near the Parker Place above Edgefield. He married a Miss Roundtrees and moved to Florida. He died about 1870. Mrs. James Turner has a molasses jug made at this pottery. She has had the jug since her marriage in 1866."[23] A check of Edgefield marriage records revealed no marriage between James Turner and a Roundtrees. However, an *Edgefield Advertiser* announcement of the marriage of Edward Turner, formerly of the Edgefield District, and Mrs. Adeline Sasser of Providence, Florida, on 11 March 1858 in Columbia County, Florida, seems to validate at least part of Mrs. Turner's story. Also, the marriage of Thomas Turner to Harriet G. Miles (sister-in-law of stoneware factory owner Lewis Miles) in 1860 may be a further indication of the involvement of the Turner family in pottery production.[24]

Mrs. Turner donated the abovementioned jug (Figure 4.11) to the Charleston Museum. The jug has a glassy, mottled olive-brown to tan-brown alkaline glaze with straw-colored patches. It is cylindrical in form with a rounded shoulder and tapers slightly inward toward the base. Other features include a flared rim and tooled rings at the shoulder.

Annual production at the Roundtree factory in 1860 totaled approximately nine thousand gallons of stoneware. By 1870 the J. P. Bodie pottery was in operation at the site. About twenty-five thousand gallons of ware valued at $2,500 were produced at the Bodie pottery in 1870. Property associated with the operation included one clay temperer and two drying pans.[25]

The Bodie pottery was in operation year-round, employing an average of eight male laborers. At least three of these workmen were white. Anglo potters William Durham, age forty-four, Isum Whatley, age forty-two, and William Horn, age

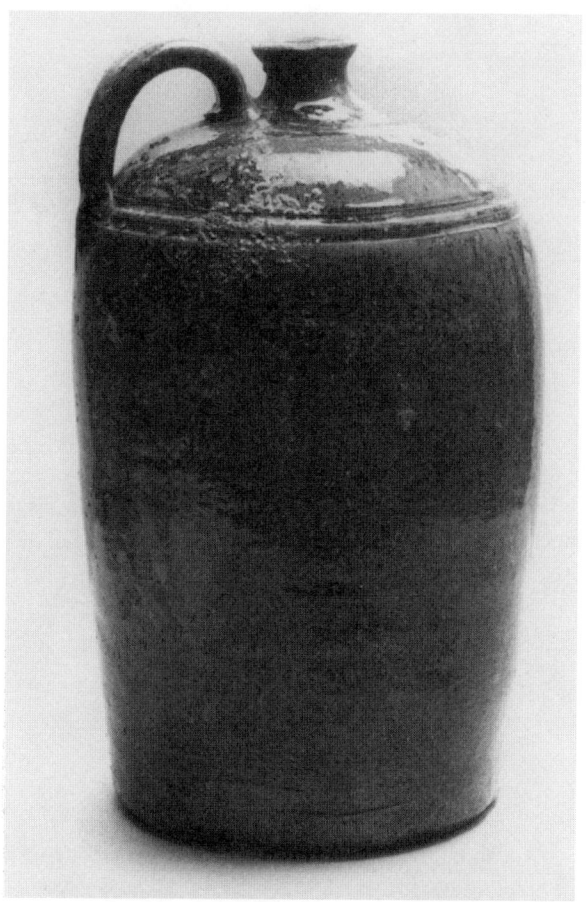

4.11   Alkaline-glazed stoneware jug, ca. 1866, attributed to James Turner, James Turner Pottery, Kirksey's Crossroads, Edgefield District, S.C. H 15½", C 30¼". Collection of the Charleston Museum, Charleston, S.C.

twenty-two, were enumerated in the 1870 census at "Kirksey's X Roads" post office with the occupation "work in potry." Durham and Whatley were listed as heads of their households, while William Horn was living in the household of his father, James Horn. Jonathan Devore, age forty-three, listed as a farmer, was living next door to the Horns in 1870.[26] In a 1920 interview Jonathan Devore's son, William J. Devore, claimed that his father had turned at the Roundtree and Bodie

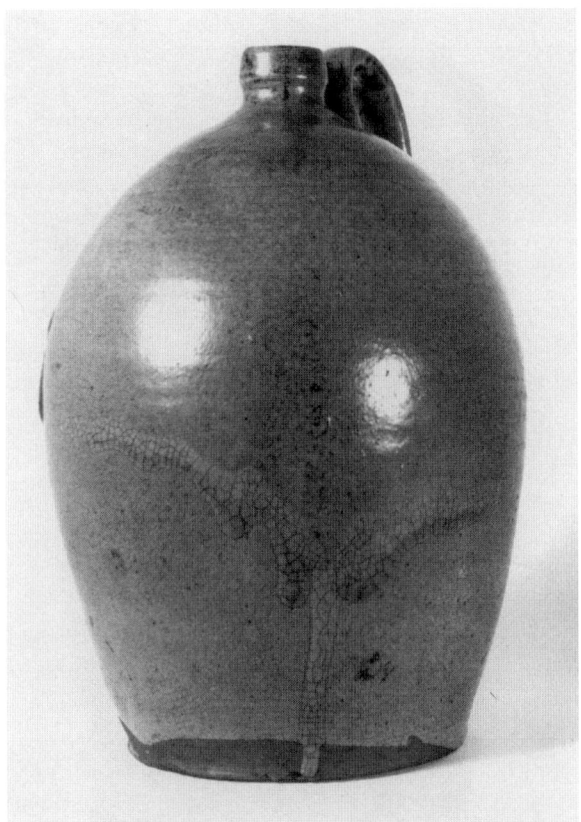

4.12   Alkaline-glazed stoneware jug, 1872, Jesse P.
Bodie Pottery, Kirksey's Crossroads, Edgefield County,
S.C. H 13″, C 28¼″. Incised script: 1872 / 2; stamped:
J. P. Bodie / Maker. Collection of Terry and Steve
Ferrell.

pottery from right after the Civil War up until
very near the time of its abandonment. A jug
signed in incised script "2 gallon / Made by /
Horne & Devore / Kirksey's X Roads / Edgefield
County / July 30th 1874" seems to substantiate
this claim (Figure 4.13). The jug is ovoid in form
with a rough, olive-brown alkaline glaze and
a single loop handle attached below the neck.
Another indication of John Devore's long association with the pottery is his appearance in the
1860 Edgefield census next to Roundtree with the
occupation "overseer."[27]

Freed blacks Lee Rodgers, age sixty-two, and

Shep Davis, age twenty-one, were also employed
at the Bodie pottery in 1870. Rodgers was listed as
the head of his household, while Davis was living
in the household of black farm laborer Andrew
Harrison. Virginia-born Lee Rodgers was the
only laborer at the pottery who was not a native of
South Carolina.[28]

Well-formed ovoid jugs, churns, and storage
jars and unusual forms such as flasks and figural bottles were produced at the Bodie factory.
Much of this ware is stamped J.P. BODIE / MAKER.
Bodie jars typically have two opposing horizontal

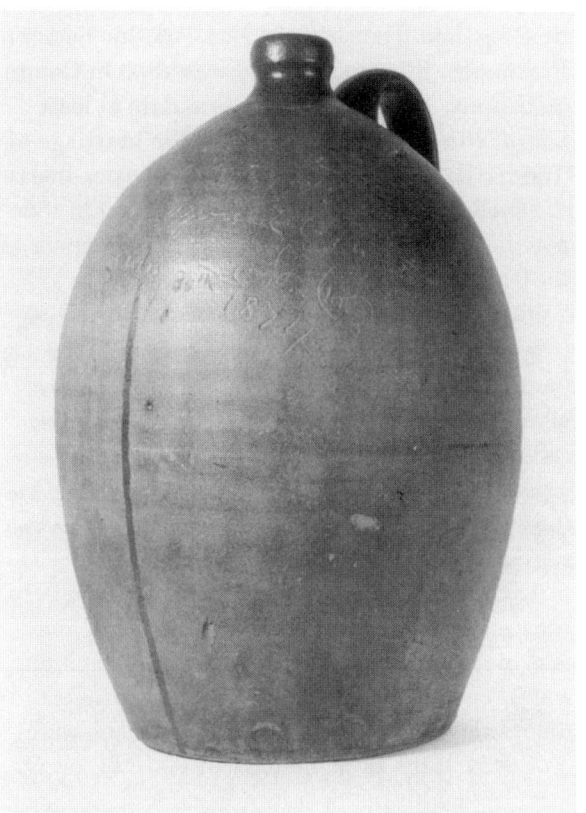

4.13   Alkaline-glazed stoneware jug with raised bands
and slip decoration, 1874, attributed to William Horne
and Semps Devore, Jessie P. Bodie Pottery, Kirksey's
Crossroads, Edgefield County, S.C. H 14⅜″, C 30¼″.
Incised script: 2 gallon / Made by / Horne & Devore /
Kirksey's X Roads / Edgefield County / July 30th 1874.
Collection of Tony and Marie Shank.

slab handles, and a collared neck with a flared rim to receive a tie-down cloth cover. Jugs produced at the factory have collared rims and strap handles attached at or below the neck. Drippy olive to olive-brown glazes and thick, glassy olive or tan-brown glazes characterize Bodie ware.

The Jesse P. Bodie factory was in operation until about 1880. Unlike many of the late nineteenth-century Edgefield-area factories, the Bodie pottery did not convert to the production of industrial-type ware. The ovoid forms and well-developed glazes identified with this Kirksey's Crossroads–area pottery remained relatively stable throughout the production period.

South Carolina Pottery

In September 1879 Lewis Miles's daughter, Sallie M. Cahill, filed a petition in the Aiken County Court of Pleas against her brother, John Miles, requesting a court order for the sale of the Miles Mill property. Proceeds from the sale were to be divided between Lewis Miles's daughters Sallie Cahill, Ella Wilcox, and America Wever, and his son-in-law, John Cahill. Lewis Miles's son, Milton Miles, had deeded his interest in the Miles Mill property to John Cahill in June 1879. Milton's brother, John Miles, evidently had deeded his share to Cahill as well because, according to the court order, Cahill was to receive John and Milton Miles's one-fifth shares of the proceeds from the sale of the property. The Miles Mill property was described in the 1879 order of sale as "all that tract or parcel of land containing one thousand eighty acres more or less—two hundred and fifty acres of which is situate in the County of Edgefield—and the remainder there of . . . being in the County of Aiken and bounded by lands of Satcher—Elbert L. Ryan—J. A. Brant—F. W. Norris—Mrs. Charles Gray—John Huit—B. F. Landrum and Henry T. Wright"[29] The property also included:

a certain clay bed in Edgefield County known as the "Presscott clay bed" containing one acre more or less: also . . . a certain clay bed situate lying and being in Edgefield County containing one acre more or less known as the "White tract" . . . a certain clay bed known as the "Frazier Sand bed" containing one acre more or less situate in the County of Edgefield on Beaver Dam Creek, . . . a certain Clay bed in Edgefield County known as the black Pond Clay bed, containing two acres more or less: . . . a certain clay bed in Edgefield County containing six acres more or less, and known as the "Allen Clay bed."[30]

It is evident from this description of the Miles Mill property that access to good clay was critical to the operation of the pottery factories at the site. Potters in the area identified locations where various types of clays were available in abundance and obtained legal rights to mine clay at these sites from their respective owners. Clays from different areas with desirable properties were often combined by the potter to produce quality stoneware clay. Provisions for access to specific clay beds were sometimes included in contracts in which pottery factories were transferred from one owner to another.

John Cahill transferred the Miles Mill property to James L. Jervey in an undated Aiken County deed probated in 1885. That same year the opening of a new pottery factory at Miles Mill was announced in the *Aiken Journal and Review*.

A factory for the manufacture of chinaware and porcelain from kaolin found in the vicinity has been erected at Miles's Mill, on the Charlotte, Columbia and Augusta Railroad, in Edgefield County, at a cost of $10,000. Messrs. Craig of New York, Jervey of Charleston and Cahill of Edgefield are the owners. Mr. Craig is fully informed in all the details of the business, having spent ten years in China. Water power will be used, furnished by Horse Creek.[31]

An 1887 sales slip from the factory, known as the South Carolina Pottery Company, bears a letterhead listing the full range of ware produced there (Figure 4.14). "A. Craig," a Scottish indus-

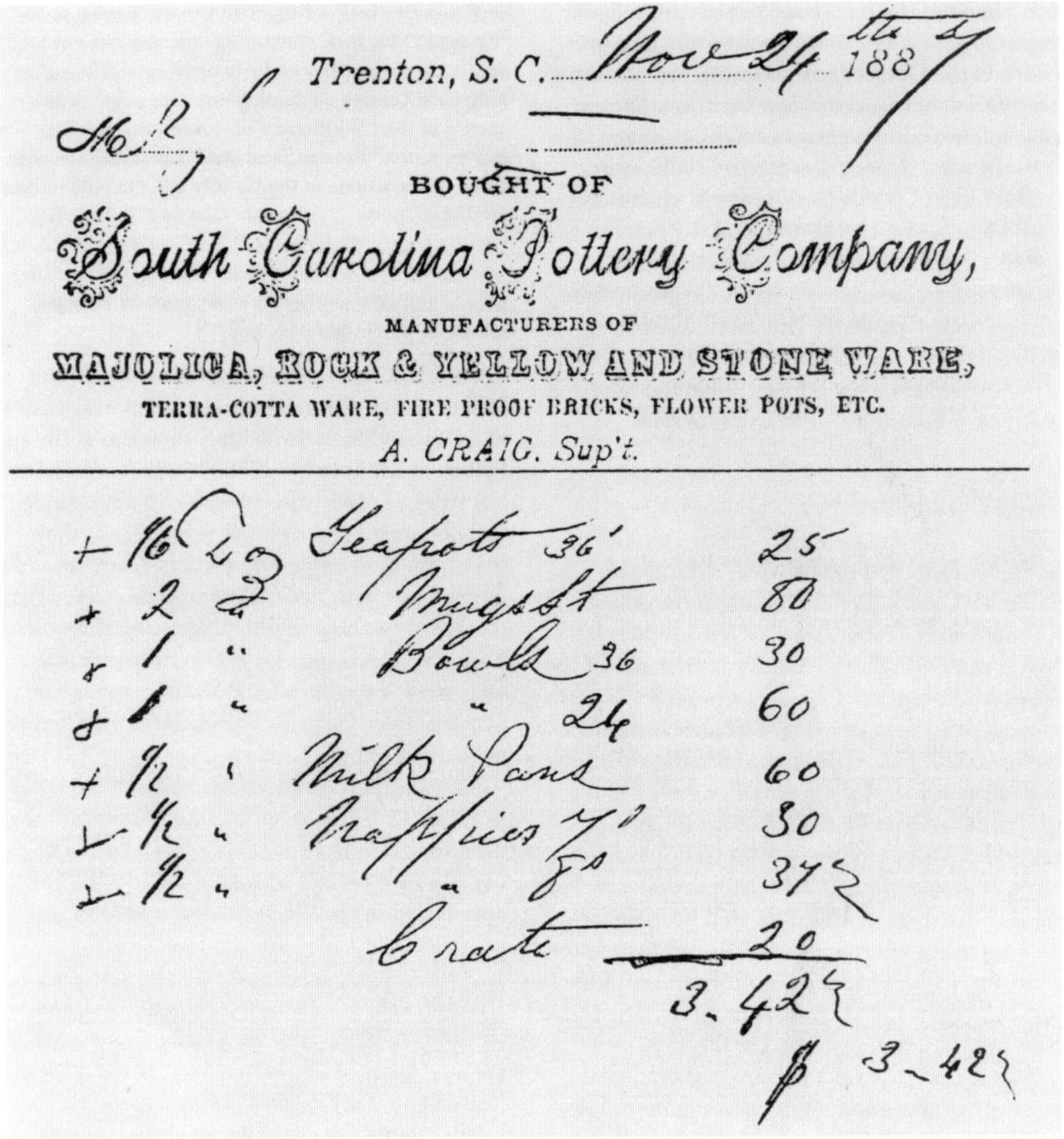

Trenton, S. C. _____ Nov 24th & 188_

M^r _____

BOUGHT OF

South Carolina Pottery Company,

MANUFACTURERS OF

MAJOLICA, ROCK & YELLOW AND STONE WARE,

TERRA-COTTA WARE, FIRE PROOF BRICKS, FLOWER POTS, ETC.

A. CRAIG. Sup't.

+	16	½ oz	Teapots 36'		25
+	2	½	Mugs ½t		80
+	1	"	Bowls 36		30
+	1	"	" 24		60
+	½	"	Milk Pans		60
✓	½	"	Nappies 7°		30
✓	½	"	" 8°		37½
			Crate		20
				3.42½
				$ 3.42½

4.14   South Carolina Pottery Company receipt. Courtesy of Harvey Teal.

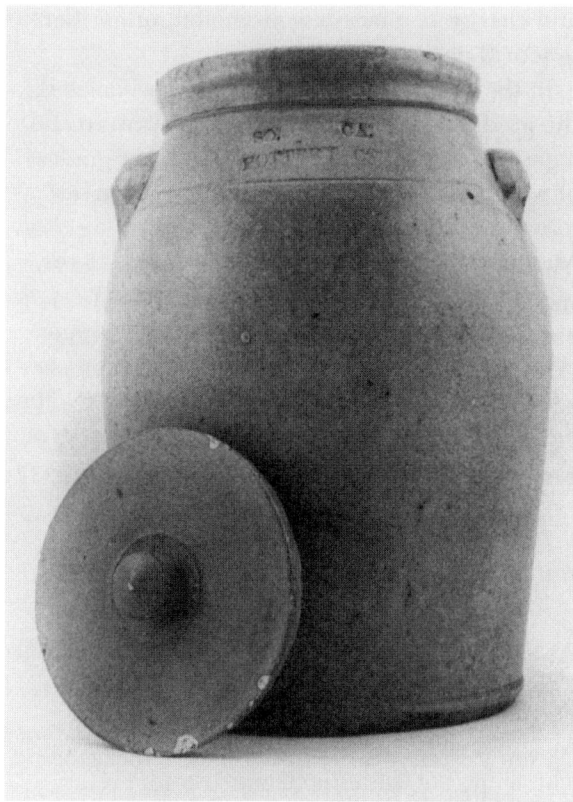

4.15 Slip-glazed stoneware churn, ca. 1887, South Carolina Pottery Company, Miles Mill, Edgefield-Aiken County, S.C. H 12″, C 28″. Stamped: SO. CA. POTTERY CO. (with a pair of parallel vertical lines after SO. and CA.). Collection of Dr. and Mrs. George V. Rosenberg.

trial potter who also worked in Atlanta, was listed as superintendent of the operation.[32] The South Carolina Pottery Company faced major setbacks during its first few years of operation. According to an April 1887 newspaper notice the company had "recently lost about one hundred cords of wood by forest fires."[33] Of even greater concern was a break in the mill dam, "caused by muskrats burrowing through, owing to the extreme dry weather and scarcity of rain."[34]

A wide range of earthenware and stoneware, including majolica, Rockingham-type ware, yellow ware, stoneware, terra-cotta ware, fireproof bricks, and flowerpots, was produced at the South Carolina Pottery Company (see Figure 4.15). Edgefield stoneware researchers Stephen and Terry Ferrell have recovered a molded bisque earthenware fragment from the site of the pottery. The sherd is a portion of a vessel body with a raised anchor and chain motif. Several Rockingham-type pitchers with identical motifs have been found locally, and some of these may be attributed to the South Carolina Pottery Company. A similar Rockingham-type pitcher, in the collection of Stephen and Terry Ferrell, bears the impressed stamp "S P Co" at the base. This vessel is tentatively attributed to the Southern Porcelain Manufacturing Company. The similarity between this pitcher and the anchor and chain pitcher fragment found at Miles Mill suggests a possible connection between the Southern Porcelain Manufacturing Company and the South Carolina Pottery Company. This connection becomes more apparent upon closer examination of the history of the Southern Porcelain Manufacturing Company and the Thomas J. Davies pottery.

Southern Porcelain Manufacturing Company

The Southern Porcelain Manufacturing Company, also known as the Kaolin factory, was located between present-day Aiken, South Carolina, and Augusta, Georgia. Edwin Atlee Barber provided a brief history of the Southern Porcelain Manufacturing Company in his book *The Pottery and Porcelain of the United States*, first published in 1893.[35]

William H. Farrar, a stockholder in the United States Pottery Company of Bennington, Vermont, established the pottery factory at Kaolin (present-day Bath), South Carolina, with the backing of a number of wealthy Augusta planters. The South Carolina legislature passed an act incorporating the Southern Porcelain Manufacturing Company on 20 December 1856. Initial investors in the company were George M. Newton, William W. Davies, Thomas Barrett, James Hope, William W. Harrison, Robert H. Gardiner, William H. Farrar, Holman, Curtis and Company, and Charles J. Jenkins.[36]

Farrar was attracted to the Bath area by the extensive kaolin deposits located there. He brought skilled laborers from Vermont to build the factory and procured potters trained in fine earthenware and porcelain production from Bennington and other factories in the North. Farrar insisted on using local clays exclusively in the production of the Kaolin factory ware, and since all the materials necessary for the production of fine porcelain were not available locally, the business was never a commercial success. Consequently, management of the factory constantly changed hands.

An unidentified English potter managed the Kaolin factory during the first year. His experiments with the local clays were unsuccessful, and most of the ware was destroyed in firing. During the second year of operation Josiah Jones, formerly a modeler for Charles Cartlidge at Greenpoint, New York, assumed management of the factory. Jones directed the first successful production of porcelain and creamware at the Kaolin factory.

In 1857 Decius W. Clark of Bennington took charge of the operation, and in February of the following year Clark's son, L. W. Clark of the New England Pottery Company, assumed the management of the pottery, thereby relieving his father. Clark sold his interests in the factory in late 1858 and returned north. Soon thereafter Christopher Webber Fenton of Bennington arrived in Kaolin to take over the management of the factory. Fenton brought with him his nephew, Jacob Fenton. Although one ceramics historian described C. W. Fenton as a "practical potter of extraordinary skill, well-nigh a genius at his trade," John Spargo, who interviewed one of the old potters who had worked with Fenton, concluded that Fenton's place in the history of American pottery "exists because of his ability

and energy as a business promoter, rather than a practical potter."[37]

In the next few years the factory specialized in the production of tableware and toilet ware and a general line of earthenware. The finer grades of ware were discontinued in 1860. At the beginning of the Civil War, the Southern Porcelain Manufacturing Company was converted to the manufacture of porcelain telegraph insulators and earthenware pipes for the Confederate government. Production ended abruptly in 1863 or 1864 when the factory was destroyed by fire. The factory resumed operation by 1866 but never fully recovered and went out of business in about 1877.

Thomas Davies Pottery

At least one Edgefield-area pottery, the Thomas Davies factory, had direct ties to the Southern Porcelain Manufacturing Company. In 1862 Anson Peeler, a carpenter and skilled mechanic who helped to build the United States Pottery at Bennington, Vermont, and the Kaolin factory at Bath, persuaded Thomas J. Davies, a local cotton planter, to establish a firebrick factory near Bath on the South Carolina Railroad. Peeler was placed in charge of the operation, and Davies provided the necessary capital and slave laborers. Large quantities of firebricks, as well as crucibles and tiles for gas-works, were produced at the factory. In 1863 the firebrick operation was converted into a pottery factory in an effort to fill the demand for tableware for the Confederate armies. Slave potters at the Davies factory turned alkaline-glazed stoneware jars, pitchers, cups, and saucers, as well as sculptural vessels, on old-fashioned kick-wheels and fired them in "large horizontal [groundhog] kilns."[38] Davies's pottery and firebrick factory was closed at the end of the war in 1865, and Davies then turned his business interests to kaolin mining.

The most distinctive ware produced at the Davies pottery was face vessels (see Figure 4.16).

These vessels were turned on the wheel and fashioned into faces by applying clay and then modeling it into desired features. Although sculpted vessels have been attributed to other Edgefield potteries, face vessels like the ones made at Bath have been directly attributed to only one other Edgefield-area pottery site—Miles Mill. The possible connection between the Southern Porcelain Manufacturing Company and the face vessels produced at the Davies pottery was discussed in Chapter 3. Both the production of modeled earthenware vessels at the Miles Mill site and the attribution to the site of alkaline-glazed stoneware face vessels point to a possible connection with the potteries at Bath. The production of modeled earthenware at Miles Mill represented a distinct departure from the local stoneware tradition. Similarities between this ware and ware attributed to the Southern Porcelain Manufacturing

Company may indicate that some of the potters who had formerly been employed at the Southern Porcelain Manufacturing Company remained in the Edgefield area after the demise of the factory and that some of these men were later employed at Miles Mill. Equipment such as molds, possibly salvaged from the Southern Porcelain Manufacturing Company factory, could also have found its way to Miles Mill.

Although stoneware was still produced at Miles Mill during the late nineteenth century, a general tendency toward more industrialized production is evident. For example, a stoneware storage jar attributed to the South Carolina Pottery Company represents a break from the alkaline-glazed stoneware tradition. The jar, stamped SO. CA. POTTERY CO, has an indented, banded rim, two horseshoe-shaped horizontal slab handles, a knob-handled lid, and a smooth tan-beige slip glaze. The use of slip glaze and the more standardized form and features of the piece distinguish it from earlier ware produced in the Edgefield area.

J. L. Jervey sold 26⅖ acres of the Miles Mill property to adjoining landowner E. L. Ryan in about 1910. About a year later Jervey sold the remaining 1,080 acres of the property to the Johnston Realty Company with the stipulation that the company would make payments totaling $900 to him by 2 January 1912 and $4,700 by 1 January 1913. A few months later the realty company mortgaged the property back to Jervey for $11,400. In January 1912 the company again mortgaged the property, this time to E. H. Beckham.

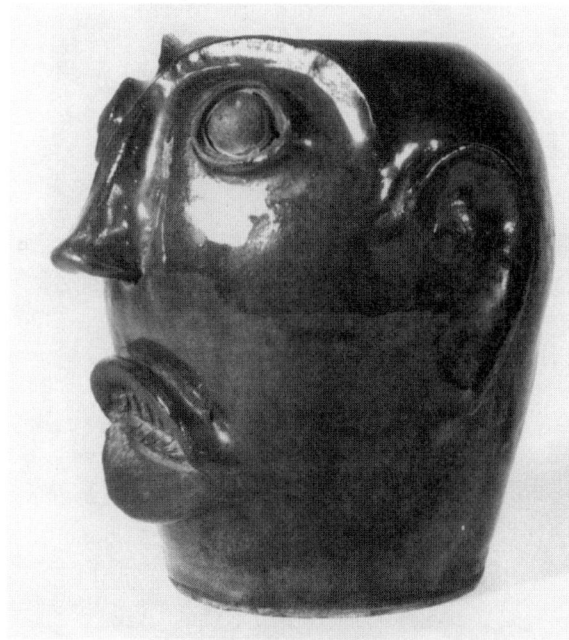

4.16 Alkaline-glazed stoneware lidded jar with applied clay features, ca. 1862, attributed to the Thomas Davies Pottery, Bath, Edgefield District, S.C. H 7⅞″, C 22¾″. Collection of the Augusta-Richmond County Museum, Augusta, Ga.

L. D. ("Duke") Harley Pottery

By 1900 Duke Harley was operating a pottery at Miles Mill. Harley was listed in the 1900 Aiken County census with the occupation "pottery and farmer," and a note reads, "rents farm Shaw township." The L. D. ("Duke") Harley pottery at Miles Mill and a pottery operated by "Dougherty

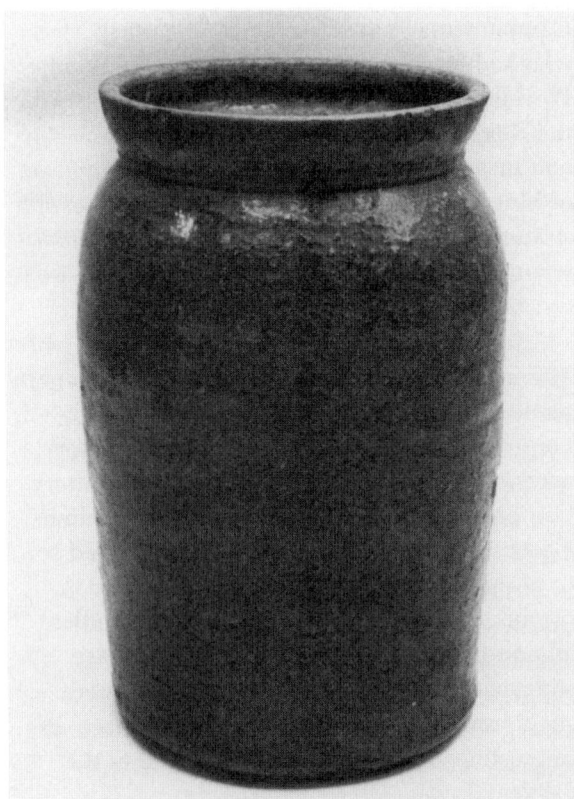

4.17   Alkaline-glazed stoneware preserve jar, ca. 1900, Miles Mill, Trenton, Edgefield-Aiken County, S.C. H 9¾″, C 20⅝″. Incised script: Made by / L. D. Harley / At Miles Mill / Post Office Trenton / S.C. Collection of the Charleston Museum, Charleston, S.C.

[var. Daugherty] and Baynham," with a post office address in Trenton, are listed in the 1908 *Handbook of South Carolina*.[39] Harley and Mrs. Mottie H. May purchased the Miles Mill tract from S. M. Smith on 3 April 1914.

The only positively identified example of the ware produced at the Harley factory is a preserve jar incised in script "Made by / L. D. Harley / At Miles Mill / Post Office Trenton / SC." The jar is cylindrical in form with a flared, collared neck and has a dark brown mottled glaze with brown-black streaks. According to notes made on the jar when it was acquired by the Charleston Museum, the glaze consists of a mixture of ash and Albany-slip glazes.

Twin brothers George and John Bennett turned ware at the Harley pottery. George Bennett and his father-in-law, C. E. Brumbeloe, are listed in the 1900 Aiken County census in Shaw Township just after L. D. Harley. Harley gave as his occupation, "pottery furnace & farm," and Bennett described himself as a "jug turner & farmer." Both men were renting farms.[40]

Camelius Brumbeloe was the son of Emanuel J. Brumbeloe of Georgia. C. E. Brumbeloe and his brother William learned the pottery craft through their association with the Bishop family of Jugtown (Upson/Pike counties), Georgia. The Bishops were one of Jugtown's earliest pottery families.[41] C. E. Brumbeloe's sons, Walter, Oscar, and

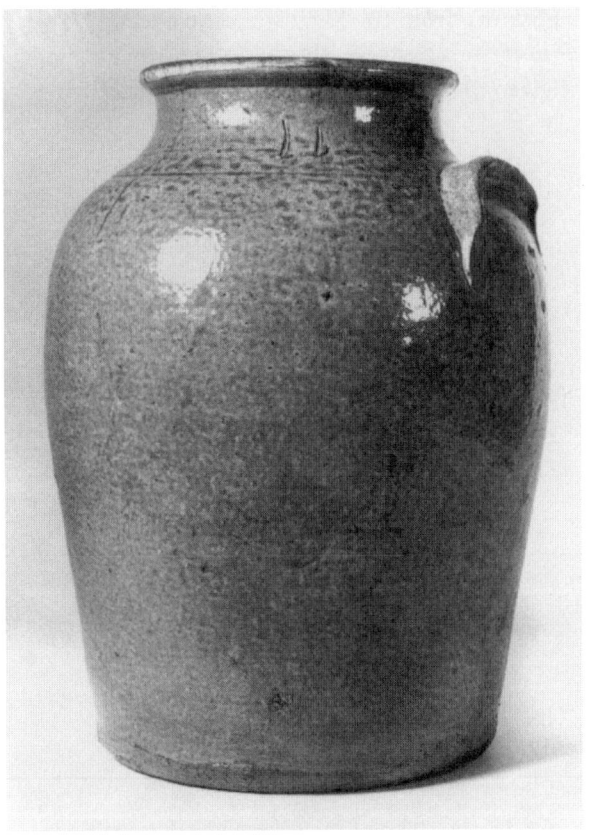

4.18   Alkaline-glazed stoneware storage jar, ca. 1900, attributed to G. U. Fletcher, Miles Mill, Edgefield-Aiken County, S.C. H 11⅞″, C 28⅜″. Collection of the Charleston Museum, Charleston, S.C.

Newt Brumbeloe, moved to Chalker in Washington County, Georgia, about 1910 where they established a pottery shop. The Brumbeloe Pottery, in operation until the late 1920s, was the last pottery in Washington County. The Brumbeloes produced Albany-slip-glazed ware in the Jugtown tradition at Chalker, hiring potters Edward L. Stork of Columbia, South Carolina, grandson of Abner Landrum, and Claude Bennett, whose father George and uncle John also helped at the shop.[42]

A vessel in the Charleston Museum collection attributed to Miles Mill may have been made by one of the Bennetts. The mottled, yellow- or orange-tan-glazed churn has a rolled, flared mouth, two opposing, horizontally attached lug handles and two horizontal tooled rings at the upper shoulder. According to John Burrison, Edward Stork produced ware glazed with Michigan slip, which sometimes fired to a burnt-orange color. The Bennetts, who were associated with Stork at Chalker, may have used a similar type of glaze.

There was evidently a lot of interaction between potters in Georgia and South Carolina during the late nineteenth and early twentieth centuries. Fred Bishop, another member of the Bishop clan, quit school at the age of eleven to go "on the road" with his father, Jugtown potter Curtis Bishop. Bishop worked for others after closing his own shop. Fred Bishop recalled accompanying his father on "stints in South Carolina with J. D. ("Jug") Johnson at Lanford (Laurens County) and the Baynhams at North Augusta."[43]

Baynham Potteries

J. G. Baynham had a well-established pottery in Aiken County by 1893. He wrote a letter to Governor Tillman on 21 March of that year in which he promised to send a sample of his jugs for the newly established South Carolina Dis-

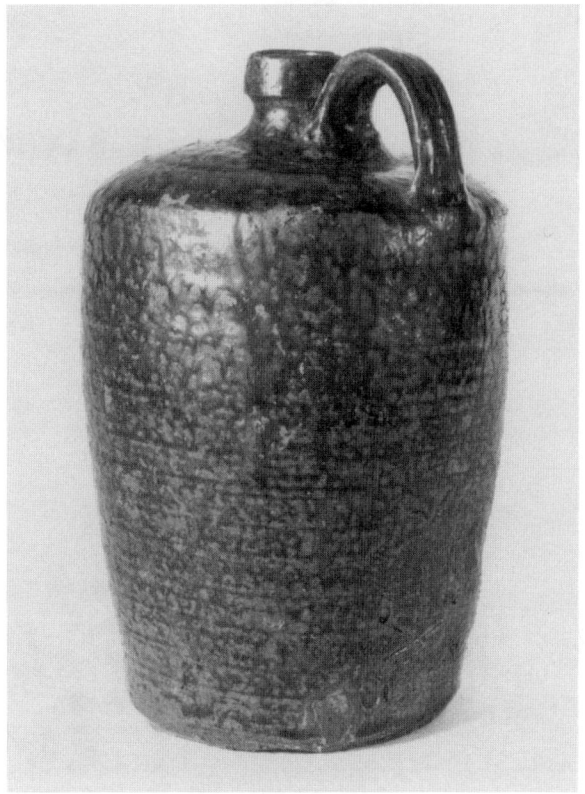

4.19 Alkaline-glazed stoneware jug, ca. 1893, attributed to the J. G. Baynham Pottery, Trenton, S.C. H 9¼″, C 18¾″. Stamped: s c DISPEN. This jug, bearing the emblem of the South Carolina Dispensary, is probably one of the 4,164 jugs produced at the J. G. Baynham Pottery for the South Carolina Dispensary. Collection of Charles Comolli.

pensary. The law providing for the creation of the South Carolina dispensary system was passed on 24 December 1892, and the system was scheduled to go into effect on 1 July 1893. Within this six-month period the state set up wholesale and retail outlets for the distribution of liquor throughout South Carolina. On 27 March Baynham sent a second letter in response to Tillman's inquiry about prices in which he stated "Carload lots 8 ct. for al. f.o.b. [freight on board]. I have special rates to Columbia. can ship 5000 gal. for $15.00." A bill of sale submitted to Tillman by J. G. Baynham on 28 June 1893 confirms Baynham's re-

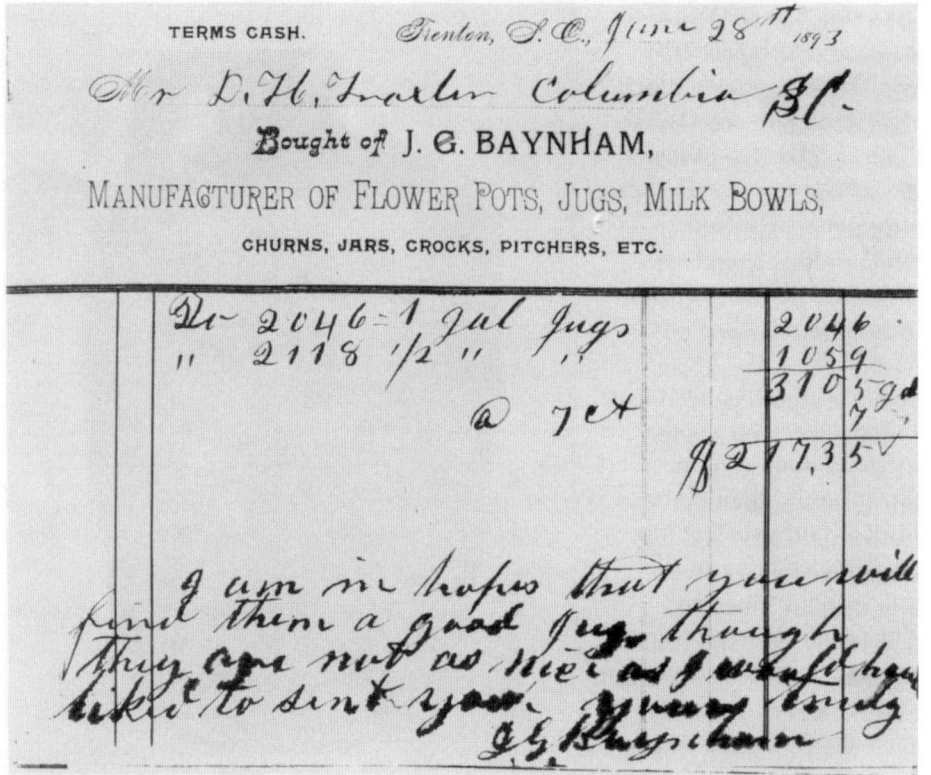

4.20 Bill of sale dated 28 June 1893 for an order of stoneware jugs produced at the J. G. Baynham Pottery for the South Carolina Dispensary. Baynham added a handwritten note at the bottom of the receipt: "I am in hopes that you will find them a good jug though they are not as nice as I would have liked to sent you." This may have been the only order of alkaline-glazed stoneware jugs commissioned for the dispensary.

ceipt of the order. According to the sales receipt, Baynham provided 2,046 one-gallon jugs and 2,118 half-gallon jugs at a total cost of $217.35 (Figures 4.19 and 4.20).[44]

A number of alkaline-glazed stoneware jugs with the South Carolina Dispensary emblem have been identified. Some, if not all of these, were undoubtedly produced at the J. G. Baynham factory. No additional documentation has been uncovered to indicate that other Edgefield area potters supplied jugs for the state dispensary system. The order filled by Baynham in 1893, then, may have been the only instance of locally made stoneware vessels having been used for the state dispensaries.

A pottery shop owned by "Dougherty and Baynham" listed in the 1908 *Handbook of South Carolina* has already been mentioned. This shop was evidently operated by Edward ("Guy") Daugherty and J. G. Baynham. Daugherty was originally from Denton, Texas. His father established a pottery shop there in about 1900 where he and his brother trained as turners. The market for pottery was not very good in Texas during the early 1900s, so the Daughertys hit the road, traveling to potteries all over the South and hiring on as turners. Daugherty later owned and operated a pottery in Kershaw County.

Horace and Mark Baynham turned ware at the shop of their father, Joseph G. Baynham, located on property adjoining the Miles Mill tract. Joseph Baynham's property and pottery were located just north of Miles Mill on a tributary of Horse Creek. A native of Virginia, J. G. Baynham appeared in the 1900 Aiken County census. According to family history, Baynham moved to

South Carolina from Kentucky. He does not appear to have been a potter, so it seems likely that his sons learned the craft from other potters in the Edgefield area. Horace Baynham, age eighteen, was also listed in the Baynham household in 1900. His elder brother Mark did not appear in the census that year, probably because he had not yet returned from serving in the Spanish-American War.

When Mark Baynham returned to South Carolina in the early 1900s he took over the operation of his father's pottery and grist mill. Conflicts between Mark Baynham and his father prompted Mark to leave the Miles Mill area and resettle in North Augusta. In 1924 Mark Baynham established his own pottery shop, the South Carolina

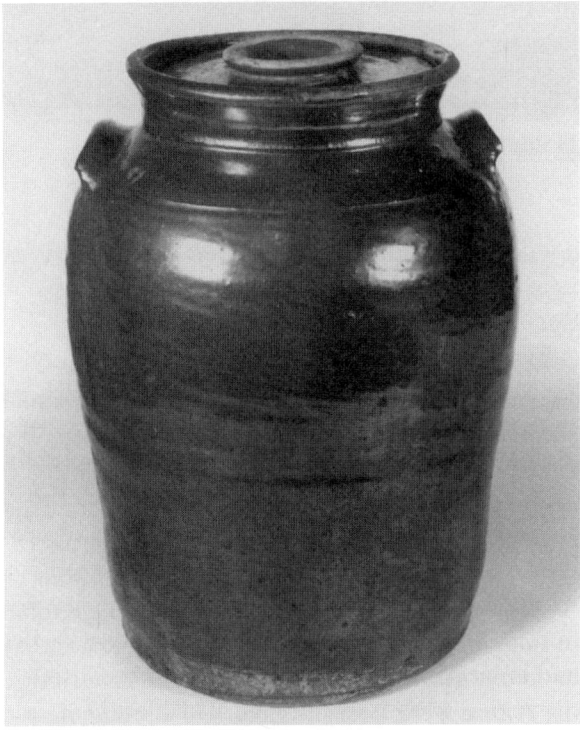

4.21 Stoneware jar, Albany-slip-glazed exterior, alkaline-glazed interior, ca. 1900–1920, attributed to Horace H. Baynham, Baynham Station, Edgefield County, S.C. H 12½″, C 30⅛″. Collection of Mrs. Frances Baynham Moseley.

Pottery, on the Savannah River in North Augusta. During the same period Mark's brother Horace established a second pottery shop on the old Baynham property, located west of Miles Mill at Baynham Station on the South Carolina Railroad.[45]

Mark's son, Hugh Baynham, claims that his father purchased pottery equipment (presses used to make flowerpots) for his North Augusta shop from a man who had operated an earlier pottery at the site. Hugh recalls that this equipment had been shipped from Great Britain. Hugh does not remember the name of the potter from whom his father bought the pottery equipment, but an English potter named H. R. Lawton, listed in the 1870 Edgefield census in Hamburg Township, most likely had obtained the equipment. A twenty-five-year-old black man, Marshal Bradley, with the occupation "works in pottery," also living in Hamburg Township that year, apparently worked at Lawton's pottery.[46] It is also possible that Mark Baynham purchased the pottery equipment for his shop from William Hahn, who established a pottery shop in North Augusta in about 1900.

The Baynhams produced alkaline-glazed stoneware in the Miles Mill area in the late nineteenth and early twentieth centuries. Mark Baynham used the alkaline glaze in North Augusta, but Horace used Albany slip almost exclusively at his shop at Miles Mill (see Figure 4.21). Mark Baynham founded a second pottery shop in North Augusta when the first was destroyed by a flood. Mark Baynham's sons, Clifton, J.A., Elmo, Hugh, Mark Junior, and Roy, worked at the South Carolina Pottery in North Augusta.

Hugh Baynham recalls that his father was quite an entrepreneur. He described how Mark Baynham made money during the Depression.

He'd stop off in North Georgia, in South Georgia [on his way back from selling a load of ware], and there would be eight or ten old poor cows out there in the

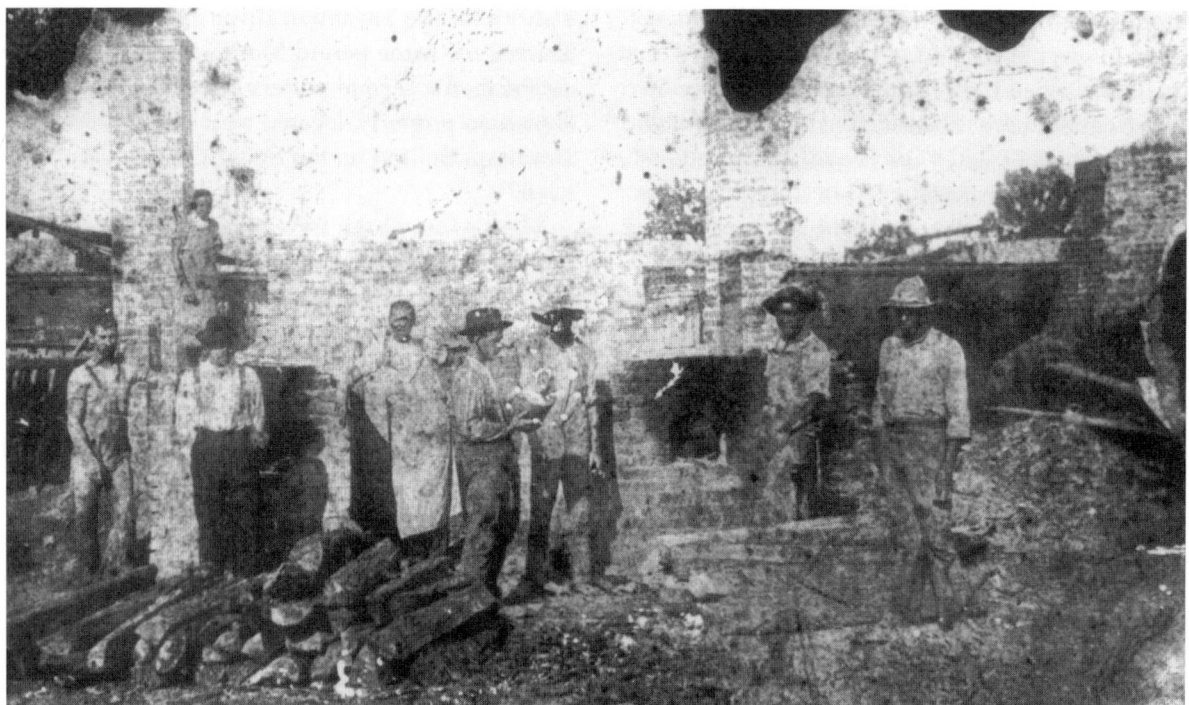

4.22   Baynham Pottery, ca. 1920, North Augusta, S.C. Mark Baynham, Sr., is at center holding a jug. Courtesy of Nancy Baynham.

field. And things was tough back in those days. It was really hard to get any money. But he would sell that load of . . . every time he'd sell a load of stuff [stoneware], he'd come back the same route and he'd stop and he'd buy a cow—a heifer or something—for about five dollars. He'd bring it home, and just turn it loose in the woods, just turn it loose, because it wasn't going nowhere, and he would leave it stay on till it got fat. He would sell it and make a few dollars off of it.[47]

Mark Baynham died in 1937. Clifton Baynham and Mark Baynham, Jr., operated a flowerpot factory on the site of the South Carolina Pottery after their father's death. Hugh Baynham later established a pottery in North Augusta. In 1958 he hired James ("Otto") Brown of Georgia and his son, Jimmy, to turn ware at the shop. Otto's brother, Javan, also turned at the Baynham shop. By this time an oil-fired kiln was used, and most of the output consisted of unglazed gardenware.

Baynham's shop was in operation for only a short time and was the last pottery established in the Edgefield area.

By the second half of the nineteenth century the focus of pottery activity in South Carolina had shifted from the Edgefield area to other pottery centers within the state. These late nineteenth-century pottery centers were increasingly influenced by the pottery traditions of other southern states, particularly Georgia and North Carolina. As itinerant turners moved throughout the region in search of jobs, the distinctive pottery styles that had emerged in the local pottery centers within the region were intermingled. This development, coupled with an evolution in form and techniques of production, resulted in a gradual shift away from the highly individualistic styles of the early nineteenth century toward a more standardized approach to stoneware production.

Richland County

Richland District (present-day Richland County) was one of the first areas in South Carolina outside the Edgefield District where alkaline-glazed stoneware was produced. Abner Landrum established the alkaline-glaze tradition in Richland District in the second quarter of the nineteenth century.

In 1885 and 1886 Abner Landrum's son, Linneaus, commissioned a survey of property that he owned in Richland County. A pottery appears on the map of his property near a tract of land that had been reserved for Dr. (Abner) Landrum in 1844 (see Figure 4.23). The pottery lay just east of Eightmile Branch and west of Almshouse (present-day Bethel Church) Road northeast of the city of Columbia.

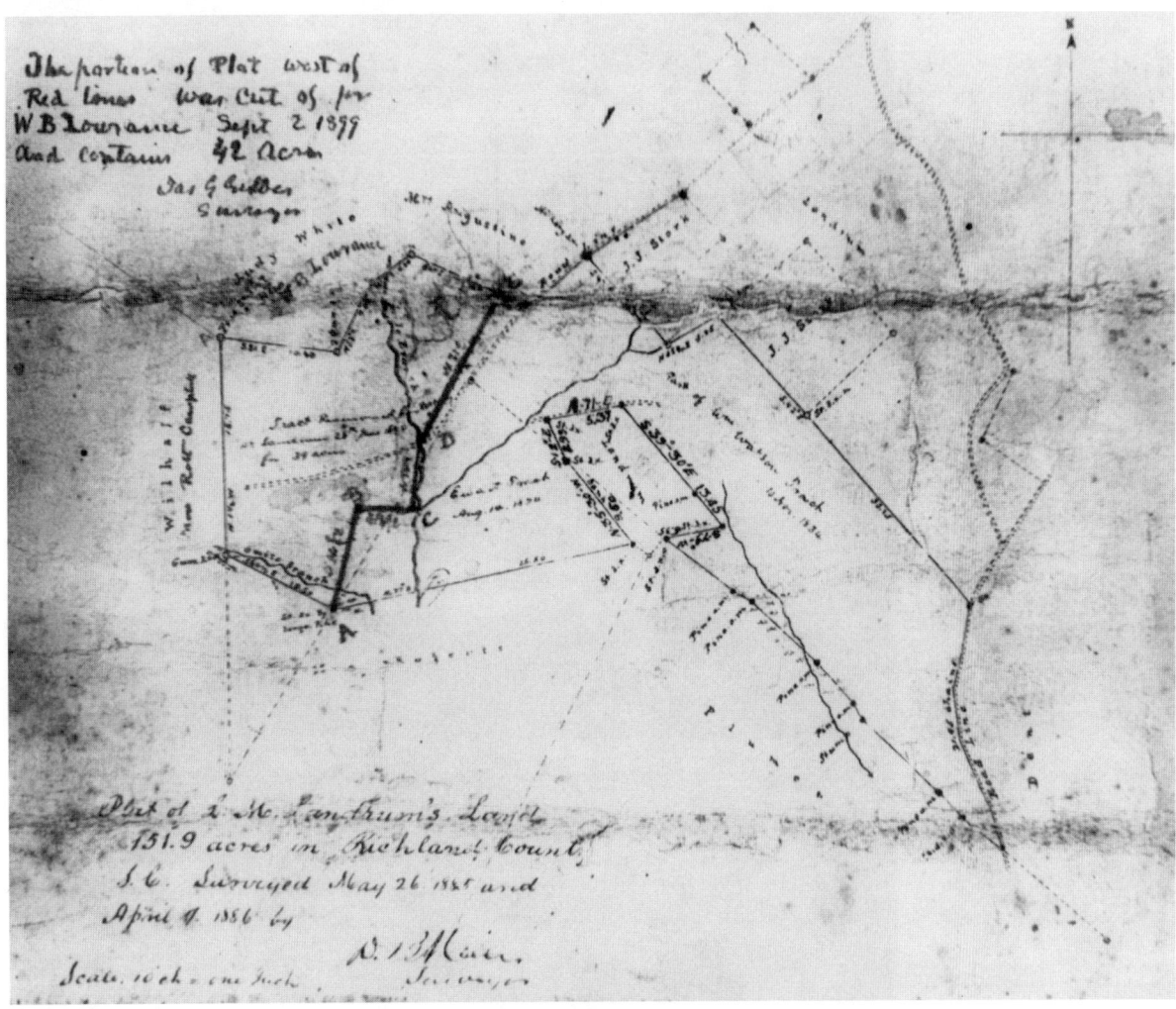

4.23   Map of land plat of property in Richland County surveyed for Linneaus M. Landrum in 1885 showing location of the pottery shop west of the thirty-nine-acre tract reserved for Dr. [Abner] Landrum. South Caroliniana Library, The University of South Carolina, Columbia, with thanks to Frank Buie.

4.24 Portrait of
Linneaus M. Landrum,
ca. 1870. Courtesy of
Maria Stork.

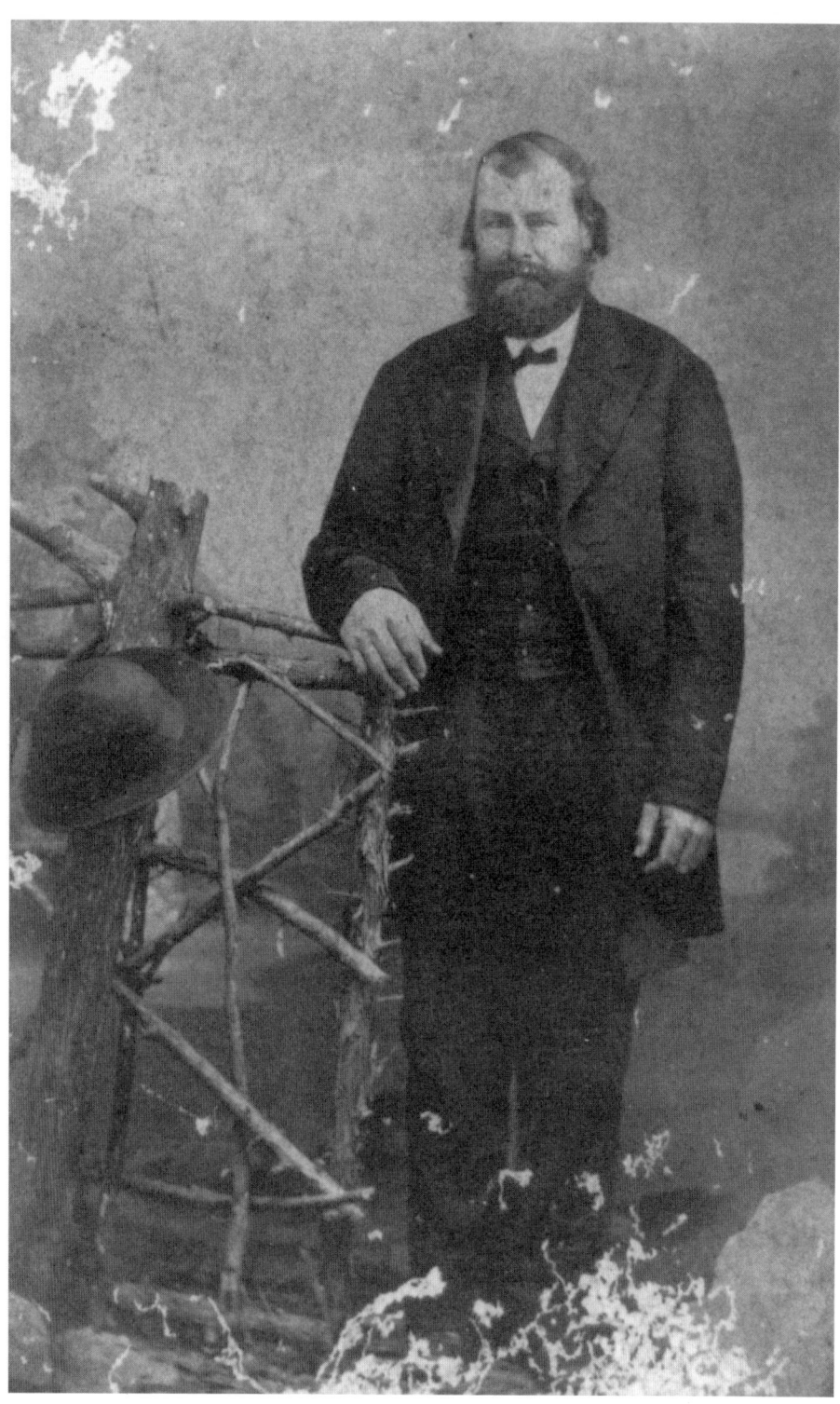

Abner Landrum's pottery is listed in the 1850 Richland District industrial census. Linneaus Landrum, then twenty-one, is known to have worked in the pottery. Some of Landrum's other sons probably also assisted in the operation. In 1840 Abner Landrum had six males in his household under the age of thirty. He had three sons—Manius (var. Manises), Palissey, and Wedgwood. Palissey became a printer and was listed as such in the 1860 census. He, Manius, and Wedgwood are said to have died in the Civil War. Family records mention three other sons—Leslie, Abner, and Manning—who may have died in infancy or as small children. Manius, Palissey, and Wedgwood, as well as Linneaus, most likely helped out in the pottery.

Power for Landrum's Columbia pottery consisted solely of hand labor. Clay valued at five hundred dollars and a total of ten cords of wood were used in the operation in 1850. From these raw materials, about twelve thousand gallons of ware were produced, valued at twelve hundred dollars. Linneaus Mead Landrum apparently inherited his father's love of clay. Linneaus became an accomplished potter under Abner's instruction and took over the pottery shop when his father died in 1859. Linneaus was listed in the 1870 Richland County industrial census as the owner of a pottery employing four adult males and two children at an annual cost of seven hundred dollars. These workers included Linneaus, John and William Stork, and neighbors George and William Augustine. According to the census report Linneaus produced about six thousand gallons of "Jugs and Jars" in 1870 valued at nineteen hundred dollars. This figure (over thirty cents per gallon) seems unusually high. Most folk potters operating in the region during the 1870s charged about ten to twelve cents per gallon for their ware.

A series of family letters written by Linneaus Landrum, his mother Mahethalan Presley Landrum, and sister Juliette Landrum Stork (wife of John Stork) to Sallie Landrum (daughter of

Abner and Mahethalan Landrum) from 1870 through 1872 include information about Linneaus's pottery.[48] The earliest reference to pottery production is found in a letter written by Juliette on 19 November 1870. In it she wrote that Linneaus had been awarded a silver knife for stoneware that he had entered in the fair. A stoneware storage jar stamped L. M. LANDRUM / COLUMBIA, S.C. attests to his proficiency as a potter (Figure 4.25). This tall, ovoid vessel is similar to ware produced in the Edgefield District in the mid-nineteenth century. It has two slab handles attached below the neck, a wide, flat, collared rim with interior lid ledge, and a light gray-green glassy alkaline glaze.

Unlike most potters, Linneaus operated his shop as a full-time business. In letters to his relatives he often mentioned the status of his stoneware business. It is apparent from these passages that the pottery was a precarious business. For example, in December 1870 he wrote, "Ware has been selling well. I have sold out all of my small jugs. I have not got much saleable ware on hand now." He went on to describe the severely cold weather, mentioning that "John [Stork] had a great deal of ware frozen." But in February 1871 Linneaus wrote, "I am not getting along with my business to suit me at all; it seems like I cannot get things to work rite; I have not been able to turn more than one day since I have been at home. I have been troubled a great deal about getting Clay." He described the difficulties that he had gone through to get clay for the pottery shop: "I went to see Shiner about getting Clay at the Bridge on Broad River; but he was sick and could not be seen, so I went to see him again about a week after; I saw him, and he promised to meet me at the Bridge on sunday evening: I went to his house sunday evening and found that he had left for New York Saturday. I saw [Stolbrand?] and got his permition to get some Clay from his brickyard." In a letter dated 5 March 1871 Linneaus responded to his sister's request

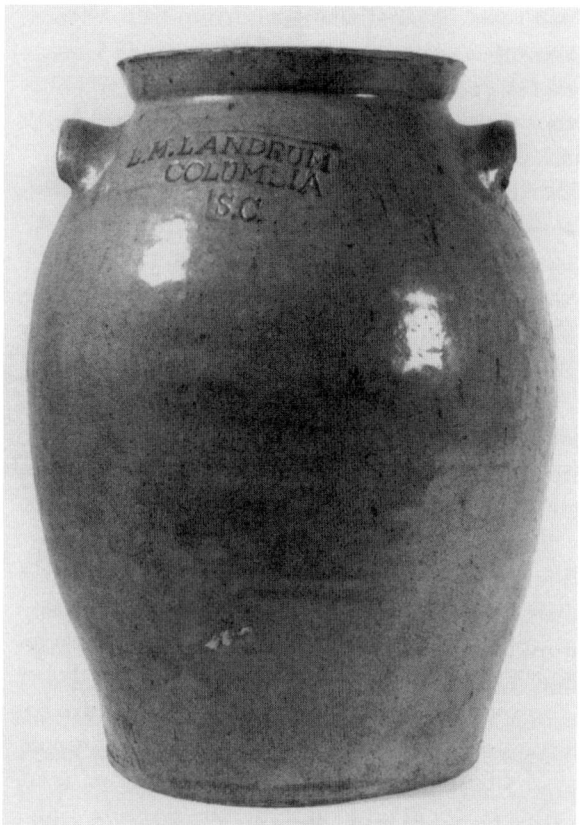

4.25   Alkaline-glazed stoneware storage jar, ca. 1860, Linneaus M. Landrum, Richland District, S.C. H 14⅝″, C 35⅞″. Stamped: L. M. LANDRUM / COLUMBIA / S.C. Collection of Tony and Marie Shank.

ness; my mule has been unable to work for a long time, and I miss his work very much. I cannot get along a plowing with the colt, he gets fretted by the roots that stop the plow, and breaks up every thing, he works clay very well, but I am afraid to work him too much in the Tub for fear of making him go blind." Linneaus's mother, Mahethalan, explained how the mule had been injured. In a December 1870 letter to Sallie, who was visiting in Edgefield, Mahethalan mentioned that she thought that Linneaus would be in Edgefield for Christmas but added that he "does not know, whether he can be there on Christmas day, or not,

for money by reminding her that "times are very hard with me. I hardly know what to do, it seems like everything works against me. My mule is swinnied, and unable to work." Later he added, "Business is very dull, my income has dwindled down to almost nothing, but my expenses continue the same. I have no alternative left, but to go in debt, or suspend business; I think I will go in debt, as I do not like to stop my business because times are dull." Later on he reiterated, "You know that my business is always dull in the spring and summer, it is particularly so this spring." And on 30 March Linneaus wrote, "I am getting along rather slowly with my busi-

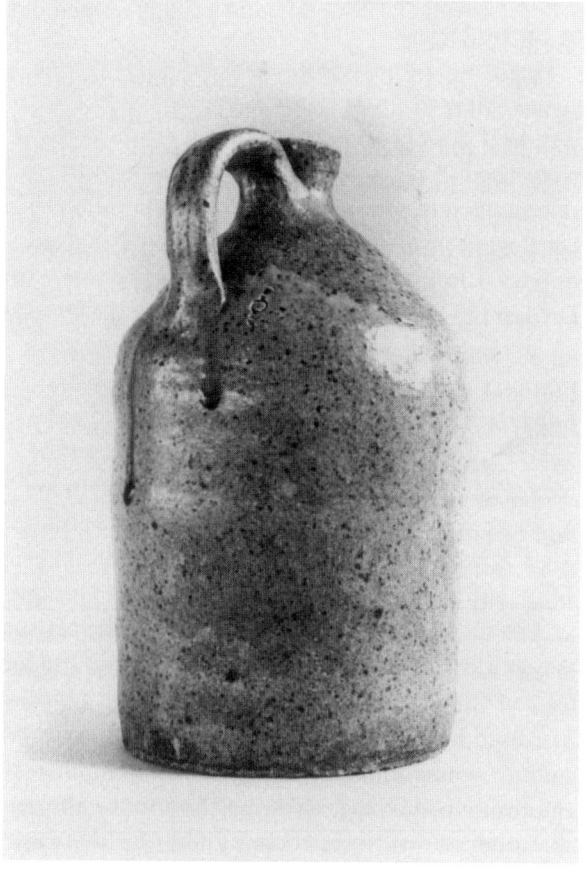

4.26   Alkaline-glazed stoneware jug, ca. 1880, attributed to the Stork Pottery, Richland County, S.C. H 9⅝″, C 18½″. Impressed circular mark right of lower handle attachment. Collection of Sylvia D. Garrett.

he has had some bad luck, his mule got crippled, the last trip they made to Camden with ware."

John Stork and his sons, Edward Leslie and Robert Manning, reportedly ran a pottery shop located on John Stork's property near present-day Highway 1 in the Dentsville community just outside Columbia. John Stork's daughter, Wilma Maude Shull, recalls that her father's pottery was located near a peach orchard. John Stork also ran a grocery store in Columbia. Edward and Robert Stork are said to have established their own pottery shop on the west side of Alms House Road (present-day Bethel Church Road) just north of Linneaus's shop.[49]

Edward and Robert Stork's pottery witnessed a period of transition. The earlier ovoid forms became more cylindrical and less precise (see Figure 4.26). Linneaus had used a glaze mixture consisting of fine sand, clay, lime, and ash with a relatively high proportion of lime, resulting in a smooth, light gray-green alkaline glaze similar to that produced by Thomas Chandler in Edgefield. Edward and Robert Stork produced thin, dark brown-black streaky ash glazes. By the turn of the century the Storks had begun using Albany slip glaze. They sometimes added lead to the slip, which produced a red-brown glaze.[50] The evolution of vessel forms and glaze types at the Stork pottery mirrors that found throughout the region. A straight-sided jug from the Stork pottery site, with a loop handle attached at the neck, a flattened collared neck and a runny, mottled olive-brown to reddish-brown ash glaze, is typical of many alkaline-glazed stoneware jugs produced in the South at the turn of the century.

Edward Stork left Columbia during the early 1900s, traveling to Alabama, Mississippi, and Georgia where he hired on at a number of shops. John Burrison outlined Stork's Georgia potting career as follows:

In Georgia he is said to have zig-zagged from Elberton, near the South Carolina border, west to Orange in Cherokee County, then south to Senoia in Coweta County, east to Chalker in Washington County, then southwest to Crawford County, moving up in a covered wagon to Alvaton, in Meriwether County about twenty miles northwest of Jugtown, where in 1907 he joined W. T. B. Gordy.

Their first shop was obtained from potter Frank Gibson, who was leaving for North Carolina. A year later they moved north to Shakerag, a settlement in Fayette County not far below Atlanta, converting an old log double-pen house into a shop. It was Stork who introduced the aboveground tunnel kiln to Gordy, who previously had known only the earth-enclosed groundhog kilns of Jugtown; Gordy would adopt the former because it attracted less moisture, making it easier to fire. After half a year they moved again to Aberdeen, near present-day Peachtree City, in the same county. The partnership dissolved in 1909 when Stork left to settle in Orange seven miles east of Canton, where, until his death in 1925, he produced a wide range of ware usually glazed with Michigan slip, which sometimes fired to a burnt-orange color.[51]

Edward created a late, indirect link with the Edgefield stoneware tradition through his association with potters in Georgia, Alabama, and South Carolina. The potters who traveled out of Edgefield in the early part of the nineteenth century had been in search of greater opportunity in the West. These men introduced the newly developed alkaline-glazed stoneware into Georgia, Alabama, Mississippi, and Texas.

Linneaus Landrum died in 1891. Eight years later Robert Stork purchased the Landrum pottery.[52] Linneaus had been producing firebrick as well as pottery, and Robert converted the operation entirely to the production of firebrick, molded ornamental ware, and gardenware. In 1914 R. M. Stork put out a promotional calendar with a letterhead that read, "Compliments of Landrum Fire Brick Works, Columbia, South Carolina." Shortly before his death in 1954 Stork took the old potter's wheel that had originally belonged to Abner Landrum out of storage and taught his son, Raymond Manning Stork, how to turn.

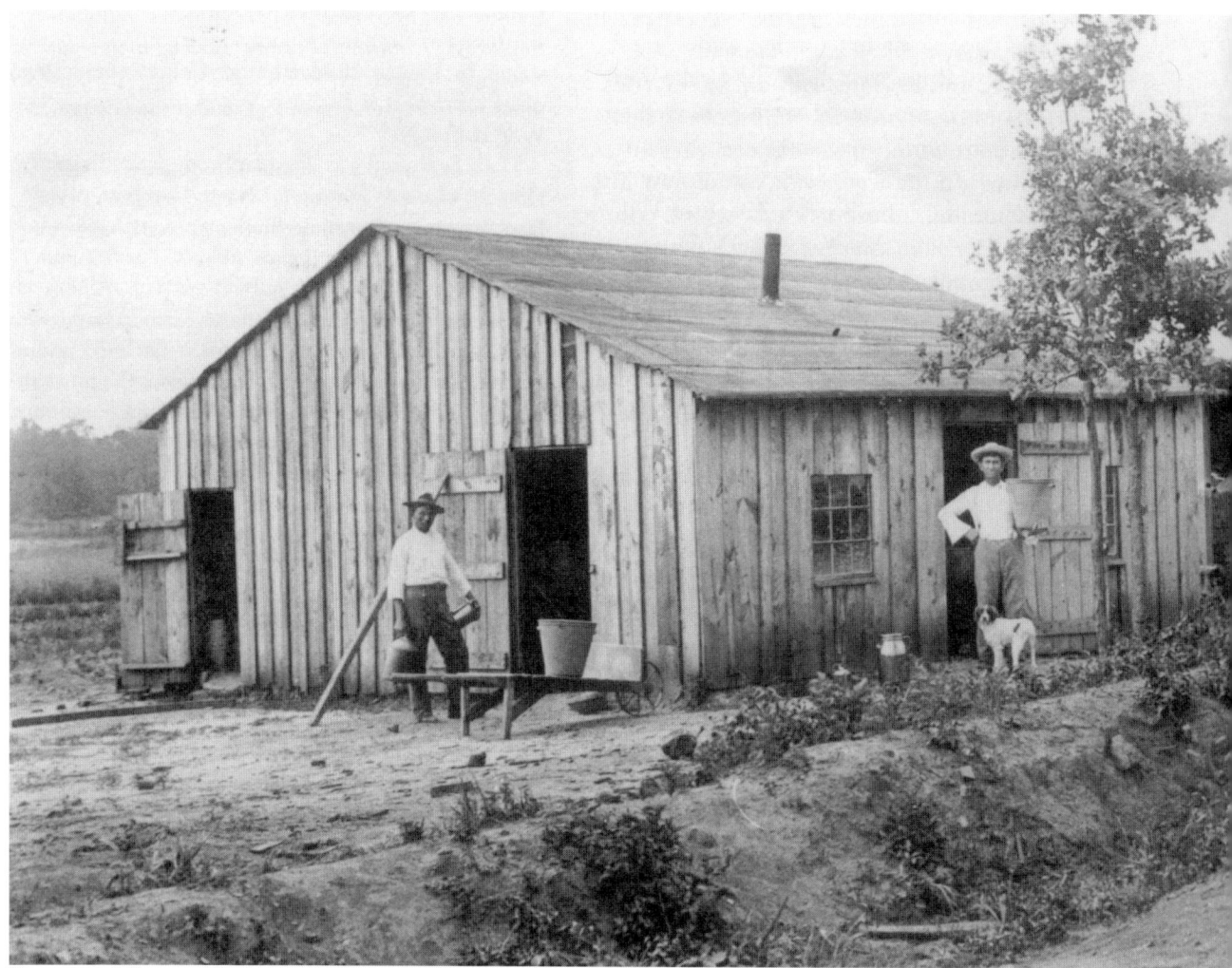

4.27   Edward L. Stork's pottery shop in Orange, Ga. Courtesy of Maria Stork.

The Brickyard Condominiums were built in 1970 on the former site of the Landrum Fire Brick Works. Prior to the construction of the condominiums, local collectors recovered a large volume of ceramic material from the site. This material included fragments of stoneware jugs, jars, churns, bowls, tableware, and a coffeepot. The presence of the coffeepot form at the Columbia pottery may be particularly significant, since early Georgia stoneware potter Abraham Massey is documented as having produced coffee boilers at his shop in Washington County as early as 1820. Coffee boilers have the baluster-shaped form typical of early stoneware pitchers but without the pinched spout. They have instead a teapot-type or tubular spout and a vertical loop handle attached opposite. Molded clay pipes, firebrick, and earthenware in a variety of forms, ranging from flowerpots to elaborately decorated planters or grave ornaments and architectural molding, were also recovered from the Landrum-Stork site.

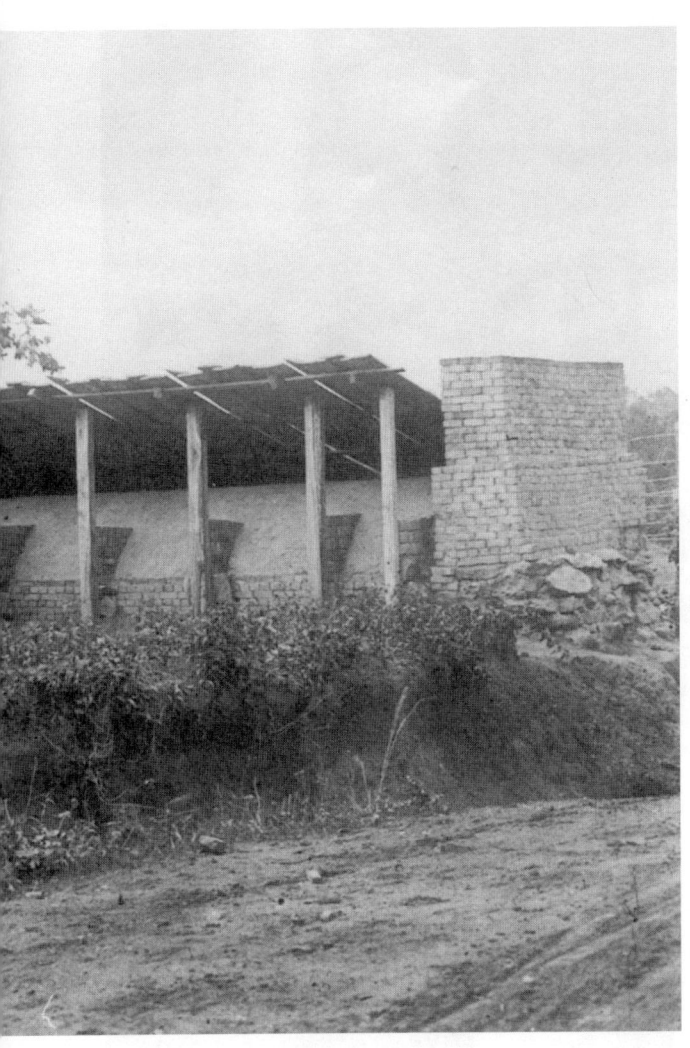

Cherokee County

Another alkaline-glazed stoneware center with direct ties to Edgefield was established in the Union District by Thomas Owensby. Owensby evidently trained as a potter in the Edgefield District. He appears as a potter in the 1850 Spartanburg County census and is known to have established a pottery in the Union District (present-day Cherokee County). Owensby's daughter, Sarah Berthine Owensby Boyle, her husband Aylie Boyle, and their children continued the pottery that he established well into the twentieth century.

The Boyles produced a dark brown-black, glassy "cinder glaze" by adding iron slag from the nearby iron foundry to their glaze mixture.[53] After the Revolutionary War, several furnaces had been erected on the Broad and Saluda rivers, and iron production soon became a major industry in the Piedmont. In 1810 U.S. Geological Surveyor Tench Coxe listed two forges in Spartanburg County, four in Pendleton County, two in Greenville County, and one in York County. By 1856 eight additional furnaces had been constructed in the area, and all but one of these were located in present-day Cherokee County. That same year the Cherokee Ford rolling mill produced 400 tons of merchant bars, and the Cherokee Ford bloomery forged 240 tons of pig iron blooms.[54] Many of the upcountry potters salvaged the iron slag from the furnaces to use in their glazes. During the Civil War the iron manufactures were important to the Confederacy, but following the war slave labor crucial to the operations was lost, and most of the capital that had been invested in the ironworks, in the form of Confederate cash, became valueless. By the end of the nineteenth century the iron industry had died out in the area. The iron glaze was reportedly used during the early period of pottery production in the area. A more refined glaze, made from white sand and lime, was used after the close of the foundries.[55]

In about 1862 Sarah Boyle secured a piece of iron from the Cherokee Ford Iron Works on the Broad River and took it to a blacksmith to have it bent into an axle to be used in the turning wheel at the pottery. The Boyles assisted Owensby in the manufacture of pottery dishes for the Confederate army during the Civil War. A jug reportedly made by Thomas Owensby, Jr., is dated 1864 and signed in incised script "Maid an Sold at / A low price fore Confedrent / Money by me / Thomas Ownbey" (see Figure 2.41).

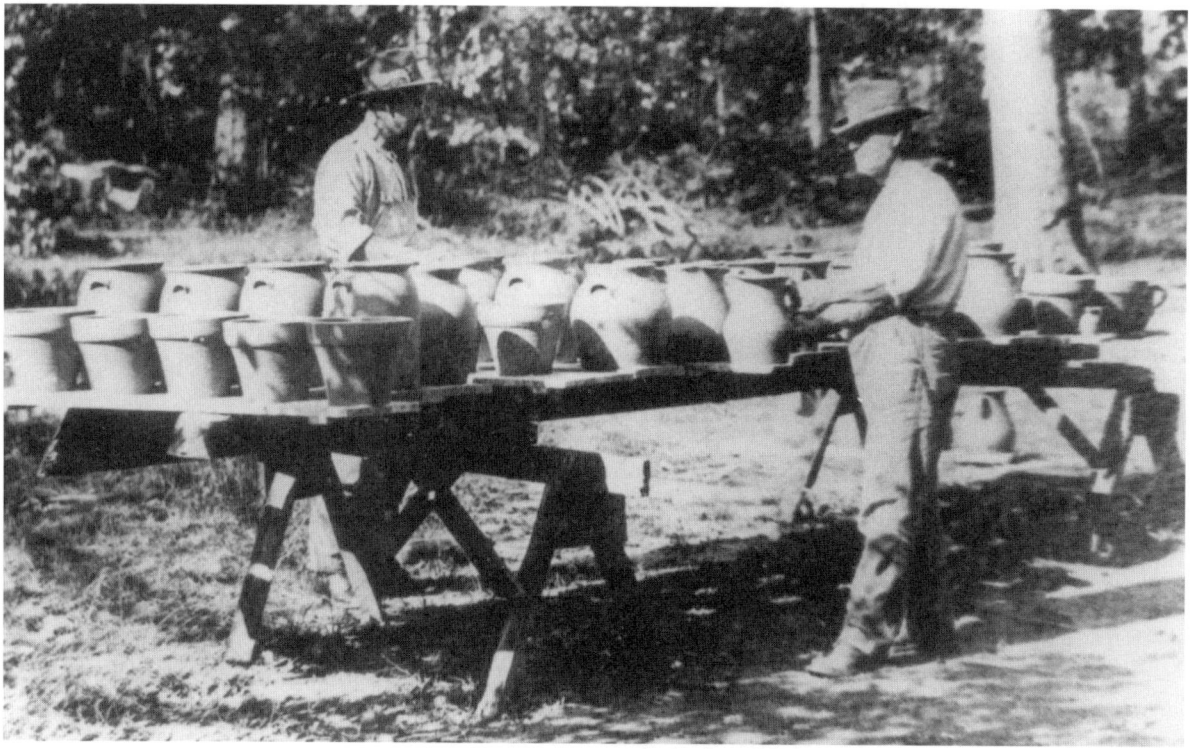

4.28   Robert Boyle and Aylie Boyle, Jr., with unfired ware at the drying tables,
Boyle Pottery, Cherokee County, S.C., ca. 1944. Courtesy of Rochelle Boyle.

Sarah and Aylie Boyle apparently took over the pottery shop after the death of Thomas Owensby, Sr., in 1878. Aylie Boyle, Sr., appears in the 1900 Cherokee County census in White Plains Township as a turner, and his wife Sarah, as a potter and farmer. Three sons, Robert L., John T., and Aylie A. Boyle, all bachelors, were also living in the household. Robert, age thirty-five, was listed as a potter, while John, age thirty, and Aylie Jr., age twenty-five, appear as farm laborers. Philip G. Petty, living nearby and listed as a jugmaker, was also potting at the Boyle shop. Petty was married to Sarah Boyle's sister Isabella, known to the family as Betts.

Early on, the Boyles transported their ware by river barge down the Broad River to Columbia. They also carried the ware throughout the area in a wagon drawn by a yoke of steers and later on

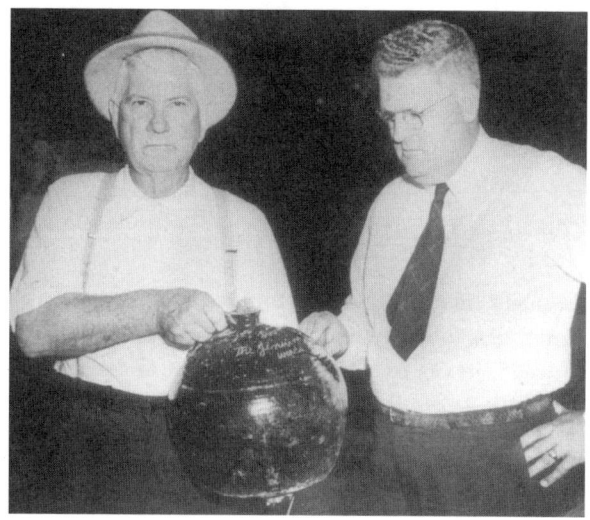

4.29   Rochelle Boyle and Aylie Boyle, Jr., holding a buggy jug made at the Boyle Pottery near Gaffney, S.C. Courtesy of Rochelle Boyle.

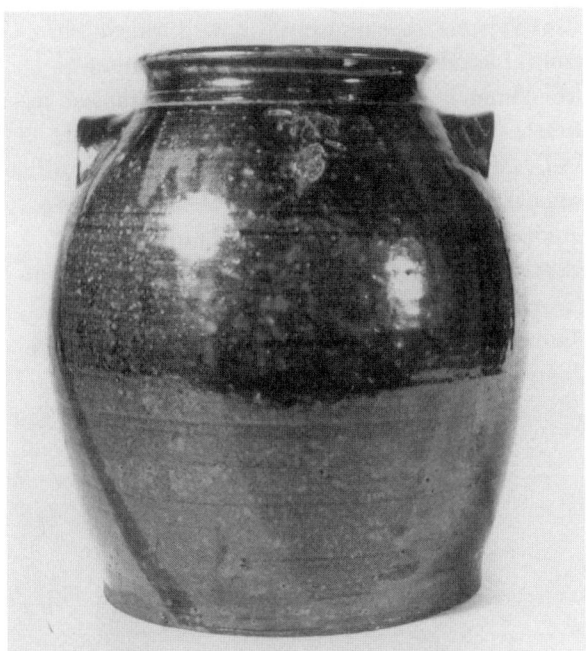

4.30 Alkaline-glazed stoneware storage jar, ca. 1930, Boyle Pottery, Cherokee County, S.C. H 11⅜″, C 33⅜″. Incised mark: RB / 3. Collection of the Charleston Museum, Charleston, S.C.

a low, wide shoulder, a rolled, gently flaring rim, and a prominently fluted pouring spout. Storage and preserve jars, milk and cream pitchers, cream risers, vases, tableware, and miniatures were also produced at the Boyle pottery shop. Larger vessels such as jars and pitchers were incised RB for Robert Boyle, who was the principal turner at the shop. Numbers indicating gallon capacity were centered directly below the maker's mark (Figure 4.30).

Thomas Owensby's in-laws, the Whelchels, were also potters. John Whelchel, who was living near Thomas Sr.'s son Joel in 1860, worked in Owensby's pottery shop. Six children were listed in the Whelchel household in 1860, including Sam L. Whelchel, age fourteen, who also became

began selling wholesale to stores in nearby towns such as Gaffney.[56]

Ware produced by Robert and Aylie Boyle, Jr., during the late nineteenth and early twentieth centuries may be readily distinguished from other southern stoneware by its distinctive forms and glazes, and sometimes by maker's marks. Boyle ware tends to be unusually wide at the shoulder. Robert Boyle produced a unique type of jug— the "buggy jug"—an extremely squat, wide-shouldered form. The buggy jug was designed to fit under the seat of a horse-drawn carriage, thereby providing drinking water and other beverages for travelers on long journeys. One buggy jug produced at the Boyle pottery is inscribed in script "From / The Jenkins Distillery works / Grover, NC" (Figure 4.29). Another distinctive form produced by Boyle, the serving pitcher, had

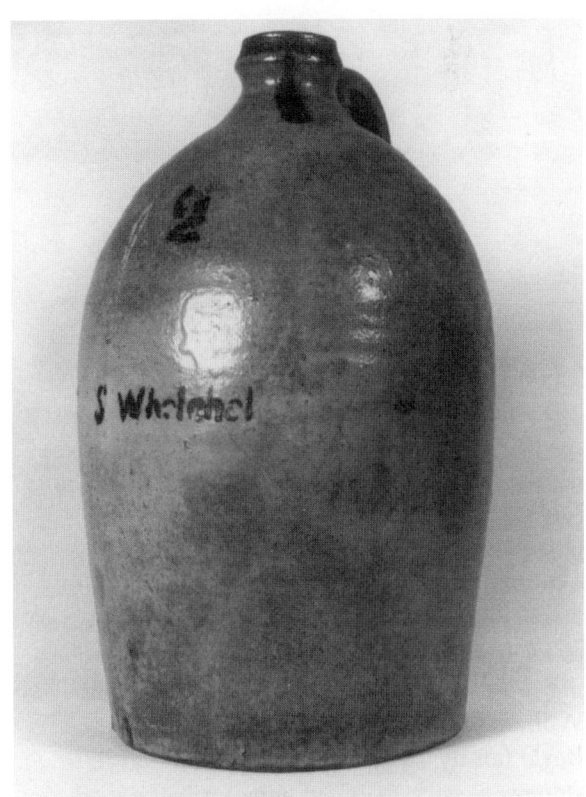

4.31 Alkaline-glazed stoneware jug, ca. 1900, Sam Whelchel, Spartanburg County, S.C. H 14⅝″, C 28¾″. Maker's mark: S Whelchel. Collection of Phil Wingard.

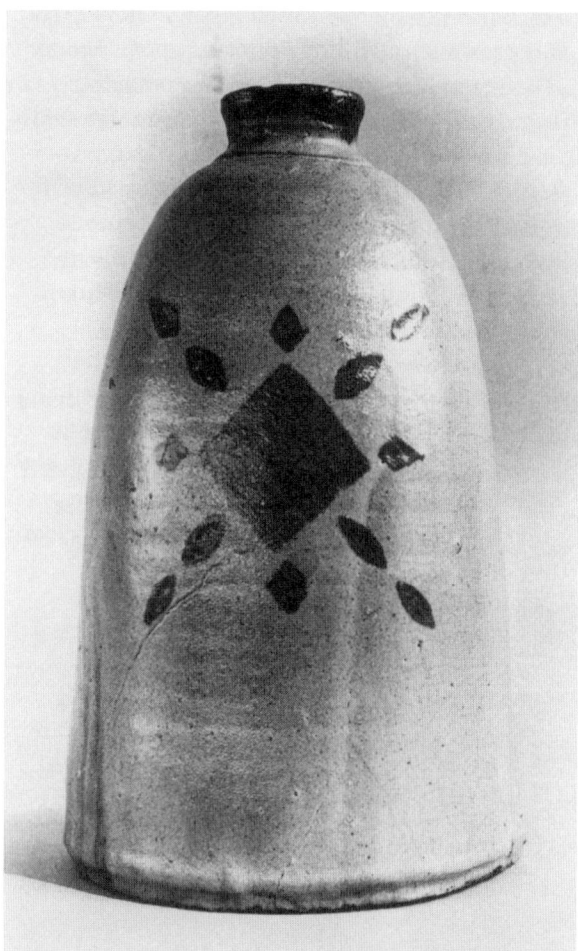

4.32   Alkaline-glazed stoneware jug with stenciled slip decoration, ca. 1900, Whelchel Pottery, Spartanburg County, S.C. H 10⅝″, C 21⅛″. Collection of Donnie F. Garrett.

a potter. Sam Whelchel and his son, William, later operated a small pottery located about two miles from the Owensby-Boyle pottery. According to folk pottery researcher Howard Smith, William Whelchel married a member of the Boyle family.[57] Hand-turned alkaline-glazed stoneware with stenciled geometrical designs in brown-black slip and molded stoneware were produced at the Whelchel pottery from about 1875 until the 1930s (see Figure 4.32).

A slip-glazed stoneware jug with raised horizontal bands around the belly is attributed to the Whelchels. This unusual vessel is incised in script, "Whelchel & Smith / Mfg. Co. Norah, S.C. / July 29th 1893" (Figure 4.33). A post office was established at Norah on 4 December 1889 and was discontinued on 11 December 1901.[58] Norah, located in Spartanburg County on Route 14 approximately halfway between Greer and Gowensville, lay in the heart of Jugtown, South Carolina's busiest upcountry pottery center.

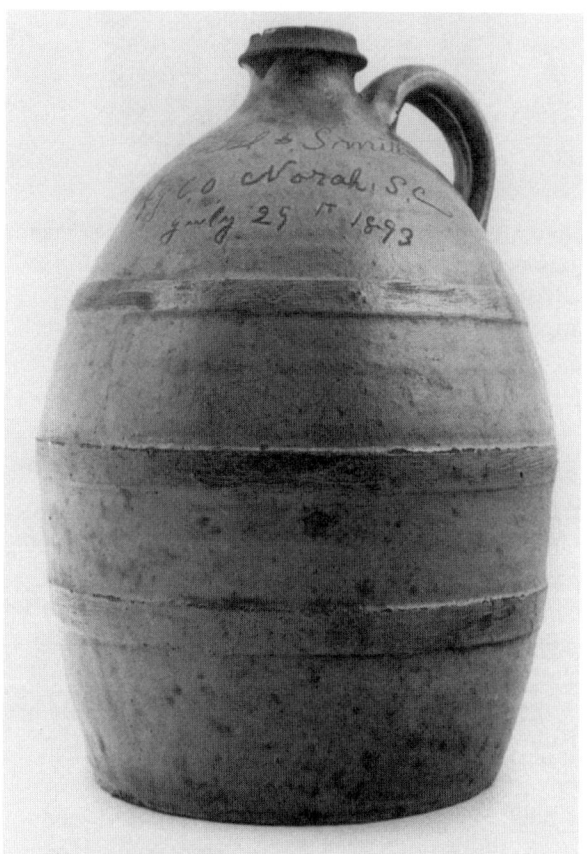

4.33   Alkaline-glazed stoneware jug, 1893, attributed to Sam Whelchel and John Smith, Norah, Greenville County, S.C. H 12⅝″, C 28¾″. Incised script: Whelchel & Smith / Mfg. Co. Norah, S.C. / July 29th 1893. Collection of Mr. and Mrs. Gary S. Thompson, Jr.

Jugtown, Spartanburg-Greenville Counties

A major center of stoneware production emerged in South Carolina during the mid-nineteenth century along the Tyger River on the Spartanburg-Greenville county line south of Gowensville. This area was South Carolina's Jugtown. Local newspaperman James Walton Lawrence, Sr., wrote in his book *Shadows of Hogback* that "at one time, the production of corn liquor was so great around the foot of Hogback Mountain [located in Greenville County, northwest of Gowensville], thirteen potteries in the Little Chicago area of Spartanburg County were kept busy turning out churns, crocks and jugs. White clay jugs were the leading product. To this very day, one of the important roads through the area is known as 'Jug Factory Road.'"[59]

Following the Revolutionary War, a federal tax was placed on whiskey, and "almost anyone could operate a distillery providing he went to the trouble to purchase a federal permit, and paid federal taxes on his output."[60] During the late 1930s, when cotton and corn were cheap, many of the local farmers made and sold liquor to supplement their incomes, and shortages of sugar necessitated the use of home-grown cane syrup, so syrup and liquor jugs were in demand. Churns were often used to make home brew (beer made of malt, yeast, and sugar) as well as to preserve food. According to one local resident, during the Depression everybody in the area had a churn, even if they did not have a cow.

Local store owner Boomer Williams recalls about a dozen potteries having been in operation within a ten-mile radius of his store in Little Chicago during the early 1900s. Henson, Tapp, Atkins, Clayton, Belcher, Williams, Fulbright, Brown, Van Patton, and Johnson are a few of the names associated with stoneware production at Jugtown.[61]

The Henson family was one of the earliest clay clans in the Jugtown area. William ("Bill") Hen-

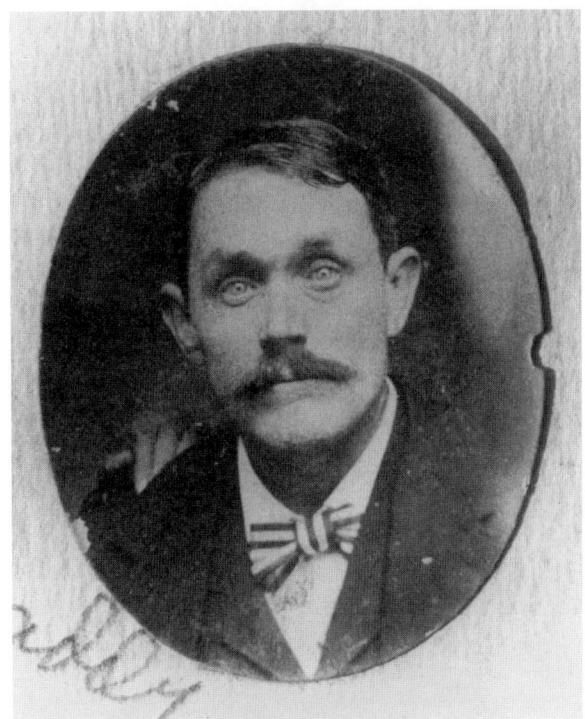

4.34 Portrait of William Thomas Henson, Jugtown, S.C. Courtesy of Pearl Henson Fowler.

son, born 15 December 1818, was the patriarch of the Henson clan. His pottery shop, located on Jordan Road in Greenville County, was reportedly one of the first established in the area. Mathias Henson, probably a relative of William Henson, appeared in the 1870 Spartanburg County census in Campobello Township as a potter. Another potter, Oliver Rofs (var. Ross), was living next door to Mathias in 1870.[62] Two of William Henson's sons, David Carr Henson and Jesse Vardry Henson, also owned pottery shops in the Mt. Lebanon community of Greenville County in the late nineteenth century. A third son, William Thomas Henson, owned a pottery shop located behind Mt. Lebanon Church. A Mr. Mason reportedly ran the shop for Henson. William Thomas Henson reportedly purchased the property on which this pottery shop was located from a man named Gum Landrum.[63] This tantalizing bit of information suggests that the Greenville-Spartanburg county stoneware tradition may have been directly influenced by the Landrum family. Although a relationship between Gum Landrum and the Landrums of Edgefield has not been positively established, one branch of the North Carolina Landrum family is known to have settled in Greenville County.

The Hensons made ovoid jugs, churns, and storage jars with alkaline glazes ranging in color from dark brown-black to olive and tan-brown (see Figure 4.35). Two storage jars attributed to Jesse Vardry Henson are similar to ware produced in the Edgefield District in the mid-nineteenth

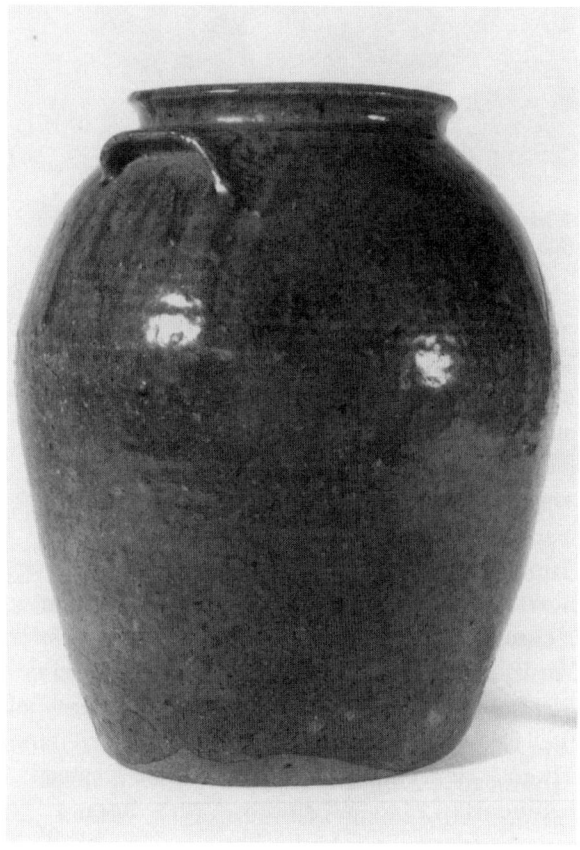

4.35   Alkaline-glazed stoneware storage jar, ca. 1880, attributed to David Carr Henson, Spartanburg County, S.C. H 12½″, C 34¼″. Collection of Billy Henson.

century. Both jars are ovoid or bulbous, with two opposing horizontal slab or lug handles and a flat, everted tie-down rim designed to receive a cloth seal. One of these storage jars has a tan-brown alkaline glaze, while the other has an olive-colored alkaline glaze. In addition to this typical ware, the Hensons also produced unusual stoneware forms such as inkwells and molded pipes.

The Hensons and another Jugtown clay clan, the Tapp family, were interrelated by marriage. Moses Foster Tapp operated a stoneware factory in Spartanburg County. According to Clarice Tapp, Moses Tapp's granddaughter, her maternal grandfather was David Carr Henson, so David Henson apparently married into the Tapp family. The Tapps, then, seem to have learned to make pottery while working for the Hensons.

Stoneware produced by the Tapps testifies to the relationship between the two families (see Figure 4.37). The Tapps made alkaline-glazed stoneware similar to that produced by the Hensons. Moses Tapp's great-grandson Kenneth Tapp and granddaughter Clarice have several vessels that they attribute to the Tapp and Henson potteries. These include several ovoid jugs, some with tan-brown glazes, others with shiny black glazes. Handles on these jugs are attached at the neck rather than below. A wide-mouthed "kraut" jar with what appears to be a local slip glaze and two opposing horizontal slab handles is attributed to David Carr Henson or Moses Tapp. Another vessel owned by the Tapps, a well-turned pitcher with a shiny black alkaline glaze, is attributed to Moses Tapp.

Moses Tapp's son, James Leroy Tapp, was also a potter. James Leroy's daughter, Clarice, recalls that her father helped dig and haul clay for the pottery, and that her father's toes had become crooked from working in the clay. An Albany-slip-glazed jug is attributed to James Leroy Tapp. The beehive-shaped jug represents a transition from the alkaline-glazed ware produced by Moses Tapp.

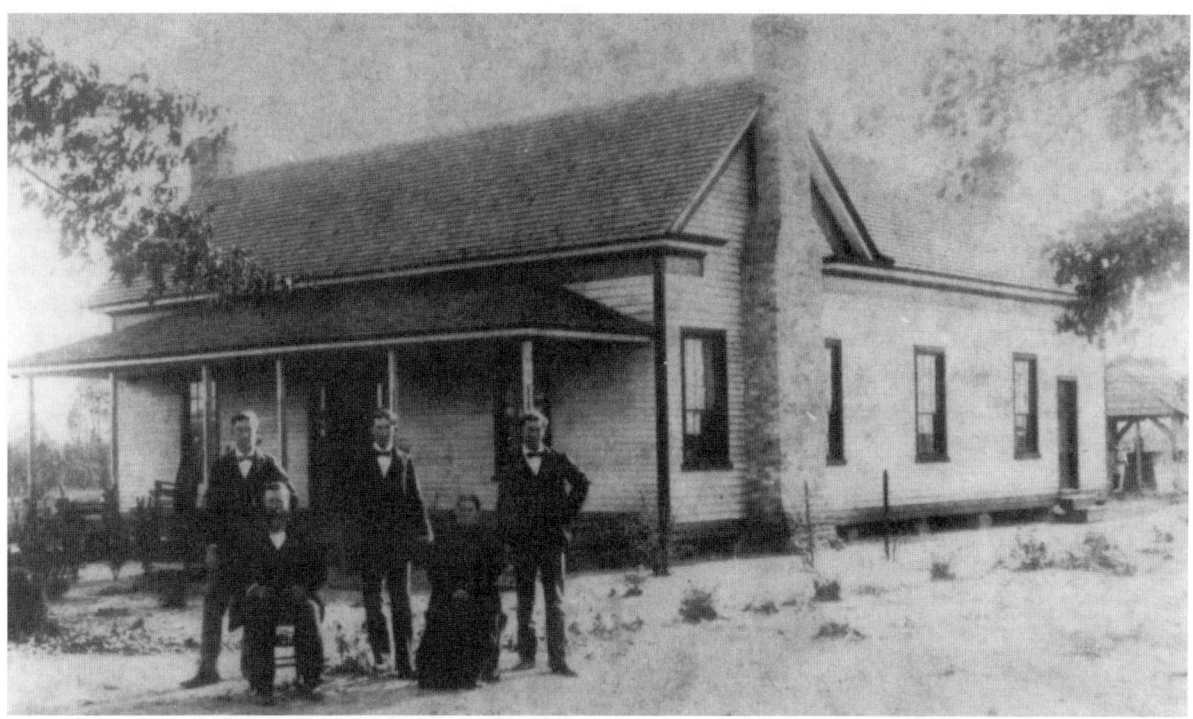

4.36　Moses Foster Tapp family. *Standing, left to right*: Willie, Judd, and James Leroy Tapp. *Sitting, left to right*: Moses Foster Tapp and wife, Mary A. Tapp. Courtesy of Kenneth and Clarice Tapp.

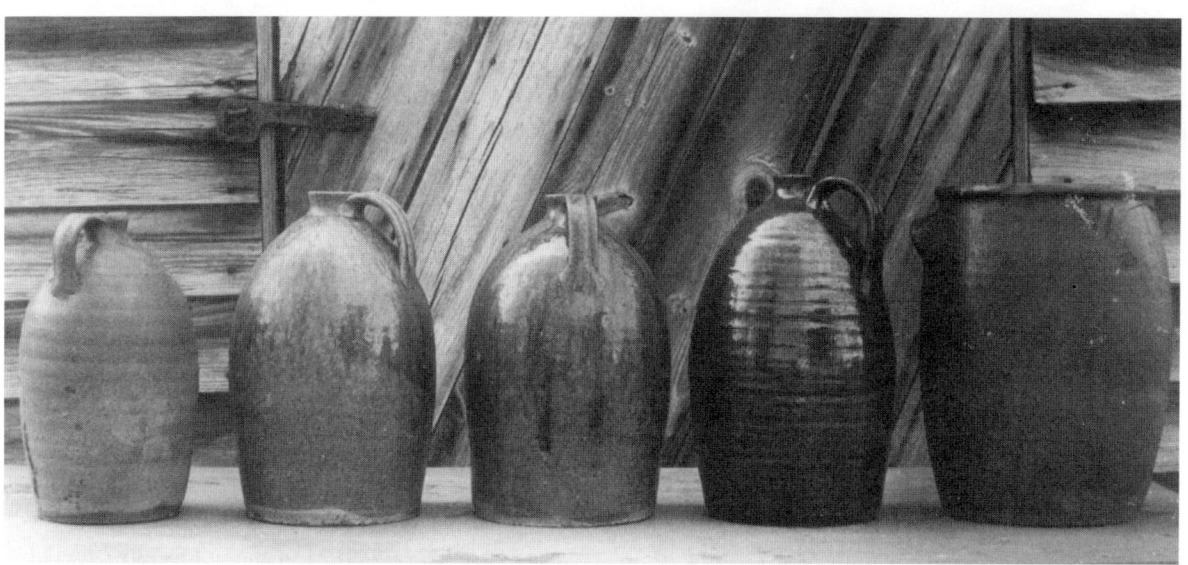

4.37　Alkaline-glazed stoneware jugs and kraut jar attributed to the Tapp and Henson families. Collection of Kenneth and Clarice Tapp.

The Atkins family of Greenville County also became involved in pottery manufacture through an association with the Hensons. John Leonard Atkins learned the pottery trade while living on property belonging to William Thomas Henson. He later established his own pottery shop on Jug Factory Road near Little Chicago, where he produced jugs, churns, jars, and, reportedly, face jugs with a glassy, black alkaline glaze (see Figure 4.38). The dark glaze color resulted from Atkins's use of feldspars obtained from North Carolina in his glazes. Leonard Atkins apparently continued his affiliation with the Henson family,

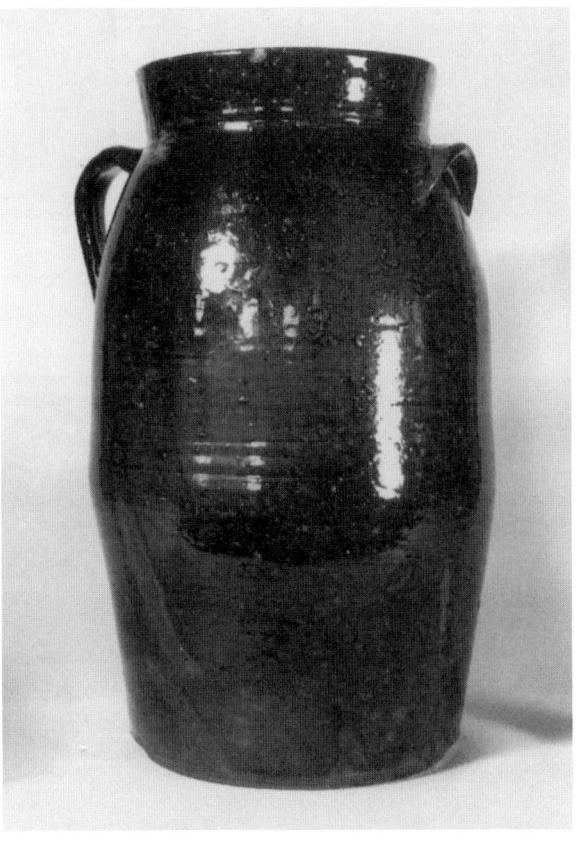

4.38 Alkaline-glazed stoneware churn, ca. 1900, John Leonard Atkins, Jug Factory Road, Greenville County, S.C. H 42″, C 32¾″. Incised mark: 5. Collection of Thomas Gentry Bab.

for B. D. Henson reportedly hauled jugs to North Carolina for Atkins.

The Henson and Atkins families may have been manufacturing stoneware together as early as 1880. Pinkney Atkins, listed as a jugmaker in the Spartanburg County census that year in Campobello Township, was probably working for the Hensons.[64] Potters James Atkins and Mathias Henson were living next door to each other, and undoubtedly potting together, in 1900 in Beech Springs Township, Spartanburg County. A Williams family was listed just before Henson in the 1900 census, and two Van Patton families were enumerated just after Atkins. Although both heads of households are listed as farmers, these families are known to have been involved in pottery manufacture in the Jugtown area.[65]

Black potter Richard ("Rich") Williams was operating a stoneware factory in the Gowensville area of Greenville County in the early 1900s. Williams, age fifty, appeared in the 1900 census as a farmer. He was listed as the head of his household and owned his farm. Other members of the household included Williams's wife Sarah, his sons James and William, and mother-in-law Lou R. Lucas. Everyone in Rich Williams's household was born in South Carolina, but it is unclear whether Williams was an Edgefield-trained potter or learned the pottery craft by working at one of the Jugtown shops.[66]

George L. Clayton founded another Jugtown-area pottery in about 1912. Clayton, who was not a potter himself, hired Jim and Gene Atkins to turn ware at the shop. Gene Atkins was the brother of Jugtown potter Leonard Atkins. Leonard, Thereon, and Fack Atkins reportedly also turned for Clayton. Leonard and Fack later established their own shops on Jug Factory Road in Jugtown. Several other turners from South Carolina, Georgia, and North Carolina later worked at the Clayton pottery. These included Albert Fulbright (who had formerly turned

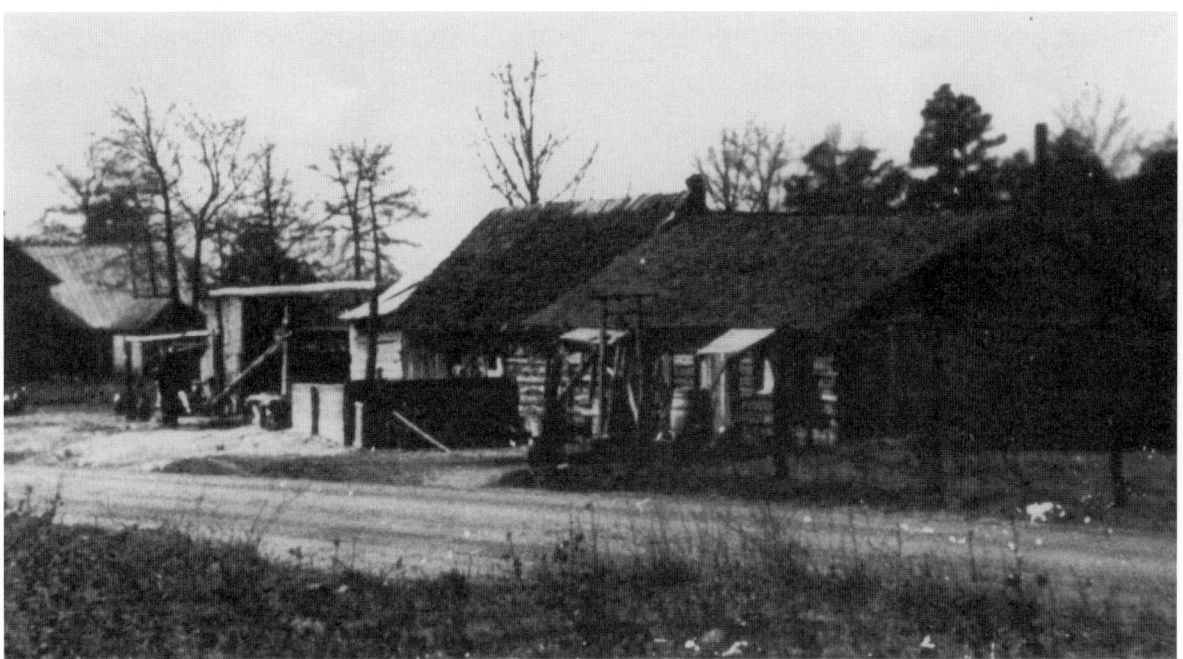

4.39 Clayton Jug Factory, Holly Springs community, Spartanburg County, ca. 1910–40. Courtesy of the Clayton family.

at Lanford Station for the Johnsons), Edward Daugherty of Texas (who later operated a pottery at Bethune, South Carolina), Missouri-born Hermann L. Jegglin (son of a German immigrant potter), Casey Meaders, Frank Gibson, and the Brown brothers of Georgia (Evan Javan, Davis P., Rufus E., and William O. ["Willie"] Brown) and James Otis Trull of North Carolina. Gibson had operated a pottery at Alvaton, Georgia, which he sold to W. T. B. Gordy and Edward Stork in 1907 before heading for North Carolina. Daugherty and Jegglin turned for W. T. B. Gordy at Alvaton.[67] Members of the Atlanta-based Brown family turned in Georgia, Alabama, Florida, South Carolina, and North Carolina. Jones ("Pete") Clayton, son of George Clayton, recalled that Javan, Rufus, and Davis Brown had worked together at the Clayton pottery before establishing their own shop at Arden, North Carolina. The Clayton shop had three "lathes"

(wheels), one for each of the Brown brothers. North Carolina potter James O. Trull was the son of Benjamin Robert Trull. J. O. Trull turned at his father's shop in Buncombe County and later for his father-in-law, James D. Rutherford, with W. M. Penland, Robert Anderson, Albert Fulbright, and Oscar Louis Bachelder.[68]

George Clayton's sons Lewis, Jones ("Pete"), Ernest, and Albert Clayton also helped out in the pottery. The Clayton pottery shop was in operation in the spring and summer months. According to Pete Clayton, specific tasks were not assigned to one individual, with the exception of turning. Pete was the only one of George Clayton's sons who became a turner. He apprenticed under Albert Fulbright, who he claimed was one of the best potters in the area. Pete's job was to turn and dry the ware, while his father and brothers were responsible for digging, hauling, and processing the clay used in the operation, glazing the ware,

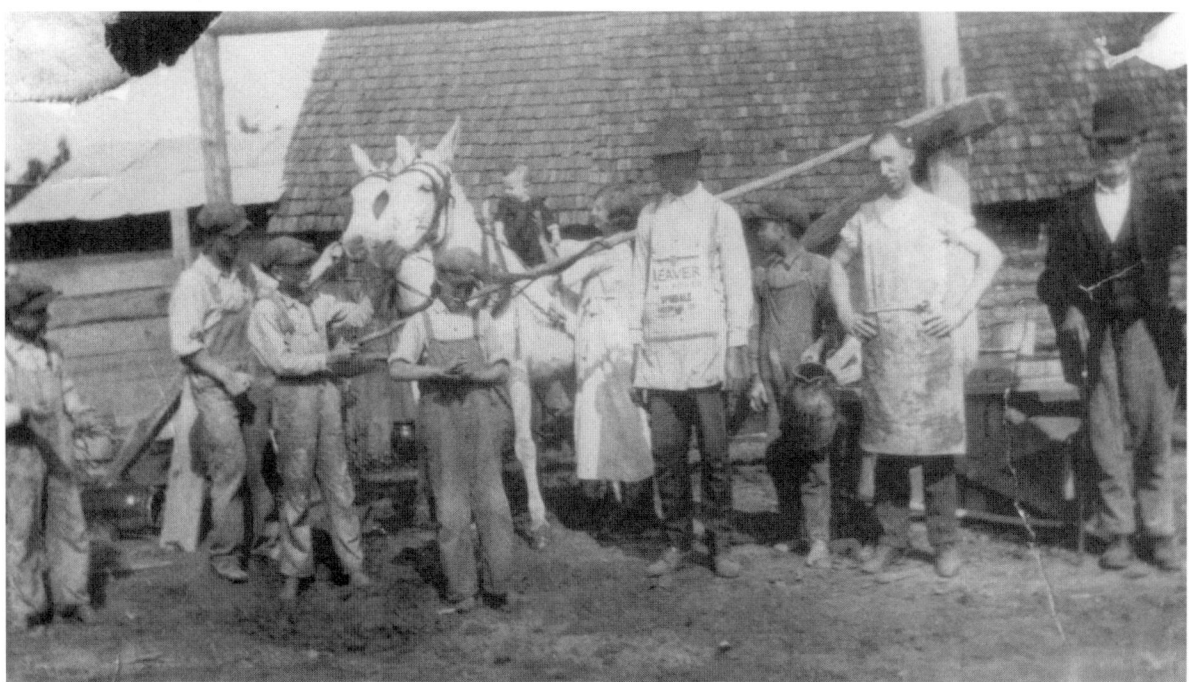

4.40   Pug mill at the Clayton Jug Factory, Spartanburg County, ca. 1920.
Left to right: Lewis, Jones ("Pete"), Ernest, and Albert Clayton, Evan Brown
(baby on mule), Madeline Brown, George ("G.L.") Clayton, Jake Clayton,
Javan Brown, and John Gowan Clayton (G.L.'s father). Courtesy of
Jake and Lewis Clayton.

"burning" it in the kiln, and hauling it to market.
Lewis Clayton became a specialist in burning the
ware. Pete recalled that about a hundred gallons
of ware per day were turned at the shop, and that
the family burned a kilnload of ware about once a
week and used about two hundred cords of wood
per year.

The Claytons dug clay from the river bottoms nearby. They mixed the clay with water
and ground it in a mule-drawn pug mill. The
clay had to be soaked before it was ground, and
two types of clay were often mixed together to
produce a clay with greater dry strength. The
grinding process took about an hour. Then the
clay was "blocked up" into cubes and stored until
ready to use. Before turning, the potter cut the
clay with a wire and slapped it together to work

out trapped air pockets. It took about six or seven
pounds of clay to make a one-gallon pitcher or
churn and about thirty pounds of clay to turn a
five-gallon churn. The turner was paid two cents
per gallon for his efforts. Pete learned to turn on
a foot-powered treadle wheel but started using an
electric wheel in 1938.

Pete first used an ash-based alkaline glaze consisting of beat-up glass mixed with wood ash
but gradually replaced the glass with feldspars.
Pete recalled that the ash-based glaze was hard
to melt, and that if too much glass was used the
glaze would "craze," creating fine cracks just
below the surface. Spanish whiting, a form of
calcium carbonate, was sometimes added to the
glaze to make it smoother.

Ware produced at the Clayton pottery was fired

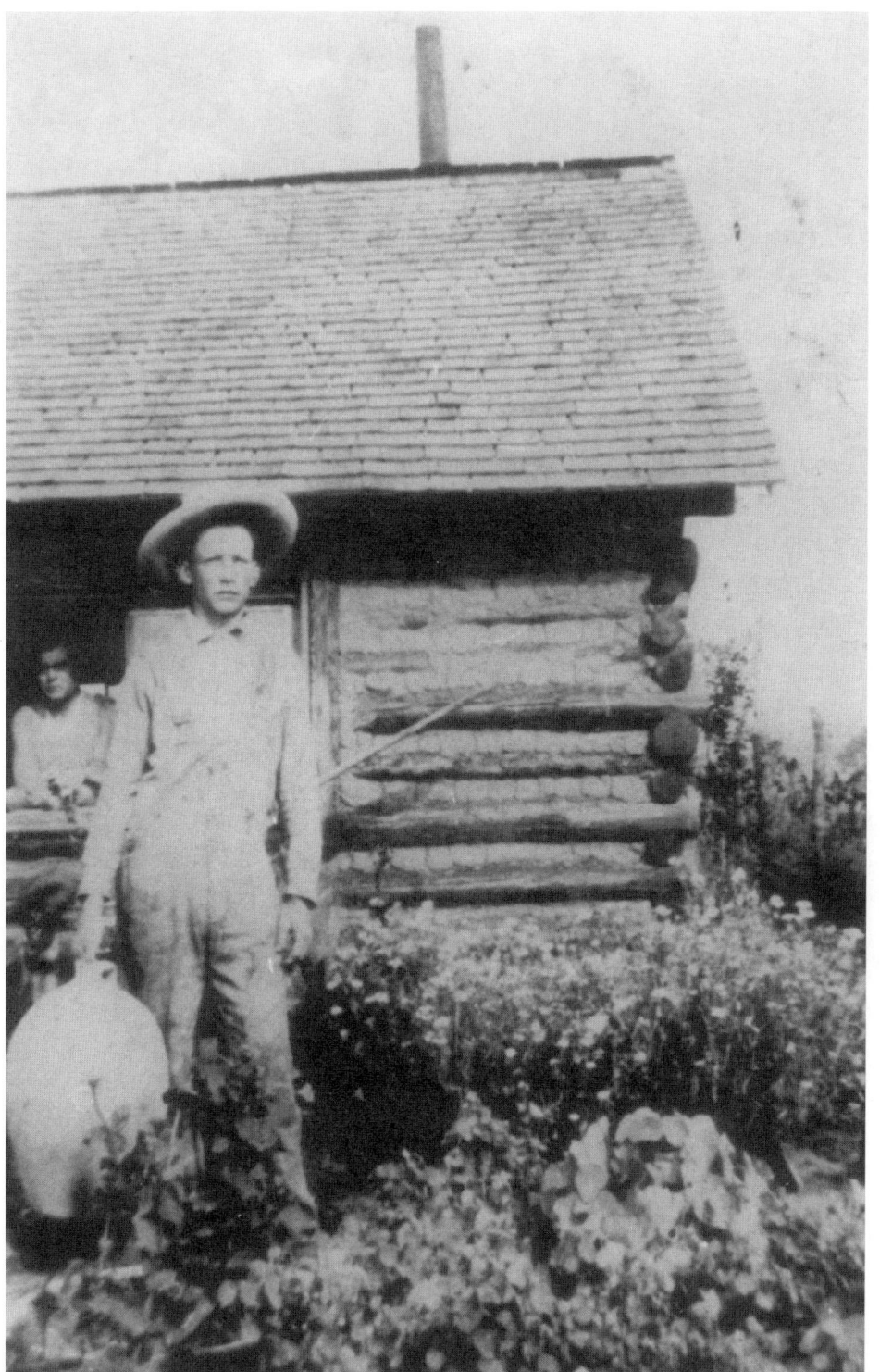

4.41 Pete Clayton with jug, Clayton Jug Factory, ca. 1920. Courtesy of Mrs. Jones ("Pete") Clayton.

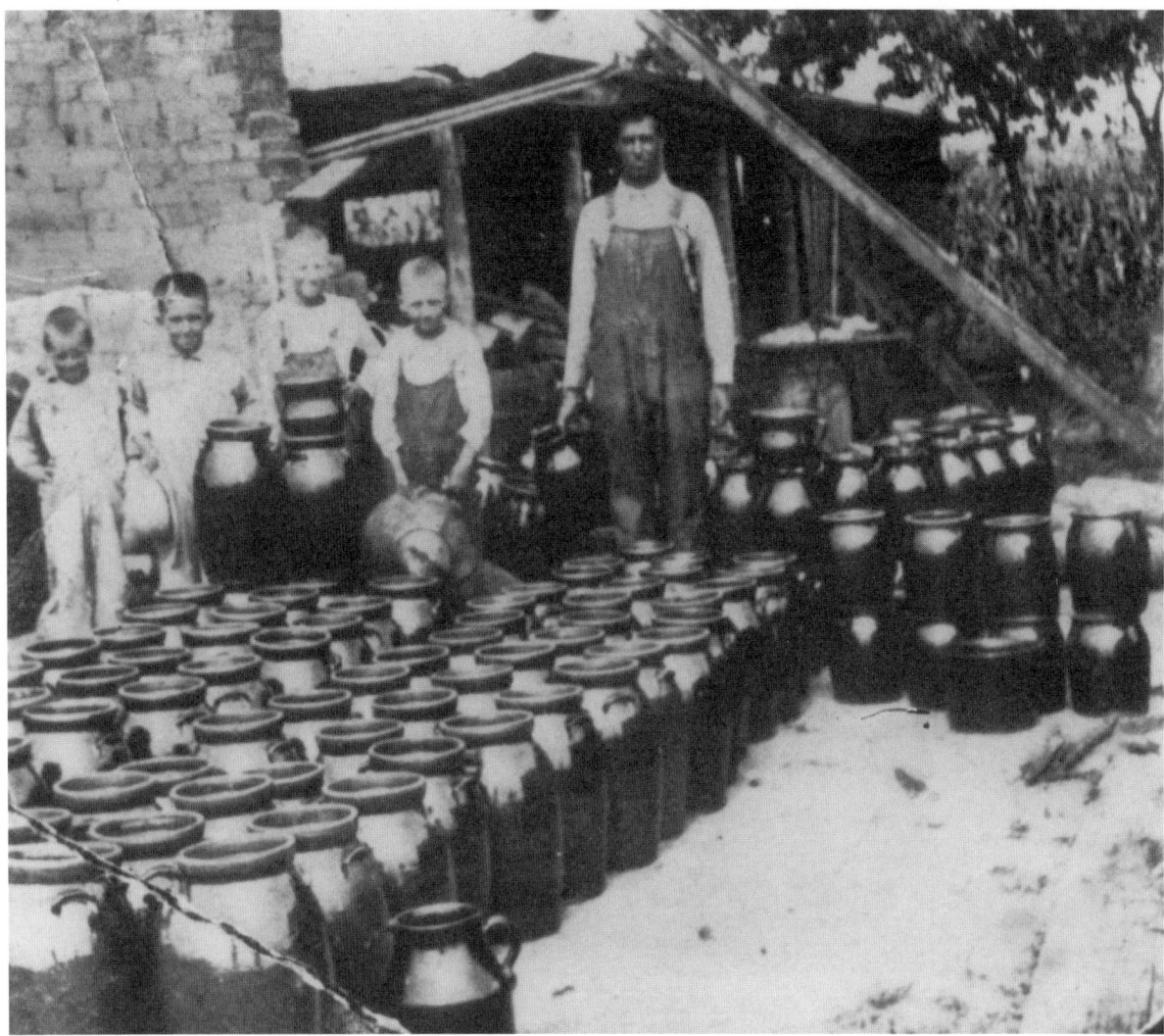

4.42   Unloading ware from the kiln at the Clayton Jug Factory, Spartanburg County, ca. 1920.
Left to right: Lewis, J.B., Ernest, Albert, and George Clayton. Courtesy of Jake and Lewis Clayton.

in a groundhog kiln. Pete Clayton described the kiln as having had a firebox at one end and a chimney opposite so that the fire went all the way through and came out the chimney. The kiln had an arched roof and a bed, or floor, of sand on which the ware was placed. Ware was stacked in the kiln.

The firing process involved building the fire up slowly at first until the ware turned cherry red. Oak was used during this initial firing stage. Quick-burning pine was introduced steadily during the final "blasting off" period until the ware became white-hot. The entire firing process took about ten to eleven hours.

Much of the finished ware produced at the pottery was hauled to Spartanburg to be sold, a trip that originally took two days by wagon. In 1917 George Clayton purchased a Model-T Ford truck to haul the ware to market, considerably shortening the trip.

In the 1920s the Claytons changed the name of their shop to Mountain View Pottery because of the beautiful view of the Blue Ridge Mountains that could be seen from the shop door. Jugs, churns, crocks, cream and milk pitchers, bean pots, slop jars, and flowerpots were produced at the Mountain View Pottery. Albert Fulbright, who managed the shop for several years, produced two basic types of stoneware—"blue ware," made with clay obtained from the Spartanburg area,

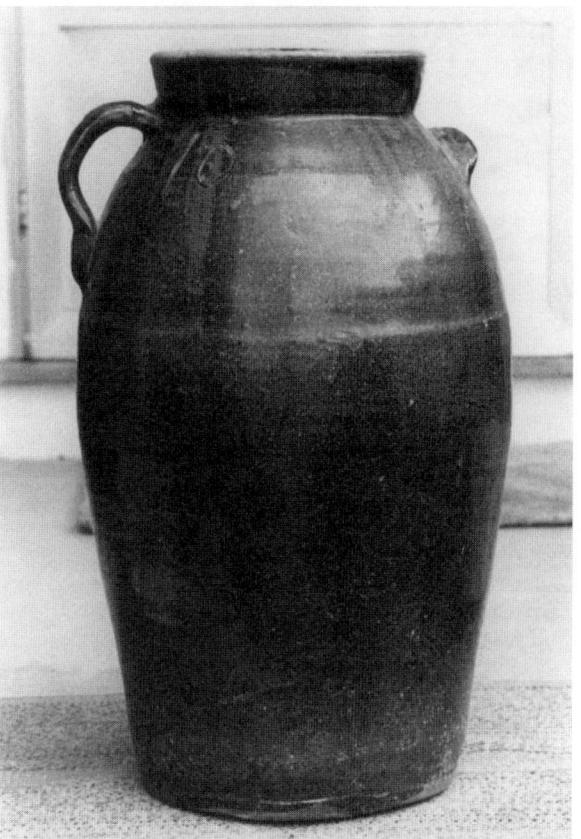

4.44 Alkaline-glazed stoneware churn, ca. 1936, Pete Clayton, Clayton Jug Factory, Holly Springs community, Spartanburg County, S.C. H 23⅛″, C 44¼″. Collection of Mrs. Jones ("Pete") Clayton.

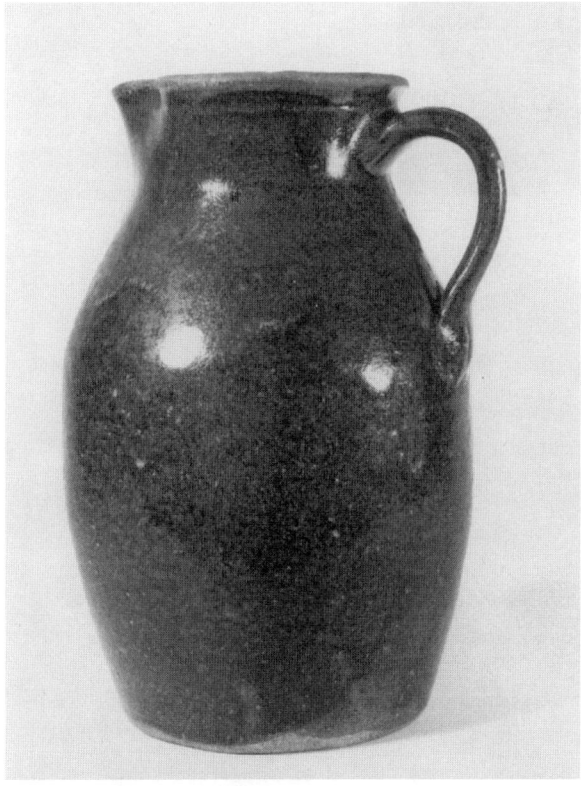

4.43 Alkaline-glazed stoneware pitcher, ca. 1910–40, Clayton Jug Factory, Holly Springs community, Spartanburg County, S.C. H 10½″, C 22″. Collection of McKissick Museum, The University of South Carolina, Columbia.

and "olive ware," a higher-fired ware made with clay from the Gaffney area.[69] Also during this period the pottery began to feature art ware and decorated tableware.

Wallace Belcher and his brother Clarence established a pottery in the Motlow Creek community of Spartanburg County in the 1930s when their father died, leaving the large family without a steady income. The Belcher pottery was also a part-time seasonal operation. Clarence Belcher ran the factory, sometimes with the aid of an assistant. Belcher produced Albany-slip-

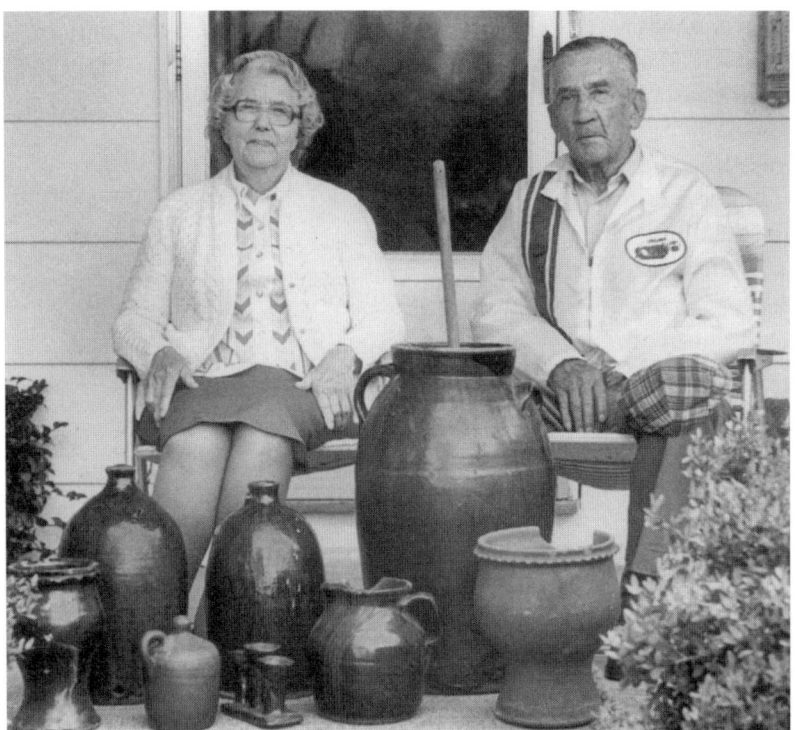

4.45 Mr. and Mrs. Jones ("Pete") Clayton with ware, 1986, Holly Springs community, Spartanburg County, S.C.

4.46 Alkaline-glazed stoneware churn and chicken waterer, ca. 1920, attributed to the Clarence Belcher Pottery, Jugtown, Spartanburg County, S.C. Collection of Mrs. Clarence Belcher.

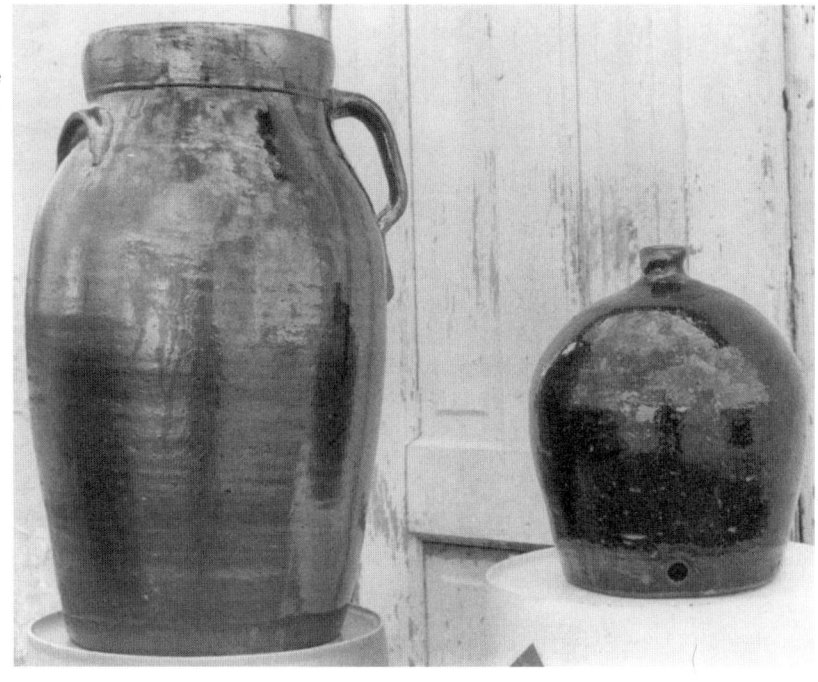

glazed jugs, butter churns, pitchers, and poultry fountains as well as earthenware flowerpots.[70]

By 1939 the shops owned by Clarence Belcher and O. J. ("Pete") Clayton were the only potteries still in operation in the Jugtown area. Both potters were using electric wheels by this time and had converted mainly to the production of gardenware. On 8 May 1940, after almost thirty years of operation, the Clayton pottery was destroyed by fire. Clarence Belcher, the last active potter in the area, was still producing pottery at his shop as late as 1945.[71]

Jugtown was South Carolina's most important upstate pottery center. Well over a dozen pottery shops were established in the Jugtown area over a span of almost a century, from about 1850 to 1940. Although no definitive connection has been established between the Jugtown potteries and the earlier Edgefield District stoneware tradition, a relationship between the two stoneware centers seems likely. The greatest migration of potters out of Edgefield took place during the second quarter of the nineteenth century, just prior to the emergence of the Jugtown stoneware tradition.

By the turn of the century stoneware potteries had been established throughout the South Carolina upcountry. Turners from Georgia, North Carolina, and other southern states came to South Carolina to work at these late nineteenth- and early twentieth-century potteries. These potters brought new stoneware forms and production techniques to the South Carolina shops.

Laurens County

Harvey M. and Joseph D. ("Jug") Johnson owned a shop in Laurens County at Lanford. Joe Johnson appeared in the 1880 Laurens County census in Youngs Township with the occupation "making jugs." Joe was living in the household of his brother Harvey, who was listed as a farmer. Both men were born in North Carolina.[72] Their father, potter Amon L. Johnson, was active at Jugtown in Catawba County, North Carolina, during the mid to late nineteenth century. Catawba Valley influence is evident in the Johnson ware produced at Lanford (see Figure 4.47).

Joe turned at the shop, and Harvey secured clay for the operation from the Enoree River near Beaver Dam Church from property owner J. P. Grey. Harvey's wife, Parthenia, made molded tobacco pipes that were sold for five cents each. The Johnsons used a glass-based alkaline glaze on the

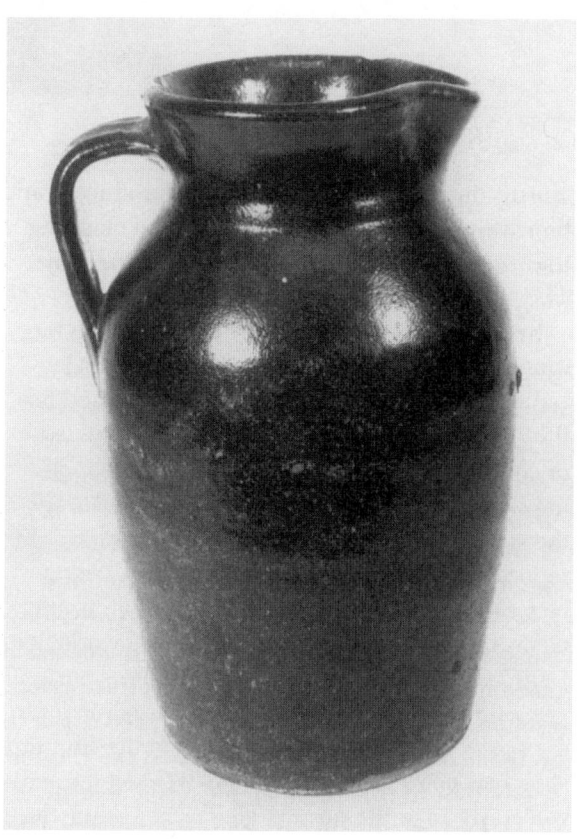

4.47 Alkaline-glazed stoneware pitcher, ca. 1880, attributed to Joe ("Jug") Johnson, Lanford Station, Laurens County, S.C. H 10¼", C 21⅛". Collection of James Henry Riddle, Jr.

4.48 Salt-glazed stoneware flower vases, ca. 1890–1900, Drury Boykin Cade Pottery, Mt. Carmel, McCormick County, S.C. Collection of Sallie Thomas Cade.

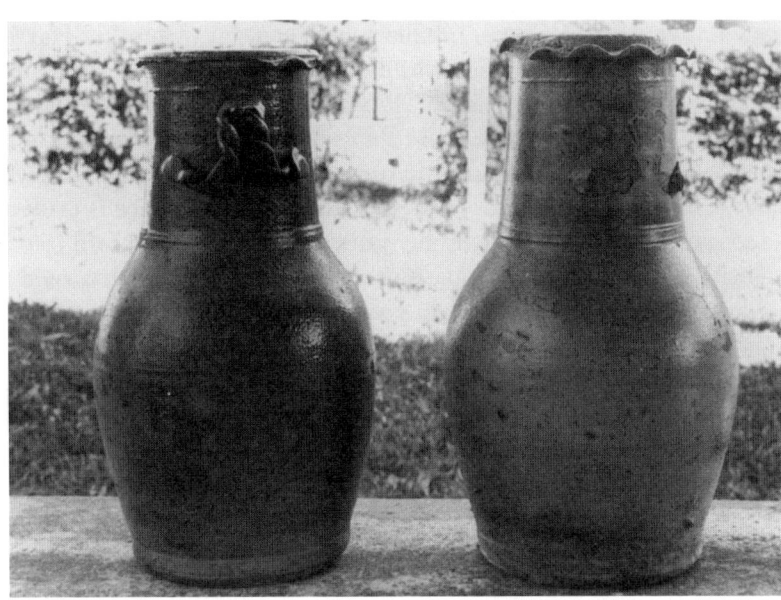

churns, jars, and pitchers that they produced, and their ware is often marked by the blue clouding that results from the use of rutile-bearing clays. They also made unglazed flowerpots.

By about 1920 the Johnsons had begun to hire itinerant potters to turn ware at the shop. Mac-Gruder Bishop of Georgia reportedly turned for the Johnsons and may have introduced the use of cobalt decoration to Lanford. Cobalt banding was routinely applied to ware produced at the shop. North Carolina potter Albert Fulbright reportedly turned for the Johnsons. Maryland Hewell, youngest son of Eli Hewell of Gillsville, Georgia, and Maryland's son Jack also worked at Lanford from 1924 to 1928.[73] During this period gasoline-powered wheels were first used. Prior to the 1920s all of the ware produced at the Lanford shop had been turned on an old-fashioned treadle wheel. By 1930 the turners had begun using electric wheels and a mechanized glass beater, and Harvey Johnson had replaced the wagon that had formerly been used to haul ware with a truck. The Johnsons' shop was closed in the early 1930s when Joe and Harvey died.

McCormick County

Although salt-glazed stoneware rarely appears in South Carolina, such ware was produced by at least one late nineteenth-century pottery shop in McCormick County. Drury Boykin Cade of Georgia established a pottery and brick factory at Mt. Carmel in McCormick County in about 1885. He hired two men from Elberton, Georgia, immigrants who had formerly been employed in the Elberton marble works, to operate the factory. Cade was from Elbert County, Georgia, and had also owned a pottery shop there. Sally Cade, Drury Cade's granddaughter, recalled vividly her childhood memories of the brick kiln at her grandfather's Mt. Carmel shop.

The kiln . . . that thing was a lot longer than this house, and much wider. And it was high up . . . I reckon, it looked like, I imagine, an old-fashioned boarding house or something. I mean, it just had brick all on the outside. But when it burnt, every other brick looked like it had an electric light in it, you know. Looked like there were windows all the way up . . . all the way up. And it must have been—ooh, it was real tall. I couldn't tell you how tall it was, but you had to hold your head back to see the top. It was covered up, up at the top, you know. All that had to be covered up, you see, all that was burnt. They had the mud there, you see. They made the brick, and put it together.[74]

This is apparently a description of a scove kiln used to fire bricks. The scove kiln was put together from unburned bricks and then disassembled after firing.

Several freed blacks worked at the Cade pottery and brick factory. Sally Cade recalled that one of

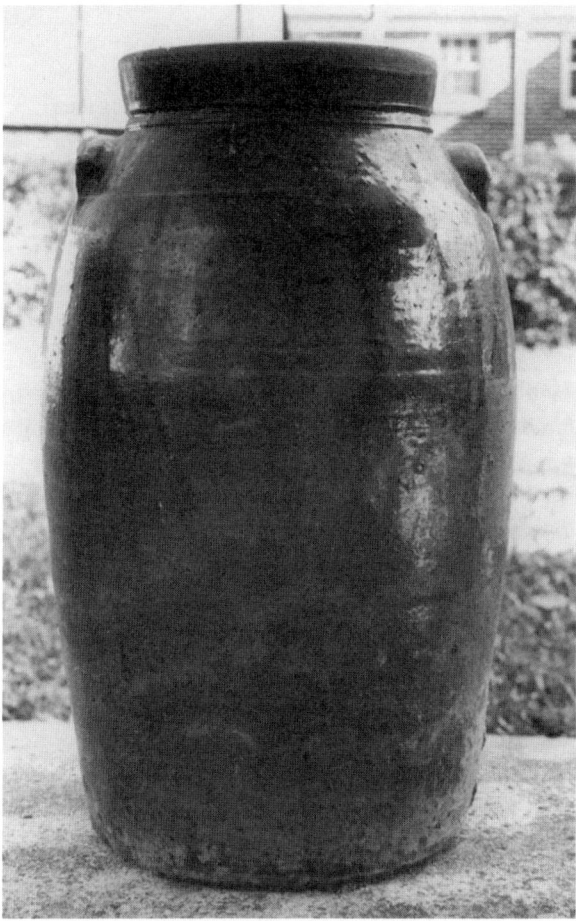

4.49   Alkaline-glazed stoneware churn, ca. 1890–1900, attributed to the Drury Boykin Cade Pottery, Mt. Carmel, McCormick County, S.C. H 16¾″, C 33¼″. Collection of Sallie Thomas Cade.

these men had fired the kiln: "I can remember one old man, that . . . old colored man. He was the tallest, blackest man I ever saw in my whole life, . . . that had charge of firing the kiln, you know. See, it had to be fired . . . somebody stayed back there day and night. They didn't leave."[75]

According to Miss Cade, her grandfather sold the brick but gave away the pottery produced at the factory. Thin-walled symmetrical cream pitchers, sugar bowls, and vases made at the Cade pottery bear the incised letters LAC in script (arranged concentrically, with a small L in the center, overlapped by a larger A, within a still larger C). These vessels have gray to tan mottled salt glazes and are decorated with fluted rims and applied clay braids (see Figure 4.48). Miss Cade claimed that they were made by her grandfather and that the letters LAC were the initials of her grandmother, Lura A. Cade.

Slip-glazed churns with horizontally placed lug handles, wide-collared rims, and interior lid ledges were also produced at the Cade pottery (see Figure 4.49). One large churn attributed to the pottery has two opposing loop handles rather than lug handles. This vessel is similar in form to ware produced by members of the Becham family of Crawford County, Georgia. A nineteenth-century potter named Cade who reportedly worked at Petersburg, Elbert County, Georgia, is listed in Burrison's checklist of Georgia potters. This information apparently is a reference to Drury Boykin Cade.[76]

Oconee County

Four brothers, Samuel Knox, James Francis, Jesse Clarence, and McCurry ("Mack") Neville, were manufacturing pottery at West Union, Oconee County, in 1900. The Nevilles used clay obtained from below Cane Creek in the production of Albany-slip-glazed stoneware jugs, churns, bowls, pitchers, jars, teapots, coffeepots, and flowerpots. Some ware produced at the shop was reportedly

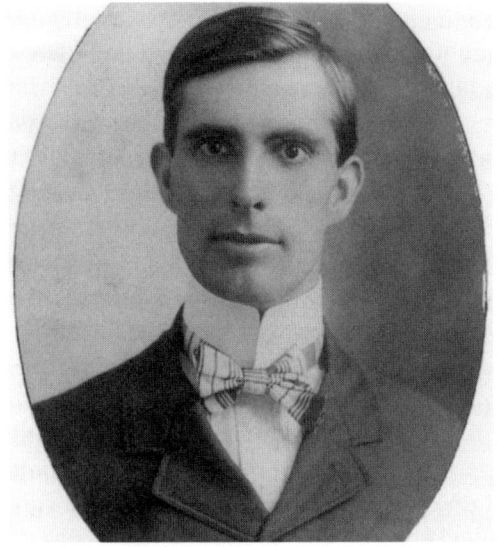

4.50   James Francis Neville, ca. 1900. Photograph by Campus Camera, Clemson, S.C. Courtesy of Mrs. Rieppe Neville Mays.

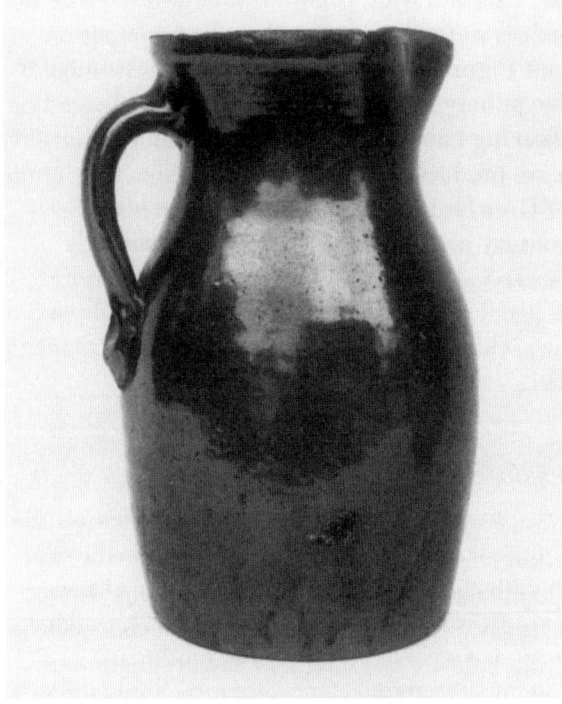

4.51   Alkaline-glazed stoneware pitcher, ca. 1900, Neville Pottery, West Union, Oconee County, S.C. Collection of Mrs. Rieppe Neville Mays.

glazed with a mixture of hickory ash, sand, and salt. The Nevilles also attempted to produce majolica and Rockingham ware but soon found that their clay was too brown for the production of fine earthenware. A Rebecca pitcher in the Charleston Museum collection from the Neville Pottery attributed to potter C. L. Rivers, trained in Trenton, New Jersey, is an example of the earthenware produced at the pottery. The Neville Pottery was in operation for about twenty-five years and was discontinued shortly after 1900.

York and Lancaster Counties

Potters trained in North Carolina established three shops in York County during the early 1900s. Martin Alexander Helton established a pottery in the York County community of Sharon. M. A. Helton was a member of the Hilton clan of North Carolina. David Hoffman's wife, Irene Hope Hoffman, was M. A. Helton's granddaughter. David Hoffman's mother-in-law, Mrs. R. W. Hope, was a first cousin of Clara Maude Hilton of Catawba County, North Carolina, so M.A. Helton apparently was the son of either Catawba Valley potter Claude Hilton or of Claude's brother Shufford Hilton. Mrs. Hope was also related to another Catawba Valley clay clan, the Shufford family.[77]

According to David Hoffman, Helton noticed the good stoneware clay deposits available in the Sharon area when he came through selling a wagonload of ware, so he decided to settle in York County. Unlike his relatives in North Carolina, who began making a more artistic pottery in the early 1900s, M. A. Helton produced only traditional stoneware in South Carolina. Several examples of Helton's work—churns and storage jars stamped with his initials MAH—are still in the Sharon community. One of these is a squat, ovoid storage jar with a dark olive-brown alkaline glaze and two opposing horizontal lug handles (Figure 4.52).

Helton was a transplanted North Carolina potter. The degree of Catawba Valley influence on Helton's work is evident in the fact that North Carolina folk pottery scholars and collectors have incorrectly attributed his ware to potter Marcus A. Holly of Lincoln County, North Carolina.[78]

William Franklin Outen established a pottery at Lancaster, South Carolina, in the early 1900s. Outen was the brother-in-law of potter James C. ("Jug Jim") Broom of Union County, North Carolina. The Outen family moved to Union County from South Carolina in about 1860. W. F. Outen worked with Jug Jim and also had a shop of his own before coming to South Carolina. A number of salt-glazed stoneware vessels stamped "W. F. Outen / Monroe / NC" are extant.[79]

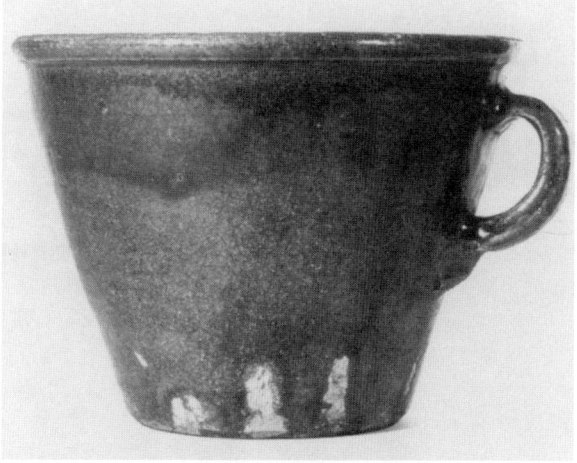

4.53 Alkaline-glazed stoneware milk pan or cream riser, ca. 1915, attributed to the W. F. Outen Pottery, Catawba, York County, S.C. H 5¾″, C 24¾″. Collection of the Charleston Museum, Charleston, S.C.

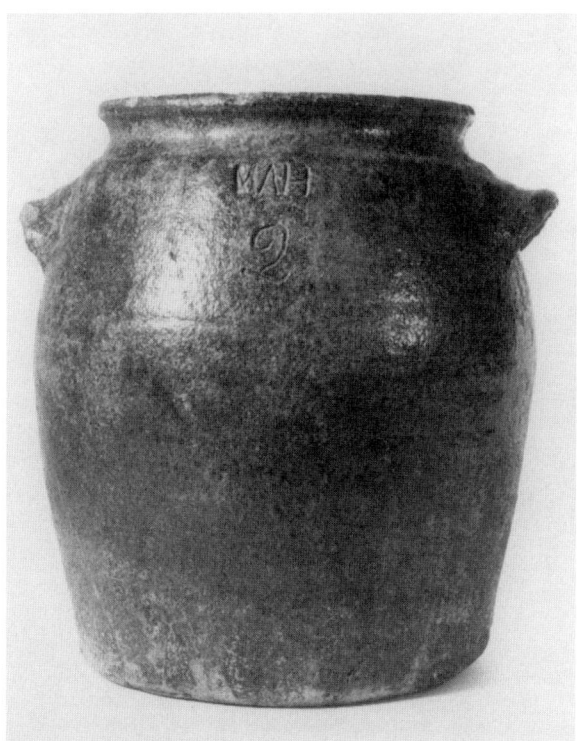

4.52 Alkaline-glazed stoneware preserve jar, ca. 1900, Martin A. Helton, Sharon, S.C. H 9⅝″, C 27⅝″. Stamped: M A H / 2 (front, between handles). Collection of McKissick Museum, The University of South Carolina, Columbia.

By 1915 Outen had established a second shop, the Catawba Pottery Company, at nearby Catawba Junction in York County. An alkaline-glazed stoneware milk crock in the Charleston Museum collection is attributed to the Hellam Pottery at Lancaster (see Figure 4.53). Hellam probably purchased the Lancaster pottery shop from Outen when he moved to Catawba. Catawba Junction was located at the junction of the Seaboard and Southern Railroad lines, five miles from the town of Lesslie. Here Outen produced stoneware glazed with a mixture of wood ashes, glass, and clay, which fired to a dark glossy brown. He made flowerpots as well as stoneware churns and jars. Outen returned to North Carolina in 1922 and established a pottery at Matthews in Mecklenburg County. E. C. Collins purchased the Catawba Pottery Company from Outen in about 1917 and hired George Fletcher to operate it for him. Fletcher, who had worked at several potteries in the Edgefield area, adopted an industrial approach to pottery production at Catawba. He had two flowerpot machines and produced flowerpots ranging in size from two to twelve inches in diameter. With the assistance of

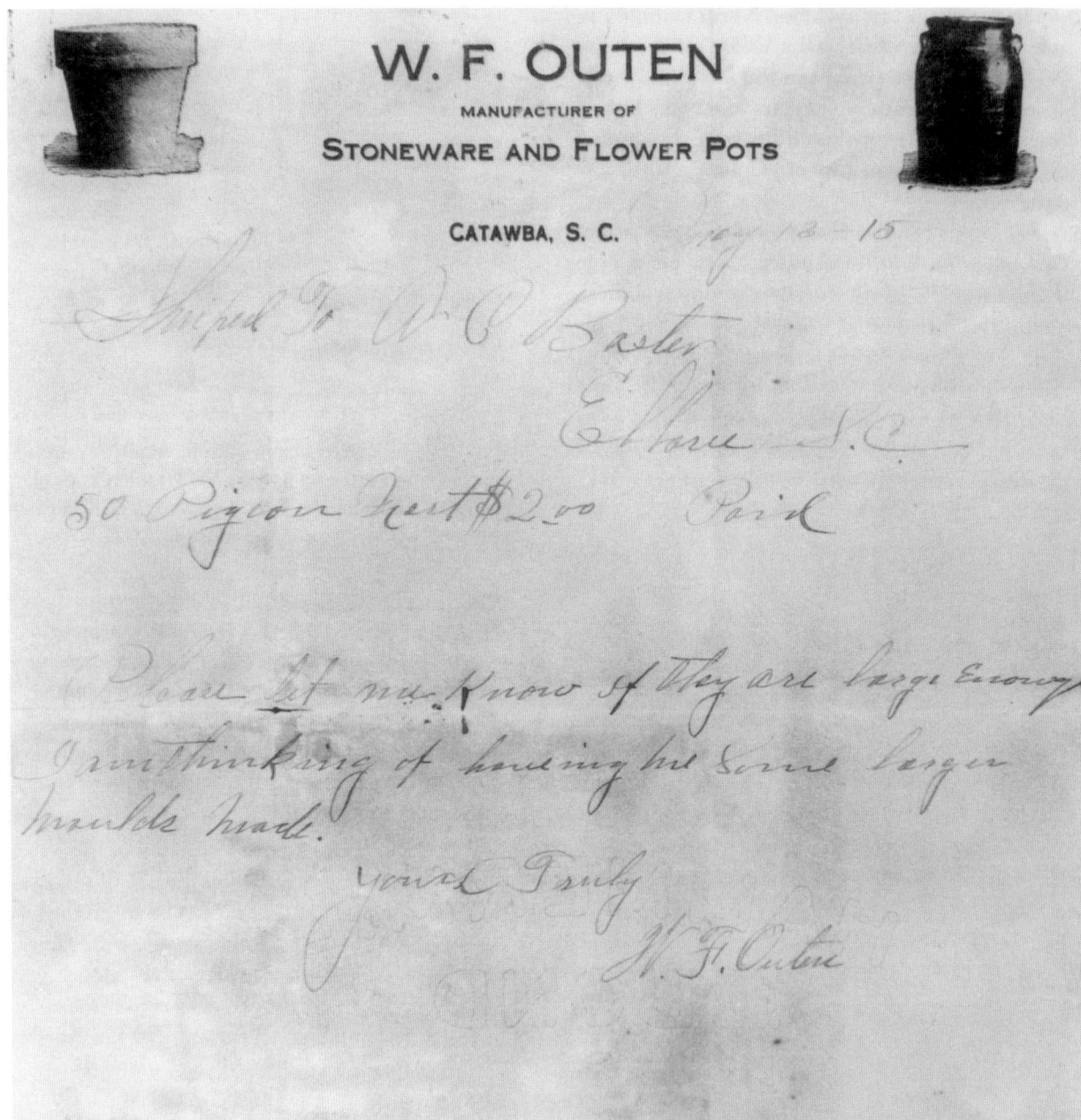

W. F. OUTEN

MANUFACTURER OF

STONEWARE AND FLOWER POTS

CATAWBA, S. C. *May 13 - 15*

Shiped To W C Baxter

&

Elbree S.C.

50 Pigeon Nest $2.00 Paid

Please let me know if they are large Enough I am thinking of having me some larger moulds made.

Yours Truly

W. F. Outen

4.54   W. F. Outen Pottery sales receipt, 13 May 1915, Catawba, S.C. Baxter Papers, South Caroliniana Library, University of South Carolina, Columbia, with thanks to Harvey Teal.

four helpers, he is said to have been able to turn out fourteen hundred six-inch pots in five hours.

Claude L. Bennett also ran a pottery at Lesslie, South Carolina. Son of George Bennett, C.L. Bennett had worked for the Brumbeloes at Chalker in Washington County, Georgia, and for Larry Daugherty (var. Dougherty) of Denton, Texas. For a year or so during the 1930s he also ran an "old-fashioned" shop located just west of Jonesboro in Clayton County, Georgia.[80] Two men named Lesslie and Glasscock owned the shop run by Bennett at Lesslie. Bennett produced flowerpots, rabbit dishes, martin jugs, and poultry fountains as well as stoneware jugs and jars. Most of the ware produced at the Lesslie pottery was unglazed, and some painted tourist ware was produced at the shop.

Kershaw County

Two of South Carolina's last traditional pottery operations were located in and near the town of Bethune in Kershaw and Chesterfield counties. The oldest of these, known as the Bethune pottery, was founded by O. E. Brumbeloe. Oscar Early Brumbeloe was the son of Camelius Brumbeloe of Georgia. Oscar and his brothers Walter and Newt had trained in the Jugtown area (Upson/Pike counties) and in about 1910 established the Brumbeloe pottery at Chalker in Washington County, Georgia. O. E. Brumbeloe came to the Bethune area in the late 1920s. He made and sold churns, flowerpots, jugs, bowls, and pitchers at Bethune, ranging in price from fifteen cents a gallon for pots, twenty cents a gallon for churns, to twenty-five cents a gallon for bowls and pitchers.[81]

A 1955 newspaper article that appeared in the *State Magazine* focuses on Guy Daugherty, the second owner of the Bethune pottery.

One of the few remaining "old time potters" in the entire Southeast is Guy Daugherty of RFD 2, Bethune.

This man, who will be 77 years young on his next birthday, made his first piece of saleable pottery in 1888 when he was only ten years old. Since then, he estimates that he has created and sold more than two million pieces of pottery.

Daugherty was born in Texas but moved to South Carolina as a young man. He came to Bethune as assistant to O. E. Brumbaloe who founded the Bethune Pottery Works in the 1920's. Daugherty bought Brumbaloe out 12 years ago and, with his two assistants, LeRoy Waters and Marion Steen, is still turning out useful and decorative products from South Carolina clay.

In addition to making souvenirs of the Palmetto State to sell to tourists who pass his U.S. Highway 1 establishment, Daugherty has shipped flue thimbles, rabbit crocks and flower pots to 47 of the 48 states. Only Oregon remains "unsold." Besides these finished items, Bethune Pottery sells modelling clay to the schools of Greenville, Columbia and Charleston, and to the U.S. Army at Fort Jackson, among other customers.

Daugherty calculates that the clay pit from which his predecessor and himself have been excavating clay will hold out for "about another hundred years, after which I plan to retire from the pottery business anyhow." He is a Mason, a Lion and a member of the American Ceramic Society. For the past 20 years, he has traveled to the New York State Fair regularly to demonstrate pottery working to citizens of the Empire State.

Although he uses an electric turning wheel primarily, Daugherty will occasionally use a "kick wheel" (one with which the power is supplied by foot) which was made in Atlanta in 1872.[82]

Daugherty bought the Bethune pottery from Brumbeloe in 1943 (O. E. Brumbeloe died in 1944) and operated it until the mid to late 1950s.

Rufus Outen and Horace Ratteree of North Carolina acquired the Bethune pottery in 1959 and hired James ("Otto") Brown and his son Otto Jr. ("Jimmy") to turn ware for them. Otto Brown was a fifth generation Georgia potter and the son of James Osborne Brown of Atlanta. Otto and his brothers William O. ("Willy"), Charles Robert ("Bobby"), Davis P., and Evan Javan ("Jay") Brown turned ware at pottery shops in Georgia, Alabama, Florida, South Carolina, and

North Carolina. Otto and Jimmy had worked in the Pine Springs community near Sulligent, Alabama, in Lamar County and at Smithville, Mississippi, Gillsville, Georgia, and North Augusta, South Carolina, before coming to Bethune. Otto turned larger ware such as jars and churns, while Jimmy specialized in smaller pieces. Otto's brother Javan, Otto's wife, Emmaus Avery Brown, and Jimmy's wife, Francis, also worked at the Bethune shop.[83] The women did the finish work, such as putting handles and legs on the "washpots." Francis recalls that they first produced washpots at Gillsville, Georgia. She also remembers Emmaus putting the faces on the face jugs made at the shop. Francis looked after the shop on weekends when Outen and Ratteree were in North Carolina.[84]

In 1962 Otto established his own pottery shop in Chesterfield County just across the Lynches River from the Bethune pottery (see Figure 4.55). Otto, Jimmy, and Javan produced gardenware— Rebekah pitchers, flowerpots, and urns—at this

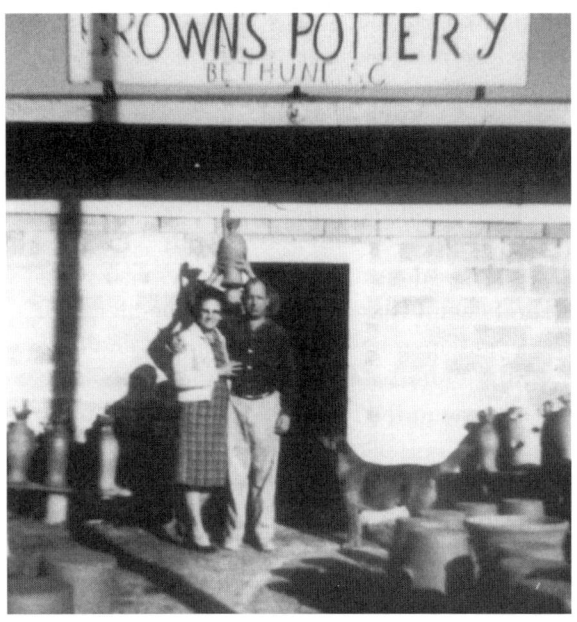

4.55   Emmaus Brown and son Jimmy at the Brown Pottery in Chesterfield County, January 1963. Courtesy of Frances Thompson.

pottery.[85] During the same period Thomas Melton purchased the Bethune pottery from Outen and Ratteree. Melton was not a potter himself, but he employed LeRoy Waters and Marion Steen who had assisted Daugherty during the 1950s. A personal conflict subsequently arose between Otto Brown and Thomas Melton regarding competition between the two potteries. Melton made tentative plans to sell his Bethune pottery operation to Leroy Stephens, who had been an employee there, but later refused to sell to Stephens when he found out that Stephens was planning to marry Otto Brown's granddaughter, Annette. Melton then sold the pottery to Otis Norris with the understanding that Norris would never sell the property to the Brown family. Nevertheless, in 1979 Stephens purchased the Bethune pottery from Norris. Although pottery is no longer produced at the Bethune shop, Stephens continues to sell local Bethune clay to potters throughout South Carolina.[86]

By the time the Browns arrived in Bethune in the late 1950s that shop was specializing in unglazed gardenware. The ware was hand-turned (with the exception of flowerpots) and was fired in an oil-burning kiln. Stoneware churns and jugs glazed with commercially prepared Albany slip were still produced occasionally, but alkaline-glazed stoneware was no longer being made. Otto and Jimmy Brown, who had worked in North Augusta before arriving in the Bethune area, were the last active folk potters in the Edgefield area, and their pottery shop near Bethune appears to have been the last traditional pottery operation in South Carolina.

The economic and social upheavals caused by the Civil War greatly affected the stoneware industry in South Carolina, resulting in the eventual decline of the factory system in Edgefield. A shift in pottery activity occurred in South Carolina during the second half of the nineteenth century as new regional pottery traditions emerged. Former Edgefield potters had established new stoneware centers in the Richland

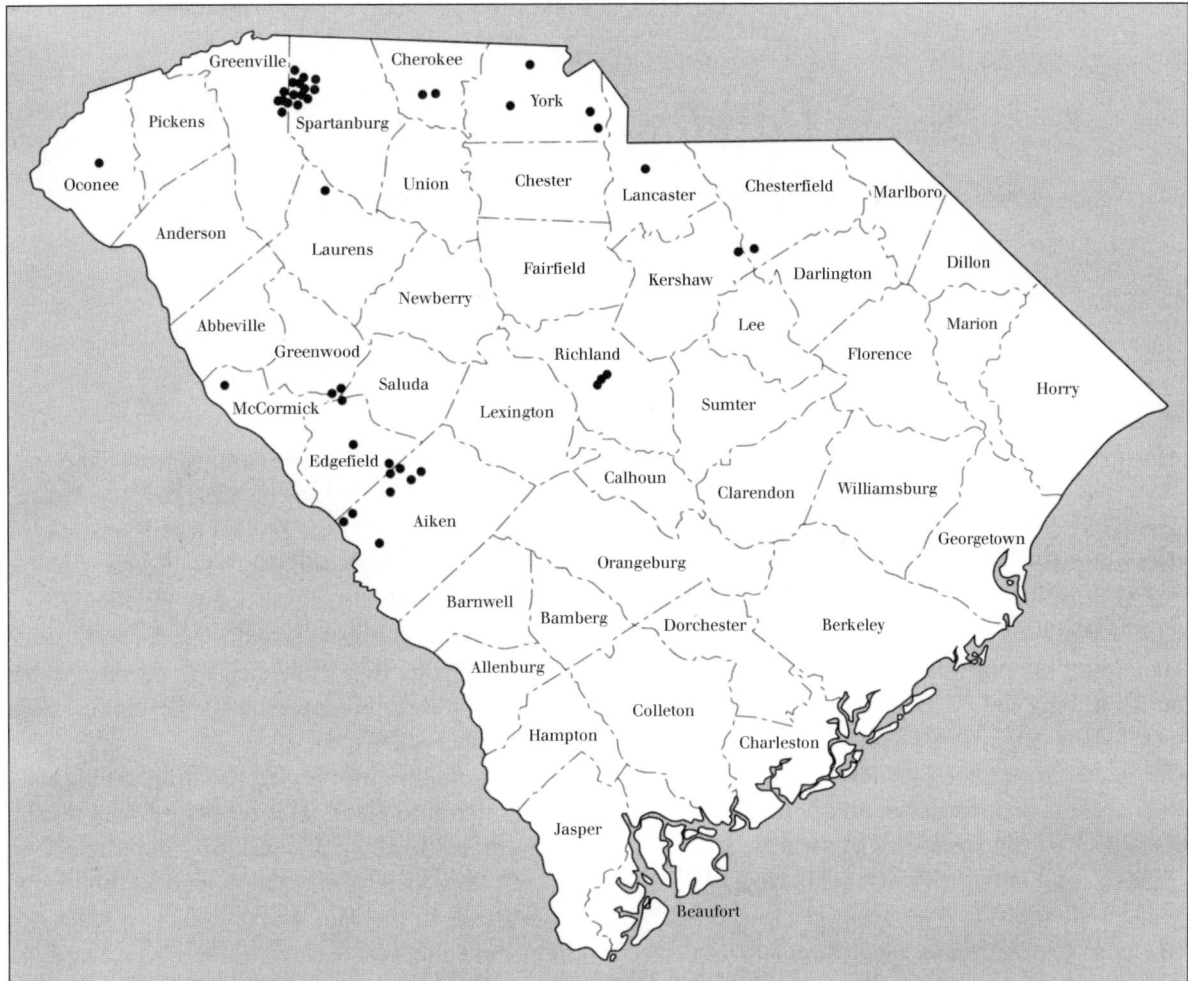

4.56   South Carolina stoneware potteries by county, ca. 1800–1970.

and Union Districts (present-day Richland and Cherokee counties) by 1850. During the same period another important pottery center with possible ties to Edgefield was emerging in the Greenville-Spartanburg county area. By the turn of the century potters from Georgia and North Carolina had established shops in five additional South Carolina counties: Laurens, McCormick, Oconee, York, and Lancaster (see Figure 4.56).[87]

Alkaline-glazed stoneware initially appears at these newly established shops, but by the early decades of the twentieth century most South Carolina potters had begun to use commercially prepared glazes and modern production methods. Gasoline- and electric-powered potter's wheels gradually replaced the earlier foot-powered treadle or "kick wheel," and oil- and gas-fired kilns took the place of traditional wood-fired groundhog kilns. A gradual changeover from the production of alkaline-glazed stoneware to the wholesale manufacture of unglazed garden-ware followed. Throughout the South, folk potters adapted their operations to these new production methods and ware types. This evolution in vernacular pottery reflected a greater pattern of change taking place in southern society.

CHAPTER FIVE

South Carolina Stoneware Glazes and Decorative Treatments

Alkaline Glaze

The characteristic feature of southern stoneware that most distinguishes it from stoneware produced in other areas of the United States is glaze type. Alkaline glaze was the principal type of glaze used on stoneware produced in the lower South during the first half of the nineteenth century. While alkaline glaze is the major feature by which much southern stoneware may be identified, a concise description and definition of the glaze is difficult. Ceramics historians, archaeologists, and decorative arts scholars have often incorrectly identified alkaline-glazed stoneware. Much of the confusion regarding alkaline glaze is due to its seemingly endless variations in color and texture. Alkaline-glazed stoneware produced in South Carolina alone ranges in color from pale gray-green and straw-yellow to olive-brown and black, and in texture from smooth and glassy to rough or sandy. Glazes may be distributed evenly across the surface of the pot, or they may run and agglutinate in thick, vertical drips along the surface.

Southern potters developed several variants of the traditional "ash and sand" alkaline glaze. These glaze types are classified according to the type of flux used. The wood ash version typically ranges in color from pale green to dark green in reduction, and from cream or tan to brown-black

in oxidation. A variegated and semitransparent glaze texture marked by vertical drips or runs along the length of the pot is characteristic of glazes containing wood ash (see Figure 5.1). Although all alkaline glazes contain some lime, the use of slaked lime in place of the wood ash usually results in a smoother, more uniform surface and a light tan-green or yellow-green glaze color (see Figure 5.2).

Many factors influenced the final appearance of the alkaline glaze. The types and amounts of ingredients in the glaze mixture, the manner in which they were prepared, as well as the firing conditions in the kiln determined to a great extent the color and texture of the glaze. The folk potter utilized locally available ingredients in his clay body and glazes, and each potter developed his own glaze recipes through trial and error. Particular glaze formulas are often associated with an individual potter or pottery center. The lime glaze, for example, was used extensively by potters in Washington, Crawford, and White counties in Georgia, important early centers of southern alkaline-glazed stoneware production.

X-ray fluorescence analysis of stoneware fragments from the Matthew Duncan site in Bastrop County, Texas, the James Kirbee site in Montgomery County, Texas, the Pound Pottery site in Randolph County, Alabama, and the Miles Mill and Rhodes-Seigler sites in Edgefield illustrates

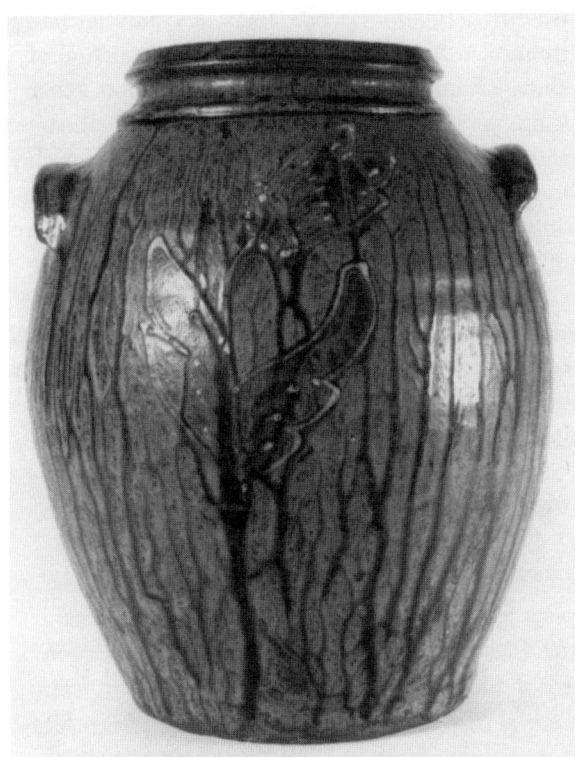

one from the Pound site most closely resembles the Chinese celadon glaze in color due to its high silica content and kaolin-rich clay body. It is light blue-green in color with a smooth, glassy transparent texture. Like the Duncan sample, it has a light gray clay body. The Rhodes-Seigler sherd has a smooth-textured olive brown glaze and a clay body that fired to a buff-brown on one side and to gray on the opposite side. A sixth stoneware fragment from the George Donkel site in Buncombe County, North Carolina, also included

5.1   Slip-decorated alkaline-glazed stoneware storage jar, ca. 1850, Collin Rhodes Factory, Shaw's Creek, Edgefield District, S.C. H 14⅛″, C 37⅜″. The presence of wood ash in the glaze mixture accounts for the drippy glaze texture of this jar. Collection of McKissick Museum, The University of South Carolina, Columbia.

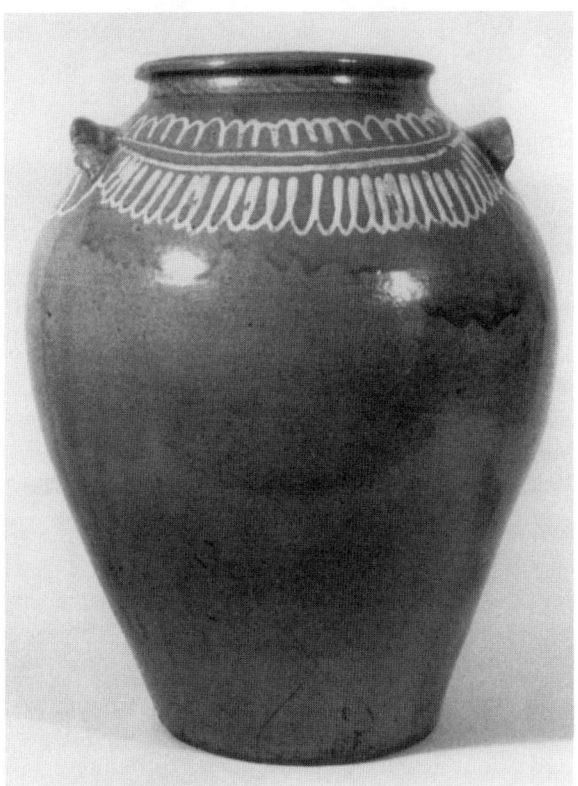

the effects of the addition of calcium or lime to the glaze formula. The glazes on each of these sherds tested as having a high calcium content, but they exhibit a variety of glaze colors and textures. The glaze sample from the Duncan site is mottled with a light gray-green glaze color and a light gray clay body, while the Kirbee sample has a dark, mottled olive-green glaze with a dark gray clay body. The Kirbee and Miles Mill samples are similar in color and texture, and both have dark gray clay bodies. Of these five glaze samples, the

5.2   Slip-decorated alkaline-glazed stoneware jar, ca. 1850, Thomas Chandler Factory, Kirksey's Crossroads, Edgefield District, S.C. H 18½″, C 50½″. Chandler may have produced this smooth, light gray-green glaze by adding silica-rich quartzite or feldspar to his finely ground glaze mixture. Collection of Dr. and Mrs. Charles M. Webb.

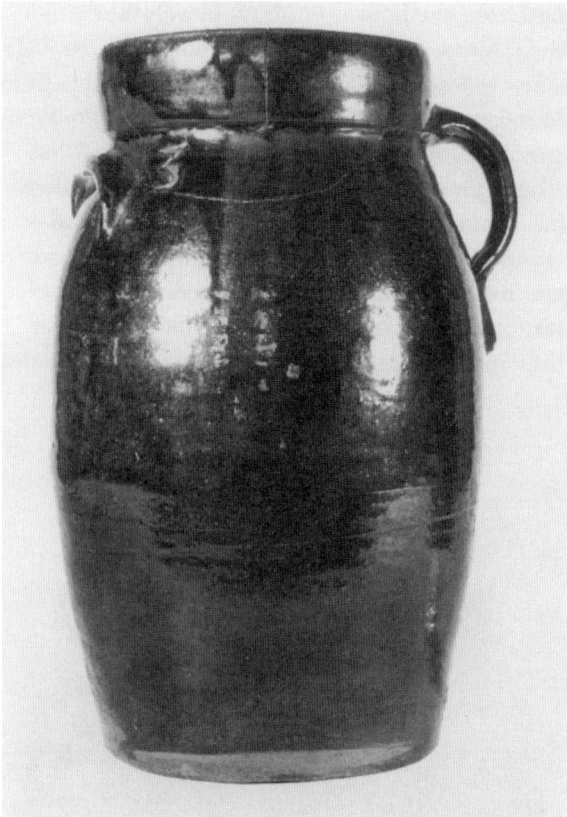

5.3   Alkaline-glazed stoneware churn with "cinder glaze," ca. 1920, attributed to the Tapp family, Spartanburg County, S.C. H 15″, C 31 ½″. Stamped: 3 (right of slab handle). Collection of Kenneth and Clarice Tapp.

in the X-ray fluorescence analysis, exhibits a very high iron content in the glaze mixture. Although the body clay fired to a light gray color, the glaze, containing a high proportion of iron, fired to a glossy black. The results of the X-ray analysis and visual inspection of these sherds demonstrate that the mineral content of the clay body (most notably, iron content) and the conditions under which a particular vessel is fired, as well as the types and amounts of ingredients used in the glaze formula, all influence glaze color and texture (see Appendix 4).[1]

The smooth, blue-green celadon-type glaze

used by Edgefield potter Thomas Chandler is thought to have contained a large proportion of silica. Chandler stamped some of his pots FLINT WARE, perhaps in reference to the use of silica-rich feldspar or quartzite in the glaze and/or clay body of his ware.[2] Fine milling and sorting probably also contributed to the smooth, even texture of Chandler's glazes.

Folk potters in South Carolina utilized a wide range of alkaline-glaze formulas. The dark "paint rock" glaze, produced by adding ground limonite or hematite to the glaze mixture, was used in Crawford County, Georgia, and in Buncombe County, North Carolina. Ware with similar glazes was also produced in the Horse Creek valley of Edgefield (see Figure 4.18). In the Union-Cherokee and Spartanburg-Greenville county pottery centers of South Carolina, as well as the Catawba Valley of North Carolina, potters often added iron slag or cinders obtained from nearby iron furnaces to their glazes. These "cinder" glazes range in color from a dark reddish-brown to brown-black due to the presence of relatively large amounts of iron (see Figure 5.3). Use of the cinder glaze most likely originated in the Catawba Valley of North Carolina since the iron furnaces in that area predate the stoneware potteries. Cinder glazes do not appear in South Carolina until the second half of the nineteenth century. Potters at the Jesse P. Bodie factory at Kirksey's Crossroads in the Edgefield District may have added pulverized glass to their glaze mixture.[3] The glass glaze was also widely used in the Catawba Valley of North Carolina.

The temperature at which ware was fired and the presence or absence of oxygen in the kiln during the firing process also affected the color and texture of the alkaline glaze. A highly oxidized kiln atmosphere, one in which oxygen was present in abundance, produced ware with cream, yellow, tan, and brown glaze colors. For instance, early Pottersville factory ware are typically light gray-beige or buttery yellow in color.

Ceramics scholar Georgeanna Greer suggests that these yellowish glaze colors are due to oxidation firing and the presence of very small amounts of iron and further speculates that the design of the kilns in which this newly developed stoneware was fired may have structural variations differing from later ones. A reduced kiln atmosphere, one in which there is insufficient oxygen available for complete combustion, also alters the glaze colors. In this instance, the clay bodies and glazes are robbed of their oxygen by the carbon compounds. Iron oxide present in the ware becomes beige, tan, reddish, or brown in oxidation but in reduction "gives cool colors of [pale green] gray, gray-green, blue-green or olive green."[4]

A lighter stoneware body yields a lighter glaze color. Thus, an alkaline glaze similar to the Chinese celadon glazes, containing a small amount of iron oxide, when applied to a light clay body (such as the kaolin-rich clays found in Edgefield) and fired in a reduced kiln atmosphere yields a pale, delicate lime green glaze. A darker clay body with the same glaze formula and similar firing conditions will produce a darker olive green glaze. The thick brown-black cinder glaze results from a different process. The high percentage of iron in the slag coupled with a reduced kiln atmosphere creates a saturated iron effect, which causes some of the iron to crystallize out onto the surface of the glaze where it is subject to oxidation.

Uneven heat distribution in the groundhog kiln further contributed to the variable nature of the alkaline glaze and presented special challenges for the folk potter. Ware with identical glazes varies widely in color and texture depending upon its placement in the kiln. For example, a jug by the slave potter Dave exhibits a white, drippy upper glaze and an olive green glaze below (Figure 5.4). The thick, white glaze was oxidized, while the olive green glaze was reduced. What appears to have been an entire kiln load of melted

ware, recovered from the Thomas Chandler Factory site in Edgefield, dramatically illustrates the effects of overfiring. The cylindrical jugs and pitchers are badly warped, the upper body walls having collapsed and slumped inward. Fragments of rough-textured ware with thin, runny glazes recovered from the Seigler site on Shaw's Creek in Edgefield exemplify the opposite extreme, whereby the kiln did not reach temperatures sufficient to mature or melt the glaze.

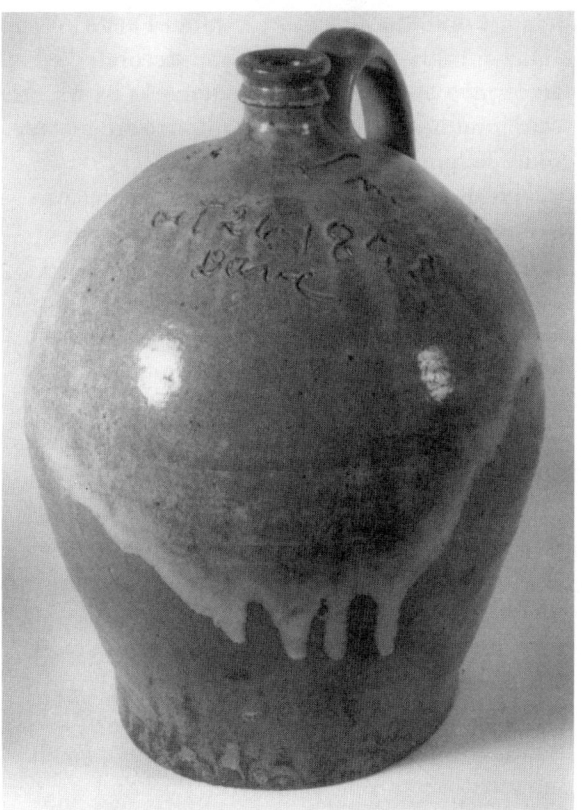

5.4 Alkaline-glazed stoneware jug, 1853, Dave (slave potter), Lewis Miles Factory, Horse Creek Valley, Edgefield District, S.C. H 15⅛″, C 37″. Incised script: Lm / oct 26 1853 / Dave. The light, drippy glaze at the upper body of this jug is the product of oxidation firing, while the darker glaze color of the lower body is the result of a reduced kiln atmosphere. Collection of Tony and Marie Shank.

Edgefield Decorated Stoneware

Widespread use of slip decoration characterized the peak period of Edgefield District stoneware production, beginning in 1840 and extending into the early 1850s. An iron-based brown-black slip and a kaolin white slip, consisting of clay mixed with water to a thick, creamy consistency, were combined or used separately in the production of a variety of decorative motifs. Four Edge-field stoneware factories—the Phoenix Factory, the Collin Rhodes Factory, the Trapp-Chandler Factory, and the Thomas Chandler Factory—specialized in the production of slip-decorated ware. Decorative motifs became trademarks by which ware produced at a particular stoneware factory could be identified.

John Burrison has observed that the decorative techniques employed in the production of Edgefield stoneware are similar to those used by English earthenware potters.[5] Most of the early Edgefield alkaline-glazed stoneware potters were of British descent. Documentary and archaeological evidence suggests that these potters were familiar with techniques of earthenware production.

Another possible influence on Edgefield decorated ware was the salt-glazed stoneware of the North. Some of the decorative motifs employed on Edgefield slip-decorated ware are similar to the cobalt decoration found on contemporaneous nineteenth-century salt-glazed stoneware produced in New England. Similar decorative treatments may also be noted. For example, on some decorated Edgefield syrup jugs and storage jars the handle attachments are outlined in brushed iron slip in a similar fashion to that used on salt-glazed cobalt-decorated stoneware.[6] There are several possibilities as to how Edgefield potters came to use these decorative techniques. A potter trained in the North may have introduced the use of this decoration to the Edgefield area. Thomas Chandler is the most likely candidate for the direct introduction of decorative techniques

from the North. Chandler enlisted in the army at Albany, New York, on 15 November 1832 and may have worked as a potter in that state.[7] Chandler was clearly a key figure in the production of Edgefield decorated stoneware, having turned ware at all of the Edgefield factories where slip decoration was widely used. Edgefield potters could also have become familiar with northern pottery styles through direct contact. River trade was important to the Edgefield area early on, and in the first half of the nineteenth century waterways became the most common means of transporting stoneware from the North. For example, the Nathan Clark Pottery of Athens, New York, owned its own boats, and salt-glazed stoneware was transported to South Carolina and Georgia as early as the 1820s by Erie Canal barge, Hudson River sloops, and ocean-going vessels.[8] The Edgefield potters repeatedly compared their stoneware to ware produced in Europe and the rest of the United States. Many of the Edgefield factory owners were knowledgeable about current developments in stoneware manufacture and were undoubtedly familiar with the methods used by the salt-glazed potters of the North.

The use of decoration on Edgefield ware may be seen as an extension of the economic effect of competition on the stoneware factories for the local market economy. The availability of rich deposits of stoneware clays in Edgefield prompted the establishment of several stoneware factories in the area during the first half of the nineteenth century. These antebellum Edgefield factories apparently produced a substantial volume of ware in comparison to other folk pottery operations in the South. Within this competitive environment, Edgefield stoneware factory owners apparently developed slip-decorated ware as part of a business strategy designed to attract customers and build up greater markets for the ware. The materials used to produce the decorative slips, kaolin and iron, were abundantly available in natural form in the local area. Since Edgefield factory owners were also slaveholders, the extra expenditures of labor to prepare these colorants would not have posed a major problem. Competition among Edgefield stoneware factory owners for markets for the ware, as well as the availability of the extra materials and labor, prompted the widespread application of slip decoration to ware produced at a few Edgefield stoneware factories.

Researchers Stephen and Terry Ferrell have recovered slip-decorated pottery fragments with no glaze visible on the surface. They believe that these are unglazed bisque sherds and assert, on the basis of their find, that Edgefield potters used a two-stage firing process in the production of slip-decorated ware—an initial firing of decorated unglazed ware to set the slip decoration and a second, higher firing after the glaze was applied. Archaeological research at the Edgefield sites where decorated ware was produced has revealed no evidence of the use of a two-stage firing process for decorated ware. Ceramics scholar Georgeanna Greer has suggested that the slip-decorated fragments that have been labeled bisque may be underfired ware with glazes that were not fully matured. Furthermore, contemporary folk potter Burlon Craig has successfully replicated the Edgefield decorated ware with only one firing.[9]

Surviving decorated ware from the Phoenix Factory illustrates an evolution in Edgefield decorative techniques and patterns. Phoenix Factory ware typically features a two-color decorative format—a brushed brown-black iron-slip base color overlain with creamy-white trailed kaolin slip. The most spectacular example of this decorative tradition is a cooler with a scene that has been interpreted by some scholars as a depiction of a slave wedding (Figure 5.5). In the scene, a male and female dressed as house servants are toasting each other. Below them stand a jug and a sow. The figures were incised into the moist clay and later brushed in with slip, the iron slip serving as a background and the kaolin used for detailing such as the woman's clothes—a hat, stockings, and a pocketbook. This tall, ovoid jug

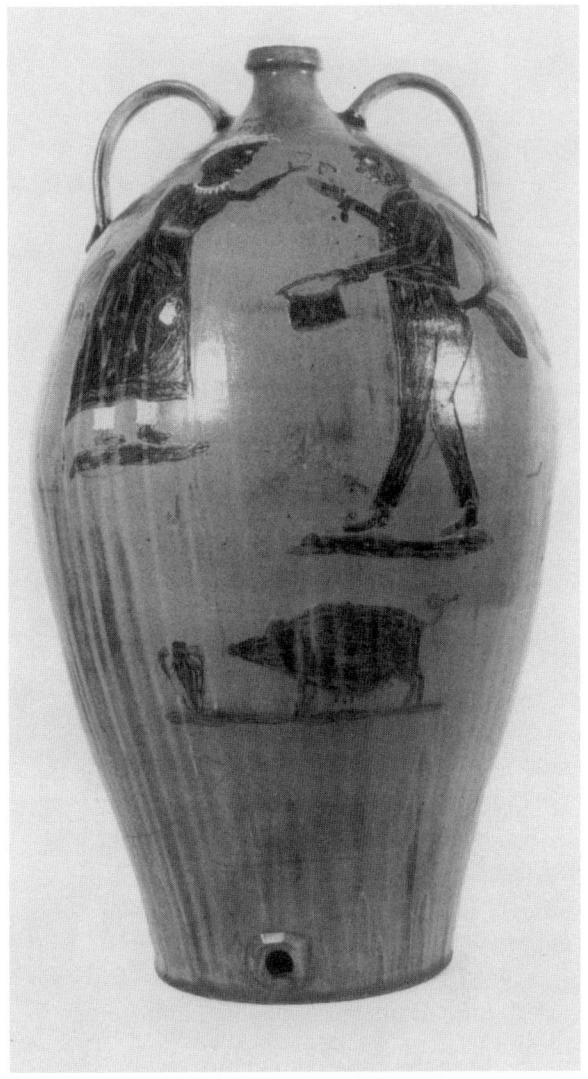

5.5 Slip-decorated alkaline-glazed stoneware cooler, ca. 1840, Thomas Chandler, Phoenix Factory, Shaw's Creek, Edgefield District, S.C. H 2′6″, C 1′6″. Stamped: PHOENIX / FACTORY / ED: SC (front and opposite, upper shoulder between handles). Collection of Tony and Marie Shank.

form, with a gently rounded, collared neck, two opposing loop handles, and a bung hole in the lower wall, is attributed to Thomas Chandler. The maker's mark, PHOENIX / FACTORY / ED: SC, is encircled by an iron slip spray or wreath, and the handle attachments are ringed in iron slip.

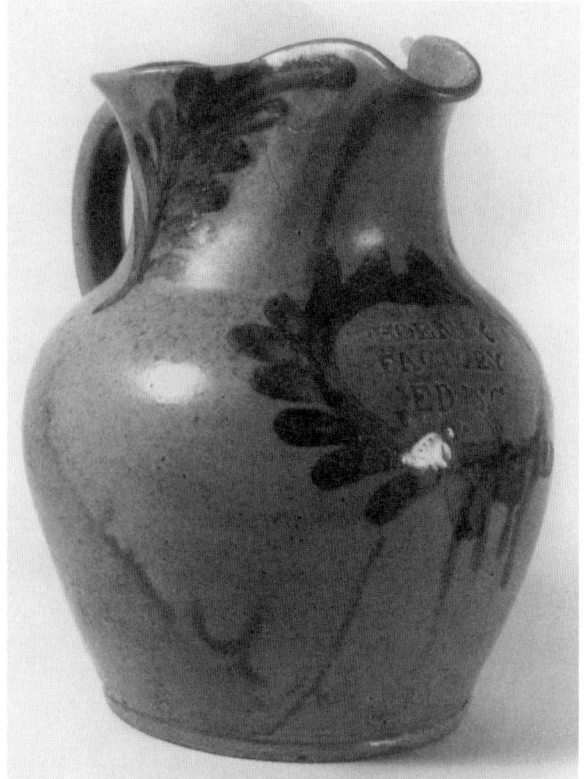

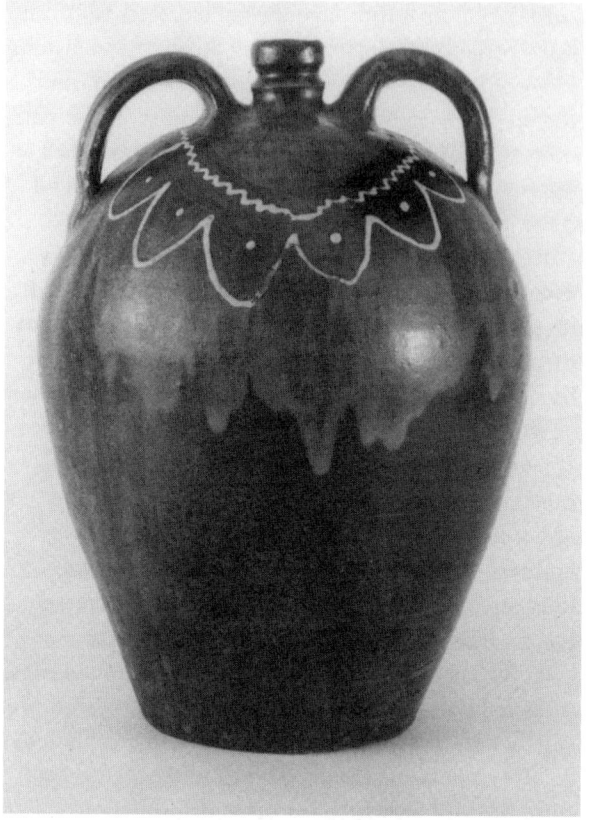

5.6 Slip-decorated alkaline-glazed stoneware pitcher, ca. 1840, Phoenix Factory, Shaw's Creek, Edgefield District, S.C. H 9⅞″, C 25¼″. Stamped: PHOENIX / FACTORY / ED. SC. Collection of Tony and Marie Shank.

A decorated pitcher, syrup jug, and storage jar also bear the Phoenix Factory stamp. The pitcher is of a squat, ovoid baluster-shaped form (Figure 5.6). An iron slip wreath similar to that found on the water cooler frames the maker's mark on this piece, with an iron slip sprig at either side of the spout. The syrup jug is decorated with a scalloped "collar" applied to the upper shoulder and between the handle attachments in iron slip with kaolin-slip detailing (Figure 5.7). This jug is bulbous in form and has two opposing loop handles and a ringed collar at the neck. In addition to the Phoenix Factory mark, it bears a stamped L at the upper shoulder.

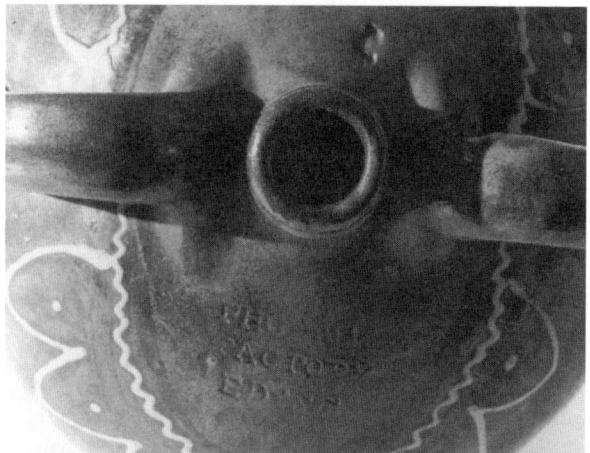

5.7 Slip-decorated alkaline-glazed stoneware syrup jug, ca. 1840, Phoenix Factory, Shaw's Creek, Edgefield District, S.C. H 16¾″, C 37¾″. Stamped: PHOENIX / FACTORY / ED: SC. Courtesy of the Museum of Early Southern Decorative Arts, Winston-Salem, N.C.

A stamped Phoenix Factory storage jar is decorated with brushed iron-slip swags overlain with a zigzag pattern in kaolin slip (Figure 5.8). The loop and swag motif, which later came to be particularly identified with Thomas Chandler, is the most common Edgefield decorative design.[10]

Several unmarked slip-decorated vessels are attributed to the Phoenix Factory. One of these is a bulbous syrup jug with a full profile of a woman in a ruffled hoop dress, executed in brown-black iron slip (Figure 5.9). A storage jar decorated in kaolin and iron slip with a profile of the bust of a man is also attributed to the Phoenix Factory. The shoulders and upper torso of the man ap-

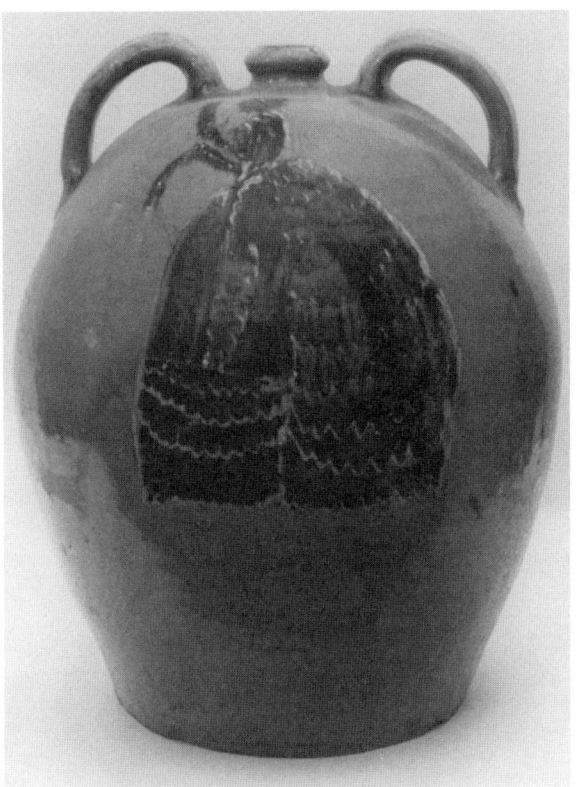

5.9　Slip-decorated alkaline-glazed stoneware syrup jug with woman in a hoop dress in kaolin- and iron-based slip, ca. 1840, Phoenix Factory, Edgefield District, S.C. H 16⅜″, C 42⅞″. Collection of Charles N. Gignilliat.

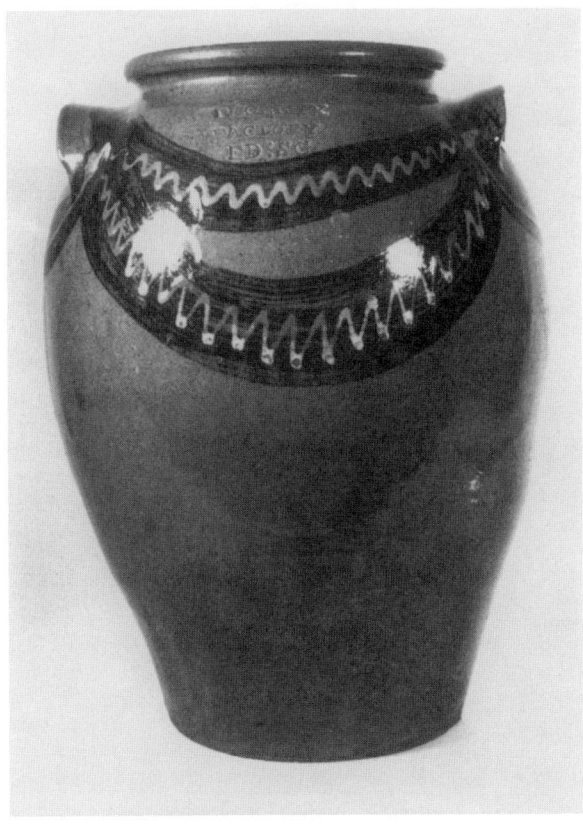

5.8　Slip-decorated alkaline-glazed stoneware storage jar, ca. 1840, Thomas Chandler, Phoenix Factory, Shaw's Creek, Edgefield District, S.C. H 16¾″, C 124″. Collection of Guy Kennedy.

pear to have been originally drawn as a flower and later incorporated into the figure of a man (Figure 5.10).

A closely related decorative style is found on as many as a half-dozen storage and preserve jars with a stamped M (perhaps the initial of Edgefield stoneware manufacturer Robert Mathis) applied at the upper shoulder of each vessel just below the neck (Figure 5.11). Each of these vessels is decorated with two opposing flowers applied in bold brush strokes to the upper shoulder of the vessel in brown-black iron slip. One flower appears on each face of the jar between the two opposing slab, or loop, handles. Archaeolo-

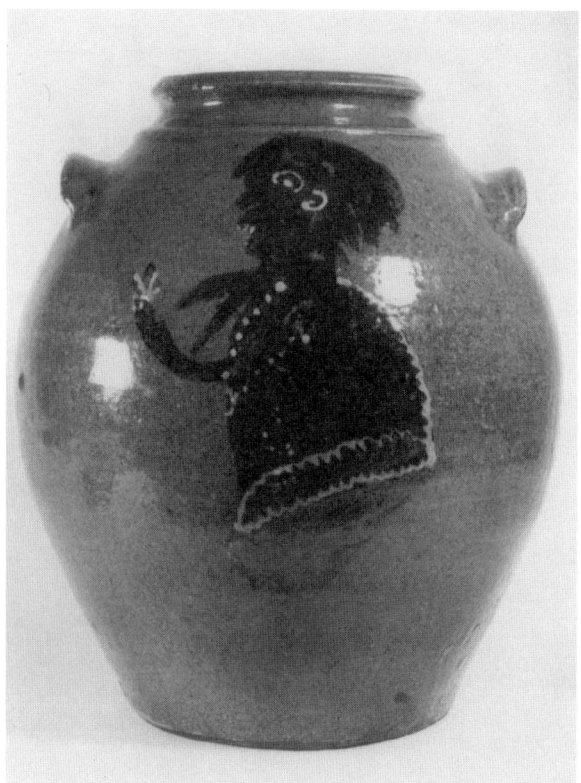

5.10 Slip-decorated alkaline-glazed stoneware storage jar with profile of man in kaolin and iron slip, ca. 1840, Phoenix Factory, Edgefield District, S.C. H 14″, C 40⅝″. Collection of Gladys Frick.

gists have recovered a stoneware fragment with a stamped M from the site of the Phoenix and C. Rhodes factories on Shaw's Creek. A similarly executed floral motif, in both kaolin and iron slip, appears on a storage jar stamped with an L (possibly Amos Landrum's mark) (see Figure 5.12).

Collin Rhodes continued the decorative tradition established at the Phoenix Factory at his stoneware factory on Shaw's Creek. Much of the ware produced at Rhodes's factory was marked "C Rhodes Maker" to distinguish it from other Edgefield ware. Decorators at Rhodes's factory applied maker's marks in at least four distinct decorative styles. The most striking example is a syrup jug with "C Rhodes Maker" written in

bold flourishing letters in iron slip horizontally along the shoulder and outlined in kaolin slip (Figure 5.13). The Rhodes maker's mark more commonly appears on jugs produced at the factory as a floral motif with "C Rhodes Maker" applied in trailed kaolin slip atop a stem with leaves (Figure 5.14). On some vessels, a stylized cartouche or medallion with a number in the center indicating gallon capacity appears above the maker's mark. A few vessels are signed in kaolin slip "Southern Make / C. Rhodes / Edgefield District / S.C." or "C Rhodes Maker" with the date below. One of these, a three-gallon jug,

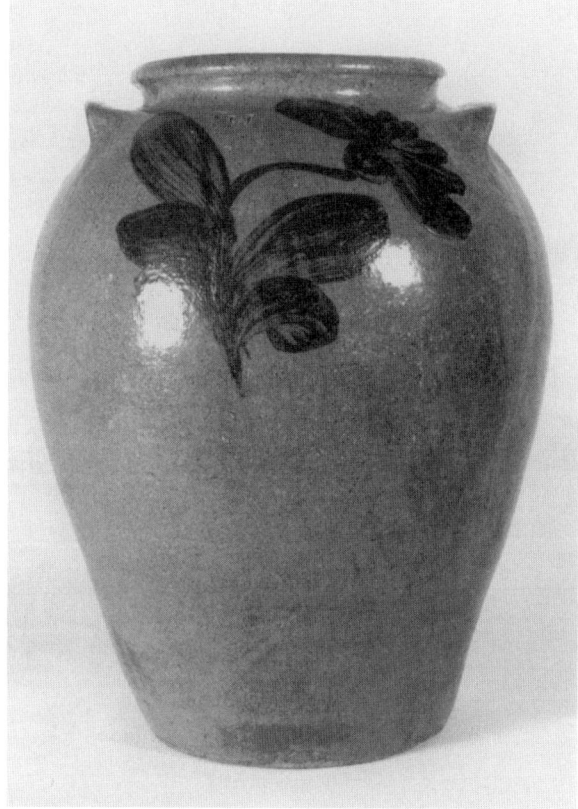

5.11 Slip-decorated alkaline-glazed stoneware storage jar, ca. 1840, attributed to the Phoenix Factory, Shaw's Creek, Edgefield District, S.C. H 14″, C 36″. Stamped: M (front, upper shoulder between handles). Collection of Mr. and Mrs. Levon C. Register.

loop handle and a ringed collar at the neck is signed in kaolin slip "James V. Lyles / Columbia / South Carolina" and "C. Rhodes / Maker" (Figure 5.17). Both a double-handled syrup jug and a storage jar with two opposing slab handles, a canted rim, and a raised band or collar at the upper shoulder are signed in kaolin slip "J.A. Hendrix & Co. / Lexington C.H. / S.C." In 1850 business associates Scott and Ewart ordered jugs with their firm's name and address, "Scott & Ewart / No. 1 Merchants Row / Columbia / S.C." (see Figure 5.18). Shop owners throughout the state and region could place an order for stoneware jugs and jars with their name and address.

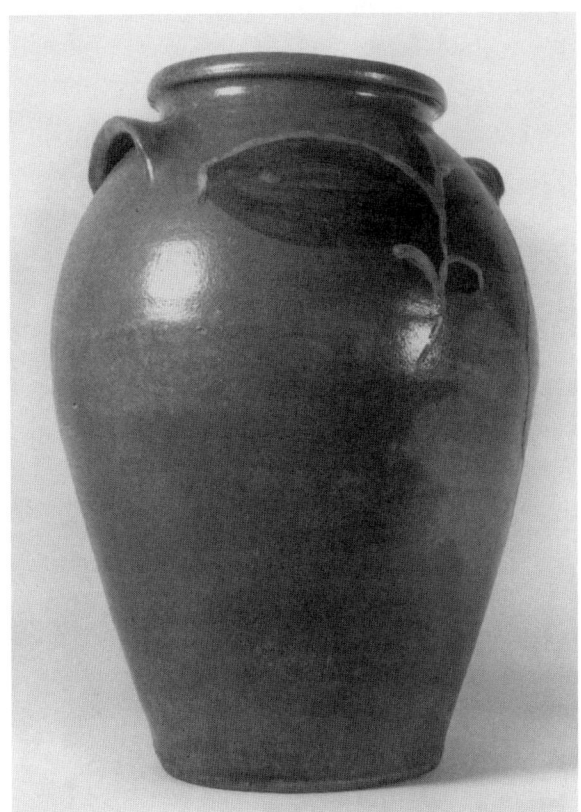

5.12 Slip-decorated alkaline-glazed stoneware storage jar, ca. 1840, attributed to the Phoenix Factory, Edgefield District, S.C. H 15⅝", C 36⅛". Stamped: L. Collection of Tony and Marie Shank.

signed in kaolin slip "C Rhodes / Maker / 1851," is elaborately decorated in kaolin and iron slip with a snake coiled along the belly and shoulder (Figure 5.15). On another Rhodes jug the "C Rhodes Maker" mark appears on a brushed iron-slip background floral wreath or spray. The maker's mark, the gallon capacity number "5," and an outline or border have been trailed onto the dark iron slip in kaolin (Figure 5.16). This decorative technique is reminiscent of the earlier Phoenix Factory ware.

Some C. Rhodes Factory ware is marked with the name of the merchant for whom it was made. For example, an ovoid jug with a single

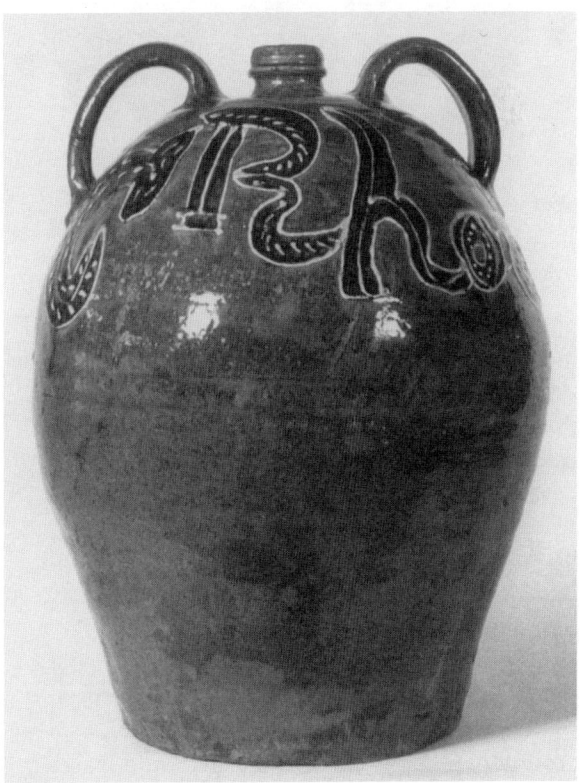

5.13 Slip-decorated alkaline-glazed stoneware syrup jug, ca. 1850, Collin Rhodes Factory, Shaw's Creek, Edgefield District, S.C. H 17", C 43¾". Maker's mark: C Rhodes Maker (in kaolin- and iron-based slip along shoulder). Collection of Tony and Marie Shank.

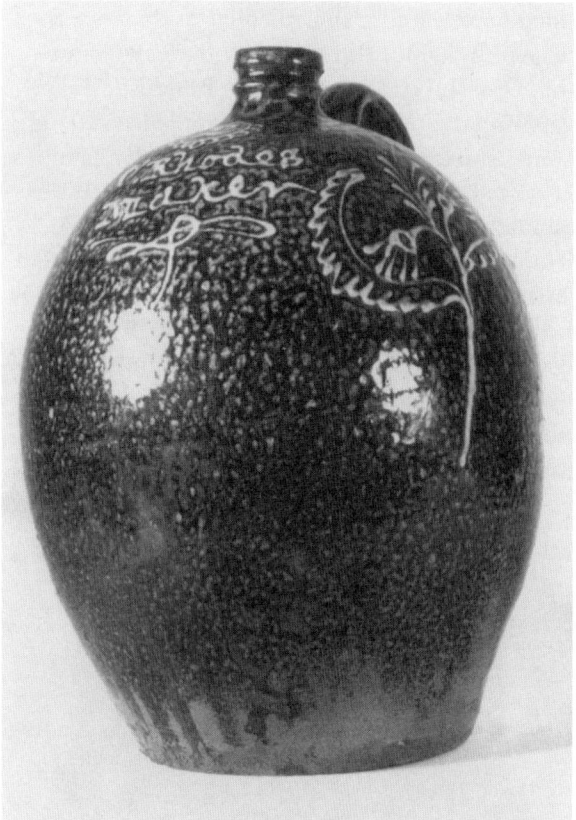 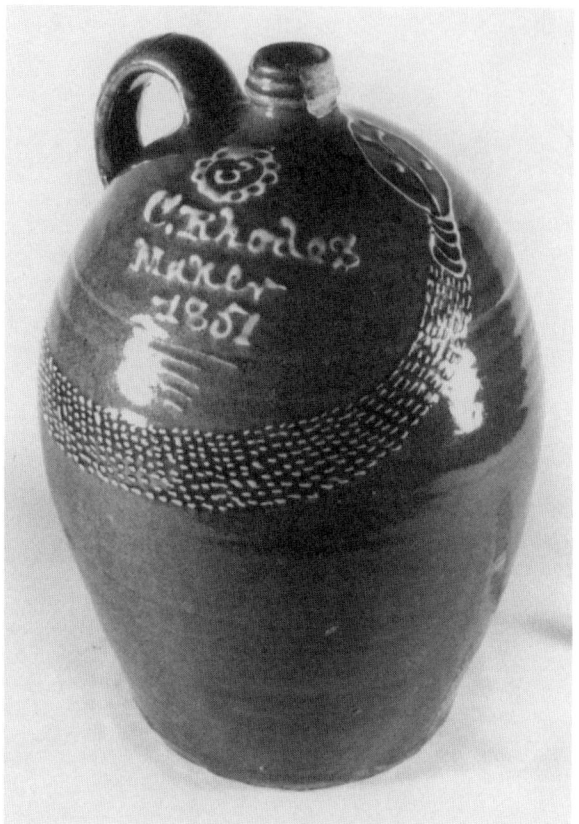

5.14 Slip-decorated alkaline-glazed stoneware jug with floral motif, ca. 1850, Collin Rhodes Factory, Shaw's Creek, Edgefield District, S.C. H 13⅜", C 32½". Maker's mark: C Rhodes Maker (in kaolin-based slip). Collection of Terry and Steve Ferrell.

5.15 Slip-decorated alkaline-glazed stoneware jug with snake motif, 1851, Collin Rhodes Factory, Shaw's Creek, Edgefield District, S.C. H 15⅜", C 35". Maker's mark: 3 / C Rhodes / Maker / 1851 (in kaolin-based slip). Collection of the Charleston Museum, Charleston, S.C.

The ware was resold to customers, thereby providing a unique form of advertisement for the merchant.

A wide variety of decorative designs appear on C. Rhodes Factory ware. Floral patterns are predominant. For example, a tulip motif, consisting of a single flower with stem and leaves drawn in iron slip with kaolin-slip detailing, appears on storage jars, double-handled syrup jugs, churns, and pitchers attributed to the C. Rhodes Factory. A variation of this motif, consisting of a stem in kaolin and iron slip with leaves topped by a numeral, combines a floral motif with a capacity mark (see Figure 5.19). An unusual South Carolina decorative technique identified with the Rhodes factory is that of applying iron-slip "rings" around the handle attachments of jugs. This technique was also employed on the salt-glazed cobalt-decorated stoneware of the North. Other decorative designs identified with the Rhodes factory include floral sprays, vines or wreaths, and feathers or plumes.

The loop and swag pattern, typically applied in iron slip, but occasionally appearing in kaolin slip, and the medallion or cartouche, encircling a capacity marking, were the most common decorative motifs employed at the Trapp-Chandler Factory (see Figure 5.20). But while the loop and swag pattern on Phoenix Factory ware consisted of an iron-slip background swag overlain with kaolin loops, the pattern appears consistently in a single slip on ware of the later Trapp-Chandler

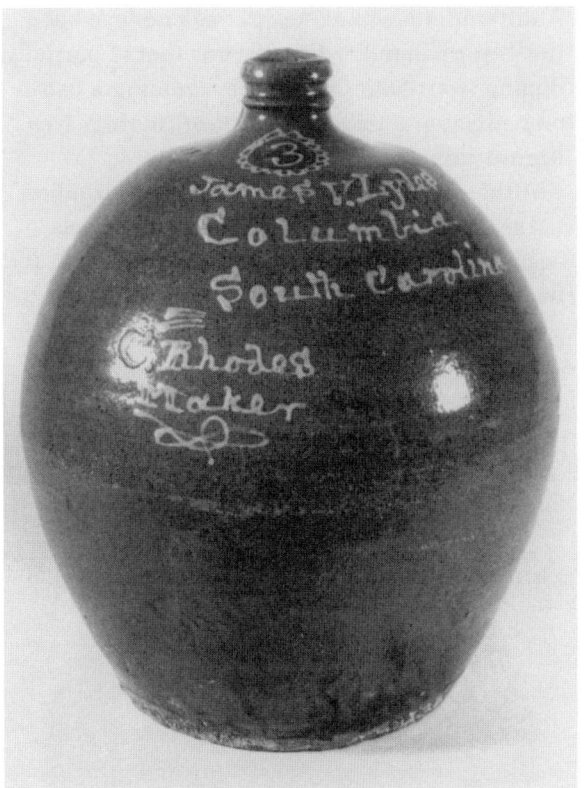

5.17 Slip-decorated alkaline-glazed stoneware syrup jug, ca. 1850, Collin Rhodes Factory, Shaw's Creek, Edgefield District, S.C. H 13″, C 37″. Merchant's and maker's mark: 3 / James V. Lyles / Columbia / South Carolina / C. Rhodes / Maker (in kaolin slip). Collection of Mr. and Mrs. Larry R. Carlson.

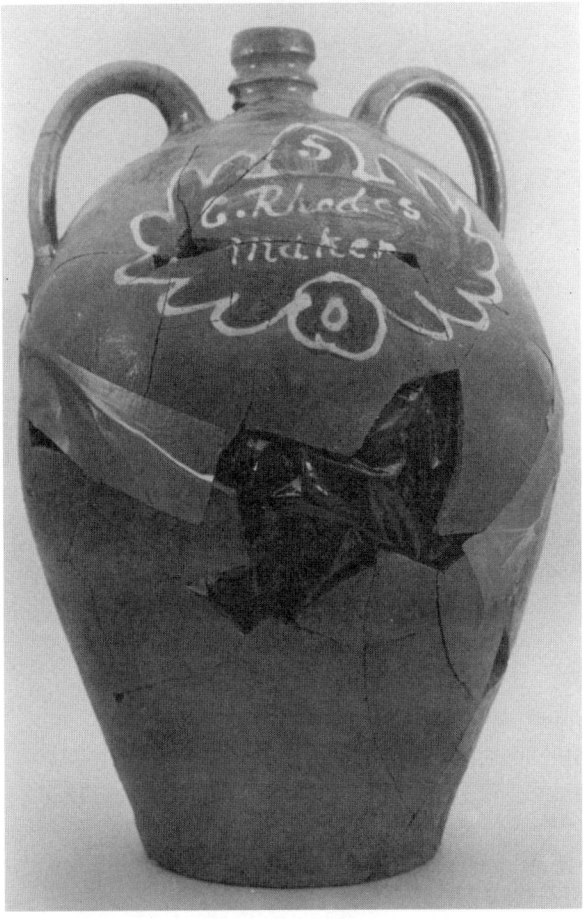

5.16 Detail of maker's mark, alkaline-glazed stoneware syrup jug, ca. 1850, Collin Rhodes Factory, Shaw's Creek, Edgefield District, S.C. H 18⅜″, C 39⅝″. Maker's mark: 5 / C Rhodes / Maker (in kaolin and iron slip within a wreath). Kaolin- and iron-based slip tulips, between handles. Collection of Matt Bramblett.

and Thomas Chandler factories. Underglaze brushed decorations, applied in iron-bearing slip before glazing, range in color from light brown to black. Slip trailing, in kaolin clay, was confined mainly to large capacity vessels, for example, churns and storage jars, although trailed slips were occasionally used on smaller bowls and jugs as well. Another decorative motif identified with the Trapp-Chandler Factory is known as the broken stem flower. This pattern consists of a single daisy with looped petals and a curved stem. Two sets of three or four leaves are arranged, one below the other, on opposing sides of the stem.

A different decorative technique employed at the Trapp-Chandler Factory was that of partially dipping ware into slip, thereby creating a two-tone effect or a pattern of concentric rings (see Figure 5.21).

Although slip decoration was usually applied to the shoulders or walls of Edgefield vessels, decorative patterns also frequently appear on the flat surfaces of pan-form bowls. For example, a

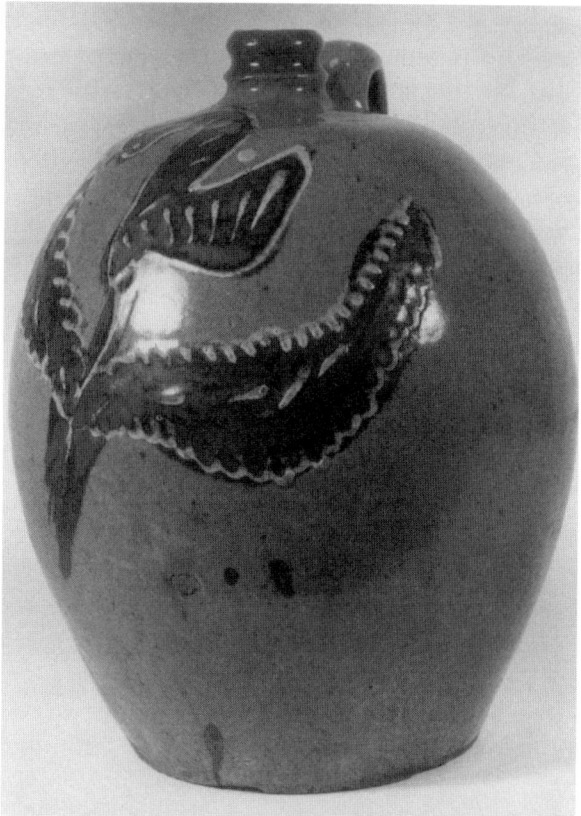

5.19 Slip-decorated alkaline-glazed stoneware jug with combined tulip motif and capacity mark in kaolin and iron slip, ca. 1850, attributed to the Collin Rhodes Factory, Shaw's Creek, Edgefield District, S.C. H 13″, C 32⅜″. Collection of Tony and Marie Shank.

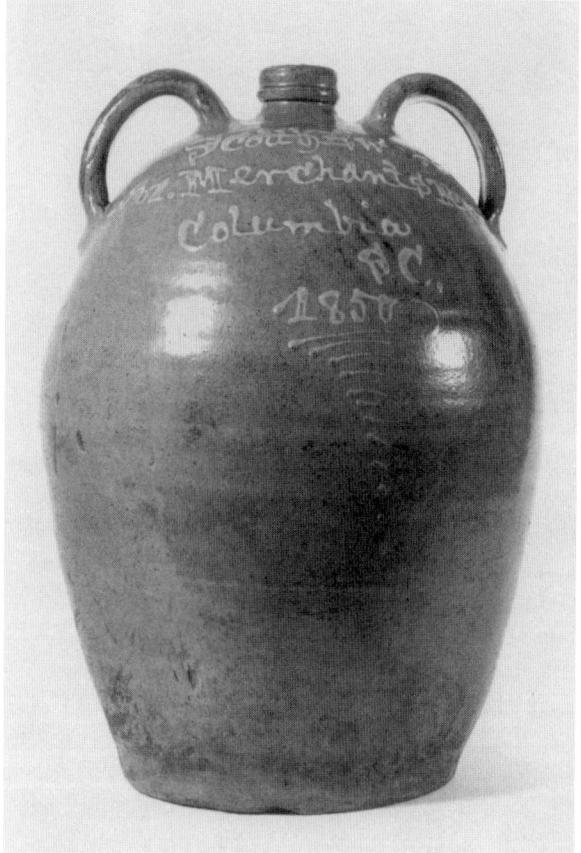

5.18 Slip-decorated alkaline-glazed stoneware syrup jug, 1850, attributed to the Collin Rhodes Factory, Edgefield District, S.C. H 16⅞″, C 39½″. Merchant's mark: Scott & Ewart / No. 1 Merchants Row / Columbia / S.C. / 1850 (in kaolin slip). Collection of McKissick Museum, The University of South Carolina, Columbia.

small serving bowl attributed to the Rhodes factory features a feather or plume motif applied in kaolin slip to the interior base and walls. Similarly decorated stoneware bowl fragments were recovered from the Rhodes site. A mixing bowl stamped TRAPP & CHANDLER has a tulip applied to the interior base in iron slip and a loop and swag pattern along the interior rim (Figure 5.22).

Thomas Chandler went so far as to use slip inscriptions as a warranty mark. Several jugs stamped with Chandler's mark have "Warranted" or "Warranted Good" written in script across the body in iron slip (see Figure 5.23). Stoneware fragments with the "Warranted" mark were recovered from the Thomas Chandler Factory site near Kirksey's Crossroads. Another common decorative motif found on Chandler factory ware, as well as ware produced at the Rhodes factory, is the medallion, a circular pattern outlined with loops, usually having a numeral in the center indicating capacity. The plumed or feathered wreath, seen on some Chandler ware, appears to be a variation of this motif.

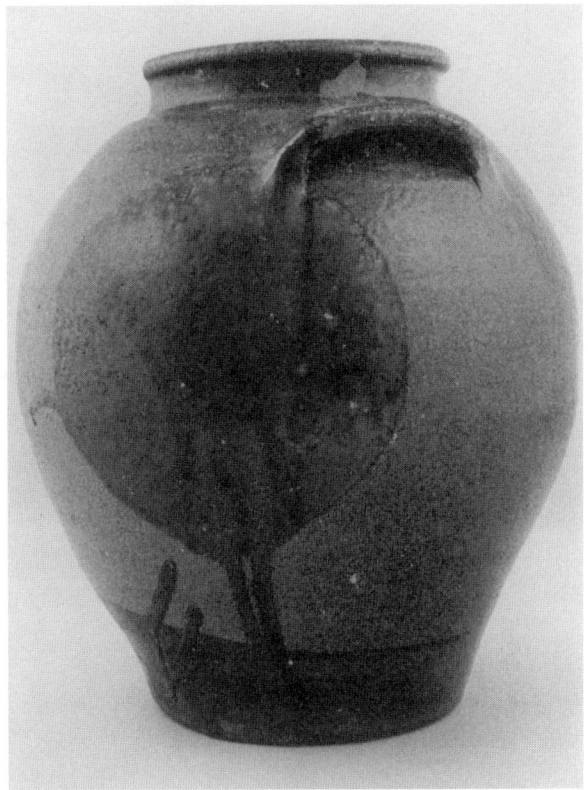

5.21 Slip-decorated alkaline-glazed stoneware jar with "dipped slip" banding, ca. 1845, attributed to the Trapp-Chandler Factory, Kirksey's Crossroads, Edgefield District, S.C. H 11″, C 31⅛″. Collection of Mr. and Mrs. Gary S. Thompson, Jr.

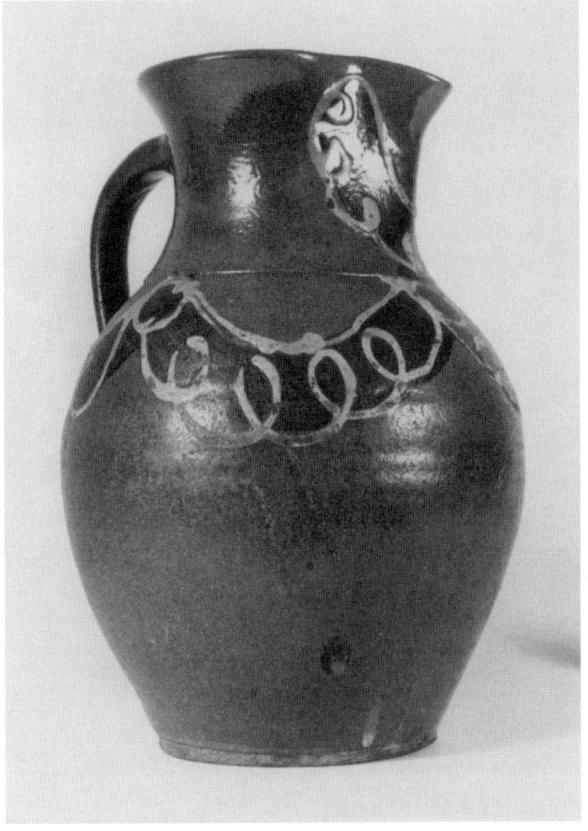

5.20 Slip-decorated alkaline-glazed stoneware pitcher with loop and swag motif, ca. 1840–50, attributed to Thomas Chandler, Trapp-Chandler Factory, Edgefield District, S.C. H 10⅞″, C 23½″. Collection of Tony and Marie Shank.

The use of slip decoration on Edgefield ware declined with the close of the large-scale stoneware factories in the district in the early 1850s. A few potters in the area, however, continued to produce slip-decorated ware into the latter part of the decade. One example of this continuation of the decorative tradition in Edgefield is a pitcher signed in kaolin slip "Rocke[s]pring Church, S.C. / 1857" and decorated with floral sprays and tulips (Figure 5.24). The pitcher is a presentation piece and was made for Rocky Springs Church in eastern Aiken County. This vessel, although

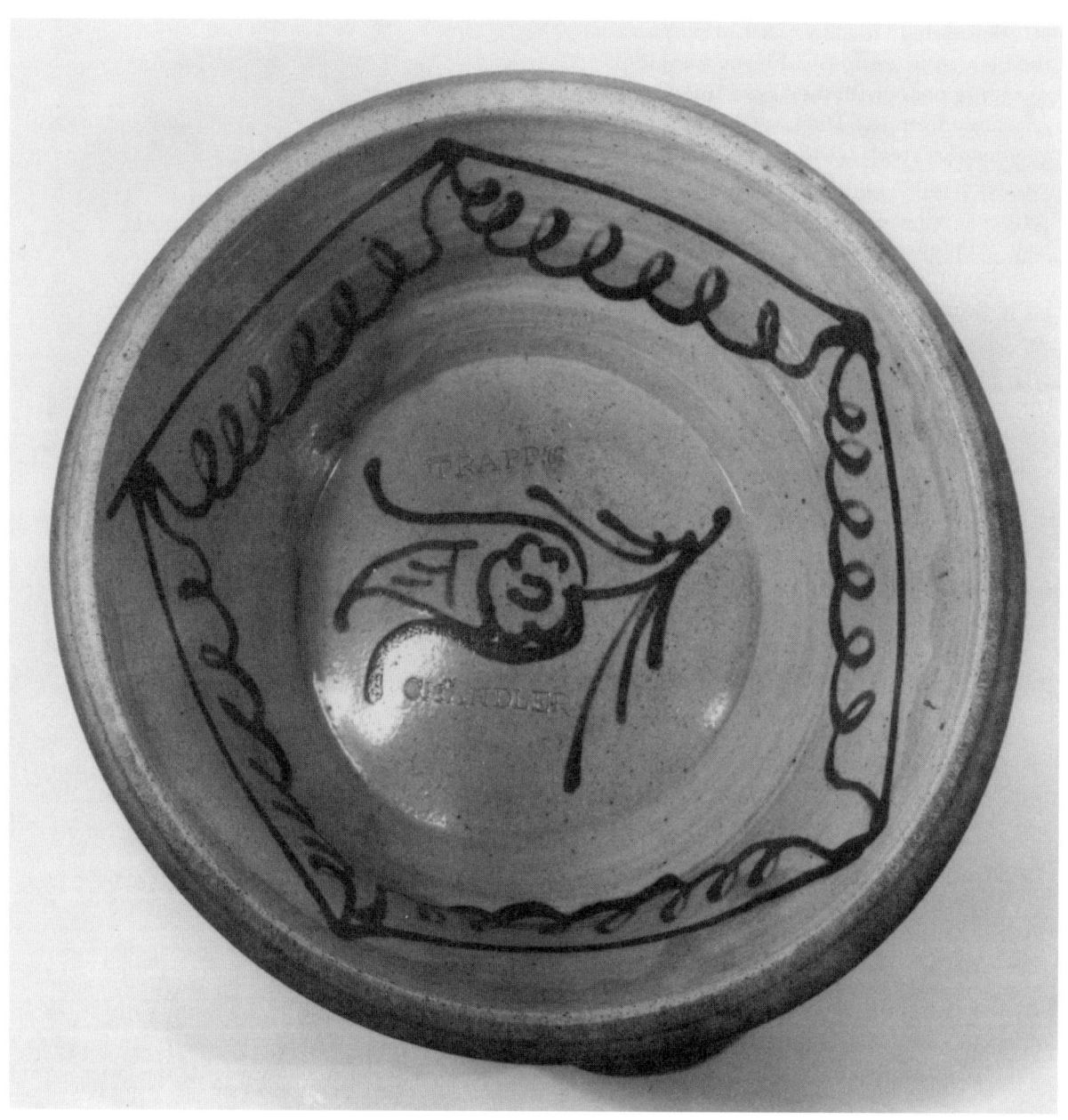

5.22 Slip-decorated alkaline-glazed stoneware bowl, ca. 1845, Trapp-Chandler Factory, Kirksey's Crossroads, Edgefield District, S.C. H 5⅝″, C 43¾″.
Stamped: TRAPP & CHANDLER. Collection of Tony and Marie Shank.

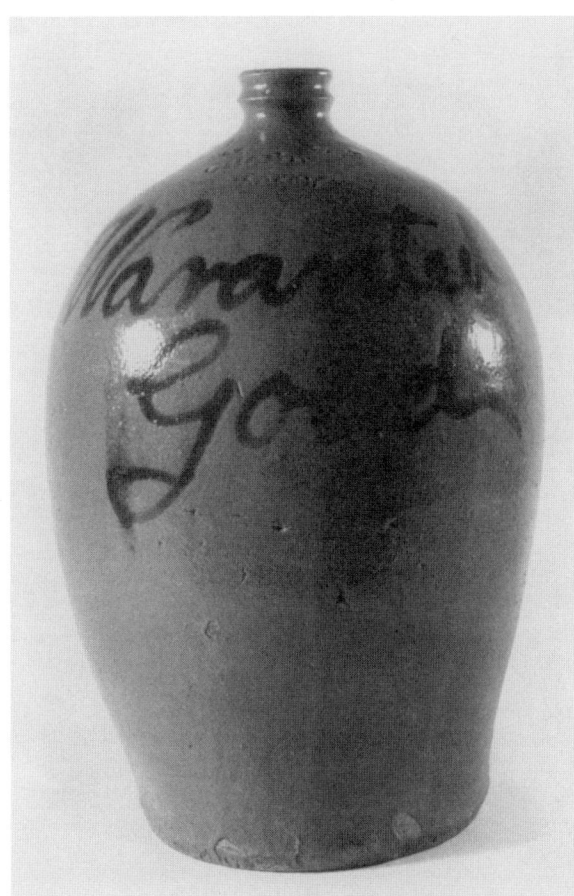

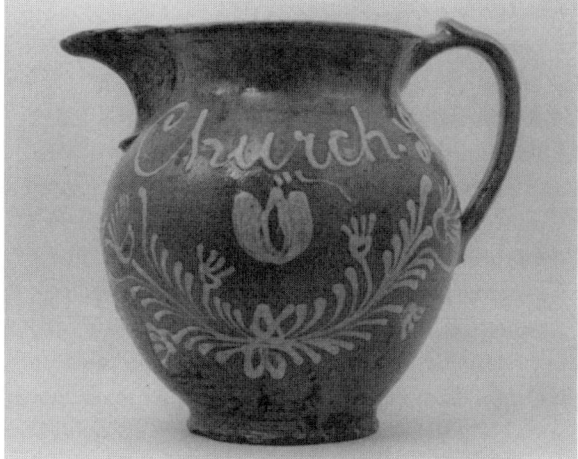

5.24 Slip-decorated alkaline-glazed stoneware pitcher, 1857, attributed to the Seigler Pottery, Shaw's Creek, Edgefield District, S.C. H 9¼", C 27". Kaolin-slip script: Rocke[s]pring Church S.C. / 1857. Collection of the Aiken County Historical Museum, Aiken, S.C.

5.23 Alkaline-glazed stoneware storage jar, ca. 1850, Thomas Chandler, Thomas Chandler Factory, Kirksey's Crossroads, Edgefield District, S.C. H 11¾", C 25¼". Stamped: CHANDLER MAKER. Iron-slip script: Warranted Good. Collection of Terry and Steve Ferrell.

slip-decorated, displays a departure in form and decorative technique from earlier Edgefield ware.

A few Edgefield potters decorated their ware by incising figures into the damp clay with a sharp tool. For example, a jug signed by slave potter Dave, dated 1 June 1856, has a crudely drawn horse and rider incised onto the lower body wall. Another Edgefield vessel, a storage jar with an incised M in bold script and attributed to the Lewis Miles Factory, is decorated with an incised bird holding a fish in its beak (Figure 5.25).

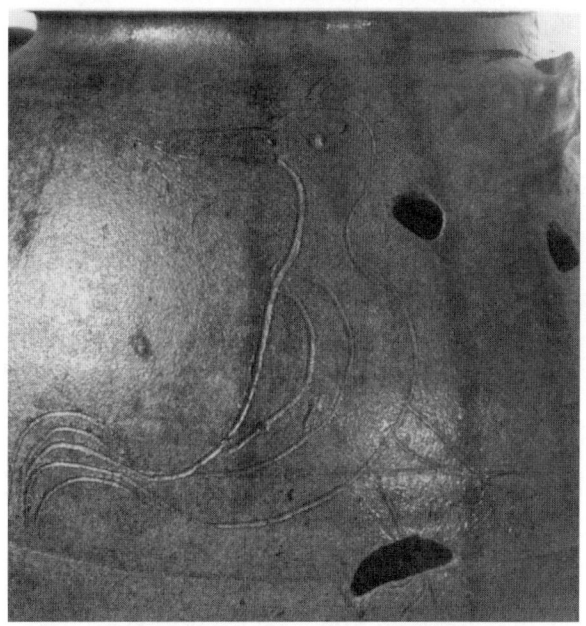

5.25 Alkaline-glazed stoneware storage jar with an incised bird with fish, ca. 1840, attributed to the Lewis Miles Factory, Edgefield District, S.C. H 18", C 51¼". Incised script: M. Collection of Mr. and Mrs. Larry R. Carlson.

Decorated Folk Pottery of Upcountry South Carolina

A few South Carolina potters outside the Edge-field District embellished their stoneware with slip decorations. The Whelchel family of Union County developed a unique style of stenciled decorations that they used on their ware. These consisted primarily of floral motifs applied in iron slip under a light-colored glaze. On a few occasions the potter also stenciled a numeral indi-cating gallon capacity onto the upper shoulder of the vessel in slip (see Figure 5.26). Slip-decorated ware from Union County may be readily dis-tinguished from Edgefield ware by its highly standardized, symmetrical designs.[11] Stenciled maker's marks and decorative motifs were com-mon throughout the country by the turn of the century. An unusual decorated jug signed by Whelchel and Smith that has raised horizon-tal bands, apparently fashioned to resemble the metal bands used to reinforce a wooden barrel, has already been described. The raised bands may have been designed as a type of reinforcement to minimize breakage of ware during shipment (see Figure 4.33). Similar bands appearing on salt-glazed stoneware seem to be an attempt to imitate a wooden barrel form.

Another upcountry potter decorated one of his jars with a series of stamped symbols. A storage jar or churn with a dark glassy "cinder glaze" and bearing the stamped maker's mark WILLIAMS on the lower wall is attributed to Greenville County potter Rich Williams (Figure 5.27). Above the maker's mark are forty-two circular impressed marks. A single vertical row of ten circular stamps with impressed tic-tac-toe patterns forms the cen-ter of the design, with diagonal rows of stamps (with impressed x patterns) radiating outward on either side, possibly representing a tree or leaf. A stamped "3" indicating gallon capacity appears in the lower right-hand corner of the stamped design. The significance of this design is

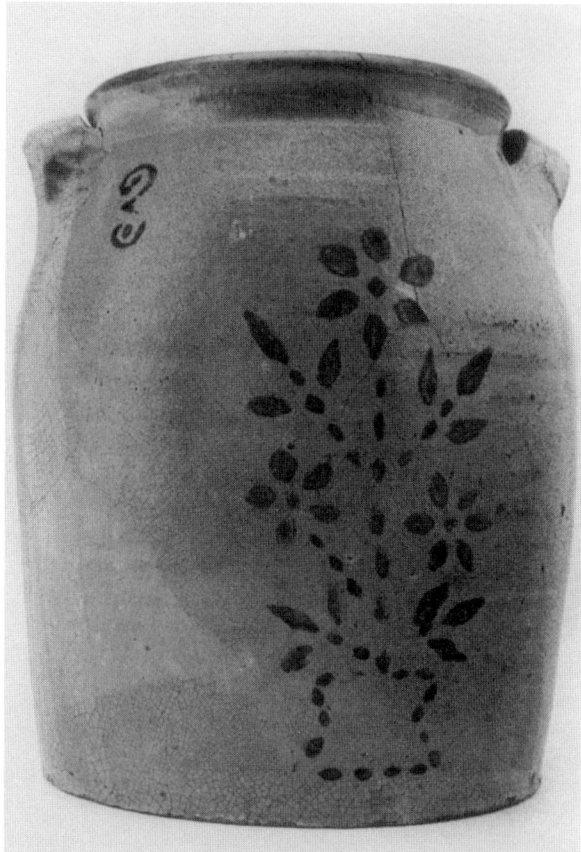

5.26   Alkaline-glazed stoneware jar with stenciled floral pattern and capacity mark, ca. 1900, attributed to the Whelchel family, Spartanburg County, S.C. H 12⅜″, C 33⅛″. Iron-slip stencil: 3. Collection of Dr. and Mrs. George V. Rosenberg.

unclear, but the impressed circle with a raised x frequently appears as a capacity mark on ware produced at the Benjamin Franklin Landrum pottery in Edgefield, suggesting that Rich Wil-liams may have been associated with potters who had worked at the Edgefield stoneware facto-ries. He may have been a relative of freed black turner Milage Williams, who in 1880 was living in Shaw's Creek Township in Aiken County.[12] Thus, decorative treatments may be useful indicators of a potter's background and training as well as of his artistic proclivities.

It is important to remember that the strong decorative tradition that emerged in the Edgefield District in the 1840s and 1850s was atypical. Even in Edgefield, slip-decorated ware appears at only a few factories. The vast majority of alkaline-glazed ware produced in the Edgefield area and throughout the state and region is not embellished with any type of decorative treatment. This ware may be appreciated for its distinctive forms, characteristic features, and well-developed glazes. These vessels speak eloquently of the agrarian society from which they originated.

South Carolina does not have a contemporary folk pottery tradition. Consequently, the archaeological record offers important information regarding early South Carolina stoneware technology and production methods. To date, only one Edgefield District pottery kiln has been excavated. Keith Landreth identified the kiln and waster dump at the Trapp-Chandler site during his 1983 investigations.[13] A proton magnetometer survey was carried out in order to define the kiln's relationship to the overall site topography and to identify internal subsurface architectural features. Based upon the results of the magnetometer survey and contour mapping of the site, Landreth was able to successfully identify the kiln features and dimensions.

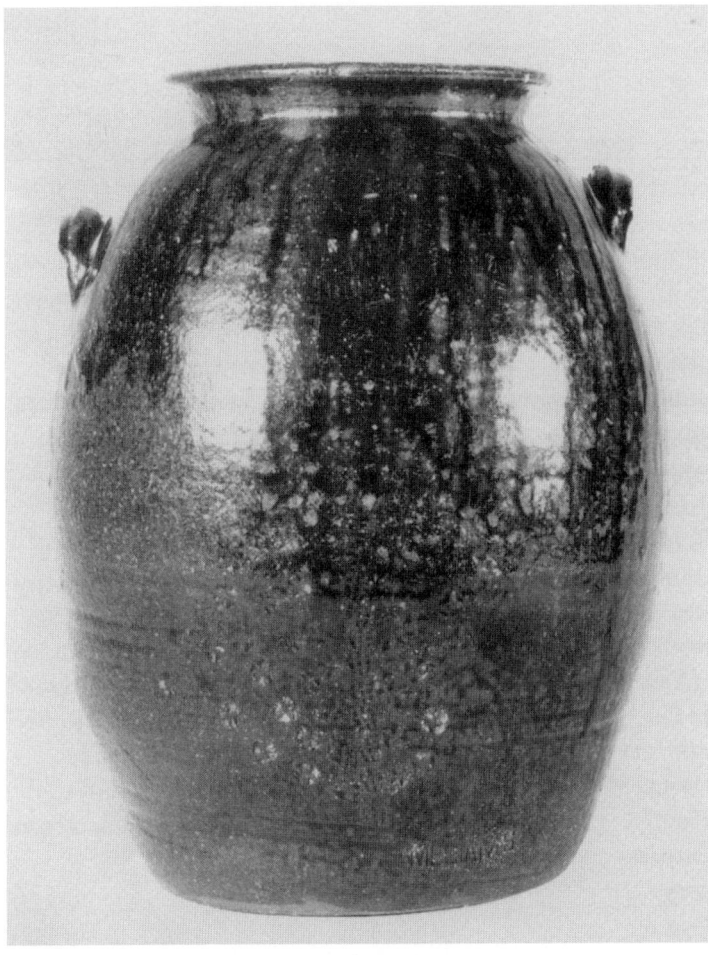

5.27 Alkaline-glazed stoneware storage jar with decorative pattern of circular stamps, ca. 1900, Rich Williams, Jugtown, Greenville County, S.C. H 13¼″, C 33″. Stamped: 4 / WILLIAMS (above base). Collection of Mr. and Mrs. Gary S. Thompson, Jr.

5.28 Burlon Craig's groundhog kiln, upper, (from Zug, *Turners and Burners*) and Trapp-Chandler kiln, lower (from Landreth, "Archaeological Investigations at the Trapp and Chandler Pottery, Kirksey, South Carolina").

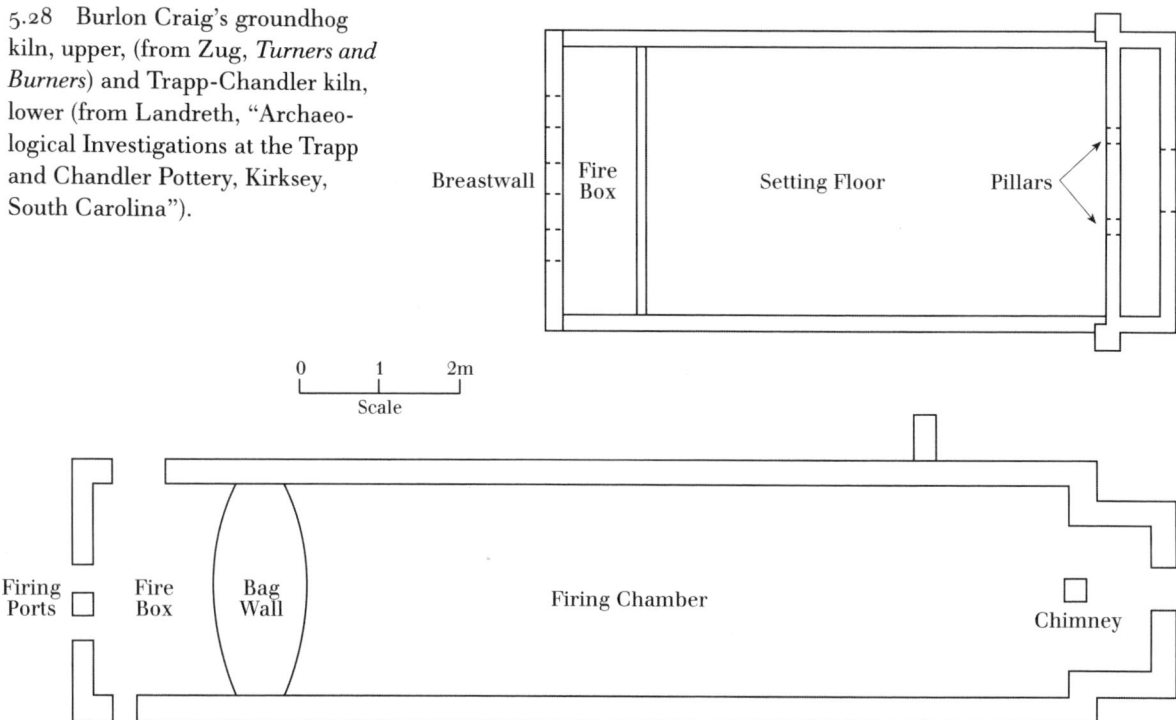

The firebox, located at the north end of the kiln, measured 8 feet by 4 feet (2.4 meters by 1.2 meters). The kiln chamber had three firing ports. Two of these ports were located on the east and west sides of the chamber, and a single smaller port was found at the north end. Landreth interpreted the number of firing ports as a factor of the kiln size and speculated that the side ports may have been used during the "blast off" period. The bagwall, a low wall of brick designed to prevent the flames in the firebox from making direct contact with the pottery, was located between the firebox and fire chamber. The firing chamber was located between the bagwall and the chimney and was an estimated 32 feet by 8 feet (9.7 meters by 2.4 meters). The chimney, located at the south end of the kiln, measured 6 feet by 6 feet (1.8 meters by 1.8 meters). These features are consistent with other nineteenth-century groundhog kilns found in the lower South except that the overall size of the Trapp-Chandler kiln, 42 feet long by 8 feet wide (12.8 meters by 2.4 meters), is much larger than the "typical" groundhog kiln described by Georgeanna Greer in 1977 as averaging 18–19 feet by 8 feet (5–6 meters by 2.5 meters).[14] On the other hand, the Kirbee kiln in Texas, measuring 35 feet by 6.6 feet (10.6 meters by 2 meters), was also considered to be exceptionally large.[15] Also, folk potter Burlon Craig of the Catawba Valley, North Carolina presently fires in a groundhog kiln measuring "24′11″ by 11′6″ overall, with an interior setting floor or ware chamber that is 20′by 10′ " (Figure 5.28).[16] The dimensions of these kilns seems to indicate that groundhog kilns in use during the mid-nineteenth century were larger in size than previously thought.

CHAPTER SIX

Put Every Bit All Between:
Stoneware Forms and Functions

An 1819 advertisement placed in the *Camden Gazette* by merchant Henry Abbott contains the earliest known description of South Carolina stoneware vessels. Abbott offered "Edgefield" water pitchers, ranging in size from two quarts to three gallons, pickling jars, from two quarts to six gallons, jugs, from two to five gallons, and two- and three-gallon churns.[1] A ledger in which Pottersville factory owners Nathaniel Ramey and John Hughes recorded their business transactions, dating from 1 January 1839 to 7 April 1840, includes entries naming jugs, pitchers, churns, crocks, jars, pans, stew pots with lids, and flowerpots. And in their 1840 advertisement announcing the opening of the Phoenix Factory, Robert Mathis and Collin Rhodes offered:

> Jars of all sizes from ½ gallon to 20 gallons.
> Jugs of all sizes do.¼ do. 20 do.
> Churns of all sizes 2 do. 5 do.
> Bowls or pans of all sizes, from ½ do. to 5 do.
> Butter Pots of all sizes from ½ do. to 3 do. with
>   covers.
> Pitchers of all sizes from ¼ do. to 3 do.
> And lids neatly made for jars and churns if desired.
> Stew Pots of various sizes & &.[2]

The documents cited above clearly establish five standard stoneware vessel forms—pitchers, jars, jugs, churns, and bowls and pans—as having been produced in South Carolina. The vast majority of stoneware vessels produced by folk potters in the state and throughout the South fall within these five categories. Due to the very nature of clay, however, there is considerable variation within each category. Even within a relatively conservative folk pottery tradition, atypical vessel forms are not uncommon. Some nonstandard forms, such as the stew pot and the cooler, were designed to fulfill specialized functions. Others, most notably sculpted face vessels, may have held special symbolic or religious meaning for the people who made and used them.

The primary relationships among various vessel forms have to do with their use or function. For purposes of this discussion, ware has been classified according to function: (1) food storage and preservation, (2) food preparation, (3) food consumption, (4) tobacco consumption, (5) household implements, (6) horticultural implements, (7) sculptural vessels, and (8) mortuary objects. The vast majority of traditional stoneware produced in South Carolina consisted of containers for the storage, preparation, and preservation of foodstuffs. Storage and preserve jars, churns, jugs, pitchers, pans, and bowls fall within these first three categories. Tobacco pipes and spittoons, used for smoking and chewing tobacco, are fairly common items, as are household articles such as chamberpots. Vessels designed for horticultural purposes include the chicken waterer or poultry fountain, which served as a drinking dispenser

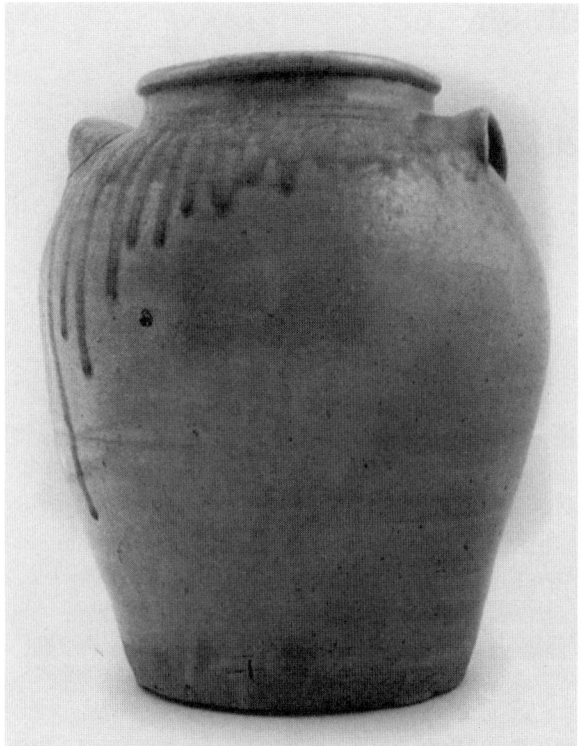

6.1   Alkaline-glazed stoneware storage jar, ca. 1810–30, Pottersville Stoneware Manufactory, Edgefield District, S.C. H 13″, C 34¾″. Stamped bracket on lower body. Collection of Mr. and Mrs. Gary S. Thompson, Jr.

for domestic fowl, and such items as flowerpots and vases. Sculpted vessels were designed as presentation pieces and in some instances may have been invested with magical or religious powers. Grave markers and cemetery urns are the best examples of mortuary objects, although other types of vessels were also used in funerary rituals.

Food Storage and Preserve Jars

The storage jar was the most basic utilitarian form produced by southern folk potters. Jars were used for the storage and preservation of a wide variety of foods. In Edgefield, folk potters produced jars ranging in size from less than a gallon

to forty gallons. Smaller preserve jars typically held pickled or preserved fruits and vegetables, while larger storage vessels were designed to hold staples such as meat and lard.

Storage jars produced before 1860 are generally ovoid or bulbous in form. One exception to this rule is a tall cylindrical storage jar attributed to the slave potter Dave (Figure 6.2). This unusual large-capacity jar may have been used for making sauerkraut.

A variety of rim treatments appear on jars but the simple rolled rim, designed for a cloth tie-down cover, is the most common. The verse "a very large jar which has four handles, / pack it full of fresh meat—then light candles" that appears on a storage jar by the slave potter Dave

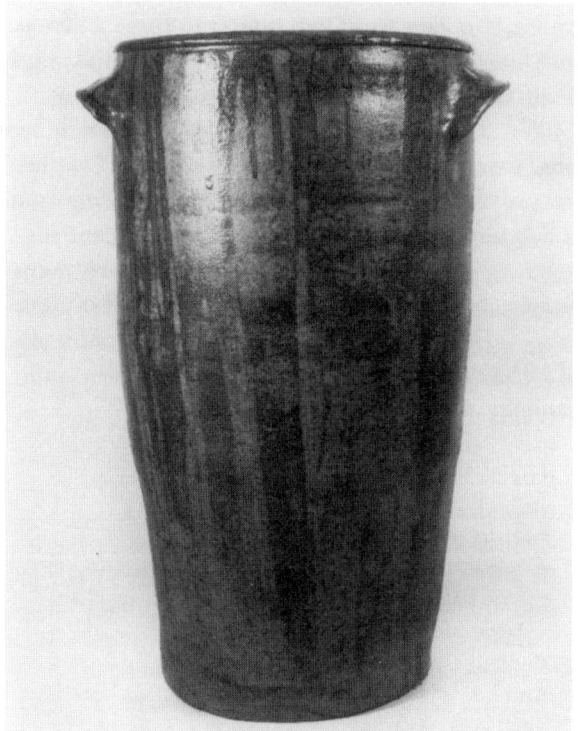

6.2   Tall cylindrical storage jar, ca. 1850, attributed to Dave (slave potter), Lewis Miles Factory, Horse Creek Valley, Edgefield District, S.C. H 27¼″, C 48⅞″. Collection of the Augusta-Richmond County Museum, Augusta, Ga.

dated April 12, 1858, alludes to another technique of sealing jars, with a coating of melted wax. The lid ledge, designed for a hanging lid was also fairly common. A few Edgefield area potters, most notably the Hahns, applied an indented groove for a metal lid. An unusual feature, the moat collar, was designed to protect the contents of jars from ants and other crawling insects (see Figure 6.3). This flange, attached to the upper shoulder of the vessel, just below the rim, acted as a barrier which, when combined with a cloth or wax seal, provided added protection for the contents of the jar.

Two opposing or four evenly spaced slab handles, attached horizontally below the rim, are also characteristic of storage jars. Most of

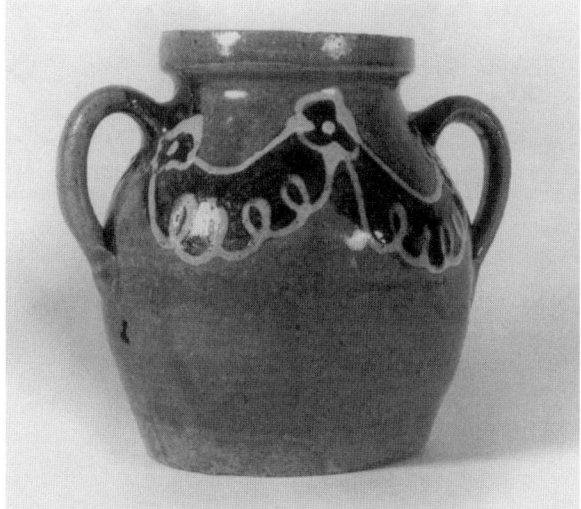

6.4 Slip-decorated alkaline-glazed stoneware preserve jar or stew pot with loop and swag design, ca. 1840–50, attributed to the Phoenix Factory or Collin Rhodes Factory, Shaw's Creek, Edgefield District, S.C. H 6⅝″, C 18¾″. Collection of Tony and Marie Shank.

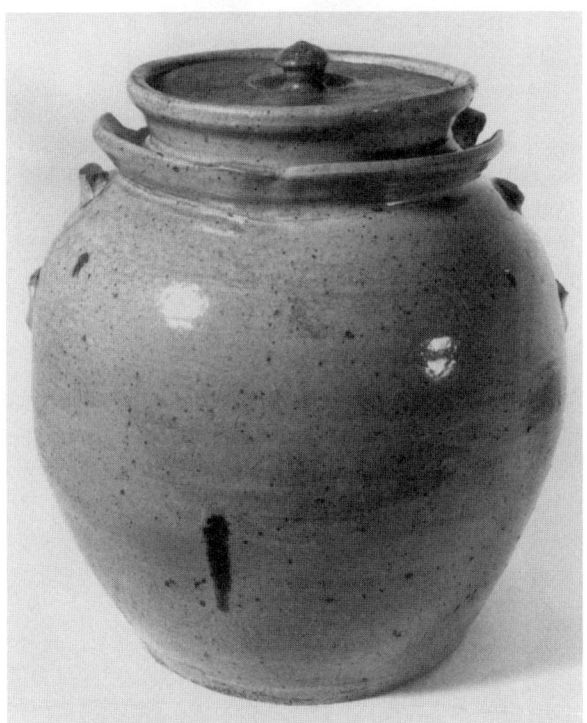

6.3 Alkaline-glazed stoneware preserve jar or home-brew jar, ca. 1820, attributed to the John Landrum Factory or the Pottersville Stoneware Manufactory, Edgefield District, S.C. H 14½″, C 41⅝″. Collection of Terry and Steve Ferrell.

these handles form a cuplike projection, but on some vessels, especially those turned by Thomas Chandler, they present a more winglike profile.

South Carolina potters produced several styles of preserve jars. Early Edgefield jars are simply smaller versions of the typical ovoid storage jars. Some of these have two horizontally attached slab handles, others have two opposing vertical loop handles, and still others have no handles. A few Edgefield examples have horizontal loop handles but this feature is rare in the South (see Figure 6.5). More cylindrical preserve jars appear at a few antebellum Edgefield factories and at late nineteenth-century pottery shops throughout the state. These straight-sided jars typically have a high, sharply defined shoulder. Most are from one-and-a-half- to two-gallon capacity and have no handles, but one unusual example, attributed to the Trapp-Chandler factory, has a single loop handle attached at and below the neck (Figures 6.6 and 6.7).

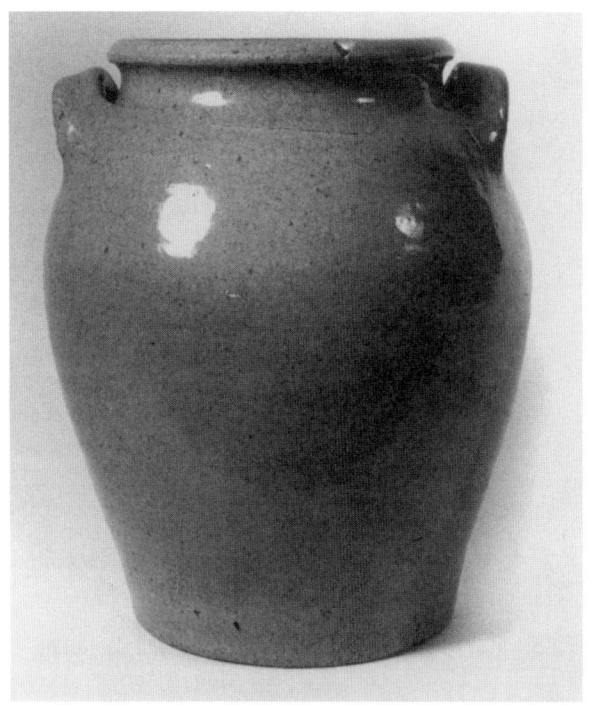

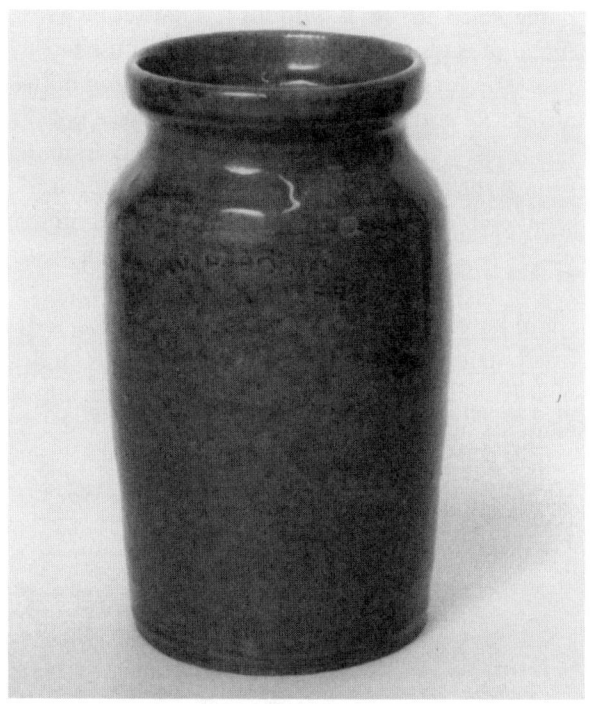

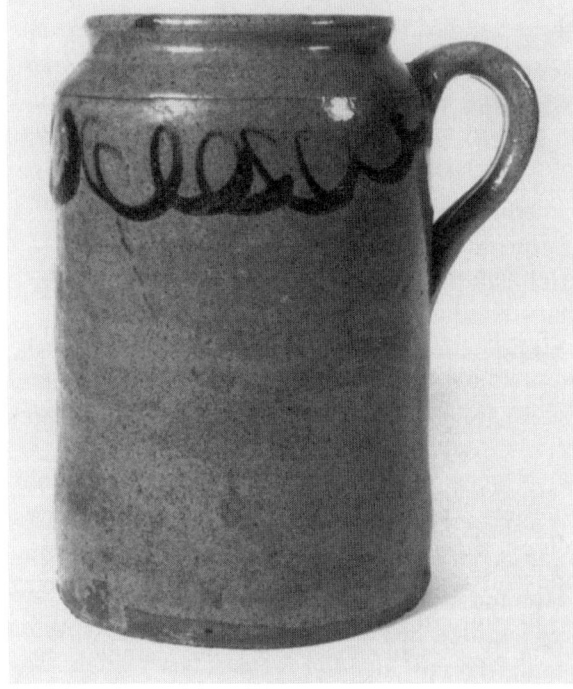

6.5 Alkaline-glazed stoneware preserve jar with horizontal loop handles, ca. 1810–30, attributed to the Pottersville Stoneware Manufactory or John Landrum Pottery, Edgefield District, S.C. H 9¼″, C 25⅛″. Stamped: I (upper handle attachment). Collection of Dr. and Mrs. Charles M. Webb.

6.6 Alkaline-glazed stoneware preserve jar, ca. 1870, Jesse P. Bodie Pottery, Kirksey's Crossroads, Edgefield County, S.C. H 8⅞″, C 18″. Stamped: J P BODIE / MAKER. Collection of Georgeanna H. Greer.

6.7 Slip-decorated alkaline-glazed stoneware preserve jar with single loop handle, ca. 1845, attributed to the Trapp-Chandler Factory, Kirksey's Crossroads, Edgefield District, S.C. H 8″, C 17½″. Collection of Dr. and Mrs. Charles M. Webb.

Churns

The churn, designed for butter-making, was a common form produced by stoneware potters throughout the state. Churns generally ranged in size from two to five gallons. Typically straight-sided or cylindrical, the churn featured a ledge inside the mouth that held a specially designed wooden or ceramic churn lid with an opening in the center for a dasher (see Figure 6.8).

Churns produced in the Edgefield District of South Carolina have two opposing lug handles, but later upcountry ware usually features an opposing strap and lug handle. The use of the

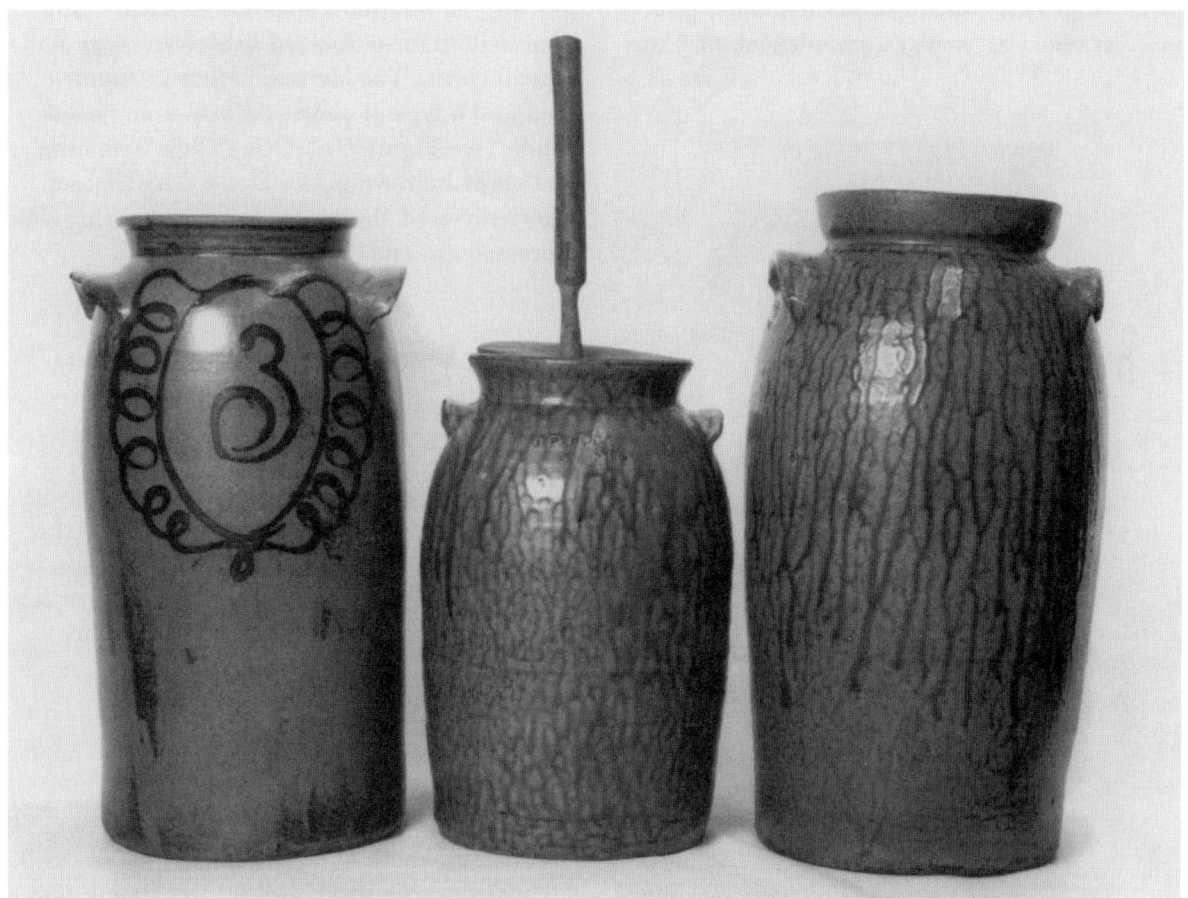

6.8 Alkaline-glazed stoneware churns from three Edgefield-area stoneware factories. *Left:* ca. 1845, attributed to the Trapp-Chandler Factory, Kirksey's Crossroads. H 16¾", C 28¼". Iron-slip looped medallion with capacity mark "3." *Center:* ca. 1870, Jesse P. Bodie Pottery, Kirksey's Crossroads. H 13", 27½". Stamped: J P BODIE / MAKER (upper shoulder). *Right:* ca. 1860–70, John W. Seigler Pottery, Shaw's Creek. H 17½", C 31¼". Stamped: J W S & CO / PINE HOUSE / S. C. (below handle). Collection of Georgeanna H. Greer.

strap handle on churns was a common practice in the Catawba Valley and the mountains of North Carolina as well as Georgia and Alabama. According to Terry Zug, "The employment of the strap handle on churns is a distinctly southern feature and was no doubt intended to facilitate pouring out the contents."[3]

Churns often served as large-capacity storage jars as well as for the preparation of dairy products. As noted previously, upcountry South Caro-

linians also produced home brew in stoneware churns.

As in Georgia and North Carolina, by the turn of the century South Carolina potters had begun to produce a smaller, more versatile "churn-jar" form. The churn-jar "incorporates characteristics of the old jar (the wide shoulder) as well as the churn (the relatively vertical form and the flaring rim with an internal flange for the lid)."[4] This combination form doubled as a pickling jar and a small churn. The Henson family of Jugtown produced a type of churn-jar with a single loop handle (see Figure 6.9). Otis ("Odie") Henson, brother of Jugtown potter David Carr Henson, reportedly used churn-jars for wine-making. Odie processed the grapes in a cider press.

Drinking Vessels and Beverage Dispensers

JUGS

Just as the storage jar was the principle folk pottery form used for food storage, the jug was the standard form designed to hold liquids. Typical early jug forms include the double-handled syrup jug, used for cane syrup, and smaller jugs for whiskey, vinegar, and drinking water (see Figures 6.10 and 6.11). More unusual types, such as ring jugs and buggy jugs, were made as presentation pieces or upon request. At his Kirksey's Crossroads factory Edgefield potter Thomas Chandler produced syrup or pouring spout jugs with wide, bowl-shaped spouts and rolled and flared rims. Another interesting secondary use of jugs reported by Mrs. Reippe Mays was for draining fields. According to Mrs. Mays, jugs with the bottoms broken out were found buried in a field adjacent to the site of the Neville pottery in West Union, Oconee County. The jugs had apparently been placed so that water that collected in the field would drain through them.

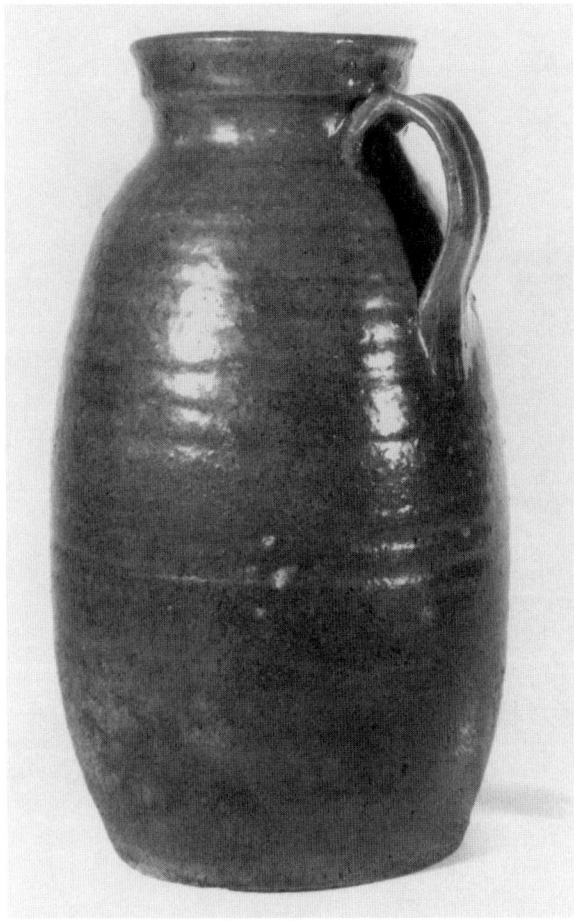

6.9   Alkaline-glazed stoneware churn-jar, ca. 1900, attributed to David Carr or Jesse Vardry Henson, Jugtown, Greenville-Spartanburg County, S.C. H 12″, C 22⅝″. Collection of Kenneth Tapp.

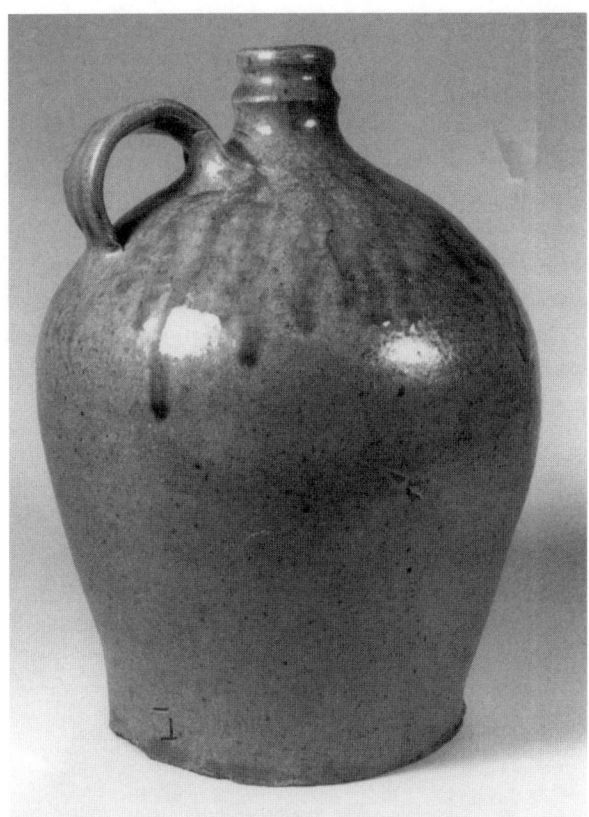

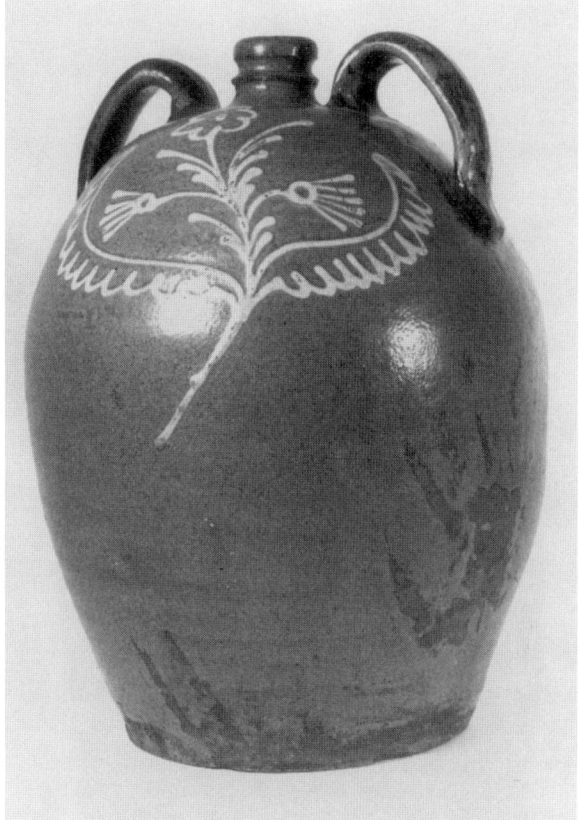

6.10   Alkaline-glazed stoneware jug, ca. 1810–30, Pottersville Stoneware Manufactory, Edgefield District, S.C. H 11″, C 26¼″. Stamped bracket on lower body. Collection of Dr. and Mrs. Charles M. Webb.

6.11   Slip-decorated alkaline-glazed stoneware syrup jug, ca. 1850, attributed to the Collin Rhodes Factory, Shaw's Creek, Edgefield District, S.C. H 15¾″, C 38⅝″. Collection of Mr. and Mrs. Levon C. Register.

Early nineteenth-century stoneware jugs produced in South Carolina exhibit a characteristic bulbous form. Most of these jugs have a wide shoulder one-third of the way down and taper sensuously to a narrow base, although some have a low shoulder and a correspondingly squat appearance. Ringed collars and wide banded collars are the most common rim treatments found on early jugs. Flattened and inverted conical mouths are found on late nineteenth-century jugs. Another distinctive feature of early South Carolina jugs is the placement of the handle attachments. Vertically placed loop handles are usually attached below the neck and at the upper shoulder on antebellum jugs. Salt- and slip-glazed jugs produced throughout the South during the late nineteenth and early twentieth centuries typically have the upper ends of handles attached at the neck. Edgefield jug handles also tend to be unusually stout, and oval in cross-section, perhaps because the jugs are so heavy.

During the late nineteenth century a variety of jug forms appear in the state. As itinerant potters traveled throughout the region, working at one shop for a few years and then moving on, new styles emerged. Potters at the Jesse Bodie

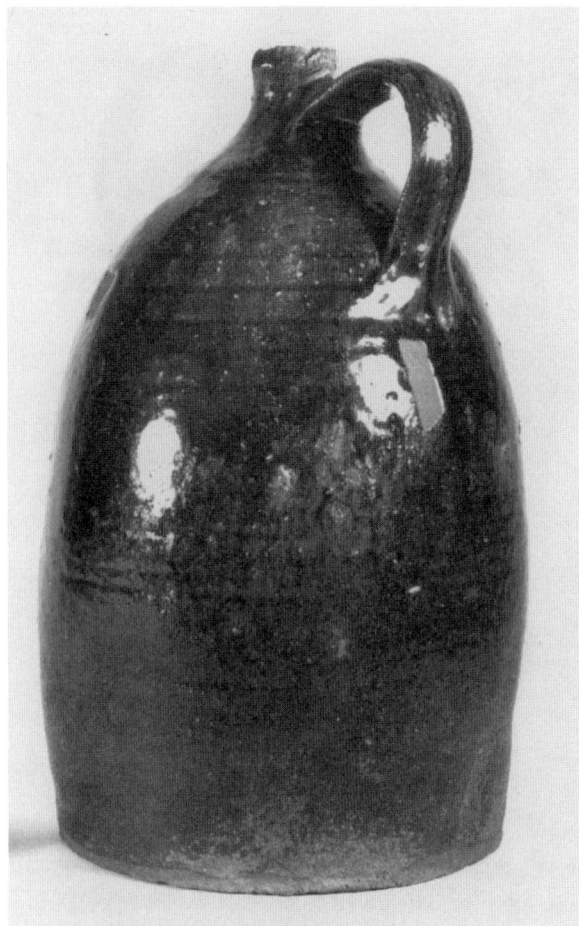

6.12 Bell-shaped alkaline-glazed stoneware jug,
ca. 1900, attributed to Jesse Vardry Henson, Jugtown,
Greenville-Spartanburg County, S.C. H 11 ¼″, C 22 ½″.
Collection of George Dewey Henson.

Factory and at Miles Mill produced pear-shaped
jugs, and the Whelchel family of Spartanburg
County produced bell-shaped jugs. The Henson
family of Jugtown produced both pear-shaped
and bell-shaped jugs (see Figure 6.12). At other
later Edgefield-area potteries, such as the W. F.
Hahn and Ben Landrum factories, cylindrical
jugs with tooled ledge shoulders replaced the
earlier ovoid types (see Figures 6.13 and 6.14).

A few Edgefield potters produced small jugs
with flattened sides. These were personal drinking vessels that could be slipped into a pocket
and carried along on trips away from home.
They usually held whiskey or rum. Thomas
Chandler made one of these flattened jugs for
Edgefield farmer Bates Wren. It is decorated
and signed in kaolin-slip script "B. Wren / N 6 /
1851" (Figure 6.15). The personalized mark identifies it as a specially designed presentation piece.
Another unusual jug flattened on opposite sides
is stamped vertically along the length J. P. BODIE /
MAKER (Figure 6.16).

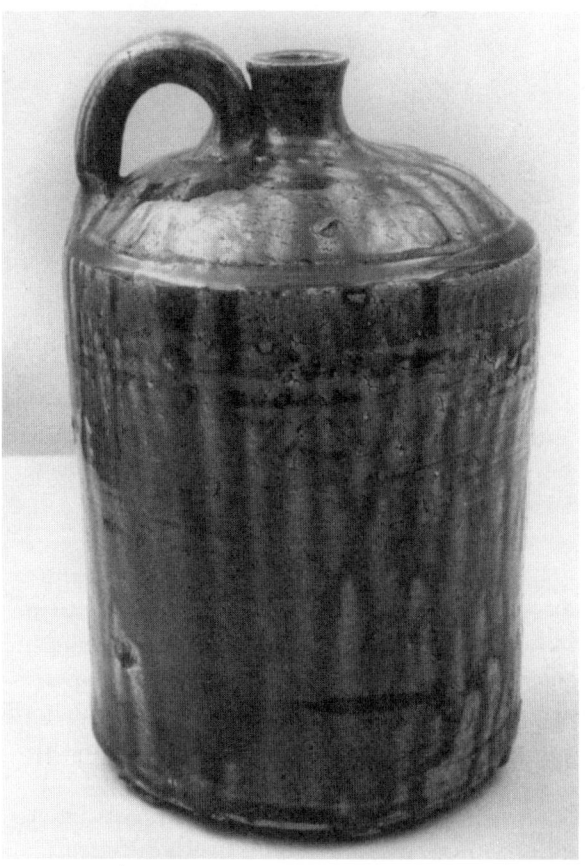

6.13 Alkaline-glazed stoneware jug with tooled shoul-
der, ca. 1900, attributed to the Benjamin F. Landrum
Factory, Horse Creek Valley, Aiken County, S.C.
H 11″, C 21 ¾″. Collection of the Charleston Museum,
Charleston, S.C.

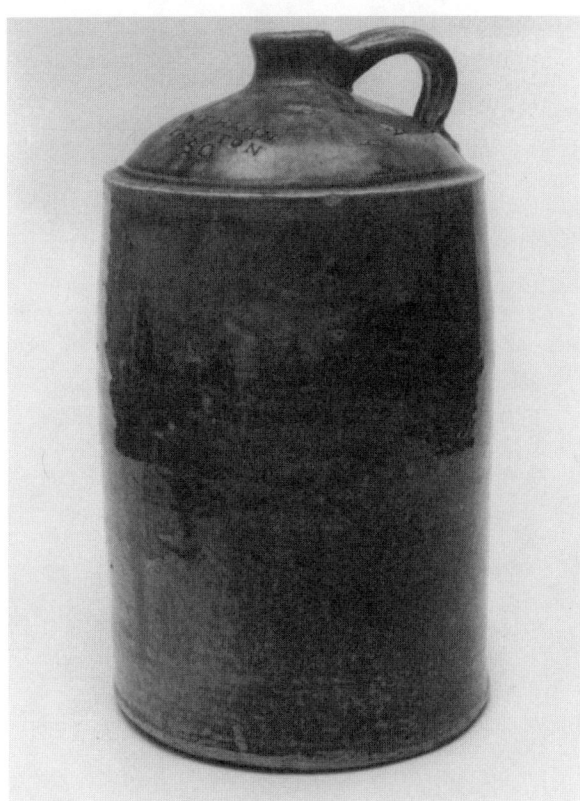

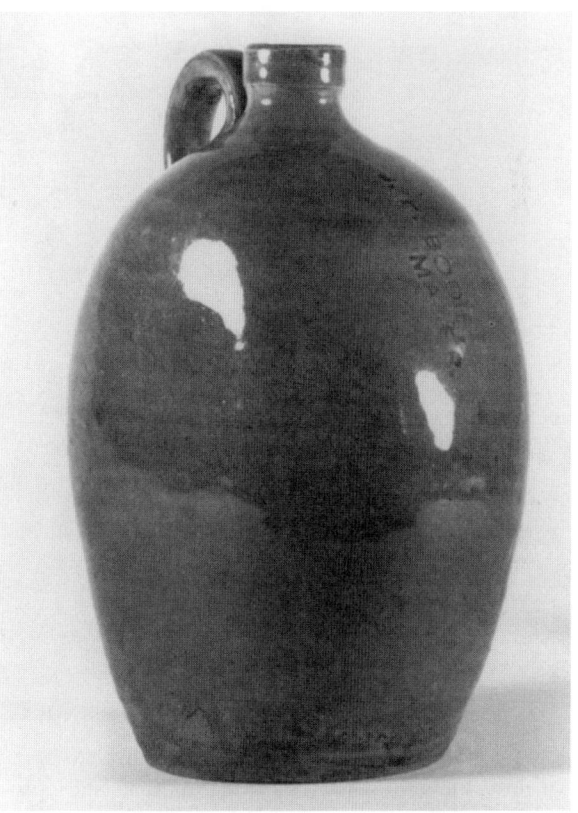

6.14 Alkaline-glazed stoneware jug with tooled shoulder, ca. 1880–1900, William F. Hahn, Trenton, S.C. H 13¾″, C 25″. Stamped: WF HAHN / TRENTON / SC (front, upper shoulder between handles); 2 (upper shoulder, right of center). Collection of Paul and Sally Hawkins.

6.15 Slip-decorated alkaline-glazed stoneware drinking jug with flattened sides, 1851, Thomas Chandler, Thomas Chandler Factory, Edgefield District, S.C. H 8½″, C 13⅝″. Kaolin-slip script: B. Wren / N 6 / 1851. Collection of Tony and Marie Shank.

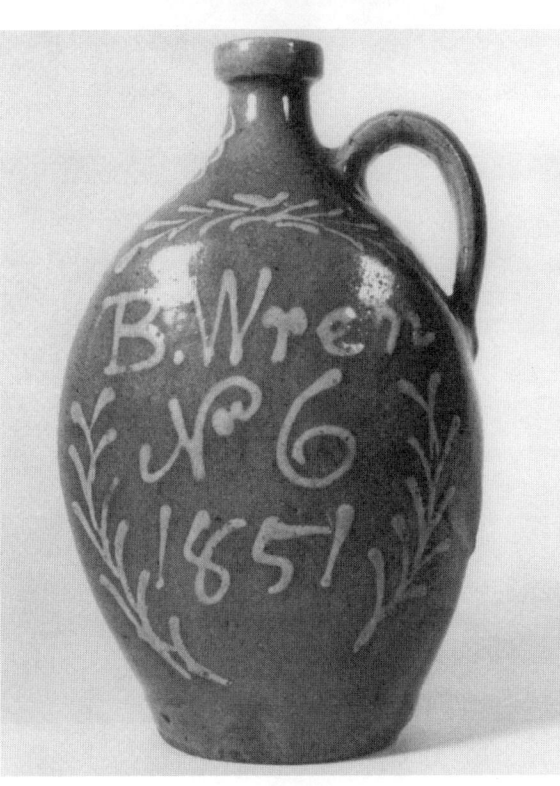

6.16 Alkaline-glazed stoneware drinking jug with flattened sides, ca. 1870, Jesse P. Bodie Pottery, Kirksey's Crossroads, Edgefield County, S.C. H 8⅞″, C 17¾″. Stamped: J. P. BODIE / MAKER (vertical, opposite handle along length of jug). Collection of Georgeanna H. Greer.

COOLERS

Thomas Chandler also produced "coolers," large
containers designed to dispense water, cider,
wine, and distilled liquors such as brandy or gin.
This vessel form, first produced at the Phoenix
Factory, consisted of an unusually tall, ovoid jug
with a jug rim or a wide flared mouth and with
a bunghole placed just above the base. Coolers
appear in Edgefield at the Phoenix Factory,
Thomas Chandler Factory, and Lewis Miles Fac-

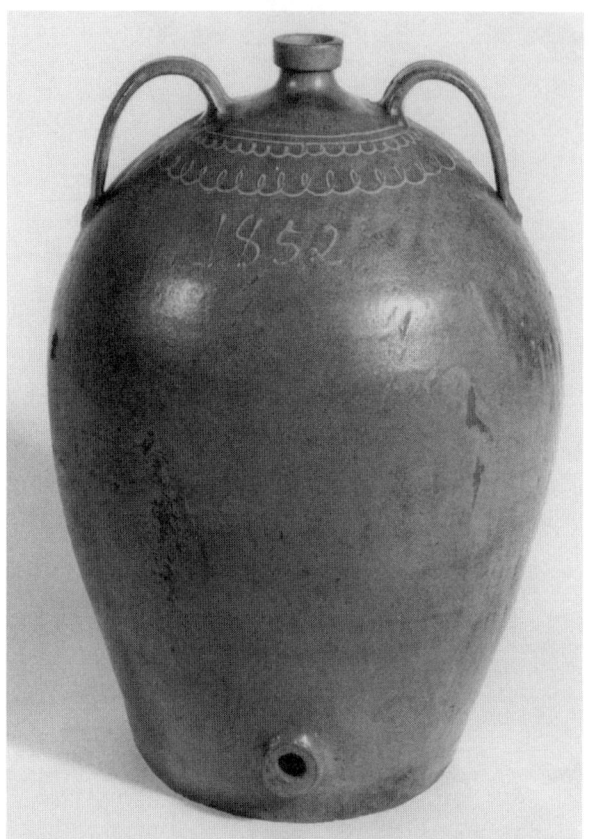

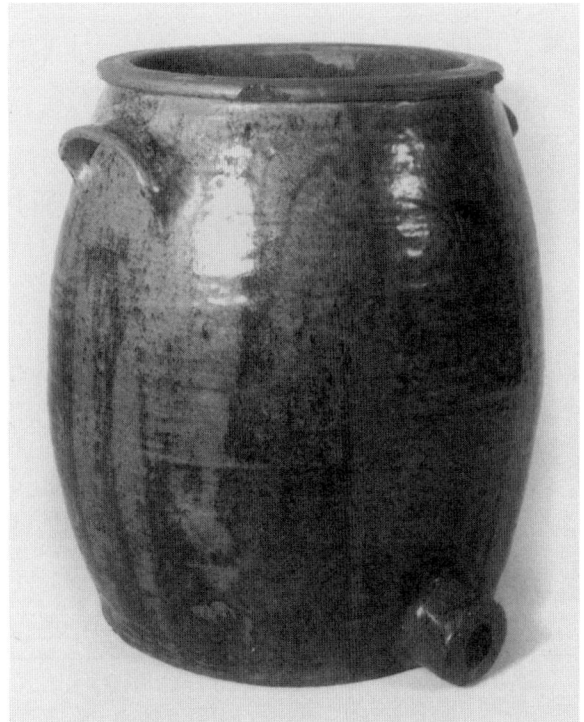

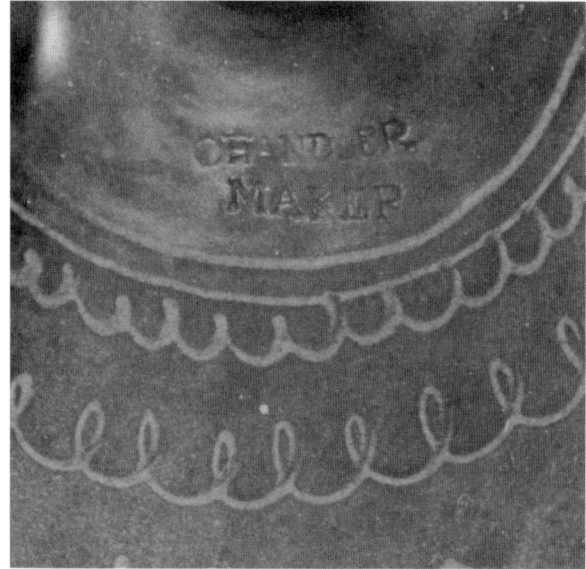

6.17 Alkaline-glazed stoneware cooler, ca. 1840–50,
attributed to an unknown African-American slave potter, Lewis Miles Factory, Horse Creek Valley, Edgefield
District, S.C. H 16⅛″, C 47¼″. The thick-walled asym-
metrical form of this cooler, in contrast to the highly
symmetrical thin-walled coolers attributed to Thomas
Chandler, is probably indicative of African-American
origins. Collection of Henry Scott Taylor.

6.18   Slip-decorated alkaline-glazed stoneware cooler with wide banded or collared jug rim, 1852, Thomas Chandler, Thomas Chandler Factory, Kirksey's Crossroads, Edgefield District, S.C. H 21⅝", C 50". Stamped: CHANDLER / MAKER (front, upper shoulder). Kaolin-slip loop and swag motif and date of manufacture, "1852," at upper shoulder and between handle attachments. Courtesy of the Museum of Early Southern Decorative Arts, Winston-Salem, N.C.

tory. Since Chandler was one of the principal turners at the Phoenix Factory, he is credited with the introduction of the cooler form to the Edgefield area. Coolers were commonly used in taverns for storing alcoholic beverages behind the bar. They were containers for holding smaller amounts of cider or wine from barrels stored in the basement or back room. "The bungs were often placed a little above the base to allow sediment to settle below the spigot."[5] The cooler, a standard form produced in the stoneware potteries of New England, offers further evidence that Thomas Chandler was introducing northern ideas to Edgefield.

KEGS

A related form, the keg, barrel, or rundlet is modeled after the wooden barrels used for similar purposes. English folk pottery scholar Peter Brears reported that "unlike those made in other parts of the country, the majority of the harvest ware made in Sussex were neither jugs nor bottles, but instead took the form of smaller kegs or flasks. The most [common] ones to have survived are the kegs which closely copied the shape and proportions of the rather elongated cane-bound casks of oak. [A]round each end of these kegs an appropriate number of raised bands was thrown to represent the cane bindings."[6]

Two distinct sizes of kegs appear in North Carolina. The smaller version is found in lead, salt, and alkaline glazes, but the larger example is represented only in alkaline-glazed stoneware by Catawba Valley potter Sylvanus Hartsoe.[7] No kegs attributed to Edgefield have been reported, but Jugtown potter Leonard Atkins produced a small keg with a dark brown-black "cinder glaze" and five horizontal tooled bands at his Jug Factory Road shop in Spartanburg County, South Carolina (see Figure 6.19). Atkins probably picked up the form from a North Carolina–trained potter who turned at one of the Jugtown-area shops.

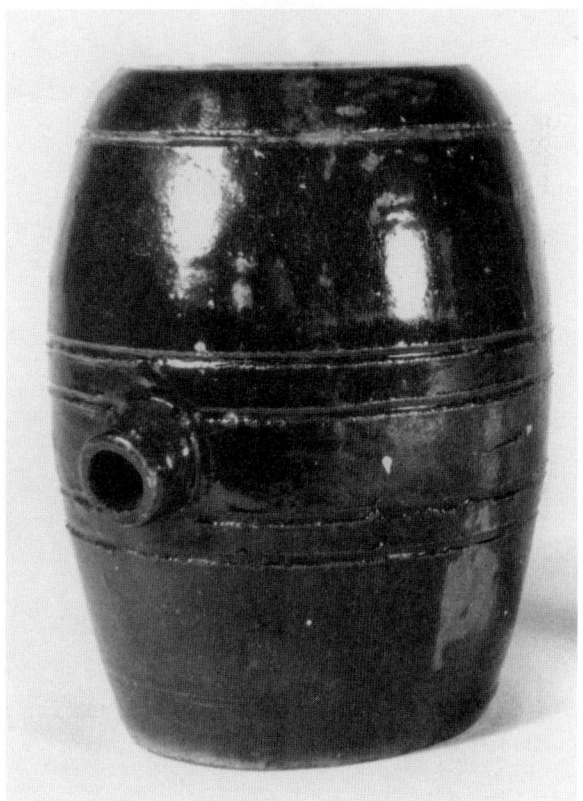

6.19   Alkaline-glazed stoneware keg with tooled bands, ca. 1900, John Leonard Atkins, Jug Factory Road, Jugtown, Greenville County, S.C. H 7⅝", C 19⅛". Collection of Thomas Gentry Bab.

MONKEY, OR HARVEST, JUGS

The "monkey," or harvest, jug, an ovoid vessel with an over-arching stirrup handle and one or two tubular spouts attached at an angle at the upper shoulder, is another unusual form produced in Edgefield. Several of the face vessels attributed to Edgefield slave potters are monkey jug forms.[8] Only one example of a slip-decorated Edgefield monkey jug has been identified (Figure 6.20). This ovoid jug has the char-acteristic overarching handle, a large spout for pouring (with a ringed collar) attached at an angle at the front upper shoulder, and a small vestigial spout designed to allow air into the vessel to make pouring easier. It is decorated in kaolin and iron slip with a loop and swag motif that is identified with the Collin Rhodes Factory.

RING JUGS

Another unusual form, the ring jug, could be hung from a saddle or up on a nail or peg for ready access. This Old World form was known in other parts of the country as a ring, harvest, or mower's bottle (see Figure 6.21).[9]

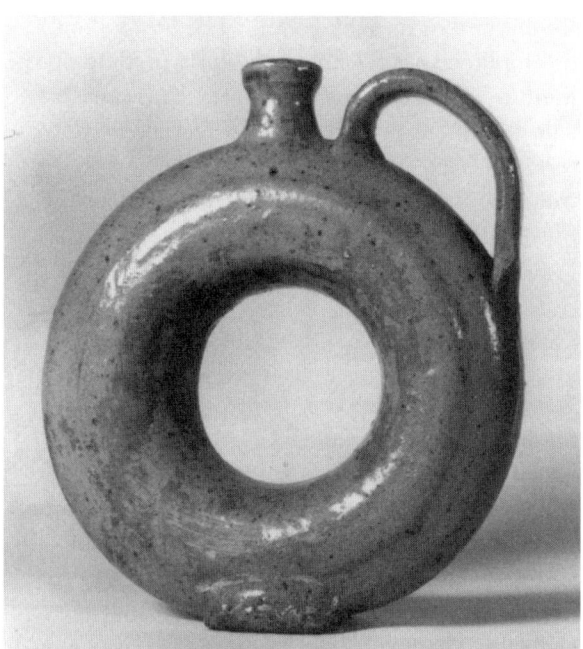

6.20   Slip-decorated alkaline-glazed stoneware "monkey" jug, ca. 1840, attributed to the Phoenix Factory, Shaw's Creek, Edgefield District, S.C. H (restored spout and handle), C 31 ¼". Kaolin- and iron-slip loop and swag motif, flowers at handle attachments, and capacity mark "3." Collection of Tony and Marie Shank.

6.21   Alkaline-glazed stoneware ring jug, ca. 1880–1900, attributed to the Landrum Pottery, Richland County, S.C. H 10⅛", C 20⅞". Collection of the Charleston Museum, Charleston, S.C.

BOTTLES

Although bottles were not commonly produced in the South, at least one South Carolina potter, Clarence Belcher of Inman, apparently turned stoneware bottles. A tall, bell-shaped bottle with a dark brown-black glaze and a simple rolled rim is attributed to the Belcher pottery (Figure 6.22).

PITCHERS

This category includes vessels used to serve beverages at the table and for washing. The pitcher is the most common serving container and was produced by potters throughout the state. South Carolina stoneware potters made two or more types of pitchers—including the common serving pitcher and the milk pitcher (see Figures 6.23 and 6.24).

Serving pitchers vary in form but are characterized by an overall baluster shape consisting of a full rounded bottom section with a cylindrical upper section. Pitchers also have a single loop handle and a fluted or pinched spout for pouring. Milk pitchers are usually ovoid rather than

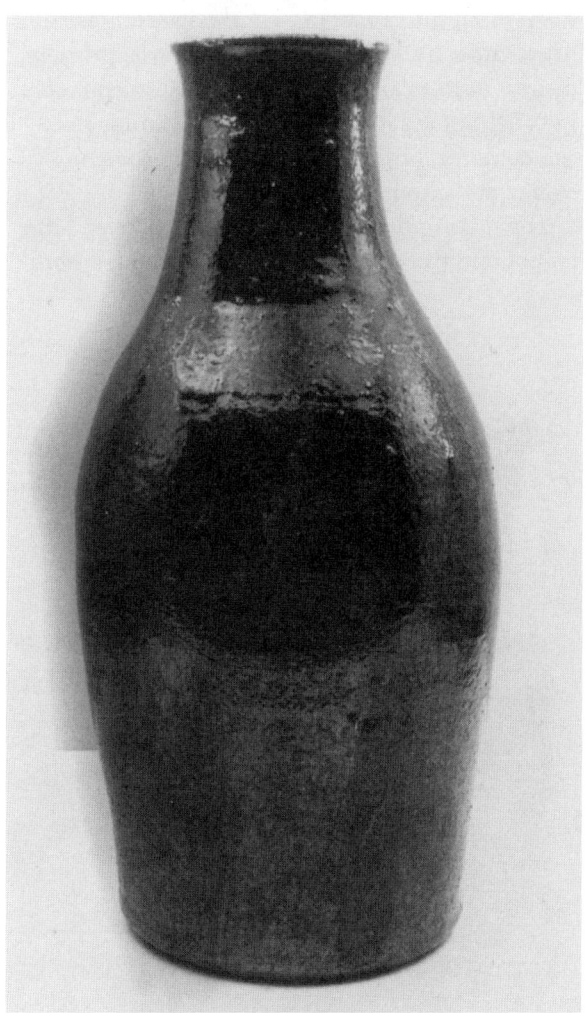

6.22 Alkaline-glazed stoneware bottle, ca. 1930, Clarence Belcher, Spartanburg County, S.C. H 19½", C 30". Collection of the Charleston Museum, Charleston, S.C.

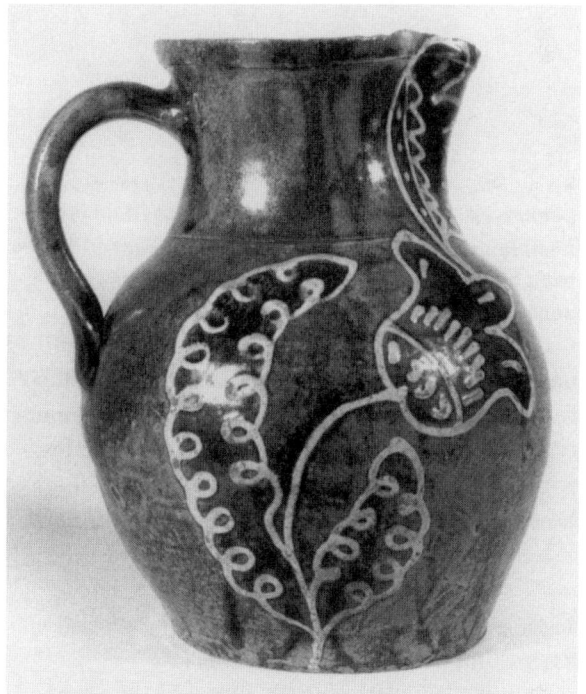

6.23 Slip-decorated alkaline-glazed stoneware serving pitcher with kaolin- and iron-slip tulips and loop and swag motif, ca. 1850, attributed to the Collin Rhodes Factory, Shaw's Creek, Edgefield District, S.C. Collection of Dr. and Mrs. James K. Smith.

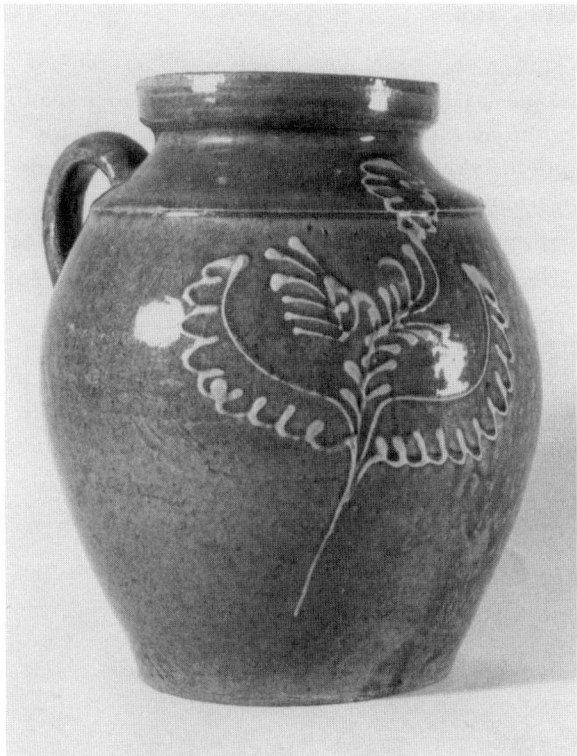

6.24 Slip-decorated alkaline-glazed stoneware milk
pitcher, ca. 1850, attributed to the Collin Rhodes
Factory or Thomas Chandler Factory, Edgefield District, S.C. H 9⅝″, C 26⅞″. Collection of Georgeanna H. Greer.

baluster-shaped. Also, while the serving pitcher
features a fluted pouring spout, the milk pitcher
typically has a circular banded rim for a lid or
cover. This special rim treatment reflects the
function of these vessels. Milk pitchers were often
filled with "sweet" (whole fresh) milk or buttermilk and placed in an icebox or springhouse,
thereby serving as storage containers as well as
for serving.

   Smaller Edgefield pitchers used at the table
were often decorated. Many examples of slip-
decorated serving pitchers have survived. Some
milk and serving pitchers have one or more raised
horizontal bands at the midpoint between the
lower neck and upper body. These also appear to
have been decorative treatments.

COFFEEPOTS AND TEAPOTS

Nineteenth-century estate inventories and newspaper advertisements attest that South Carolinians enjoyed their coffee and tea. Coffee was
listed among the stock of goods offered for sale
by Pottersville factory owners J. Gibbs and Company in 1843.[10] During the same year Hamburg
merchant H. A. Kenrick offered "a general assortment of china, crockery and glassware consisting
of common and fine teas, plates, bowls, pitchers,
dishes, flowers and basins, granite and china tea
setts."[11] Some local potters took advantage of
the demand for these beverages by producing
stoneware teapots and coffeepots.

   The distinguishing characteristic between the
teapot and the coffeepot is form. Although both

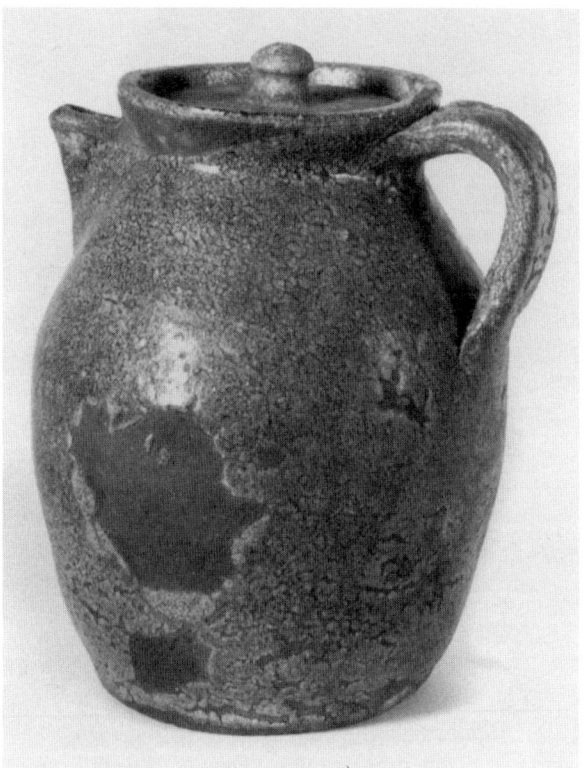

6.25 Alkaline-glazed stoneware coffee boiler, ca.
1850–60, Landrum Pottery, Columbia, Richland
District, S.C. H 7¾″, C 19″. Collection of Tony and
Marie Shank.

vessels may feature either a tubular or a V-shaped spout, the teapot is typically spherical in form, while the coffeepot is cylindrical or baluster-shaped.

Teapot or coffeepot fragments found at the John Landrum site in the Edgefield District may be similar in form to the "coffee boilers" listed in the 1820 industrial census as having been produced by Georgia potter Abraham Massey. Massey had migrated to Georgia from Edgefield and may have produced the coffee boiler form in South Carolina before coming to Georgia.

A coffeepot recovered from the Stork-Landrum pottery site in Richland County is the only known whole vessel of its type that may be directly attributed to the Landrum family (Figure 6.25). The Richland County coffeepot is baluster-shaped and has a flared rim, with an interior lid ledge and a knob-handled lid, an applied V-shaped spout, and opposing loop handle. The glaze color and texture of this vessel are difficult to ascertain, since the vessel was improperly fired. This rough-textured glaze is gray in color and has "crawled" along the surface of the pot, leaving unglazed patches.

Bowls, Cream Risers, and Butter Pots

South Carolina stoneware potters produced a variety of pan-form bowls designed for food preparation and serving. Larger mixing bowls, cream risers, and butter pots often have two opposing lug handles attached at the rim. Flattened and indented banded rims are the most common type of rim treatment found on bowls. Most bowls have straight sides that taper inward toward the base, but a few serving bowls with gently rounded sides have been identified (see Figure 6.26).

The wide-mouthed milk pan or cream riser was designed for separating cream. Antebellum Edgefield potters produced this form in a variety of sizes. In post–Civil War Edgefield, cream risers or clabber bowls took the form of squat pitchers,

frequently without spouts. The thick cream that rose to the top of the fresh milk placed in the pan could be easily skimmed off to be used in the preparation of butter and buttermilk. Once the cream was converted into butter it was stored in an icebox or springhouse in straight-sided butter pots with heavy lids (see Figure 6.27).

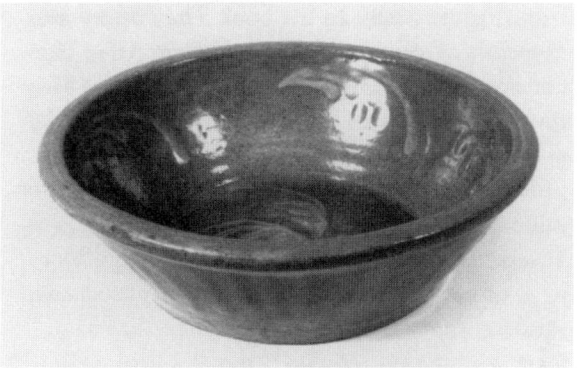

6.26 Slip-decorated alkaline-glazed stoneware bowl, ca. 1850, attributed to the Collin Rhodes Factory or the Thomas Chandler Factory, Edgefield District, S.C. H 2¾″, C 28¾″. Collection of James Henry Riddle, Jr.

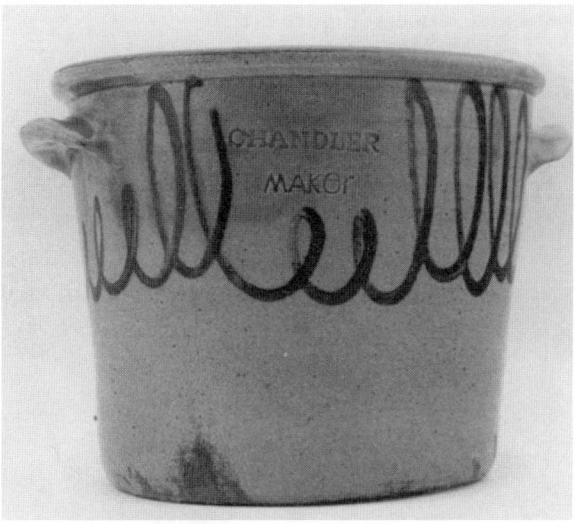

6.27 Slip-decorated alkaline-glazed stoneware butter pot, ca. 1850, Thomas Chandler Factory, Kirksey's Crossroads, Edgefield District, S.C. H 7⅛″, C 27⅞″. Stamped: CHANDLER MAKER. Collection of Dr. and Mrs. George V. Rosenberg.

Tableware

South Carolina stoneware potters produced tableware such as cups, mugs, saucers, and plates
throughout the nineteenth century but never
on a large scale. A slip-decorated master salt,
used for salting foods at the table, is attributed
to the Phoenix Factory in the Edgefield District (Figure 6.28). In his book *The Pottery and
Porcelain of the United States* Edwin Atlee Barber wrote that during the time of the Civil War
the Thomas Davies Palmetto Fire Brick Works
at Bath, South Carolina, was converted to the
production of tableware for the Confederate hospitals. According to family history, turners at the
Owensby pottery contributed to the war effort
by producing cups and saucers for Confederate
soldiers. These were specialty items that were
usually made on request. After the turn of the
century some potters such as Albert Fulbright
of the Mountain View Pottery near Inman produced fancy decorated tableware. Fulbright's line
of ware included a cobalt-decorated table setting
consisting of a teapot, sugar and creamer, and
cups and saucers (Figure 6.29).

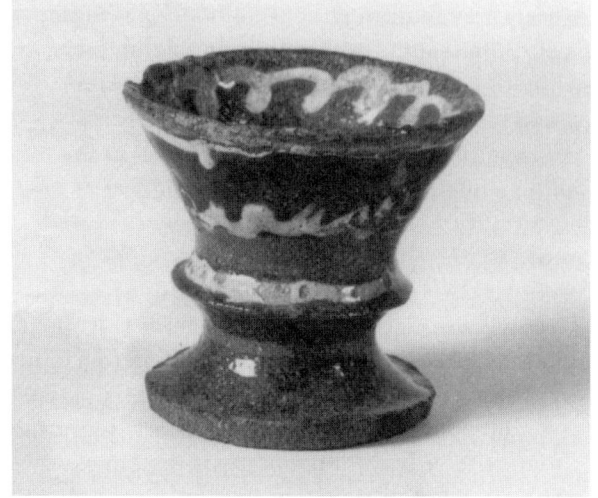

6.28   Slip-decorated alkaline-glazed stoneware mas-
ter salt, ca. 1840, attributed to the Phoenix Factory,
Shaw's Creek, Edgefield District, S.C. H 2⅜″, C 8¼″.
Collection of Tony and Marie Shank.

6.29   Cobalt-decorated alkaline-glazed stoneware tea
set, ca. 1920, attributed to Mountain View Pottery (formerly the Clayton Jug Factory), Inman, S.C., cream
pitcher in background at far right, ca. 1927, Hilton Pottery Works, Hickory, N.C. Collection of the Charleston
Museum, Charleston, S.C.

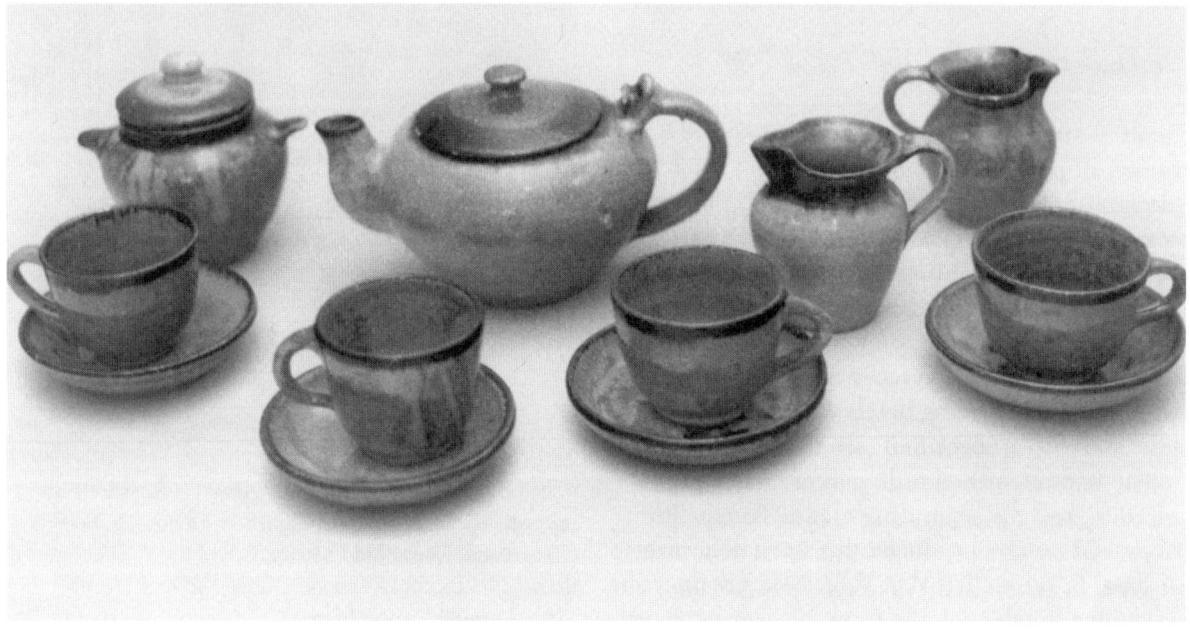

Pipes and Spittoons

Molded clay tobacco pipes were an important sideline for South Carolina stoneware potters throughout the nineteenth century, and some individuals specialized in pipe-making. For example, Sarah Garner appears in the 1860 Edgefield District census with the occupation "pipe making." [12] Members of the Horne family apparently also made tobacco pipes in Edgefield. Mrs. M. W. Watson of Ridge Springs reported in a 1920 interview that members of the family came to her grandmother's plantation, known as the King Plantation, to get "a very fine clay to make fancy clay pipes." [13] Alkaline-glazed stoneware tobacco pipes have been recovered from the site of the John Landrum pottery, and molded tobacco pipes were also found at the site of the Landrum Fire Brick Works in Richland County.

The spittoon, another vessel related to tobacco use, also appears in stoneware. A doughnut-shaped spittoon with an opening at the side through which the tobacco juice was drained is attributed to the Benjamin Franklin Landrum factory in Edgefield (Figure 6.30). This vessel has a smooth, glassy olive brown alkaline glaze.

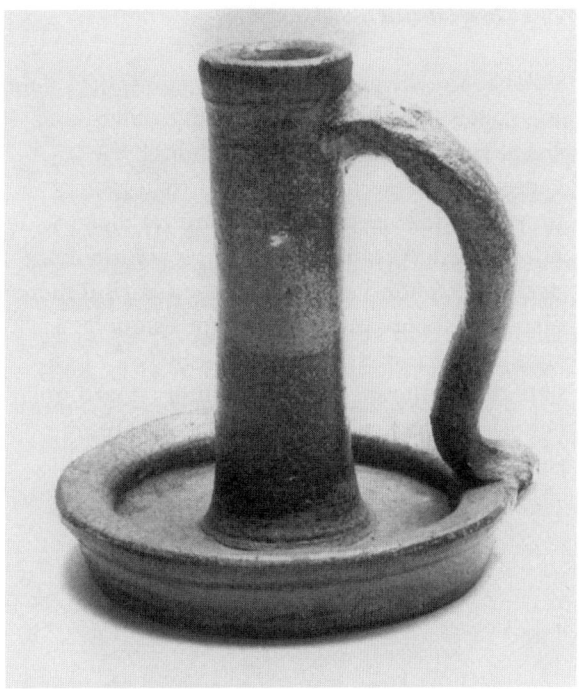

6.31 Alkaline-glazed stoneware candlestick, ca. 1930, Clarence Belcher Pottery, Jugtown, Spartanburg County, S.C. H 6⅜″, C 18⅛″. Collection of the Charleston Museum, Charleston, S.C.

Personal Hygiene Implements

The chamberpot and pitcher were the most common toilet articles produced in stoneware. The chamberpot is shaped like a large teacup with an everted rim. Chamberpots appear at several of the early Edgefield pottery sites and were apparently one of the earliest forms produced in alkaline-glazed stoneware in the state.

Tin basins were probably more commonly used for personal washing than were stoneware bowls, but large-capacity stoneware pitchers (holding up to two gallons) were designed for carrying water for bathing.

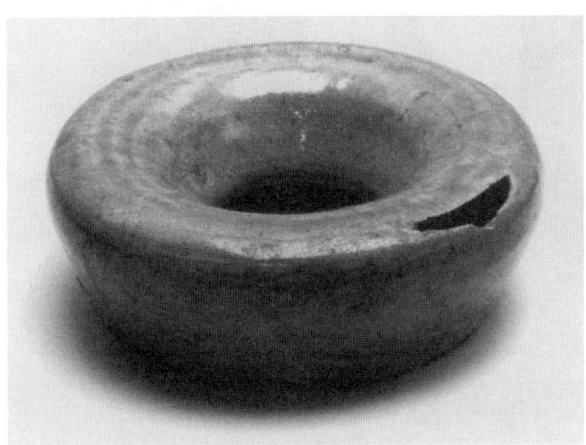

6.30 Alkaline-glazed stoneware spittoon, ca. 1900, Benjamin F. Landrum Pottery, Aiken County, S.C. H 2½″, C 23¼″. Collection of the Charleston Museum, Charleston, S.C.

Lighting Implements

Prior to the advent of electricity, household lighting consisted of the open hearth, candles, and simple fuel-burning lamps. Although the invention of the kerosene lamp in 1859 largely precluded the need for stoneware candlesticks, after World War I the demand grew for a more decorative pottery. Potters responded with more elaborate forms and glazes.[14] For example, a stoneware candlestick produced by C. L. Bennett at the Clarence Belcher Pottery near Inman is in the collection of the Charleston Museum (Figure 6.31).

Toys and Miniatures

Unglazed clay marbles were among the artifacts recovered from the Pottersville factory site in Edgefield. Marbles were easy to make and are commonly found in stoneware. Some South Carolina potters also produced miniature vessels. These were designed as toys for children and as giveaways, advertisements, or promotionals. The Nevilles produced miniature jugs at their pottery in West Union, and Albert Fulbright of the Mountain View Pottery made "cuckoo jugs" (miniature jugs used as whistles) and "little brown jugs" to sell at the Spartanburg fair. Although jugs were the most popular type of miniature, potters made miniatures in a variety of forms. For example, Aylie Boyle, Jr., made miniature churns at the Boyle factory in Cherokee County (see Figure 6.32).

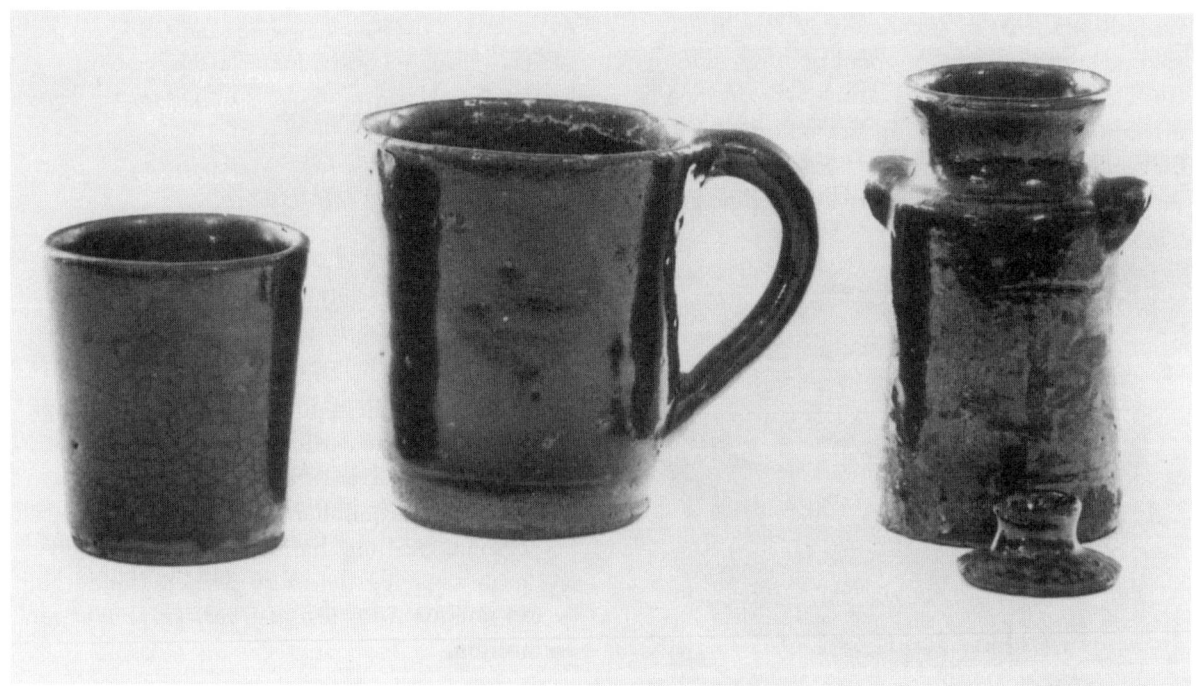

6.32   Alkaline-glazed stoneware goblet, mug, and miniature churn, ca. 1930, Boyle Pottery, Union (present-day Cherokee) County, S.C. Collection of Kye Boyle.

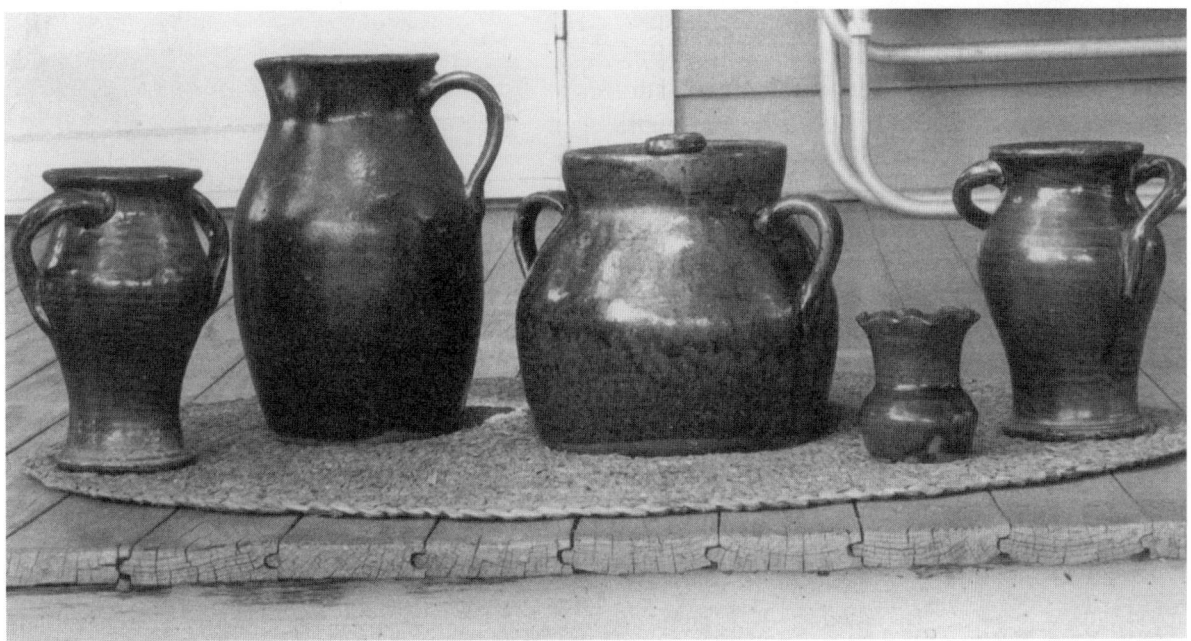

6.33   Clayton Jug Factory ware: flower vases, pitcher, and stew pot.
Collection of Mrs. Jones ("Pete") Clayton.

Horticultural Implements

By the turn of the century stoneware potters throughout the South were facing competition from increasingly available and cheaper mass-produced glass and metal containers. Most potters converted to the production of garden and tourist ware in order to survive.

Many potters produced gardenware such as flowerpots, vases, and urns along with their regular line of stoneware. Flowerpots were unglazed, as were the large urns or planters used in the yard and in the cemetery. Urns, planters, and vases were often further embellished with decorative handles, fluted rims, and tooled rings (see Figure 6.33).

South Carolina potters also produced vessels used in animal husbandry. The chicken waterer or poultry fountain appears in alkaline-glazed stoneware in the Edgefield District as well as in the upcountry region of the state.

Sculpted Vessels

Sculpted vessels are attributed to several Edgefield-area stoneware factories. These vessels take two main forms—the figural vessel and the face vessel. Figural vessels are statuettes consisting of a vessel base onto which a complete figure has been modeled in applied clay. Details such as facial features are typically rendered in dark iron-bearing slip or white kaolin slip. The face vessel also involves modeling features in clay onto a thrown base, but instead of a complete figure, the potter created a head with well-defined facial features. Mid-nineteenth-century South Carolina face vessels may be distinguished from later versions by the type of material used for the eyes and teeth. Early Edgefield potters inserted pure kaolin into the hollow openings of the eyes and mouth. The round eyeballs occasionally bear a single puncture mark where they were pierced with a sharp tool. Details of the teeth vary widely, with some potters simply smoothing the kaolin into the mouth and others meticulously incising one or two rows of vertical lines onto the clay divided by a single horizontal line across the length of the mouth. Another Edgefield potter applied a row of diagonal lines for the teeth. Although some twentieth-century potters have produced face vessels with eyes fashioned from kaolin, the teeth typically consist of broken fragments of earthenware. The jagged "teeth" are inserted into the mouth individually. The possible origins and significance of these unusual vessels have already been discussed in Chapter 3. Twentieth-century South Carolina potters who produced face vessels include the Brown family of Bethune and John R. Smith in the Jugtown area.

Mortuary Objects

Pottery grave markers, made to be placed on a grave as a marker or planter, are found from southwestern Pennsylvania to Texas. Few South Carolina examples have survived, but these vessels were probably fairly commonly produced in the late nineteenth century.

A vessel signed in iron-slip script "John Trapp / Edgefield District / SC / January 13, 1846" may be a rare example of an antebellum South Carolina cemetery urn or planter (Figure 6.34). This unusual pot, attributed to the Trapp-Chandler Factory at Kirksey's Crossroads, has a smooth olive brown alkaline glaze, a tooled rim, and a wide, footed base.

In a 1967 *Ceramics Monthly* article Bennie Lee and Don Lewis wrote about their discovery of over thirty large cemetery urns and a grave marker in a local cemetery.[15] The vessels illustrated in the article were unglazed but were decorated with fluted rims, incised markings, and tooled rings. They exhibited a wide range of forms. One of the most recent examples was

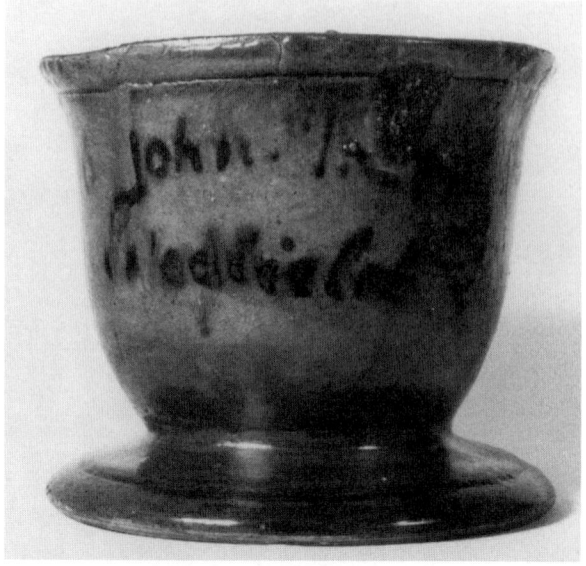

6.34   Alkaline-glazed stoneware cemetery urn, 1846, Trapp-Chandler Factory, Kirksey's Crossroads, Edgefield District, S.C. H 6⅛″, C 23⅛″. Iron-slip script: John Trapp / Edgefield District / SC / January 13, 1846. Collection of Tony and Marie Shank.

a tall footed urn with a pedestal-type base and fluted rim (Figure 6.36). This was one of the most sophisticated pieces, having been turned in two pieces. Two other pots were baluster-shaped, and a third was short and squat with a high, wide shoulder and an everted rim. The simplest pot in form and decoration was a wide-mouthed flowerpot with three sets of wavy combed bands.

The makers of these vessels were not identified, but Lee and Lewis observed that the ware represented the skills of at least a half-dozen different potters. The grave ornaments have long since disappeared, but the cemetery where they were found, Mt. Lebanon Church in Greenville County, is located in the heart of Jugtown. Several potters, most notably the Hensons, Atkinses, and Tapps, operated shops in the Mt. Lebanon community. Thomas Gentry Bab, stepson of

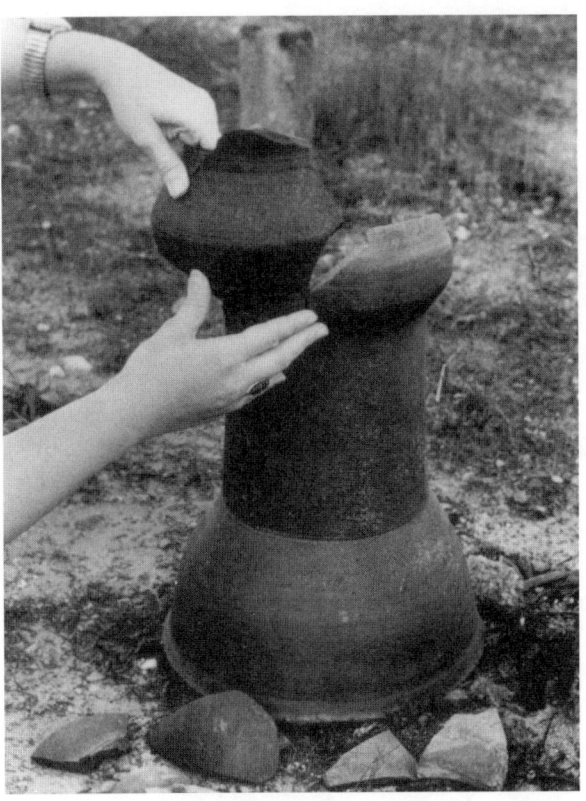

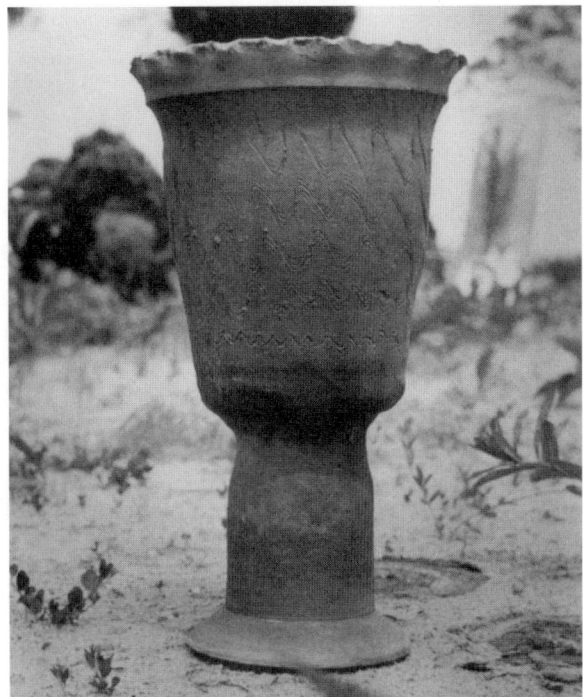

6.35   Unglazed stoneware grave marker with incised inscription, ca. 1930, Jugtown, Mt. Lebanon Church, Greenville County, S.C. From Lee and Lewis, "Graveyard Pots," with thanks to Don Lewis.

6.36   Unglazed stoneware cemetery urn with incised decoration, ca. 1930, Jugtown, Mt. Lebanon Church, Greenville County, S.C. From Lee and Lewis, "Graveyard Pots," with thanks to Don Lewis.

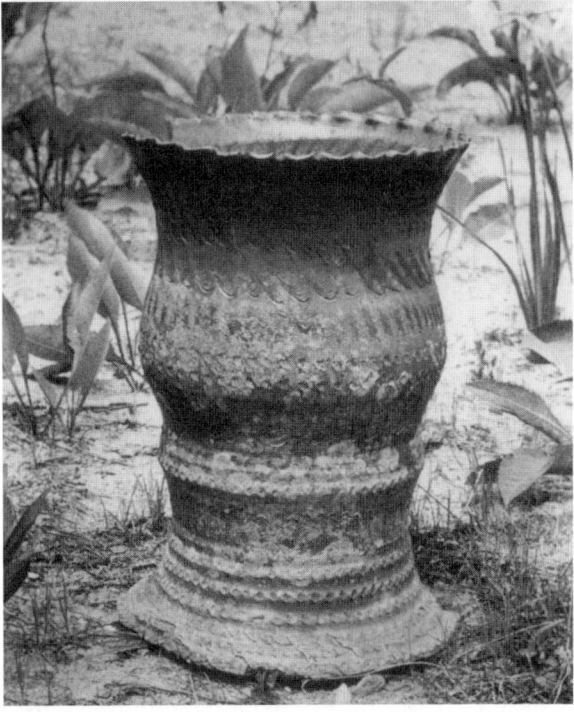

6.37   Unglazed stoneware cemetery urn with incised decoration, ca. 1930, Jugtown, Mt. Lebanon Church, Greenville County, S.C. From Lee and Lewis, "Graveyard Pots," with thanks to Don Lewis.

were much less expensive than stone markers. Moreover, as Greer explained, "Many of these markers were made for members of potter's families."[17]

Early nineteenth-century South Carolina stoneware may be identified by its characteristic forms and features. Ware produced in South Carolina prior to 1860 is generally ovoid in form with ware gradually becoming more cylindrical during the late nineteenth century. Early Edgefield District ware tends to have thick body walls and heavy bases. Jugs have pulled strap handles attached below the neck and at the upper shoulder. Most early Edgefield jugs have flattened rolled handles that are oval-shaped in cross section. Churns and jars typically have two opposing slab-type handles attached horizontally at the upper shoulder. Large-capacity storage jars, espe-

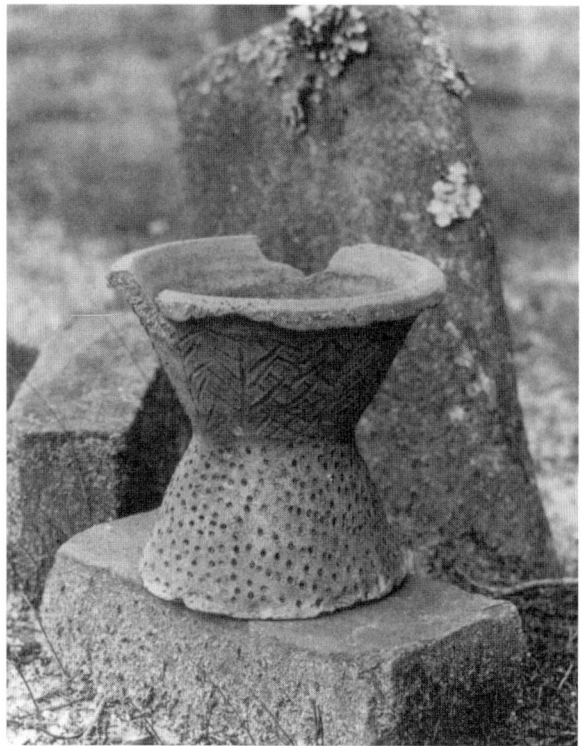

6.38   Unglazed stoneware cemetery urn with incised decoration, ca. 1930, Jugtown, Mt. Lebanon Church, Greenville County, S.C. From Lee and Lewis, "Graveyard Pots," with thanks to Don Lewis.

Jugtown potter Leonard Atkins, recently sold a similar cemetery urn that he claimed had been made by his stepfather. The unglazed stoneware urn or planter is cylindrical with a widely flared footed base and a flared and scalloped rim. It is decorated with a series of wavy horizontal incised lines. According to Mr. Bab, Atkins made a number of these vessels. Atkins, then, was apparently one of the Jugtown area potters who produced the "graveyard pots" found at Mt. Lebanon Church.

Burrison has observed that "the tradition of ceramic grave markers seems to have been stimulated by depressed economic conditions following the Civil War, when many families could not afford stone markers."[16] Stoneware grave markers

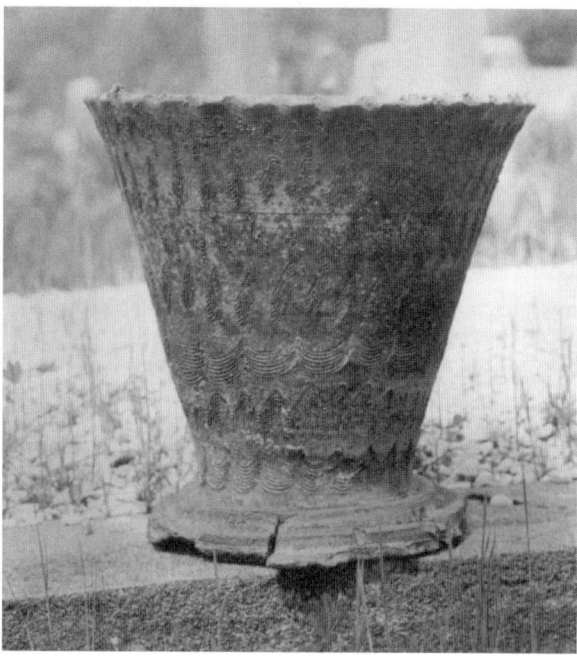

6.39   Unglazed stoneware cemetery urn with incised decoration, ca. 1930, Jugtown, Mt. Lebanon Church, Greenville County, S.C. From Lee and Lewis, "Graveyard Pots," with thanks to Don Lewis.

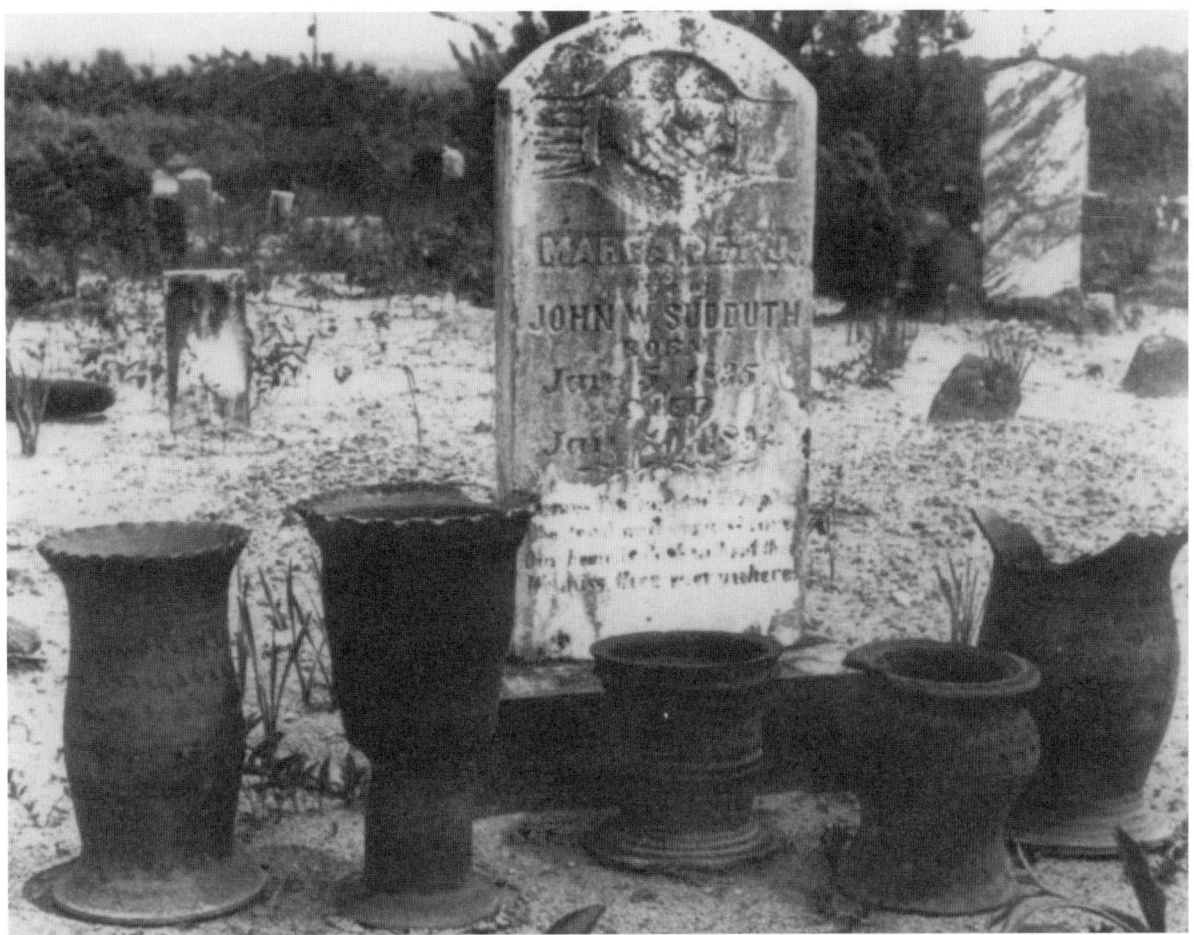

6.40 Unglazed stoneware cemetery urns and grave marker, with incised decoration, ca. 1930, Jugtown, Mt. Lebanon Church, Greenville County, S.C. From Lee and Lewis, "Graveyard Pots," with thanks to Don Lewis.

cially those produced by Edgefield potter Thomas Chandler, may have four evenly spaced handles.

Another important feature of South Carolina stoneware that distinguishes it from ware produced in other southern states is the composition of the clay body and glaze mixture. South Carolina clays, particularly those found in the Edgefield District, typically contain a high pro-

portion of kaolin. Consequently, South Carolina ware tends to have relatively light-colored clay bodies and glazes. This combination of characteristic vessel forms and features, as well as clay composition and glaze color, identify South Carolina alkaline-glazed stoneware as a distinctive regional pottery tradition.

Decline and Renewal of the Southern Folk Pottery Tradition

The twentieth century marked a period of transition for stoneware pottery production in South Carolina. By the turn of the century pottery shops had been established throughout the upstate region. Potters from Georgia moved through South Carolina en route to the pottery centers of the Catawba Valley and Buncombe County in western North Carolina. A few North Carolina potters such as M. A. Helton moved southward and established shops in South Carolina. The demand for locally produced pottery remained high in the rural areas where there was less access to outside markets. But potters encountered increasing competition from other shops and were faced with the problem of finding more specialized markets for their ware. The depression years of the 1920s and 1930s prompted a resurgence of the stoneware pottery tradition in South Carolina. In addition to filling the demand for inexpensive containers for food storage and preservation, some stoneware potters specialized in the production of jugs for the illicit liquor trade.

By the 1940s the once vital pottery traditions of the South had begun to disappear. Although the greater availability of efficient glass and metal containers contributed to this decline, a number of factors led to the demise of the local stoneware industry in the region. The demand for stoneware syrup jugs decreased in proportion to the drop in cane syrup production as store-bought sugar became commonplace. John Burrison has noted that "with the rise of commercial dairies in the 1920s many farmers found it uneconomical to keep their own cows, and so the ware that accompanied milk processing—milk crocks, 'cream risers,' churns and buttermilk pitchers—often were abandoned. At the same time, the substitution of the icebox and, later, the refrigerator for older ways of cooling dairy products (such as the springhouse) made its contribution."[1] The expansion of job markets in the South during and after World War I and the subsequent changes in southern life also had a negative impact on the pottery tradition in the South.

During the handicrafts "revival" movement of the 1920s and 1930s, Laura Bragg, then director of the Charleston Museum, initiated the first project aimed at documenting the folk pottery traditions of South Carolina. This project was limited in scope, however, and did not produce any permanent document.

Unlike in the surrounding states of North Carolina and Georgia, the South Carolina stoneware tradition was not directly influenced by the arts and crafts movement. There were actually two revivals. The first occurred in the 1920s and 1930s in North Carolina. Outsiders (most notably the Busbees at Jugtown) came in with new ideas to redirect the old tradition, and a new clientele of tourists traveling up and down Route 1 to and from Florida provided a ready market for the new ware. During the late 1960s and early 1970s a second revival, inspired by the commemorative celebrations and activities surrounding America's bicentennial and popular books such as Mary Emmerling's *American Country*, revitalized the folk pottery traditions of North Carolina and Georgia.

Both revivals bypassed South Carolina, whose potters did not have the same advantages as their counterparts in North Carolina and Georgia. Although a few folk potters were still producing stoneware in the state during the late 1940s and early 1950s, there had been no direct introduction of new ideas from outside South Carolina. Also, South Carolina did not have a strong market for the new "art" pottery. Despite these disadvantages, a few potters took advantage of the tourist trade to develop new markets for their ware. The Nevilles of West Union, for example, made miniatures that they gave to tourists from Charleston who visited the nearby resort town of Walhalla via the Blue Ridge Railroad during the early 1900s. Neville ware was also reportedly used at the Biemann Hotel in Walhalla, a luxury hotel that catered to lowcountry tourists. Albert Fulbright of the Clayton jug factory (renamed the Mountain View Pottery during the 1920s) developed a line of tableware, and tourist items such as "cuckoo jug" whistles and "little brown jugs" that he sold at the county fair in Spartanburg. The Bethune Pottery, located on Highway 1 in Kershaw County, like the potteries of Moore and Chatham counties in eastern North Carolina, catered to the Florida tourist trade as well as to the local demand for utilitarian stoneware. These are relatively isolated examples, however, and were not directly connected with the arts and crafts revival.

Renewed interest in southern folk pottery within the past two decades has resulted in the organization of a number of major exhibitions

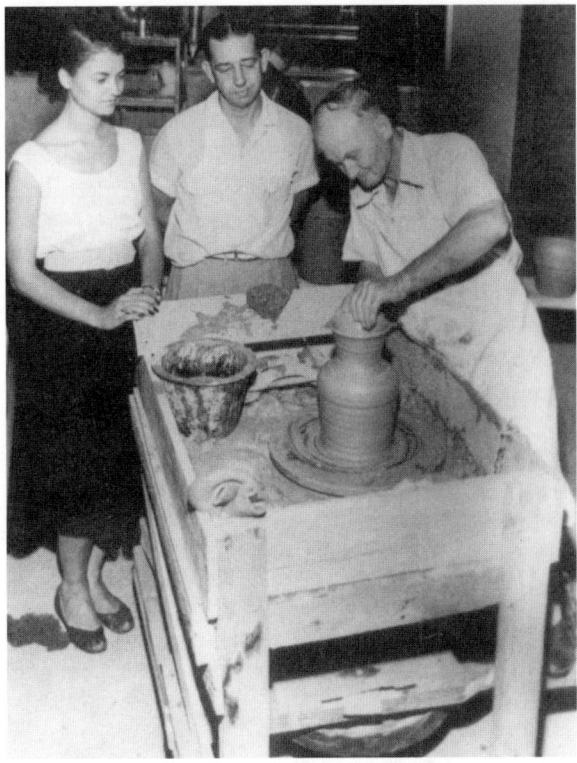

E.1 Claude Bennett turning ware at Hugh Baynham's shop in North Augusta, S.C., ca. 1960. Courtesy of Hugh Baynham.

and the publication of several important books on the subject. *American Stonewares: The Art and Craft of Utilitarian Potters*, by Georgeanna H. Greer, published in 1981, was a pioneering work that demonstrated the role of the southern folk pottery tradition in the development of American stoneware. The exhibition and catalog *Early Decorated Stoneware of the Edgefield District, South Carolina*, organized by the Greenville County Museum of Art in 1976, was the first focused museum exhibition dealing specifically with South Carolina's alkaline-glazed stoneware tradition. The catalog for this exhibition, written by local collectors Stephen and Terry Ferrell, continues to be an important reference for collectors and scholars alike. In 1983 John A. Burrison published the first in-depth study of the folk pottery traditions of a particular state within the South. Entitled *Brothers in Clay: The Story of Georgia Folk Pottery*, it is a sensitive and thorough account of Georgia's stoneware traditions. Several other exhibitions and their accompanying catalogs have generated interest in southern stoneware. These include *Southern Make: The Southern Folk Heritage* and *Carolina Folk: The Cradle of a Southern Tradition* at the McKissick Museum, University of South Carolina, by George D. Terry and Lynn Robertson Myers; John Burrison's exhibit

"Tangible Traditions: Folk Crafts of Georgia and Neighboring States" at the Atlanta Historical Society; *The Traditional Pottery of Alabama* at the Montgomery Museum of Fine Arts by E. Henry Willett and Joey Brackner; *Potters of the Catawba Valley, North Carolina* at the Mint Museum, edited by Daisy Wade Bridges; and *The Traditional Pottery of North Carolina* at the Ackland Art Museum, University of North Carolina, by Charles G. Zug III. A second statewide survey, entitled *Turners and Burners: The Folk Potters of North Carolina* by Zug was published in 1986.

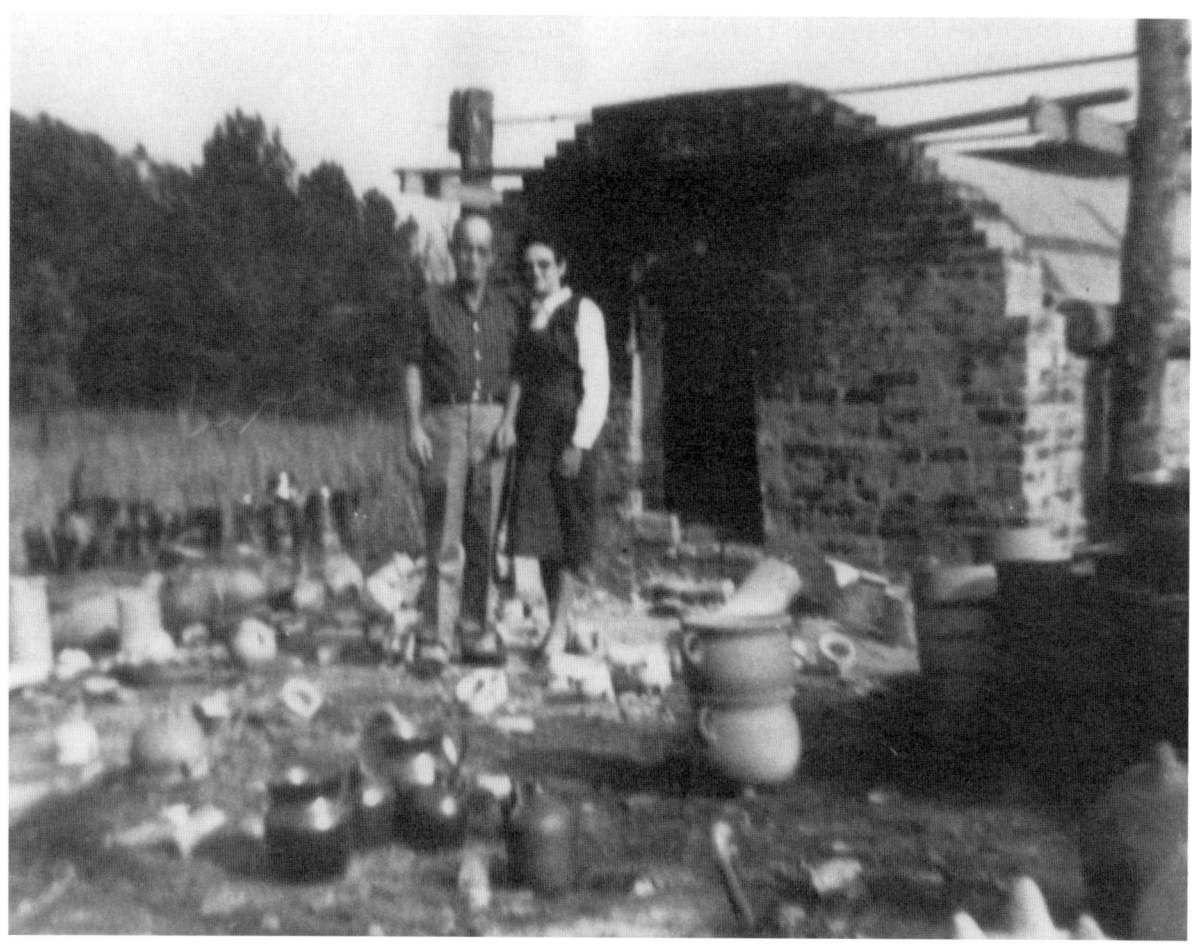

E.2   Otto Brown, Sr., and wife Emmaus Avery Brown at the Brown Pottery, Chesterfield County, S.C., January 1963. Courtesy of Frances Thompson.

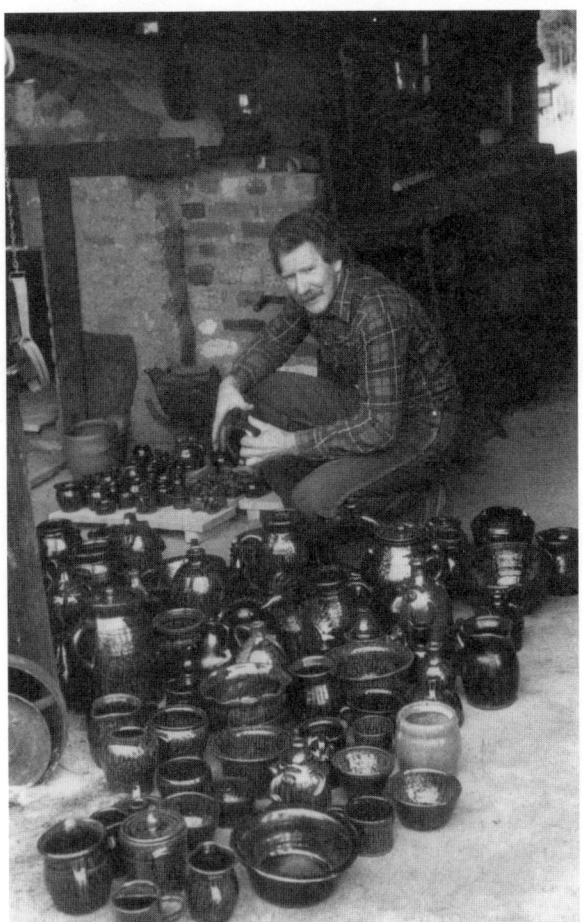

E.3 Billy Henson at his second kiln opening, 5 March 1990, Lyman, S.C.

Like *Brothers in Clay*, *Turners and Burners* is the definitive study of North Carolina's folk pottery traditions.

In Georgia, Alabama, and North Carolina, a few folk potters, notably Lanier and Cleater Meaders, Chester Hewell, Jerry Brown, and Burlon Craig, still produce traditional stoneware. Although no folk potters have been active in South Carolina since the 1950s, Billy Henson, a descendant of the Henson family of Jugtown, South Carolina, is learning the craft. Billy recently built a pottery shop complete with a treadle wheel, glaze mill, and tunnel kiln, and is turn-

ing stoneware in the tradition of his grandfather, Jesse Vardry Henson. Through talking with local turners such as Pete Clayton and members of the Brown family of Arden, North Carolina, and by reading recently published studies on southern folk pottery, Billy is reintroducing the pottery tradition to South Carolina. Billy's involvement in the craft stems from an interest in preserving the history of his family and community and from a respect for the "old ways." "I love to see things did the old way," he explains. "I feel like I was born a hundred years too late." He describes how he became interested in making pottery. "Back when I was a kid my Dad used to . . . we'd walk down across the branch, and he'd tell me about his father doing pottery. At the time I wasn't interested. Then in '84 when the book came out on . . . *Foxfire*, had the pottery in it, I got to reading about it. And I got to talking to my uncle, and he remembered a lot about it. He used to go to the mountains with his Dad to haul pottery with the mules and wagon, and he said they would camp out on Green Creek . . . went in a covered wagon. They would go two wagon loads at a time." When questioned about his talent for working with his hands and using tools he replies, "Most people that lived on a farm did things like that. When you don't have much money, you have got to learn to do things. A person that's got a lot of money can get on the telephone and call the plumber, electrician, whatever, you know. But if you don't have the money to do it, you do the best you can. It's survival . . . learn to survive." Billy's efforts are a hopeful sign because they indicate a renewed interest in and increasing recognition of the vital role that the pottery tradition has played in the lives of South Carolinians during the past two hundred years.

A landmark event that helped bring South Carolina's alkaline-glazed stoneware tradition to the attention of the public was the 1990–91 exhibition "Crossroads of Clay" organized by the McKissick Museum. McKissick also initiated preliminary research on several Edgefield District stoneware pottery sites. Since there is no continuing pottery tradition in Edgefield, archaeology has been an important component of the South Carolina stoneware research. These efforts will hopefully enable South Carolinians to have a greater understanding of and appreciation for the stoneware traditions of their state and region. These "great and noble jars" and the people who made them represent a fundamental part of the history and culture of South Carolina and the South. Our recognition of these traditions is a validation and reaffirmation of our cultural heritage.

Appendixes

Landrum Family Pottery Dynasty

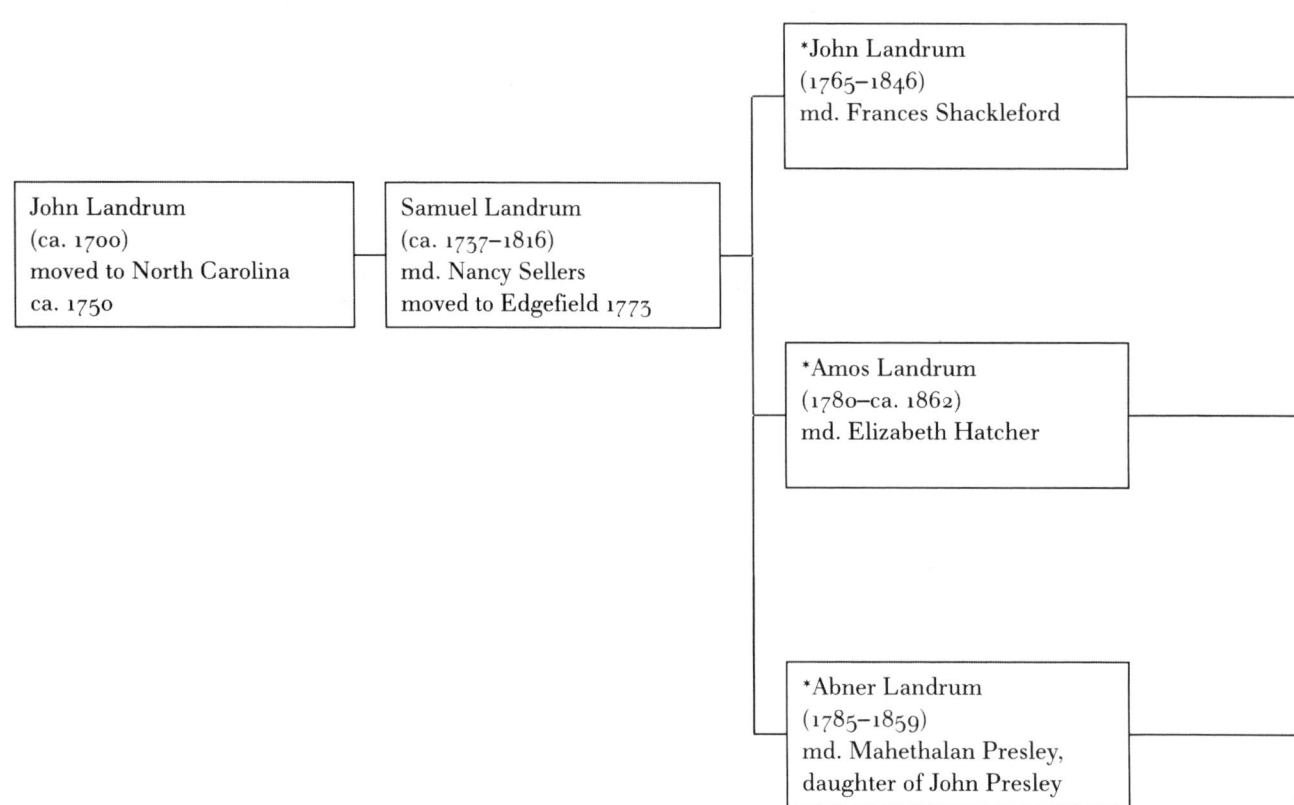

John Landrum
(ca. 1700)
moved to North Carolina
ca. 1750

Samuel Landrum
(ca. 1737–1816)
md. Nancy Sellers
moved to Edgefield 1773

*John Landrum
(1765–1846)
md. Frances Shackleford

*Amos Landrum
(1780–ca. 1862)
md. Elizabeth Hatcher

*Abner Landrum
(1785–1859)
md. Mahethalan Presley,
daughter of John Presley

*Stoneware potters

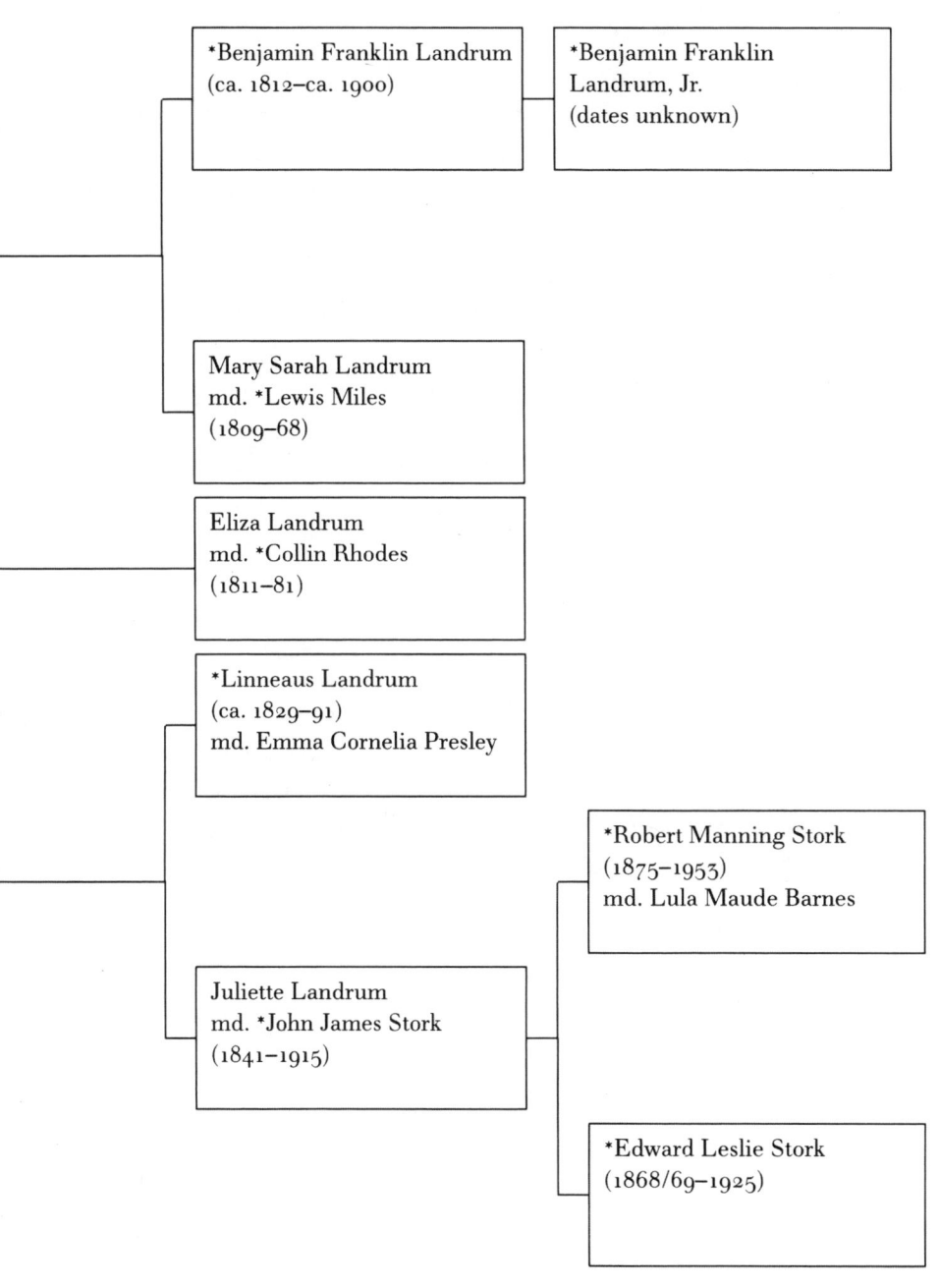

*Benjamin Franklin Landrum
(ca. 1812–ca. 1900)

*Benjamin Franklin
Landrum, Jr.
(dates unknown)

Mary Sarah Landrum
md. *Lewis Miles
(1809–68)

Eliza Landrum
md. *Collin Rhodes
(1811–81)

*Linneaus Landrum
(ca. 1829–91)
md. Emma Cornelia Presley

Juliette Landrum
md. *John James Stork
(1841–1915)

*Robert Manning Stork
(1875–1953)
md. Lula Maude Barnes

*Edward Leslie Stork
(1868/69–1925)

Ownership Chronology for the Pottersville Stoneware Manufactory

Date	Firm Name or Transfer	Investor-Owners
ca. 1815–28	Pottersville Stoneware Manufactory	Abner Landrum
1828–32	Drake Factory	Harvey Drake Reuben Drake
1832–36	Drake and Rhodes Factory	Reuben Drake Collin Rhodes
January 1836	Drake, Rhodes and Company	Reuben Drake Collin Rhodes Nathaniel Ramey
September 1836– June 1838	Ramey, Rhodes and Company	Nathaniel Ramey Collin Rhodes Robert Mathis
1838–39	Rhodes, Ramey and Gibbs	Collin Rhodes Nathaniel Ramey Jasper Gibbs
January 1839	N. Ramey and Company	Nathaniel Ramey Jasper Gibbs John Hughes
October 1839	Gibbs sold his interest in the factory.	Nathaniel Ramey John Hughes
April 1840	Ramey and Hughes mutually dissolved their partnership; Ramey deeded his interest in the factory to James W. Gibbs and Jasper Gibbs.	James W. Gibbs Jasper Gibbs
1841	J. Gibbs and Company	Jasper Gibbs Sandford Gibbs John D. Nance
1842	The factory was divided into six shares.	John Hughes James W. Gibbs Jasper Gibbs Sandford Gibbs John D. Nance (sixth partner unknown)
1850	Pickens purchased the factory between 1842 and 1850.	Francis W. Pickens

Sources: This information was compiled from a series of Edgefield deeds, plats, equity records, business agreements, and newspaper advertisements.

Verses Appearing on Ware Produced by the Slave Potter Dave

"Put every bit all between / surely this jar will hold 14"
(12 July 1834)
South Carolina State Museum, Columbia, S.C.

"Better thing I never saw / When I shot off the Lions
jaw" (9 November 1836)

"Give me silver or either gold; / though they are
dangerous; to our soul" (27 June 1840)
Anonymous collection

"Ladys & Gentlemens Shoes / Sell all you can &
nothing you'll lose" (29 January 1840)

"Dave belongs to Mr. Miles / wher the oven bakes & the
pot biles" (31 July 1840)
Charleston Museum, Charleston, S.C.

"Another trick is worse than this / Dearest Miss, spare
me a kiss" (26 August 1840)
Collection of William L. Cox

"I wonder where is all my relations / Friendship to all—
and every nation" (17 May 1857)
Collection of Larry Carlson

"I made this jar for cash / Though its called mere trash"
(22 August 1857)
Collection of Tony and Marie Shank

"Pretty little girl on a verge / volca[n]ic mountain, how
they burge" (24 August 1857)
*McKissick Museum, University of South Carolina,
Columbia, S.C.*

"I made this for our, Sott / it will X never—never,—rott"
(31 March 1858)
Pottersville Museum, Edgefield, S.C.

"This noble jar will hold 20 / fill it with silver then you'll
have plenty" (8 April 1858)
Collection of Georgeanna Greer

"A very large jar which has four handles / pack it full of
fresh meat—then light candles" (12 April 1858)
Collection of John Burrison

"I saw a leppard & a lion's face, / then I felt the need
of—grace" (3 November 1858)
Collection of Tony and Marie Shank

"Hive is eighteen; hundred + fifty nine / unto you all I
fill in ———, cline" (18 April 1859)
Anonymous collection

"Good for lard or holding fresh meats / blest we were,
when Peter saw the folded sheets" (3 May 1859)
Collection of Tony and Marie Shank

"Made at Stoney Bluff / for Making lard Enuff"
(13 May 1859)
Charleston Museum, Charleston, S.C.

"Great & Noble jar, / hold sheep, goat and bear"
(13 May 1859)
Charleston Museum, Charleston, S.C.

"The fourth of July is surely come / to sound the fife and
beat the drum" (4 July 1859)
Collection of John Burrison

"A noble jar, for pork or beef / then carry it a round to
the indian chief" (9 November 1860)
Collection of Tony and Marie Shank

"I—made this Jar all of cross / If you dont repent, you
will be lost" (3 May 1862)
Collection of Tony and Marie Shank

Weight of Major Elements in Glaze and Clay Body of Selected Alkaline-glazed Stoneware Samples from Texas, Alabama, South Carolina, North Carolina, and Georgia (%)

	Silica	Titanium	Aluminum	Iron	Manganese	Magnesium	Calcium	Sodium	Potassium	Phosphorus	Summary
							Oxides Used				
Matthew Duncan Site, Bastrop County, Tx.											
Glaze	68.83	.60	12.24	2.41	.085	.20	15.38	.14	1.246	.442	101.18
Clay body	71.97	.82	15.73	2.269	.020	.539	.52	.12	1.826	.065	93.88
James Kirbee Site, Montgomery County, Tx.											
Glaze	66.02	.46	11.52	4.88	.226	.30	16.14	.02	.910	.412	100.88
Clay body	65.69	.77	15.90	4.306	.063	.90	3.13	.07	1.124	.171	92.13
Pound Pottery Site, Randolph County, Ala.											
Glaze	60.81	.41	12.72	4.12	.559	1.25	15.22	.46	1.843	.339	97.74
Clay body	66.01	.76	19.23	3.029	.040	.480	.64	.53	2.340	.048	93.11
Miles Mill Site, Horse Creek Valley, Edgefield District, S.C.											
Glaze	57.69	.79	13.03	3.65	.985	1.65	16.55	.18	1.160	.445	96.12
Clay body	54.05	1.91	26.46	4.459	.105	.970	1.89	.15	1.652	.073	91.73
Rhodes-Seigler Site, Shaw's Creek, Edgefield District, S.C.											
Glaze	53.06	1.08	13.29	2.89	.616	2.48	18.02	.15	.765	.172	92.53
Clay body	56.93	1.94	26.91	3.388	.043	.352	.58	.02	.644	.046	90.81
George Donkel Site, Buncombe County, N.C.											
Glaze	61.58	.25	7.24	17.92	.058	1.03	8.88	6.33	1.236	.433	104.94
Clay body	56.45	1.40	20.14	4.027	.036	.634	.40	1.02	.881	.027	85.02

Notes

CHAPTER ONE

Carolina Clay: Early Influences on the Stoneware Tradition in South Carolina

1. Quoted in Winberry, "The Cultural Hearth of the Southern Pottery Tradition," 7.
2. Ramsay, *American Potters and Pottery*, 90.
3. Kovacik and Winberry, *South Carolina: A Geography*, 13–29.
4. Tuomey, "Report on the Geological and Agricultural Survey of South Carolina," 44.
5. Ceramics scholar Georgeanna Greer notes that high alumina clays do not take salt well. High silica clays are required for proper development of the salt glaze, which consists mainly of sodium silicate. This may partially explain why Edgefield potters developed the alkaline glaze rather than producing salt-glazed stonewares. Georgeanna Greer, personal communication, 7 May 1989.
6. Robinson, Buie, and Johnson, *Common Clays of the Coastal Plain of South Carolina*, 13.
7. Grimshaw, *The Chemistry and Physics of Clays and Allied Ceramic Materials*, 36, 272, 338–40, 899.
8. Swanton, "The Indians of the Southeastern United States"; Fewkes, "Catawba Pottery-Making," 69–124; Harrington, "Catawba Potters and Their Work," 399–407; Speck, "Indian Notes and Monographs"; Simms, *The Magnolia*, 3:222–23.
9. Baker, "Catawba Indian Trade Pottery of the Historic Period"; Merrell, *The Indians' New World*, 267–71.
10. Spargo, *Early American Pottery and China*, 7–18.
11. Rhodes, *Stoneware and Porcelain*, 29–33.
12. "A letter signed Philolethes," 2 March 1763, *Papers of Henry Laurens*, 3:314, SCL; "An Expedition in Search of Cherokee Clay, 1767–1768," in Merens, *The Colonial South Carolina Scene*, 243–45.
13. Quoted in Barber, *The Pottery and Porcelain of the United States*, 59–60.
14. Henry Laurens to Thomas Mears, 24 January 1757, *Papers of Henry Laurens*, 2:431, SCL.
15. Caleb Lloyd to Richard Champion, 25 July 1765, in Owen, *Two Centuries of Ceramic Art in Bristol, Being a History of the True Porcelain by Richard Champion*, 8.
16. Henry Laurens to Andrew Williamson, 30 October 1764, *Papers of Henry Laurens*, 4:486, SCL.
17. Henry Laurens to William Williamson, Westminster, 28 November 1771, *Papers of Henry Laurens*, 8:55, SCL; Terry, "Pottery Manufacturing in South Carolina, 1750–1830." See also Rauschenberg, "'A Clay White as Lime . . . of Which There is a Design Formed by some Gentlemen to Make China': The American and English Search for Cherokee Clay in South Carolina, 1745–75," 67–80.
18. Myers, "A Survey of Pottery Manufacture," 1–13.
19. Burrison, *Brothers in Clay*, 101; Giannini, "Anthony Duche," 201; Watkins, *Early New England Potters and Their Wares*, 34–38.
20. *South Carolina Gazette*, 5 April 1735, p. 3, SCL; quoted in Burrison, *Brothers in Clay*, 102.
21. Current research suggests that Duche used clays from western North Carolina in these experiments. Personal communication, Bradford Rauschenberg, fall 1987. For a more detailed account of Andrew Duche's pottery ventures in South Carolina and Georgia, see Rauschenberg,

"Andrew Duche: A Potter 'a Little Too Much Addicted to Politicks,'" 1–101.

22. The Philadelphia firm of Gouse Bonnin and George Anthony Morris launched the first successful American attempt to make porcelain in 1769. They first produced porcelain in 1771, but the few examples of their ware that have been identified are not hard enough to be called true porcelain. Like many early American potting ventures, Bonnin and Morris was short-lived, lasting only until 1772. Claims that Anthony Duche was associated with Bonnin and Morris appear to be unfounded. See Prime, *The Arts and Crafts in Philadelphia, Maryland, and South Carolina, 1721–1785*, 117; Hood, *Bonnin and Morris*.

23. Terry, "Pottery Manufacturing in South Carolina, 1750–1830"; South Carolina Judgments, no. 59A, p. 3, August 1768, SCDAH. George Terry kindly shared his research notes regarding John Bartlam and the export of Carolina clay to England. See also, Rauschenberg, "John Bartlam Who Established 'new Pottworks in South Carolina' and Became the First Successful Creamware Potter in America," 1–66.

24. South Carolina Court of Common Pleas, Judgment Rolls, 1768, roll 64, box 76B, no. 59A, p. 4, SCDAH.

25. South Carolina Mortgages, 3A, p. 343, 21 May 1768, SCDAH. Recent archaeological investigations carried out by Stanley South, Carl Steen, and Bradford Rauschenberg at the site of Bartlam's Cainhoy pottery may yield important additional information regarding this early South Carolina pottery operation.

26. *South Carolina Gazette & Country Journal*, 16 May 1769, p. 4, col. 3, and 6 June 1769, suppl. p. 1, col. 3, SCL.

27. South Carolina Journal of Commons House of Assembly, no. 38, pt. 2, SCDAH.

28. *South Carolina Gazette*, 4 October 1770, p. 3, col. 1; *South Carolina Gazette & Country Journal*, 20 November 1770; *South Carolina Gazette*, 11 October 1770, suppl., p. 2, col. 1, SCL; quoted in Terry, "Pottery Manufacturing in South Carolina, 1750–1830," 6.

29. Finer and Savage, eds., *The Selected Letters of Josiah Wedgwood*, 29.

30. Wedgwood, "An Address to the Workmen."

31. Schulz, "The Rise and Decline of Camden," 26–27, 92; Lewis, *Camden: A Frontier Town in Eighteenth-Century South Carolina*, 169–73; Charleston Inventories (1776–84), Charleston County Probate Court, book BB, p. 214, CCCH.

32. Bivens, *The Moravian Potters in North Carolina*, 7.

33. William Hill, York County Office of the Clerk, William McGill, 25 August 1856, SCL. Tom Cowan uncovered this reference while researching South Carolina iron foundries.

34. Grimshaw, *The Chemistry and Physics of Clays and Allied Ceramic Materials*, 36.

35. Early European kilns were a simple updraft type based on Roman prototypes. Greer, *American Stonewares*, 16–17; Rhodes, *Stoneware and Porcelain*, 3–34.

36. Rhodes, *Stoneware and Porcelain*, 29–33.

37. Barber, *The Pottery and Porcelain of the United States*, 60.

38. Grimshaw, *The Chemistry and Physics of Clays and Allied Ceramic Materials*; Rhodes, *Stoneware and Porcelain*, 3–34.

39. Graham and Wedgwood, *Wedgwood*. See also Finer and Savage, eds., *The Selected Letters of Josiah Wedgwood*; Wedgwood and Wedgwood, *The Wedgwood Circle*; Honey, *Wedgwood Ware*; Dawson, *Masterpieces of Wedgwood in the British Museum*; Macht, *Classical Wedgwood Designs*; Reilly and Savage, *Wedgwood: The Portrait Medallions*.

40. Zug, *Turners and Burners*, 23.

41. Bordley, *Essays and Notes on Husbandry and Rural Affairs*, 456–57. Howard Smith kindly provided this reference.

42. Ramsay, *American Potters and Pottery*, 83; Barka, "The Kiln and Ceramics of the 'Poor Potter' of Yorktown," 291–318.

43. Myers, "A Survey of Pottery Manufacture," 4.

44. Ketchum, *Early Potters and Potteries of New York State*, 20–32.

45. See Burrison, *Brothers in Clay*, 138–39.

46. Pendrill-Church, *William Cookworthy, 1705–1780*; Greer, "Preliminary Information on the Use of the Alkaline Glaze," 156.

47. Quoted in Zug, *Turners and Burners*, 72.

48. Abner Landrum attended the Willington Academy in Abbeville District and studied with a prominent doctor in Augusta, Georgia. Founded in about 1804 by teacher-minister Moses Waddel, the Willington Academy was established as "an American Eton," specializing in classical studies. Prominent Willington graduates include John C. Calhoun, William H. Crawford, Hugh S. Legare, George McDuffie, and A. B. Longstreet. W. W. Mims, personal communication, 20 November 1989. Lyon, "Moses Waddel and the Willington Academy."

49. Vlach, "International Encounters at the Crossroads of Clay."

50. Mills, *Statistics of South Carolina*, 523–24.

51. Castille, Baldwin, and Steen, *Archaeological Survey*.

52. South Carolina Legislative Papers, 1831–59, Public Improvements—Manufacturing, Petition of Abner Landrum regarding porcelain manufacture to the Committee, SCDAH.

53. Rhodes, *Kilns*, 45–50.

54. Zug, *Turners and Burners*, 207–9.

55. Burrison, *Brothers in Clay*, 81–84.

56. Zug, *Turners and Burners*, 160.

57. Ramsey, *American Potters and Pottery*, 87.

58. Brackner, "Traditional Pottery of Mobile Bay." The demographics of Alabama and Mississippi are such that the alkaline glaze was predominant in eastern and southern Alabama and in eastern Mississippi. The use of the salt glaze dips deeply into northwestern Alabama and western Mississippi. In Alabama the dividing line between the two glaze types generally followed the Piedmont and the major river systems, which served as natural geographical boundaries. Joey Brackner, personal communication, 17 July 1990.

CHAPTER TWO

The Edgefield District Stoneware Factories: Origins of a Regional Folk Pottery Tradition

1. Kovacik and Winberry, *South Carolina: A Geography*, 13–23.

2. Burton, *In My Father's House Are Many Mansions*, 15.

3. Lockwood, *A Geography of South Carolina*, 78.

4. See "Guide Maps to the Development of South Carolina Parishes, Districts and Counties," compiled by the South Carolina Department of Archives and History, WPA Records Survey, for an analysis of South Carolina parish, district, and county origins.

5. Chapman, *History of Edgefield County*, 40–42, 52–55; Jones, *South Carolina*, 40–42, 52–55.

6. Ramsay, *History of South Carolina*, quoted in Burton, *In My Father's House Are Many Mansions*, 18.

7. Winberry, "The Cultural Hearth of the Southern Pottery Tradition."

8. Mills, *Statistics of South Carolina*, 520.

9. Lockwood, *A Geography of South Carolina*, 78.

10. Burton, *In My Father's House Are Many Mansions*, 35.

11. Jones, *South Carolina*, 128.

12. *Carolina Gazette*, Charleston, S.C., 11 September 1800, p. 2, col. 4, SCL.

13. Lockwood, *A Geography of South Carolina*, 78.

14. Burton, *In My Father's House Are Many Mansions*, 34; Mills, *Statistics of South Carolina*, 253–54.

15. Coleman, ed., *A History of Georgia*, 172.

16. Burton, *In My Father's House Are Many Mansions*, 28–30.

17. *Edgefield Hive*, 26 March 1830, Edgefield District, S.C., SCL. "Chalk" is the folk name for kaolin in the South.

18. Castille, Baldwin, and Steen, *Archaeological Survey*, 32–33; Neuffer, "Edgefield County Towns and Communities," 31.

19. Nancy C. Mims, personal communication, January 1989; Edgefield Wills, vol. 52, pp. 138–42, SCDAH; Burton, *In My Father's House Are Many Mansions*, 34.

20. Burrison, *Brothers in Clay*, 43–52; Zug, *Turners and Burners*, 237–49.

21. Shedd, *The Landrum Family of Fayette County, Georgia*, 6; Zug, *Turners and Burners*, 74; Smith, *Index of Southern Potters*, 92–97.

22. Letter from O. B. Anderson, Ridge Realty Company, Johnston and Edgefield, S.C., to the Charleston Museum, 2 September 1927, Charleston Museum, Charleston, S.C. Mrs. Woodson's account contains several errors. The kaolin sent from North Carolina for use in the Wedgwood

potteries came from Franklin, North Carolina, which is far to the west of Asheville and not in the locality of Salisbury, as Mrs. Woodson states. According to North Carolina folk pottery expert Charles Zug, the North Carolina potters did not use kaolin in stoneware or earthenware production, as Mrs. Woodson suggests. Also, the "mixing basin in which the potters used to mix the clay" to which Mrs. Woodson refers may have been a glaze mill or querne. Finally, she fails to make a distinction between the kaolin and stoneware clays in her notes.

23. Zug, *Turners and Burners*, 11–12, 15.

24. Mills, *Statistics of South Carolina*, 253–54.

25. *Camden Gazette*, 3 June 1819, SCL.

26. Castille, Baldwin, and Steen, *Archaeological Survey*, 47.

27. Edgefield Deeds, 1827–29, book 43, pp. 359–60, Edgefield County Probate Office, ECCH.

28. Edgefield Deeds, book 45, pp. 373–74, Edgefield Probate Records, apt. 9, pkg. 304, Edgefield County Probate Office, ECCH; Edgefield Deeds, vol. 47, pp. 441–42, and vol. 48, pp. 29–30, SCDAH.

29. Edgefield Equity Records, pkg. 739, frames 0–7, roll JR4086–87, SCDAH; *Edgefield Advertiser*, 4 April 1839, SCL.

30. *Edgefield Advertiser*, 4 April 1839, SCL; Edgefield Equity Records, pkg. 590, frames 105–10, roll JR4083–84, SCDAH.

31. South Carolina Miscellaneous Records, Edgefield District, vol. K, pp. 416–18, SCDAH.

32. *Edgefield Advertiser*, 4 April 1839, p. 3, col. 3, and 13 February 1840, p. 3, col. 2, SCL.

33. Edgefield Conveyances, 1840–69, book CCC, p. 72, Edgefield County Conveyance Office, ECCH.

34. *Edgefield Advertiser*, 16 April 1840, p. 3, col. 4, and 15 February 1843, p. 3, SCL.

35. *Edgefield Advertiser*, 12 April 1843, SCL.

36. Patricia H. Rhodes, personal communication, 12 February 1991; Georgeanna Greer, personal communication, 4 September 1984.

37. Holcombe and Holcombe, "South Carolina Potters and Their Wares."

38. Edgefield County Probate Judge, deed book 12,

1795–96, p. 452, WPA typescript, 1937, p. 101, SCL.

39. Alabama folk pottery scholar Joey Brackner points out that kiln furniture was used on alkaline-glazed stoneware pottery sites in Alabama, for stacking small objects or for leveling large ones. Joey Brackner, personal communication, 16 April 1990.

40. Rinzler and Sayers, *The Meaders Family*, 79; Burrison, *Brothers in Clay*, 91; Zug, *Turners and Burners*, 209. Georgeanna Greer, personal communication, 21 September 1988.

41. Castille, Baldwin, and Steen, *Archaeological Survey*, 83–85.

42. Edgefield Deeds, book 31, p. 6; Edgefield Plats, book 3, p. 48, Edgefield County Conveyance Office, all in ECCH. Edgefield Equity Records, no. 737, roll JR4086–87, SCDAH.

43. *Edgefield Advertiser*, 3 February 1847, p. 3, SCL.

44. *Edgefield Advertiser*, 3 November 1847, p. 3, SCL.

45. Interview with Frank Landrum and Rebecca Steele, Charleston Museum, Charleston, S.C.

46. *Edgefield Advertiser*, 16 July 1862, p. 3, SCL.

47. *Edgefield Advertiser*, 6 November 1867, p. 2, col. 3, SCL.

48. Edgefield Deeds, vol. 47, pp. 94–95; South Carolina Miscellaneous Records Edgefield District, vol. 1, pp. 231–32, both in SCDAH.

49. *Edgefield Advertiser*, 2 April 1840, p. 3, col. 4, SCL.

50. Siegling, "The Best Friend of Charleston," 19–23.

51. Cooper, *The Conservative Regime*, 116–17.

52. Court of Pleas and Quarto Sessions, Mecklenburg County, North Carolina, 21 December 1857. Howard Smith kindly provided this reference.

53. Edgefield Deeds, book 46, p. 78, Edgefield County Conveyance Office, ECCH; U.S. Bureau of the Census, 1840, Edgefield District, SCDAH.

54. *Edgefield Advertiser*, 28 May 1840, p. 3, col. 5; 15 October 1840, p. 5, SCL.

55. Patricia H. Rhodes, personal communication, 12 February 1991. *Edgefield Advertiser*, 17 September 1840, p. 4, SCL.

56. Edgefield Deeds, book CCC, p. 371, Edgefield County Conveyance Office, ECCH.

57. Woodson, *History of the Edgefield Baptist Association*.

58. Horn's Creek Baptist Church Book, 1824–59, Edgefield, WPA typescript, SCL.

59. Landreth, "Archaeological Investigations." Landreth excavated the Trapp-Chandler site in 1983.

60. Landreth, "Archaeological Investigations," 20; Edgefield Equity Records, pkg. 921, Edgefield County Probate Office, ECCH.

61. McClendon, *Edgefield Marriage Records*, 32.

62. Landreth, "Archaeological Investigations," 64–65.

63. *Edgefield Advertiser*, 15 May 1850, p. 3, col. 4, SCL.

64. Landreth, "Archaeological Investigations," 86–88; Castille, Baldwin, and Steen, *Archaeological Survey*, 63, 67–68.

65. Ferrell and Ferrell, *Early Decorated Stoneware*.

66. Coroner's Book of Inquisitions, 1851–59, Edgefield County Judge of Probate, Edgefield, WPA typescript, 1937, no. 165-33-7172, SCL; U.S. Bureau of the Census, 1850, Edgefield District, p. 30, line 29.

67. For example, members of the Kirkland and Duncan families were living in Barnwell District in the early decades of the nineteenth century. These families were later involved in pottery manufacture in Georgia, Alabama, and Texas.

68. Barka, "The Kiln and Ceramics of the 'Poor Potter' of Yorktown"; Guilland, *Early American Folk Pottery*, 171.

69. Burrison, *Brothers in Clay*, 122–23.

70. Castille, Baldwin, and Steen, *Archaeological Survey*, 115.

71. Greer, "Out of Edgefield."

72. Edgefield Deed Book 32, p. 441, ECCH; Edgefield Deeds, vol. 32, p. 88, SCDAH. The Abner Landrum deed signed by Abraham Massey is cited in Burrison, *Brothers in Clay*, 123. Georgeanna Greer kindly provided a copy of the John Landrum deed signed by Cogburn, Massey, and Kirkland.

73. Burrison, *Brothers in Clay*, 122–23.

74. Castille, Baldwin, and Steen, *Archaeological Survey*, 85, from John Landrum site, 38AK497; collection of Stephen T. Ferrell, Piedmont, South Carolina, from Phoenix Factory site, 38AK495.

75. Burrison, *Brothers in Clay*, 122–24.

76. Clerk's Confessions, 1821–44, Edgefield County Judge of Probate, Edgefield, WPA typescript, p. 88, SCL.

77. Burrison, *Brothers in Clay*, 44–45.

78. Ibid., 144.

79. South Carolina State Grants, vol. 9, p. 221, 6 March 1786, SCDAH; Edgefield Conveyances, book 3, pp. 319–20, SCDAH.

80. Zug, *Turners and Burners*, 74–82.

81. Quoted in Zug, *Turners and Burners*, p. 83.

82. *Edgefield Advertiser*, 12 August 1841, p. 3, SCL.

83. *Edgefield Advertiser*, 5 August 1841, p. 3, SCL.

84. Zug, *Turners and Burners*, 93–98.

85. Coroner's Book of Inquisitions, 1851–59, Edgefield County Judge of Probate, Edgefield, WPA typescript, 1937, no. 165-33-7172, SCL; U.S. Bureau of the Census, 1840, Edgefield District, SCDAH.

86. Brewster, *Summer Migrations*, 63–64.

87. Zug, *Turners and Burners*, 65–69.

88. *Edgefield Advertiser*, 10 January 1849, p. 3, col. 3, SCL.

89. Greer, "Out of Edgefield."

90. See Willett and Brackner, *The Traditional Pottery of Alabama*, 30–36.

91. Edgefield Conveyances, 1840–69, book BBB, p. 213, ECCH.

92. Malone, Greer, and Simons, *Kirbee Kiln*, 8.

93. Brackner, "The Wilson Potteries," 45–51.

94. Some slaves took the surnames of their masters after emancipation. Slaves attached particular importance to preserving names through naming traditions, and blacks created family identities through the use of surnames. See Burton, *In My Father's House Are Many Mansions*, 165.

95. Zelinsky, *The Cultural Geography of the United States*.

96. Jones, *South Carolina*, 139.

97. Hennig, *Columbia*, 226–29.

98. Quoted in Jones, *South Carolina*, 145.

99. Hennig, *Columbia*, 229.

100. *Edgefield Advertiser*, 30 January 1838, SCL.

CHAPTER THREE

The African-American Presence in the Edgefield District Stoneware Tradition

1. Noel Hume, "An Indian Ware of the Colonial Period."

2. Handler and Lange, *Plantation Slavery in Barbados*, 135–44. See also Wood, *Black Majority*.

3. Ferguson, "Looking for the 'Afro' in Colono-Indian Pottery," 68–83; Ferguson, *Uncommon Ground*.

4. Blue ribbon cane was grown in the lowlands throughout the 1800s. Sorghum, a variety of sugar cane introduced from China in the 1850s, thrived in the uplands. Both types of cane yield cane syrup, sometimes called molasses, although in some areas molasses meant an especially thick form of cane syrup. John Burrison, personal communication, 5 July 1989.

5. Loverling, "A Detailed Account of Experiments"; Rawick, *South Carolina*, pt. 1, 53, vol. 2 of *The American Slave*. As late as 1947, around 17,818,000 gallons of sorgo syrup were consumed by humans in the United States. Paul W. Chapman wrote that "practically every farm in the Gulf Coast region has a patch of cane used for the making of syrup to meet home requirements." See Chapman, *Southern Crops*, 384.

6. Rawick, *Georgia*, pt. 3, 234, vol. 13 of *The American Slave*. Quoted in Burton, *In My Father's House Are Many Mansions*, 162.

7. Burton, *In My Father's House Are Many Mansions*, 161.

8. Rawick, *Arkansas*, pt. 6, 103–5, and *Georgia*, pt. 2, 61, vols. 10 and 12, respectively, of *The American Slave*. Quoted in Burton, *In My Father's House Are Many Mansions*, 161.

9. Plantation Record Book, "General Directions as to Treatment of Negroes," 21–23, 60–61, Francis Wilkinson Pickens Papers, Duke University, Perkins Library, Durham, N.C. Quoted in Burton, *In My Father's House Are Many Mansions*, 161.

10. Rawick, *Florida*, 47–52, and *Georgia*, pt. 3, 234, vols. 17 and 13, respectively, of *The American Slave*. Quoted in Burton, *In My Father's House Are Many Mansions*, 162.

11. Rawick, *South Carolina*, pt. 4, 71–74, and *South Carolina*, pt. 2, 215, vols. 3 and 2, respectively, of *The American Slave*. Quoted in Burton, *In My Father's House Are Many Mansions*, 162.

12. Reitz, Gibbs, and Rathbun, "Archaeological Evidence for Subsistence on Coastal Plantations."

13. Ibid.

14. Reitz, Gibbs, and Rathbun, "Archaeological Evidence for Subsistence on Coastal Plantations"; Burton, *In My Father's House Are Many Mansions*, 161; Rawick, *South Carolina*, pt. 2, 238, vol. 2 of *The American Slave*.

15. Bridenbaugh, *The Colonial Craftsman*, 15–16, 139–41.

16. Burton, *In My Father's House Are Many Mansions*, 163.

17. Edgefield Deeds, book 46, p. 78; Edgefield Conveyances, 1840–69, book CCC, p. 72, both in ECCH.

18. Edgefield County, Judge of Probate, Deed Book 12, 1795–96, p. 100, SCL.

19. *Edgefield Advertiser*, 17 September 1840, p. 4; 30 April 1840, p. 3; 15 February 1843, p. 3; 3 February 1847, p. 3, all in SCL.

20. Edgefield Conveyances, 1840–69, book GGG, pp. 383–84, Edgefield County Conveyance Office, ECCH.

21. Brackner, "The Wilson Potteries."

22. Palmetto Fire Brick Works business ledger, Thomas J. Davies Papers, SCL.

23. The "furnice" mentioned in the coroner's inquisition was probably the stove used to heat the pottery shop rather than the pottery kiln.

24. Coroner's Book of Inquisitions, 1844–50, Edgefield County Judge of Probate, Edgefield, WPA typescript, 1937, no. 165-33-7172, SCL.

25. *Edgefield Advertiser*, 1 April 1863, p. 2, SCL.

26. Barber, *The Pottery and Porcelain of the United States*, 466.

27. Ibid.

28. Vlach, "International Encounters at the Crossroads of Clay." This cup is in the collection of the Augusta-Richmond County Museum, Augusta, Ga.

29. Slave rental or hiring out was often a prelude to buying a slave. Some whites who rented slaves

could be cruel, and some slaveholders opposed the practice. Burton, *In My Father's House Are Many Mansions*, 171–73.

30. Thompson, "African Influence on the Art of the United States," 139; Vlach, "International Encounters at the Crossroads of Clay."

31. Curtin, *The Atlantic Slave Trade*; Vlach, *The Afro-American Tradition in Decorative Arts*, 85–86; Vlach, "International Encounters at the Crossroads of Clay"; Thompson, "African Influence on the Art of the United States," 145–46.

32. *Drums and Shadows*, 26, 32–33, 53, 106.

33. Thompson and Cornet, *The Four Moments of the Sun*, 99–102.

34. Vlach, "International Encounters at the Crossroads of Clay."

35. Barber, *The Pottery and Porcelain of the United States*, 189–91, 248–51.

36. Montgomery, "Survivors from the Cargo of the Negro Slave Yacht *Wanderer*."

37. *Drums and Shadows*, 183–85.

38. Montgomery, "Survivors from the Cargo of the Negro Slave Yacht *Wanderer*," 614.

39. Castille, Baldwin, and Steen, *Archaeological Survey*, A75–A77. Note the similarity of this story to the one told by Floyd White of St. Simons Island that appears above.

40. Thompson and Cornet, *The Four Moments of the Sun*, 99–102.

41. Palmetto Fire Brick Works business ledger, Thomas J. Davies Papers, SCL.

42. Watson, *Greenwood County Sketches*, 39–40.

43. Thompson, "African Influence on the Art of the United States," 135; Vlach, "Black Creativity in Mississippi," 28–32.

44. Lanier currently specializes in the production of face vessels because of their popularity among folk art collectors.

45. Zug, *Turners and Burners*, 384.

46. Hall, "Brother's Keeper: Some Research on American Face Vessels and Some Conjecture on the Cultural Witness of Folk Potters in the New World," 197.

47. Vlach, *The Afro-American Tradition in Decorative Arts*, 86; Chase, *Afro-American Art and Craft*, 57. According to Alice Sanders, great granddaughter

of Thomas J. Davies, African-Americans in the Beech Island community still use the term "monkey" to warn against the dangers of drinking too much water, or water that is too cold, while working in the hot sun.

48. Vlach, *The Afro-American Tradition in Decorative Arts*, 89–90; Georgeanna Greer, personal communication, 27 January 1989; John Burrison, personal communication, 5 July 1989. Burrison agrees with Greer and concludes that the form originated in the Mediterranean.

49. Thompson and Cornet, *The Four Moments of the Sun*, 157–63.

50. Thompson, "African Influence on the Art of the United States," 142.

51. Puckett, *Folk Beliefs of the Southern Negro*, 105.

52. *Drums and Shadows*, 58–59, 95, 130.

53. Herskovits, *The Myth of the Negro Past*, 63; Thompson, "African Influence on the Art of the United States," 122–70.

54. Davis, "Negro Folklore in South Carolina," 248; Vennie Deas Moore, personal communication, 24 August 1989. This practice also continues today in Georgia, for example, at Buena Vista in Marion County. John Burrison, personal communication, 5 July 1989.

55. Vlach, "Arrival and Survival."

56. Lander, "The Iron Industry in Ante Bellum South Carolina"; Dew, "David Ross and the Oxford Iron Works"; Steffen, "The Pre-Industrial Iron Worker."

57. Morley, *The Carolina Mountains*, 187–89.

58. This kiln type is known as a "groundhog" kiln when it is earth-enclosed, or a "tunnel" kiln when it is open.

CHAPTER FOUR
Post–Civil War Stoneware Production in South Carolina

1. Jones, *South Carolina*, 128.

2. Freedmen's Bureau Reports, Orders and Circulars, frames 680–83, roll no. 34, SCDAH.

3. Ibid.

4. Burton, *In My Father's House Are Many Mansions*, 225–30.

5. Freedmen's Bureau Reports, Orders and Circulars, frames 680–83, roll no. 34, SCDAH.

6. Freedman's Bureau Reports Relating to Contracts, roll no. 42, SCDAH.

7. Freedmen's Bureau Reports, Orders and Circulars, frames 680–83, roll no. 34, SCDAH.

8. Ibid.

9. Ibid., frames 773–74, SCDAH.

10. U.S. Bureau of the Census, 1880, Aiken County, Products of Industry, SCDAH.

11. U.S. Bureau of the Census, 1870, Edgefield County, pp. 431B, 433B, SCDAH.

12. Notes from an interview with George Fletcher, Charleston Museum, Charleston, S.C.

13. U.S. Bureau of the Census, 1880, Aiken County, p. 255, line 41, SCDAH.

14. *Edgefield Advertiser*, 6 March 1851, SCL.

15. U.S. Bureau of the Census, 1860, Edgefield District, p. 13, lines 20 and 25, SCDAH.

16. Asbill Family Papers, SCL.

17. E. B. Chamberlain, notes made on trip to Seigler's Pottery, near Eureka, S.C., 4 October 1930, Charleston Museum, Charleston, S.C.

18. Ibid.

19. U.S. Bureau of the Census, 1870, Edgefield County, p. 433B, lines 20–22; p. 433A, lines 12 and 31, both in SCDAH.

20. Neuffer, "Edgefield County Towns and Communities," 31.

21. Burton, *In My Father's House Are Many Mansions*, 29–30. Edgefield and Hamburg were the only incorporated cities in the antebellum Edgefield District.

22. Interview with Hugh Baynham on 25 March 1986; Burrison, *Brothers in Clay*, 119, 292; Ladd, *A Preliminary Report*, 152–54. Burrison notes that although Augusta developed a brick-making industry, few other potters ever worked in the area. George Ladd mentions a pottery at Grovetown in Columbia County, about fifteen miles west of Augusta.

23. Field notes on collecting trip of P. M. Rea to Edgefield County, 24 April 1919, Charleston Museum, Charleston, S.C.

24. McClendon, *Edgefield Marriage Records*, 162.

25. U.S. Bureau of the Census, 1860, Edgefield District, Products of Industry; U.S. Bureau of the Census, 1870, Edgefield County, Products of Industry, SCDAH.

26. U.S. Bureau of the Census, 1870, Edgefield County, p. 130A, lines 1, 10, 13, 24, 27, 33, SCDAH.

27. Interview with W. J. Devore, 13 July 1920, Ninety Six, S.C., Charleston Museum, Charleston, S.C.; U.S. Bureau of the Census, 1860, Edgefield District, p. 14, lines 21 and 24, SCDAH.

28. U.S. Bureau of the Census, 1870, Edgefield County, p. 130A, SCDAH.

29. Aiken County Court of Common Pleas, pkg. no. 9324, ACCH.

30. Aiken County Deeds, vol. D, pp. 292A–292B, SCDAH.

31. *Aiken Journal and Review*, 1 July 1885, p. 4, col. 2, SCL.

32. Smith, *Index of Southern Potters*, 36; South Carolina Pottery Company bill of sale, dated 24 November 1887. Harvey Teal kindly provided a copy of this document.

33. *Aiken Journal and Review*, 20 April 1887, p. 3, col. 1, SCL.

34. Ibid.

35. Barber, *The Pottery and Porcelain of the United States*, 186–91.

36. Reports and Resolutions of the General Assembly of the State of South Carolina proposed by the Annual Session of 1856, 490–91.

37. Spargo, "The Fentons—Pioneer American Potters."

38. Barber, *The Pottery and Porcelain of the United States*, 248–50.

39. Watson, *Handbook of South Carolina*, 143.

40. U.S. Bureau of the Census, 1900, Aiken County, p. 123, lines 9, 18, 21, SCDAH.

41. Burrison, *Brothers in Clay*, 171–72.

42. Ibid., 126–28.

43. Ibid., 170.

44. South Carolina Dispensary Records, SCDAH, with special thanks to Harvey Teal.

45. Interview with Hugh Baynham, 25 March 1986.

46. U.S. Bureau of the Census, 1870, Edgefield

County, p. 259B, lines 14–20; p. 255, line 33, both in SCDAH.

47. Interview with Hugh Baynham, 25 March 1986.

48. Landrum-Stork family letters written to Sallie Landrum over a thirty-five-year period, SCFARC.

49. Mrs. Broddus Shull, personal communication, 31 May 1989.

50. Notes from an interview with R. M. Stork, Charleston Museum, Charleston, S.C.

51. Burrison, *Brothers in Clay*, 172–73.

52. Notes from an interview with R. M. Stork, Charleston Museum, Charleston, S.C.

53. The "cinder glaze" was also used in the Catawba Valley of North Carolina. See Zug, *Turners and Burners*, 180–83.

54. Moss, "Cooperville: Iron Capital of South Carolina," 32–35.

55. Stepp and Rowland, "Adventures in Small-Scale Rural Enterprises in South Carolina."

56. Ibid.

57. Smith, *Index of Southern Potters*, 187.

58. Gary S. Thompson, personal communication, 26 September 1989. Norah is indicated on an 1896 postal map located in the South Carolina Room of the Greenville County Library.

59. Lawrence, *Shadows of Hogback*, 1–2.

60. Ibid., 36.

61. A vessel in the Charleston Museum collection is attributed to the Jones brothers, who reportedly ran a pottery shop located four miles from Spartanburg, probably in the Jugtown area. Potters James A. and John Wesley Jones, sons of North Carolina–born Wilson Jones, are known to have established a shop at Young Cane, Union County, Georgia, by 1879. Two of John Wesley's sons, Dock and Henry, were also potters, and his younger children also helped out at the shop. After his father retired in 1903, Dock continued to operate the shop for several years, closing it about 1912. The Jones Pottery produced mainly whiskey and syrup jugs. Ash glaze was used exclusively at the shop at first, but later ware was glazed mostly with Albany slip. Burrison, *Brothers in Clay*, 116–18.

62. U.S. Bureau of the Census, 1870, Spartanburg County, p. 344, lines 30 and 37, SCDAH.

63. A Montgomery Landrum appears in the 1880 Spartanburg County census. U.S. Bureau of the Census, 1880, Spartanburg County, p. 70A, line 34, SCDAH.

64. U.S. Bureau of the Census, 1880, Spartanburg County, p. 111B, line 1, SCDAH.

65. U.S. Bureau of the Census, 1900, Spartanburg County, p. 19B, SCDAH.

66. U.S. Bureau of the Census, 1900, Greenville County, p. 174A, line 35, SCDAH.

67. Burrison, *Brothers in Clay*, 172–74; John Burrison, personal communication, 7 August 1989.

68. Zug, *Turners and Burners*, 98.

69. Laura M. Bragg and E. B. Chamberlain, notes collected on trip to various potteries, 24–26 June 1930, Charleston Museum, Charleston, S.C.

70. The Belchers, perhaps a branch of the South Carolina family, also produced stoneware in DeKalb County, Alabama. John Burrison, personal communication, 7 August 1989.

71. Lofton, "Holly Springs Pottery Maker"; Tindall, "Pottery-Making Art Still Thrives in Holly Springs Section of County."

72. U.S. Bureau of the Census, 1880, Laurens County, p. 296, lines 12 and 17, SCDAH.

73. Zug, *Turners and Burners*, 87; Burrison, *Brothers in Clay*, 180, 228–29; Gary S. Thompson, personal communication, 25 July 1989.

74. Interview with Sallie Cade, 6 December 1985.

75. Ibid.

76. Burrison, *Brothers in Clay*, 70, 312.

77. Zug, *Turners and Burners*, 397–98, 87.

78. Ibid., 440.

79. Ibid., 66, 68, 442.

80. Burrison, *Brothers in Clay*, 201–2.

81. Robert K. Demarest, "Pottery Manufacture in Kershaw County," Work Projects Administration Index File H-1-76, SCL.

82. Lavisky, "Old Time Potter," 3–5.

83. Emmaus Avery Brown was a member of the Avery family, a well-known Georgia clay clan.

84. Outen and Ratteree lived in North Carolina but traveled to Bethune to oversee the pottery operation during the weekdays. Interview with Francis Brown Thompson on 25 July 1990.

85. The Rebekah pitchers that the Browns pro-

duced were hand-turned vessels without any exterior decoration. The term "Rebekah" refers to the form of the pieces rather than to a decorative motif.

86. Burrison, *Brothers in Clay*, 195–98; Mack, "Turned to Tradition," 10–11. Interview with Frances Brown Thompson, 25 July 1990.

87. B. C. Matthews reportedly also operated a pottery located in Newberry County. No further information is available on this pottery. Matthews, however, may have been related to Georgia potter James L. Matthews. James Matthews was potting in Columbus, Muscogee County, Georgia, in 1898. Charleston Museum Notes, Charleston, S.C.; Burrison, *Brothers in Clay*, 318.

CHAPTER FIVE
*South Carolina Stoneware Glazes
and Decorative Treatments*

1. Karl, "Folk Pottery: The X-Ray Fluorescence Analysis of Some Glazes." Ceramics scholar Georgeanna Greer points out that the presence of lime in the glaze, whether it is the purposeful addition of a form of lime or a high lime content in the clay used in the glaze, will make the glaze have a little higher gloss and cause the final color to have a yellowish cast, often resulting in olive green glaze colors. When lime is substituted entirely for the wood ash, the surface texture of the glaze fades out, producing a glassy appearance with very few runs and a lighter, often more transparent, glaze.

2. Lime glazes used elsewhere in the South (most notably, in Georgia) appear more glassy and do not have the soft, unctious look of the Edgefield glazes. Greer suggests that the lime glazes found in Edgefield may have contained wood ash and extreme amounts of silica but their composition has not been positively established. Georgeanna Greer, personal communication, 7 May 1989.

3. Glass was also used as a form of decoration on at least one vessel produced at the Bodie site, a figural bottle attributed to freed black potter Jim Lee. See chapter 3.

4. Rhodes, *Clay and Glazes*, 266. Quoted in Zug, *Turners and Burners*, 225.

5. Burrison, *Brothers in Clay*, 74–75.

6. See also Webster, *Decorated Stoneware Pottery of North America*, 165, and Watkins, *Early New England Potters and Their Wares*. A three-gallon "serving jug," stamped "Cognac-Brandy / 1820" within a border of cobalt blue, attributed to the Nathan Clark Pottery of Athens, New York, is illustrated by Webster. A similarly decorated mark with a border of iron-bearing clay slip glaze is found on an Edgefield water cooler stamped "Phoenix Factory / Edgefield S.C." A water cooler illustrated by Watkins made in Hartford, Connecticut, is similarly decorated.

7. Court of Pleas and Quarto Sessions, Mecklenburg County, North Carolina, 21 December 1857.

8. MacFarlane, "Nathan Clark, Potter."

9. Ferrell and Ferrell, *Early Decorated Stoneware*; Zug, *Turners and Burners*, 76.

10. Georgeanna Greer noted that the swag and drape decorative motifs, as well as the classic wreath design, were popular patterns used by both northern and southern potters of the early nineteenth century. They were abstracted to suit the potter's taste and are a reflection of the neoclassic period seen in architecture and all forms of decorative art.

11. Howard Smith has noted that William Whelchel's wife, a member of the Boyle family, was a quiltmaker and that some of the stenciled designs used by William may have been copied from quilt patterns. Smith, *Index of Southern Potters*, 187.

12. Files in the Charleston Museum indicate that Milage Williams was a turner at Miles Mill. Charleston Museum, Charleston, S.C.

13. Landreth, "Archaeological Investigations," 44–55.

14. Greer, "Groundhog Kilns."

15. Malone, Greer, and Simons, *Kirbee Kiln*.

16. Zug, *Turners and Burners*, 203.

CHAPTER SIX
Put Every Bit All Between:
Stoneware Forms and Functions

1. *Camden Gazette*, 3 June 1819, SCL.
2. *Edgefield Advertiser*, 14 May 1840, p. 3.
3. Zug, *Turners and Burners*, 317.
4. Ibid., 302.
5. Guilland, *Early American Folk Pottery*, 206. Quoted in Zug, *Turners and Burners*, 337.
6. Brears, *The Collector's Book*, 68.
7. Zug, *Turners and Burners*, 335.
8. The possible origins of this vessel form are discussed in chapter 3.
9. Zug, *Turners and Burners*, 375.
10. *Edgefield Advertiser*, 13 February 1843, SCL.
11. *Edgefield Advertiser*, 13 December 1843, SCL.
12. U.S. Bureau of the Census, 1860, Edgefield District, p. 16, line 29, SCDAH.
13. James D. Lee, Field Report from Ridge Springs, Saluda County, 2 July 1920, Charleston Museum, Charleston, S.C.
14. Zug, *Turners and Burners*, 343–45.
15. Lee and Lewis, "Graveyard Pots."
16. Burrison, *Brothers in Clay*, 68.
17. Greer, *American Stonewares*, 125.

EPILOGUE
Decline and Renewal of the Southern
Folk Pottery Tradition

1. Burrison, *Brothers in Clay*, 277.

Bibliography

Interviews

Unless otherwise noted, all interviews were conducted by the author.

Bab, Claude. Greer, S.C., 18 September 1990.
Bab, Thomas Gentry. Greer, S.C., 4 March 1986.
Baynham, Hugh. North Augusta, S.C., 25 March 1986.
Belcher, Mrs. Clarence. Campobello, S.C., 4 March 1986.
Buie, B. F. Columbia, S.C., 21 April 1986.
Byars, R. Paul. Columbia, S.C., 6 November 1984.
Clayton, Mr. and Mrs. Jones ("Pete"). Campobello, S.C., 21 May, 28 October 1986.
Gingrey, Irene. Edgefield, S.C., 24 July 1987.
Henson, Billy. Lyman, S.C., 15 August 1990.
Henson, Dewey, Allie Wilson Henson, and Billy Henson. Lyman, S.C., 18 March 1986.
Hoffman, David. Sharon, S.C., 15 November 1985.
Lee, Robert. Trenton, S.C., 26 August 1987.
Mathis, E. C. Trenton, S.C., 8 September 1987.
Mays, Mrs. H. E. Walhalla, S.C., 18 August 1989.
Murray, Rosa Henderson. Greenville, S.C., 21 July 1989.
Shull, Maude Stork. Williston, S.C., 16 November 1984.
Steele, Harold, Sr. Columbia, S.C., 5 August 1987.
Tapp, Kenneth, and Clarice Tapp. Lyman, S.C., 3 March 1986.
Thompson, Frances. Camden, S.C., 25 July 1990.
Thurmond, Lucinda. Aiken, S.C., 10 December 1987.
Williams, J. B. Campobello, S.C., 4 March 1986.

Archival and Manuscript Sources

AIKEN COUNTY COURT HOUSE (ACCH)
Aiken County Court of Common Pleas

CHARLESTON COUNTY COURT HOUSE (CCCH)
Charleston Inventories (1776–84)

EDGEFIELD COUNTY COURT HOUSE (ECCH)
Edgefield Conveyances
Edgefield Deeds
Edgefield Equity Records
Edgefield Plats

SOUTH CAROLINA DEPARTMENT OF ARCHIVES AND HISTORY, COLUMBIA (SCDAH)
Aiken County Deeds
Edgefield Deeds
Edgefield Equity Records
Freedmen's Bureau Reports, Orders and Circulars
Freedmen's Bureau Reports Relating to Contracts
South Carolina Court of Common Pleas, Judgment Rolls
South Carolina Journal of Commons House of Assembly
South Carolina Legislative Papers, 1831–59
South Carolina Miscellaneous Records, Edgefield District
South Carolina Mortgages
U.S. Bureau of the Census, 1820, Edgefield District
U.S. Bureau of the Census, 1840, Edgefield District
U.S. Bureau of the Census, 1850, Edgefield District
U.S. Bureau of the Census, 1860, Edgefield District
U.S. Bureau of the Census, 1870, Edgefield County
U.S. Bureau of the Census, 1870, Spartanburg County
U.S. Bureau of the Census, 1880, Aiken County

U.S. Bureau of the Census, 1880, Laurens County
U.S. Bureau of the Census, 1880, Spartanburg County
U.S. Bureau of the Census, 1900, Aiken County
U.S. Bureau of the Census, 1900, Greenville County
U.S. Bureau of the Census, 1900, Spartanburg County

SOUTH CAROLINA FOLK ARTS RESOURCE CENTER, MCKIS-
  SICK MUSEUM, UNIVERSITY OF SOUTH CAROLINA,
  COLUMBIA (SCFARC)
SOUTH CAROLINIANA LIBRARY, UNIVERSITY OF SOUTH
  CAROLINA, COLUMBIA (SCL)

NEWSPAPERS
Aiken Journal and Review
Camden Gazette
Carolina Gazette
Edgefield Advertiser
Edgefield Hive
South Carolina Gazette
South Carolina Gazette & Country Journal

MANUSCRIPTS AND TYPESCRIPTS
Asbill Family Papers
Clerk's Confessions, 1821–44, Edgefield County Judge
  of Probate, Edgefield, WPA, typescript
Coroner's Book of Inquisitions, Edgefield County
  Judge of Probate, 1844–50, Edgefield, WPA 1937
  typescript
Edgefield Deeds, Edgefield County Judge of Probate,
  Edgefield, WPA, typescript
Edgefield Equity Records, Edgefield County Judge of
  Probate, Edgefield, WPA, typescript
Horn's Creek Baptist Church Book, 1824–59, Edge-
  field, WPA, typescript
Work Projects Administration Index Files
York County Office of the Clerk

Published Sources

Baker, Steven G. "Catawba Indian Trade Pottery of
  the Historic Period." Columbia, S.C.: Columbia
  Museum of Art, 1973. Exhibition catalog.
———. *Colono-Indian Pottery from Cambridge, South
  Carolina, with Comments on the Historic Catawba
  Pottery Trade.* South Carolina Institute of Archae-
  ology and Anthropology Notebook 4, no. 1. Colum-
  bia: University of South Carolina, 1972.

Barber, Edwin Atlee. *The Pottery and Porcelain of
  the United States: A Historical Review of American
  Ceramic Art from the Earliest Times to the Present.*
  1893. Reprint. New York: Feingold and Lewis, 1976.
Barka, Norman F. "The Kiln and Ceramics of the
  'Poor Potter' of Yorktown: A Preliminary Report." In
  Ceramics in America, edited by Ian M. G. Quimby,
  292–315. Winterthur Conference Report, 1972. Char-
  lottesville: University Press of Virginia, 1973.
Bivens, John, Jr. *The Moravian Potters in North Caro-
  lina.* Chapel Hill: University of North Carolina
  Press, 1972.
Bordley, John Beak. *Essays and Notes on Husbandry
  and Rural Affairs.* 2d ed. with additions. Philadel-
  phia: Budd and Bartram, 1801.
Brackner, Elmer Joe, Jr. "The Wilson Potteries." M.A.
  thesis, University of Texas at Austin, 1981.
Brackner, Joey. "Traditional Pottery of Mobile Bay."
  Alabama Heritage, no. 7 (Winter 1988): 30–41.
Brackner, Joey, and Ron Countryman. *Pottery from the
  Mountains of Alabama.* Bessemer, Ala.: Bessemer
  Hall of History, 1986. Exhibition catalog.
Brears, Peter C. D. *The Collector's Book of English
  Country Pottery.* North Pomfret: David & Charles,
  1974.
Brewster, Lawrence Fay. *Summer Migrations and
  Resorts of South Carolina Lowcountry Planters.*
  Historical Papers of the Trinity College Historical
  Society, series 26. Durham, N.C.: Duke University
  Press, 1947.
Bridenbaugh, Carl. *The Colonial Craftsman.* 1950.
  Reprint. Chicago: University of Chicago Press, 1974.
Burrison, John A. "Alkaline-Glazed Stoneware: A
  Deep-South Pottery Tradition." *Southern Folklore
  Quarterly* 39, no. 4 (December 1975): 377–403.
———. *Brothers in Clay: The Story of Georgia Folk
  Pottery.* Athens: University of Georgia Press, 1983.
Burton, Orville Vernon. *In My Father's House Are Many
  Mansions: Family and Community in Edgefield,
  South Carolina.* Chapel Hill: University of North
  Carolina Press, 1985.
Castille, George, Cinda Baldwin, and Carl Steen.
  *Archaeological Survey of Alkaline-Glazed Pottery
  Kiln Sites in Old Edgefield District, South Caro-
  lina.* Columbia: McKissick Museum and the South
  Carolina Institute of Archaeology and Anthro-
  pology, 1988.

Chapman, John A. *History of Edgefield County from the Earliest Settlements to 1897.* Newberry, S.C.: Elbert H. Aull, 1897.

Chapman, Paul W. *Southern Crops.* Atlanta: Turner E. Smith and Company, 1947.

Chase, Judith Wragg. *Afro-American Art and Craft.* New York: Van Nostrand Reinhold Company, 1971.

Coleman, Kenneth, ed. *A History of Georgia.* Athens: University of Georgia Press, 1977.

Cooper, William J., Jr. *The Conservative Regime: South Carolina, 1877–1890.* Baltimore: The Johns Hopkins University Press, 1968.

Curtin, Philip D. *The Atlantic Slave Trade: A Census.* Madison: University of Wisconsin Press, 1969.

Davis, Henry C. "Negro Folklore in South Carolina." *Journal of American Folklore* 27 (July–September 1914): 241–54.

Dawson, Aileen. *Masterpieces of Wedgwood in the British Museum.* London: British Museum Publications, 1984.

Dew, Charles B. "David Ross and the Oxford Iron Works: A Study of Industrial Slavery in the Early Nineteenth-Century South." *William and Mary Quarterly* 31, no. 1 (1974): 189–224.

Drums and Shadows: Survival Studies Among the Georgia Coastal Negroes. Savannah Unit, Georgia Writers' Project, Work Projects Administration. 1940. Reprint. Athens: University of Georgia Press, 1986.

Ferguson, Leland. "Looking for the 'Afro' in Colono-Indian Pottery." *Conference on Historic Site Archaeology Papers* 12:68–83. Columbia: South Carolina Institute of Archaeology and Anthropology, University of South Carolina, 1978.

———. "Looking for the 'Afro' in Colono-Indian Pottery." In *Archaeological Perspectives on Ethnicity in America*, edited by R. Schuyler, 14–28. Farmingdale, N.Y.: Baywood Publishing Co., 1980.

———. *Uncommon Ground: Archaeology and Colonial African-America, 1650–1800.* Washington, D.C.: Smithsonian Institution Press, 1992.

Ferrell, Stephen T., and Terry M. Ferrell. *Early Decorated Stoneware of the Edgefield District, South Carolina.* Greenville, S.C.: Greenville County Museum of Art, 1976. Exhibition catalog.

Fewkes, Vladimir J. "Catawba Pottery-Making, with Notes on Pamunkey Pottery-Making, Cherokee Pottery-Making, and Coiling." *Proceedings of the American Philosophical Society* 88, no. 2 (July 1944): 69–124.

Finer, Ann, and George Savage, eds. *The Selected Letters of Josiah Wedgwood.* New York: Born & Hawes Publishing Company, 1965.

Giannini, Robert L., III. "Anthony Duche, Sr., Potter and Merchant of Philadelphia." *Antiques* 119, no. 1 (January 1981): 201.

Graham, John Meredith, II, and Hensleigh Cecil Wedgwood. *Wedgwood.* New York: Tudor Publishing Company, 1948.

Greer, Georgeanna H. *American Stonewares: The Art and Craft of Utilitarian Potters.* Exton, Pa.: Schiffer Publishing Co., 1981.

———. "Groundhog Kilns: Rectangular Kilns of the Nineteenth and Early Twentieth Centuries." *Northeast Historical Archaeology* 6, nos. 1–2 (1977): 42–54. Council for Northeast Historical Archaeology, California, Pennsylvania.

———. "Out of Edgefield: The Migration of Alkaline-Glazed Stoneware Potters in the Lower South." In *Crossroads of Clay: The Southern Alkaline-Glazed Stoneware Tradition*, edited by Catherine Wilson Horne, 89–105. Columbia: McKissick Museum, University of South Carolina, 1990. Exhibition catalog.

———. "Preliminary Information on the Use of the Alkaline Glaze for Stoneware in the South, 1800–1970." In *The Conference on Historic Site Archaeology Papers* 5, edited by Stanley South, 155–70. Columbia: Institute of Archaeology and Anthropology, University of South Carolina, 1971.

Thomas Griffiths, "An Expedition in Search of Cherokee Clay, 1767–1768." In *The Colonial South Carolina Scene: Contemporary Views, 1697–1774*, edited by H. Roy Merrens, 243–45. Columbia: University of South Carolina Press, 1977.

Grimshaw, Rex W. *The Chemistry and Physics of Clays and Allied Ceramic Materials.* London: Ernest Benn, 1971.

Guilland, Harold F. *Early American Folk Pottery.* Philadelphia: Chilton Book Company, 1971.

Hall, Michael D. "Brother's Keeper: Some Research on American Face Vessels and Some Conjecture on the Cultural Witness of Folk Potters in the New World." In *Stereoscopic Perspective: Reflections on American Fine and Folk Art*, edited by Michael D.

Hall. Contemporary American Art Critics, no. 11, Donald Kuspit, series editor. Ann Arbor, Mich.: UMI Research Press, 1988.

Hamer, Philip M., ed. *The Papers of Henry Laurens*. 12 vols. Columbia: University of South Carolina Press, 1968–90.

Handler, Jerome, and Frederick W. Lange. *Plantation Slavery in Barbados: An Archaeological and Historical Investigation*. Cambridge: Harvard University Press, 1978.

Harrington, M. R. "Catawba Potters and Their Work." *American Anthropologist* 10, no. 3 (1908): 399–407.

Hennig, Helen Kohn. *Columbia: Capital City of South Carolina, 1786–1936*. Columbia Sesqui-Centennial Commission. 1936. Reprint. Columbia, S.C.: State-Record Company, 1966.

Herskovits, Melville J. *The Myth of the Negro Past*. Boston: Beacon Press, 1958.

Holcombe, Joe L., and Fred E. Holcombe. "South Carolina Potters and Their Wares: The Landrums of Pottersville." *South Carolina Antiquities* 18, nos. 1–2 (1986): 47–62.

Honey, W. B. *Wedgwood Ware*. London: Faber and Faber, 1948.

Hood, Graham. *Bonnin and Morris of Philadelphia: The First American Porcelain Factory, 1770–1772*. Chapel Hill: University of North Carolina Press, 1972.

Horne, Catherine Wilson, ed. *Crossroads of Clay: The Southern Alkaline-Glazed Stoneware Tradition*. Columbia: McKissick Museum, University of South Carolina, 1990. Exhibition catalog.

Jones, Lewis P. *South Carolina: A Synoptic History for Laymen*. Columbia, S.C.: Sandlapper Press, 1971.

Karl, Kevin. "Folk Pottery: The X-Ray Fluorescence Analysis of Some Glazes." Unpublished research paper on file at South Carolina Folk Arts Research Center, Columbia.

Ketchum, William C., Jr. *Early Potters and Potteries of New York State*. New York: Funk and Wagnalls, 1970.

Kovacik, Charles F., and John Winberry. *South Carolina: A Geography*. Boulder, Col.: Westview Press, 1987.

Ladd, George E. *A Preliminary Report on a Part of the Clays of Georgia*. Geological Survey of Georgia Bulletin, no. 6A. Atlanta: State Printer, 1898.

Lander, Ernest M., Jr. "The Iron Industry in Ante Bellum South Carolina." *Journal of Southern History* 20 (1954): 350–55.

Landreth, Gerald K. "Archaeological Investigations at the Trapp and Chandler Pottery, Kirksey, South Carolina." M.A. thesis, University of Idaho, 1985.

Lavisky, Saul. "Old Time Potter: Guy Daugherty Has Been Turning Out Clay Products for 66 Years." *The State Magazine*, January 16, 1955, 3–5.

Lawrence, James Walton, Sr. *Shadows of Hogback*. Landrum, S.C.: News Leader, 1979.

Lee, Bennie, and Don Lewis. "Graveyard Pots." *Ceramics Monthly* 15 (1967): 20–21.

Lewis, Kenneth E. *Camden: A Frontier Town in Eighteenth-Century South Carolina*. Anthropological Studies 2. Columbia: Institute of Archaeology and Anthropology, University of South Carolina, October 1976.

Lockwood, Thomas P. *A Geography of South Carolina*. Charlestown: J. S. Burges, 1832.

Lofton, John. "Holly Springs Pottery Maker Turns Out 3,200 Pieces of Artistic Work Yearly." *Spartanburg Herald-Journal*, section 2, p. 1, December 30, 1945.

Loverling, Joseph S. "A Detailed Account of Experiments and Observations upon the Sorghum Saccharatum, or Chinese Sugar Cane Made with the View of Determining Its Value as a Sugar-Producing Plant, Together with a Compilation of Articles on the Subject, from Other Sources, by William Glaze, Proprietor of the Palmetto Iron Works." Columbia, S.C.: I. C. Morgan, 1858.

Lyon, Ralph M. "Moses Waddel and the Willington Academy." *North Carolina Historical Review* 8, no. 3 (July 1931): 284–99.

McClendon, Carlee T. *Edgefield Marriage Records*. Columbia, S.C.: R. L. Bryan Company, 1970.

MacFarlane, Janet R. "Nathan Clark, Potter." *Antiques* 55, no. 1 (July 1951): 42–44.

Macht, Carol. *Classical Wedgwood Designs*. New York: M. Barrows and Company, 1957.

Mack, Randy. "Turned to Tradition: The Folk Pottery of Today's South." *Collections* 1, no. 1 (Fall 1988): 9–14. Columbia, S.C.: Columbia Museum of Art.

Malone, James M., Georgeanna H. Greer, and Helen Simons. *Kirbee Kiln: A Mid-Nineteenth-Century Texas Stoneware Pottery*. Office of the State Archaeologist

Report, no. 31. Austin: Texas Historical Commission, 1979.

Merens, H. Roy, ed. *The Colonial South Carolina Scene: Contemporary Views, 1697–1774*. Columbia: University of South Carolina Press, 1977.

Merrell, James H. *The Indians' New World: Catawbas and Their Neighbors from European Contact Through the Era of Removal*. Published for the Institute of Early American History and Culture, Williamsburg, Virginia. Chapel Hill: University of North Carolina Press, 1989.

Mills, Robert. *Statistics of South Carolina*. Charleston: Hurlbut and Lloyd, 1826.

Montgomery, Charles J. "Survivors from the Cargo of the Negro Slave Yacht *Wanderer*." *American Anthropologist* 10 (1908): 611–23.

Morley, Margaret W. *The Carolina Mountains*. New York: Houghton Mifflin Company, 1913.

Moss, B. G. "Cooperville: Iron Capital of South Carolina." *South Carolina History Illustrated* 1, no. 2 (May 1970): 32–35.

Myers, Susan M. "A Survey of Pottery Manufacture in the Mid-Atlantic and Northeastern United States." *Northeast Historical Archeology* 6 (1977): 1–13.

Neuffer, Claude. "Edgefield County Towns and Communities." In *Names in South Carolina*, vol. 30. Columbia: Department of English, University of South Carolina, 1983.

Noel Hume, Ivor. *A Guide to Artifacts of Colonial America*. New York: Alfred A. Knopf, 1969.

———. "An Indian Ware of the Colonial Period." *Quarterly Bulletin, Archaeological Society of Virginia* 17, no. 1 (September 1962).

Olsen, Frederick L. *The Kiln Book*. 2d ed. Bassett, Calif.: Keramos Books, 1973.

Owen, Hugh. *Two Centuries of Ceramic Art in Bristol, Being a History of the True Porcelain by Richard Champion*. Glouster, England, 1873.

Pendrill-Church, John. *William Cookworthy, 1705–1780: A Study of the Pioneer of True Porcelain Manufacture in England*. Truro, Cornwall: D. Bradford Barton, 1972.

Prime, Alfred Cox, comp. *The Arts and Crafts in Philadelphia, Maryland, and South Carolina, 1721–1785*. Philadelphia, 1929.

Puckett, Newbell Niles. *Folk Beliefs of the Southern Negro*. New York: Dover Publications, 1969.

Ramsay, David. *History of South Carolina from Its First Settlement in 1670 to the Year 1808*. Charleston, 1809.

Ramsay, John. *American Potters and Pottery*. Ann Arbor, Mich.: Ars Ceramica, 1976.

Rauschenberg, Bradford L. "Andrew Duche: A Potter 'a Little Too Much Addicted to Politicks.'" *Journal of Early Southern Decorative Arts* 17, no. 1 (May 1991): 1–101.

———. "'A Clay White as Lime . . . of Which There is a Design Formed by some Gentlemen to Make China': The American and English Search for Cherokee Clay in South Carolina, 1745–75." *Journal of Early Southern Decorative Arts* 17, no. 2 (November 1991): 67–80.

———. "John Bartlam Who Established 'new Pottworks in South Carolina' and Became the First Successful Creamware Potter in America." *Journal of Early Southern Decorative Arts* 17, no. 2 (November 1991): 1–66.

Rawick, George P., ed. *The American Slave: A Composite Autobiography*. 12 vols. Westport, Conn.: Greenwood Publishing Company, 1972. Supplement Series 2, 10 vols., 1979.

Reilly, Robin, and George Savage. *Wedgwood: The Portrait Medallions*. London: Barrie and Jenkins, 1973.

Reitz, Elizabeth J., Tyson Gibbs, and Ted A. Rathbun. "Archaeological Evidence for Subsistence on Coastal Plantations." In *The Archaeology of Slavery and Plantation Life*, edited by Theresa A. Singleton, 163–91. New York: Academic Press, Harcourt Brace Jovanovich, 1985.

Reports and Resolutions of the General Assembly of the State of South Carolina Proposed by the Annual Session of 1856. Columbia, S.C.: Edward H. Button, State Printer, 1856.

Rhodes, Daniel. *Clay and Glazes for the Potter*. Radnor, Penn.: Chilton Book Co., 1973.

———. *Kilns: Design, Construction and Operation*. Radnor, Penn.: Chilton Book Company, 1968.

———. *Stoneware and Porcelain: The Art of High-Fired Pottery*. Radnor, Penn.: Chilton Book Company, 1959.

Rinzler, Ralph, and Robert Sayers. *The Meaders Family: North Georgia Potters*. Smithsonian Folklife Studies, no. 1. Washington, D.C.: Smithsonian Institution Press, 1980.

Robinson, G. C., B. F. Buie, and H. S. Johnson, Jr.

Common Clays of the Coastal Plain of South Carolina, no. 25. Columbia, S.C.: Division of Geology, State Development Board, 1961.

Schulz, Judith Jane. "The Rise and Decline of Camden as South Carolina's Major Inland Trading Center, 1751–1829: A Historical Geographic Study." M.A. thesis, Wayne State University, 1972.

Shedd, Joel P. *The Landrum Family of Fayette County, Georgia.* Washington, D.C.: Moore and Moore, 1972.

Siegling, H. Carter. "The Best Friend of Charleston." *South Carolina History Illustrated* 1, no. 1 (February 1970): 19–23.

Simms, William Gilmore. *The Magnolia.* Vol. 3 (1841).

Smith, Howard. *Index of Southern Potters.* Vol. 1. Mayodan, N.C.: Old America Company, 1982.

Spargo, John. *Early American Pottery and China.* New York: Garden City Publishing Company, 1926.

———. "The Fentons—Pioneer American Potters." In *The Art of the Potter*, edited by Diana Garrison and J. Garrison. Clinton, N.J.: Main Street Press, 1977.

Speck, Frank G. "Indian Notes and Monographs." *Museum of the American Indian* 1, no. 5 (1928).

Steffen, Charles G. "The Pre-Industrial Iron Worker: Northampton Iron Works, 1780–1820." *Labor History* 20, no. 1 (1979): 89.

Stepp, J. M., and Gil Rowland. "Adventures in Small-Scale Rural Enterprises in South Carolina." South Carolina Agricultural Experiment Station, circular no. 67 (January 1944): 5–8. Clemson, S.C.: Clemson Agricultural College.

Swanton, John R. "The Indians of the Southeastern United States." *Bureau of American Ethnology*, no. 137. Washington, D.C.: U.S. Government Printing Office, 1946.

Sweezy, Nancy. *Raised in Clay: The Southern Pottery Tradition.* Washington, D.C.: Office of Folklife Programs, Smithsonian Institution Press, 1984.

Terry, George. "Pottery Manufacturing in South Carolina, 1750–1830." Southeastern College Art Conference, Harrisonburg, Virginia, 1983. Unpublished manuscript.

Thompson, Robert Farris. "African Influence on the Art of the United States." In *Black Studies in the University: A Symposium*, edited by Armstead L. Robinson, Craig C. Foster, and Donald H. Ogilvie, 122–70. New Haven: Yale University Press, 1969.

Thompson, Robert Farris, and Joseph Cornet. *The Four Moments of the Sun: Kongo Art in Two Worlds.* Washington, D.C.: National Gallery of Art, 1981.

Tindall, J. F. "Pottery-Making Art Still Thrives in Holly Spring Section of County." *Spartanburg Herald-Journal*, May 7, 1939, p. 3.

Tuomey, M. "Report on the Geological and Agricultural Survey of South Carolina." Columbia, S.C.: A. S. Johnston, 1844.

Vlach, John M. *The Afro-American Tradition in Decorative Arts.* Cleveland, Ohio: Cleveland Museum of Art, 1978. Exhibition catalog.

———. "Arrival and Survival: The Maintenance of an Afro-American Tradition in Folk Art and Craft." In *Perspectives on American Folk Art*, edited by Ian M. G. Quimby and Scott T. Swank, 177–217. New York: W. W. Norton and Company, 1980.

———. "Black Creativity in Mississippi: Origins and Horizons." In *Made by Hand: Mississippi Folk Art*, 28–32. Jackson: Mississippi State Historical Museum, Mississippi Department of Archives and History, 1980. Exhibition catalog.

———. "International Encounters at the Crossroads of Clay: European, Asian, and African Influences on Edgefield Pottery." In *Crossroads of Clay: The Southern Alkaline-Glazed Stoneware Tradition*, edited by Catherine Wilson Horne, 17–39. Columbia: McKissick Museum, University of South Carolina, 1990. Exhibition catalog.

Watkins, Lura Woodside. *Early New England Potters and Their Wares.* Cambridge: Harvard University Press, 1950.

Watson, E. J. *Handbook of South Carolina: Resources, Institutions and Industries of the State.* 2d ed. Columbia, South Carolina: State Department of Agriculture, Commerce, and Immigration, 1908.

Watson, Margaret. *Greenwood County Sketches: Old Roads and Early Families.* Greenwood, S.C.: Attic Press, n.d.

Webster, Donald Blake. *Decorated Stoneware Pottery of North America.* Rutland, Vt.: Charles E. Tuttle Company, 1975.

Wedgwood, Barbara, and Hensleigh Wedgwood. *The Wedgwood Circle: Four Generations of a Family and Their Friends, 1730–1897.* London: Studio Vista, 1980.

Wedgwood, Josiah, F.R.S. "An Address to the Workmen in the Pottery on the Subject of Entering into the Service of Foreign Manufacturers." Newcastle, Staffordshire: J. Smith, 1783.

Whatley, L. McKay. "The Mount Shepherd Pottery: Correlating Archeology and History." *Journal of Early Southern Decorative Arts* 6, no. 1 (1980): 21–57.

Willett, E. Henry, and Joey Brackner. *The Traditional Pottery of Alabama*. Montgomery, Ala.: Montgomery Museum of Fine Arts, 1983. Exhibition catalog.

Winberry, John. "The Cultural Hearth of the Southern Pottery Tradition: The Historical Geographic Framework." In *Crossroads of Clay: The Southern Alkaline-Glazed Stoneware Tradition*, edited by Catherine Wilson Horne, 5–15. Columbia: McKissick Museum, University of South Carolina, 1990. Exhibition catalog.

Wood, Peter H. *Black Majority*. New York: Alfred A. Knopf, 1974.

Woodson, Hortense, and Church Historians. *History of the Edgefield Baptist Association*. Edgefield, S.C.: Edgefield Advertiser Press, 1957.

Zelinsky, Wilbur. *The Cultural Geography of the United States*. Foundations in Cultural Geography Series, Richard E. Dahlberg, series cartographer. Englewood Cliffs, N.J.: Prentice-Hall, 1973.

Zug, Charles G., III. *Turners and Burners: The Folk Potters of North Carolina*. Chapel Hill: University of North Carolina Press, 1986.

South Carolina Potters

Abram [slave]
Edgefield District, 1795: bill of sale for a "negro boy, Abram" from Samuel Landrum to John Landrum; 1830: named in Pottersville business agreement between Harvey and Reuben Drake; 1839: named in an indenture between John Hughes and Collin Rhodes as part of Pottersville Stoneware Manufactory property; 1840: named as a turner in a deed in which James W. Gibbs sold his one-sixth share in the "Pottersville Stone Ware Manufacturing establishment" to Jasper Gibbs; 1842: named as a turner in a mortgage in which J. D. Nance released his one-third share in the "Pottersville Manufacturing concern" to Jasper Gibbs.

Allen, James W., Sr.
Edgefield training, with Leopards, Prothros, and Duncans; Randolph County, Ala., 1840, 1850; Bastrop and Lee counties, Tex., 1859–1900. Son-in-law of Matthew Duncan.

Anderson, William M. (1800/1820 [S.C.]–?)
Fayette County, Ala. (Division), 1850: potter.

Artemus, William (ca. 1827–?)
Spartanburg County, 1870: jug manufacturer.

Atkins, Early
Spartanburg County, ca. 1900; Pickens County, ca. 1920. Brother of John L., Gene, and Smiley.

Atkins, Gene
Spartanburg County, ca. 1912, for George L. Clayton. Brother of John L., Smiley, and Early.

Atkins, James B. (ca. 1863–?)
Spartanburg County, Beech Springs Township, 1900: potter.

Atkins, John Leonard (ca. 1876–1957)
Spartanburg County, Jug Factory Road, ca. 1920. Brother of Gene, Smiley, and Early.

Atkins, L. Fack (1874–1928)
Spartanburg County, Jug Factory Road; ca. 1920, for George L. Clayton.

Atkins, Pinkney (ca. 1820–?)
Spartanburg County, 1880: jugmaker.

Atkins, Smiley
Pickens County, ca. 1920. Brother of John L., Gene, and Early.

Atkins, Thereon
Spartanburg County, ca. 1920, for George L. Clayton.

Augustine, George (ca. 1858–?)
Richland County, 1870: works in pottery.

Augustine, William (ca. 1854–?)
Richland County, 1870: works in pottery.

Baddler [slave]
Lewis Miles Factory, Edgefield District, 1859: storage jar signed "Dave and Baddler" and dated 13 May 1859 with verse, "Great & Noble jar / hold sheep, goat and bear," and jar signed "Dave and Baddler" and dated 13 May 1859 with verse, "Made at Stoney Bluff / for Making lard Enuff."

Bain, William (ca. 1805 [Scotland]–?)
Edgefield District, 1860: agent in pottery.

Barnes, John (1825 [S.C.]–1887)
Randolph County, Ala. (Rock Mills), 1860: potter.
Randolph County, Ala., 1887: potter.

Bartlam, John (ca. 1736 [England]–1781)
Cainhoy area from Staffordshire by 1765: potter. Charleston, 1770: potter. Camden area by 1776: potter.

Baur, William
Edgefield County, 1860: potter.

Baynham, Clifton (1904–1971)
North Augusta, Aiken County, South Carolina Pottery. Son of Mark Sr.

Baynham, Elmo (1907–1930)
North Augusta, Aiken County, South Carolina Pottery. Son of Mark Sr.

Baynham, Horace H.
Baynham Station, Trenton, Edgefield County, ca. 1920. Son of Joseph G. Baynham.

Baynham, Hugh (b. 1910)
North Augusta, Aiken County, South Carolina Pottery. Son of Mark Sr.

Baynham, Joseph A. (1905–1975)
North Augusta, Aiken County, South Carolina Pottery. Son of Mark Sr.

Baynham, Joseph G. (1841 [Va.]–?)
Aiken County, Shaws Township, 1900: farmer?

Baynham, Mark, Sr. (1878–1937)
North Augusta, Aiken County, 1924: established South Carolina Pottery.

Baynham, Mark Andrew (1918–1985)
North Augusta, Aiken County, South Carolina Pottery. Son of Mark Sr.

Baynham, Roy (1920–1985)
North Augusta, Aiken County, South Carolina Pottery. Son of Mark Sr.

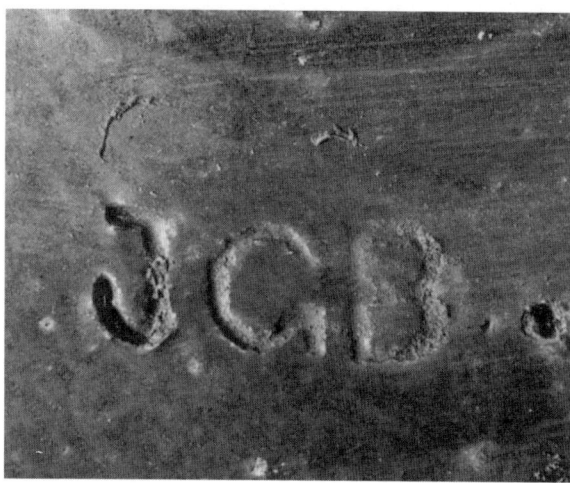

Stoneware fragment with maker's mark JGB recovered from the Baynham site (38ED221). From Castille, Baldwin, and Steen, *Archaeological Survey of Alkaline-Glazed Pottery Kiln Sites in Old Edgefield District, South Carolina.*

Becham, John, Jr.
Ninety-Six District, 1784: purchased property on Gilders Creek and Peters Creek.

Becham [var. Beckham], John, Sr. (ca. 1795 [S.C.?]–184?)
Washington County, Ga.; Crawford County, Ga., 1830.

Becham [var. Beckum], Thomas
Ninety Six District, Edgefield County, 1789: sold plantation on Horn's Creek to Aquilla Miles.

Belcher, Clarence
Spartanburg County, ca. 1930: potter.

Bennett, Claude L.
Lesslie, York County, Glasscock and Bennett Pottery. Son of George.

Bennett, George
Aiken County, 1900: jug turner. Md. (1) Roxy Brumbeloe, daughter of Camelius E. Brumbeloe.

Bennett, John
Aiken County, ca. 1900. Twin brother of George.

Bishop, Curtis Grover, Sr. (1891/92–1961)
Jugtown, Ga., 1927–28, for Rufus S. Rogers; Lanford, Laurens County, ca. 1920–30, for J. D. ("Jug") Johnson; North Augusta, Aiken County, ca. 1930, for the Baynhams. Son of W. Davis Bishop.

Bishop, Fred (b. 1918)
Jugtown, Ga., 1930s; Lanford, Laurens County, ca. 1920–30, for J. D. ("Jug") Johnson; North Augusta, Aiken County, ca. 1930, for the Baynhams. Son of Curtis Sr.

Bodie, Jesse P. (1826–1884)
Edgefield County, 1870: potter.

Boyle, Aylie (1819–1912)
Cherokee County. Md. (1) Sarah Berthine Owensby Boyle.

Boyle, Aylie, Jr. (1876–?)
Cherokee County. Son of Aylie Sr. and Sarah Berthine Owensby.

Boyle [var. Boils], Robert L. (1864–1937)
Cherokee County, 1900: potter and farmer. Son of Aylie Sr. and Sarah Berthine Owensby.

Boyle [var. Boils], Sarah Berthine Owensby (1832–1917)
Cherokee County, 1900: potter and farmer. Daughter of Thomas Owensby.

Bradley, Marshall (ca. 1845–?) [black]
Edgefield County, Hamburg Township: works in pottery.

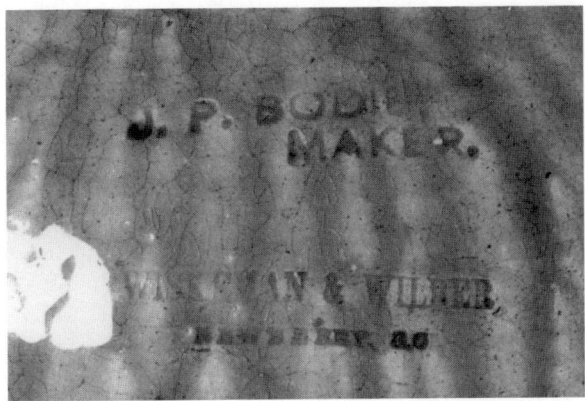

Detail of maker's mark J. P. BODIE / MAKER with merchants' name and address, WISKEMAN & WILBER / NEWBERRY S.C. Alkaline-glazed stoneware storage jar, ca. 1870, Jesse P. Bodie Pottery, Kirksey's Crossroads, Edgefield County, S.C. Collection of Georgeanna H. Greer.

Brannon, A. F.
Edgefield District, 1823: signed and dated jar (Agnes Brannon is listed as a head of household in the 1820 Abbeville District census).

Brooks, Esau
Edgefield District, Kirksey's Crossroads, 1841: appears with John Presley and John Trapp in a court notice announcing the sale of property at a pottery factory on the Martin Town Road.

Brown, Davis Pennington (1895–1967 [N.C.])
Inman area, Spartanburg County, ca. 1920, from Atlanta, Ga. Son of James Osborne.

Brown, Evan Javan ("Jay") (1897–1980 [N.C.])
Inman area, Spartanburg County, ca. 1920, from Atlanta, Ga. Son of James Osborne Brown.

Brown, James Otto (1899 [Ga.]–1980)
Inman area, Spartanburg County, ca. 1920.

Brown, James Otto, Jr. ("Jimmy") (1930–1976)
Smithville, Miss., Suggs Pottery, ca. 1955; Gillsville, Ga., ca. 1956, for Harold Hewell; North Augusta, Aiken County, 1958, for Hugh Baynham; Bethune, Kershaw County, 1959–60, for Rufus Outen and Horace Ratteree; Chesterfield County, Brown's Pottery, 1961–80. Son of James Otto Sr.

Brown, Marshall (ca. 1855–?) [black]
Edgefield County, Hamburg Township, 1870: works in pottery.

Brown, Rufus Edwin (1901–?)
Inman area, Spartanburg County, ca. 1920, from Atlanta, Ga. Son of James Osborne Brown.

Brown, William O. ("Willie") (1887–ca. 1966)
Inman area, Spartanburg County, ca. 1920, from Atlanta, Ga. Son of James Osborne.

Brumbeloe, Camelius E. (1836–?)
Jugtown, Ga.; Stockton, Lanier County, Ga., 1880; Aiken County, 1900: L. D. Harley Pottery with son-in-law George Bennett; Jugtown, Ga., 1906: potter. Son of Emanuel.

Brumbeloe, Oscar Early (1871–1944)
Jugtown, Ga., 1900: potter; moved to Washington County, Ga., ca. 1910; Bethune, Kershaw County, late 1920s. Son of Camelius. Md. (1) Ella Hahn.

Burnett, J. H.
Edgefield County, Kirksey's Crossroads, ca. 1870; reportedly sold stoneware factory to Jesse P. Bodie.

Buster (ca. 1790–?) [slave]
Edgefield District, 1835: named as a turner in an indenture in which Amos Landrum released his property on Shaw's Creek to Reuben Drake and Jasper Gibbs.

Cade, Drury Boykin
Petersburg, Elbert County, Ga.; Mt. Carmel, McCormick County, ca. 1885–1900.

Champion, Richard (1743–1791)
Plymouth, England, 1768: copartnership in porcelain factory with William Cookworthy; Bristol, England, 1773: Castle Green Pottery; Camden, 1784. Md. (1) Julia [var. Judith] Lloyd.

Chandler, Thomas (1810 [Va.]–1854 [N.C.])
Shaw's Creek, Edgefield District, 1840: turner at Phoenix Factory; Kirksey's Crossroads, 1843: Trapp-Chandler Factory (co-owner with John Trapp); 1850: stoneware manufactory. Md. (1) Margaret Durham.

Chestus, Fortune (ca. 1850–?) [black]
Miles Mill: former slave of Lewis Miles.

Clayton, Oliver Jones ("Pete") (1906–1988)
Holly Springs Community, Spartanburg County, ca. 1930–40: Clayton Jug Factory, trained under Albert Fulbright.

Cogburn, Cyrus [var. Silas] (1782 [N.C.]–ca. 1855 [Tex.])
Edgefield, 1814: witnessed deed in which John Lan-

drum purchased property on Horse Creek. Washington County, Ga., 1820: stoneware manufacturing; Talbot County, Ga., 1830; Macon County, Ala., 1840; Rusk County, Tex., 1850.

Craig, A.
South Carolina Pottery Company, Trenton, Edgefield County, 1887: Superintendent.

Crow, Josiah (1819 [S.C.]–?)
Russell County, Ala., 1850: potter.

Cumberland, James (1824 [S.C.]–?)
Marion County, Ala., 1850: potter.

Daniel [slave]
Edgefield District, 1840: named as a turner in a deed in which James W. Gibbs sold his one-sixth share in the "Pottersville Stone Ware Manufacturing establishment" to Jasper Gibbs; 1842: named as a turner in a mortgage in which J. D. Nance released his one-third share in the "Pottersville Manufacturing concern" to Jasper Gibbs.

Daugherty, Edward ("Guy") (1878 [Tex.]–ca. 1970)
Bethune area, 1943: purchased shop from O. E. Brumbeloe.

Dave (ca. 1780–ca. 1863) [slave]
Edgefield District, 1840: turner at Lewis J. Miles Factory; also known as "Dave Pottery"; associated with the *Pottersville Hive* newspaper; probably trained at the Pottersville and/or John Landrum factory; specialized in large-capacity storage jars incised in script with factory mark "Lm," signature "Dave," date of manufacture, and rhymed verses.

Davies, Thomas J. (1830–1902)
Edgefield District, 1862: established Palmetto Fire Brick Works with Anson Peeler (slaves at this factory produced alkaline-glazed stoneware face vessels and utilitarian ware).

Davis, Shep (ca. 1849–?) [black]
Edgefield County, 1870: works in pottery (cannot read or write).

Devillin, Andrew
Edgefield County, 1850: stoneware manufacturing.

Devillin [var. Devlin], Francis
Edgefield District, 1850: appeared as a witness in a coroner's inquisition into the drowning death of Thomas Chandler's son; Buncombe County, N.C., 1860: jugmaker.

Devore, Jonathan (1827–?)
Greenwood County, Kirksey's Crossroads, ca. 1867–85: Roundtree and Bodie Pottery.

Devore, Semps
Aiken County, ca. 1880: journeyman potter.

Dickson, Carey (also known as Carey Posey)
Aiken County, ca. 1880: Seigler Pottery.

Dixon, P. [K. or R.?] (ca. 1841–?)
Greenville County, 1870: potter.

Drake, David (ca. 1800–?) [black]
Edgefield County, 1870: turner.

Drake, Harvey (?–1832)
Edgefield District, 1827–32: Pottersville Stoneware Manufactory.

Drake, Reuben
Edgefield District, 1827–32: Pottersville Stoneware Manufactory; 1832–36: Drake and Rhodes Factory; 1836: Drake, Rhodes and Company; by 1850: Natchitoches Parish, La.

Duche, Andrew (1710 [Pa.]–1778 [Pa.])
Charleston by 1735 from Philadelphia: potter; New Windsor, ca. 1836; Savannah, Chatham County, Ga., 1738–43: potter. Son of Anthony.

Duncan [var. Dunkin], Matthew (ca. 1796 [S.C.]–ca. 1881 [Tex.])
Edgefield District, 1810; Coweta County, Ga., by ca. 1828–30; Randolph County, Ala., 1840; Bastrop County, Tex. 1856–80: potter.

Duncan [var. Dunkin], Samuel
Edgefield, 1810; Coweta County, Ga., 1830; Randolph County, Ala., 1840, 1850; Chambers County, Ala., 1880. Probably related to Matthew Duncan.

Durham, Isaac
Edgefield District, Shaw's Creek, 1840: turner at Phoenix Factory; 1843: appeared in property conveyance as owner of land located adjacent to that of John Trapp at Kirksey's Crossroads; Alabama, 1850.

Durham, John
Edgefield District, 1843: sold property and "stone factory" located on "Martin Town Road" to John Trapp.

Durham, M. J. (? [S.C.]–ca. 1900)
Guadalupe County, Tex., by 1865, from Edgefield District with a freed black named John Chandler. Probably related to Durham family of Edgefield.

Durham, Stewart
Edgefield District, 1850: associated with Thomas Chandler.

Durham, William
Edgefield, 1820: probably father of John and/or Isaac Durham.

Durham, William (ca. 1826–?)
Edgefield County, 1870: works in pottery.

Easter [slave]
Edgefield District, Kirksey's Crossroads, 1852: listed as part of Thomas Chandler's property in a trust deed filed for Chandler's wife, Margaret, and their children.

Effurt [var. Efford, Efurd], Adam (?–1822)
Camden District, by 1784: potter; Ninety Six District, by 1791; Edgefield District, 1810, 1820.

Ellis, William
Camden, S.C., from Staffordshire, England: worked for John Bartlam; Bethabara, N.C., 1771; Salem, N.C., 1773: introduced fancy Queensware and tortoiseshell ware to the North Carolina Moravians; returned to Staffordshire by 1783.

Emanuel, Peter R.
Graniteville, near Aiken: storage jar dated 1879.

Ferguson [var. Fergerson], Charles H. (1793–1878/79)
Edgefield District, 1820; migrated to Jackson (present-day Barrow) County, Ga., in 1846 and established a shop near present-day Statham.

Fletch, George (ca. 1862 [Germany]–?)
Aiken County, Schultz Township, 1900: potter (immigrated from Germany in 1880).

Fletcher [var. Flesher], George U. [black]
Reportedly worked at Miles Mill and several other potteries in the Aiken-Edgefield County area; Lesslie, York County, ca. 1917, for E. C. Collins.

Forbes, Daniel J. (1848 [S.C.]–?)
York County, Kings Mountain Township, 1900: farmer.

Foreman, Glover G. (1835 [S.C.]–1900)
Stockton, Lanier County, Ga., 1881, 1883.

Fulbright, Albert M. (ca. 1867–?)
Jugtown, Buncombe County, N.C., 1910: potter; Arden, Buncombe County, N.C.; Lanford Station, Laurens County, ca. 1920; Inman area, Spartanburg County, ca. 1930: Mountain View Pottery.

Galledge, John (ca. 1833 [S.C.])
Greenville District, 1860: turner?

Gibbs, Jasper (1810–1877)
Edgefield District, Pottersville, 1838–39: Rhodes, Ramey and Gibbs; 1839: N. Ramey and Co.; 1840–42: J. Gibbs and Co. Md. (1) Laura Jane Drake, daughter of Harvey Drake.

Glasscock, ———
Lesslie, York County, G and B Pottery (co-owner of a shop run by Claude L. Bennett).

Green, Isaac (ca. 1850–?)
Richland County, 1910: potter in pottery.

Grice, William (ca. 1816–?)
Edgefield District, 1850: turner.

Gunter, Allen (1801–ca. 1860?)
Montevideo/Coldwater, Hart County, Ga., 1830, from Edgefield District; 1850: jars and jugs.

Guthery, D. D. (1829 [S.C.]–1909)
Marion County, Ala. 1850: potter.

Hahn, P. L. (ca. 1871–?)
North Augusta, Aiken County, 1900: potter.

Hahn, William F. (ca. 1861–?)
Trenton, Aiken County, ca. 1880; North Augusta, Aiken County, 1900: potter (owns and manages business).

Hance, George W. (ca. 1827–?)
Union District, 1830; York County, Kings Mountain Township, 1840; Union County, N.C., 1850: potter; 1860: potter.

Harley, Langley Duke ("L.D.") (1861–1925)
Aiken County, 1900: potter and farmer; preserve jar signed in incised script "made by L. D. Harley, Miles Mill."

Harry [slave]
Edgefield District, 1840: named as a turner in a deed in which James W. Gibbs sold his one-sixth share in the "Pottersville Stone Ware Manufacturing establishment" to Jasper Gibbs; 1842: named as a turner in a mortgage in which J. D. Nance released his one-third share in the "Pottersville Manufacturing concern" to Jasper Gibbs.

(Old) Harry [slave]
Edgefield District, 1839: named in an indenture between John Hughes and Collin Rhodes as part of the Pottersville Stoneware Manufactory property.

(Young) Harry [slave]
Edgefield District, 1839: named in an indenture be-
tween John Hughes and Collin Rhodes as part of the
Pottersville Stoneware Manufactory property.

Hatcher, John (ca. 1836–?)
Edgefield District, 1860: turner.

Helton, Martin Alexander (1843–1921)
Sharon, York County, ca. 1900.

Henson, Billy Walker (b. 1941)
Jugtown, Spartanburg-Greenville County. Grandson
of Jesse Vardry.

Henson, David Carr (1848–1925)
Jugtown, Spartanburg-Greenville County: potter.
Son of William Marquis.

Henson, Jesse Vardry (1857–1933)
Jugtown, Spartanburg-Greenville County: potter.
Son of William Marquis.

Henson, Mathias B. (ca. 1842–?)
Spartanburg County, 1870: potter; 1900: potter.

Henson, William Marquis ("Bill") (1818–1904)
Jugtown, Spartanburg-Greenville County: potter.

Henson, William Thomas (1859–1922)
Jugtown, Spartanburg-Greenville County: potter.
Son of William Marquis.

Hershinger, John
Saxe Gotha Township, 1742: potter.

Hewell, Jack (b. 1914 [Ga.])
Gillsville, Ga.; Lanford Station, Laurens County,
1924–28. Son of Maryland.

Hewell, Maryland ("Bud") (1891 [Ga.]–1964 [Ga.])
Gillsville, Ga.; Lanford Station, Laurens County,
1924–28. Son of Eli.

Hill, J. C. (1815 [N.C.]–ca. 1870?)
In Georgia by 1844, from South Carolina.

Hill, James F. (1842 [S.C.]–?)
Duck Creek, Walker County, Ga., 1870, 1880: pot-
ter; 1883, 1886: jug manufacturer; Cleburne County,
Ala., 1900, 1910: potter. Son of John C.

Hill, John C. (1824 [N.C.]–?)
Benton County, Ala. (adjacent to present-day Randolph County), 1850: potter. Md. [1] Sarah in South
Carolina, ca. 1837; children born in South Carolina,
1838–42. Son of James.

Horn, William (ca. 1848–?)
Edgefield County, Gray Township, 1870: works in
pottery.

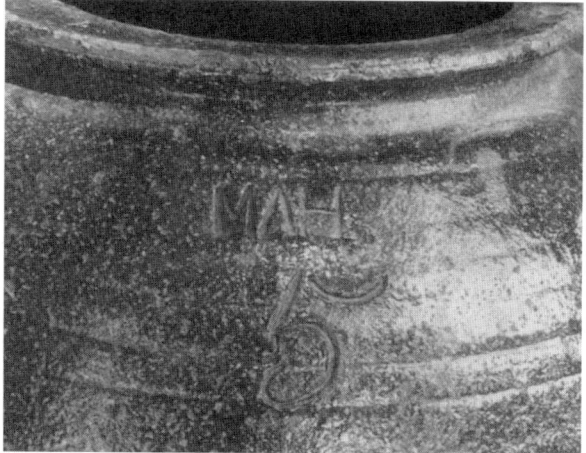

Detail of maker's mark MAH / 5. Alkaline-glazed
stoneware storage jar, ca. 1900, Martin A. Helton Pottery, Sharon, S.C. Collection of Susie E. Ramsey.

Howard, P[eter?] (1812–?)
Amicalola District, Lumpkin County, Ga., by 1850,
from South Carolina.

Hughes, John
Edgefield District, Pottersville, 1839: N. Ramey and
Company; 1840–42: J. Gibbs and Company.

Jegglin, Hermann (ca. 1860 [Mo.]–?)
Jugtown, Ga., ca. 1905–10, for Wiley Rogers; Alva-
ton, Meriwether County, Ga., for W. T. B. Gordy;
Spartanburg County, ca. 1920, for George L. Clay-
ton. Son of John, a German potter who settled at
Boonville, Mo.

John (ca. 1834–?) [slave]
Edgefield District, Kirksey's Crossroads, 1852: slave
listed as part of Thomas Chandler's property in a
trust deed filed for Chandler's wife, Margaret, and
their children.

Johnson, A. (ca. 1822–?)
Spartanburg County, 1850: potter.

Johnson, Harvey M. (1846–1931)
Lanford Station, Laurens County: owner of shop
operated by his brother, Joseph D. Md. (1) Parthenia M. Lanford.

Johnson, Joseph D. ("Jug") (1848 [N.C.]–ca. 1948)
Lanford Station, Laurens County, 1880: jugmaker.
Brother of Harvey M.

Johnson, Parthenia M. (1850–1916)
Lanford Station, Laurens County: maker of molded clay smoking pipes. Md. (1) Harvey M. Johnson.

Jones, ———
Spartanburg County: Jones brothers reportedly ran a pottery shop located near Spartanburg.

Jones, Brewster [black]
Seigler Pottery, Edgefield County, ca. 1875.

Jones, Mark (ca. 1835–?) [black]
Edgefield County, 1870: turner.

Jones, Thomas (ca. 1852–?) [black]
Edgefield County, 1870: works in pottery.

Kent, James M. (1829 [S.C.]–?)
Shelby County, Ala. (Hillsboro P.O.), 1870: potter.

Kinard, Wash (ca. 1860–?) [black]
Schultz Township, Aiken County, 1900: potter (owns and manages business).

Kirbee [var. Kirby], James (1790 [S.C.]–1860 [Tex.])
Edgefield District, 1810, 1820; Elbert County, Ga., 1830; Harris County, Ga., 1840; Montgomery County, Tex., late 1840s; 1850: potter; 1860: potter.

Kirbee, Lewis (1821 [S.C.]–? [Tex.])
Montgomery County, Tex., 1850: stoneware manufacturer. Son of James.

Kirbee, M. J. (Jefferson) (? [S.C.]–?)
Montgomery County, Tex., 1850: potter. Son of James.

Kirkland, Benjamin, Sr.
Henry County, Ala., 1840; Randolph County, Ala., 1850: in close association with other potters; Rusk County, Tex., 1890.

Kirkland, Isaac
Edgefield District, 1814: witnessed deed in which John Landrum purchased property on Horse Creek.

Landrum, Abner (1785–1859)
Edgefield District, ca. 1810–28: owner of the Pottersville Stoneware Manufactory; Richland District, 1850: pottery. Md. (1) Mahethalan Presley. Son of Samuel.

Landrum, Amos (1780–ca. 1862)
Edgefield District, 1810, 1830, 1836: granted property

to Reuben Drake and Jasper Gibbs including Buster, a slave, listed as a turner; 1850: farmer (in household of Christian Hatcher). Md. (1) Elizabeth Hatcher. Son of Samuel.

Landrum, Benjamin Franklin [B. F.], Sr. (ca. 1812–ca. 1900)
Edgefield District, 1850: stoneware manufacturer; 1860: stoneware maker. Son of John.

Landrum, Benjamin Franklin, Jr. ("Ben")
Aiken County, 1880: Stone Ware Factory (owner). Son of Benjamin Franklin Landrum, Sr.

Landrum, John, Rev. (1765 [N.C.]–1846)
Edgefield District, ca. 1810–40. Son of Samuel.

Landrum, Linneaus [var. Lineous] Mead (ca. 1829–1891)
Richland County, 1870: potter; 1880: potter. Son of Abner.

Landrum, Samuel (ca. 1737–1816)
Edgefield District, from North Carolina by 1786. Not established as a potter.

Lawton, H. R. (ca. 1823 [England]–?)
Edgefield County, 1870: potter.

Lee, Jim (ca. 1860–?) [black]
Roundtree-Bodie Pottery, Edgefield District, ca. 1860: figural bottle.

Leopard, Daniel
Edgefield District, 1820.

Leopard, Emmanuel [var. Manuel]
Edgefield, 1800, 1810, 1820.

Leopard, Holland (ca. 1812 [S.C.]–?)
Fayette County, Ga., 1830, from Edgefield District; Randolph County, Ala., 1840: manufacturer; Winston County, Miss., 1850: potter. Son of Emmanuel.

Leopard, John D. (1803 [S.C.]–1881 [Tex.])
Edgefield, 1820; Fayette County, Ga., 1830; Randolph County, Ala., 1840; Rusk County, Tex., 1850: jugmaker; 1860: jugmaker; 1870: potter; 1880: potter. Son of Emmanuel.

Leopard, Lewis (1807 [S.C.]–?)
Chambers County, Ala. (Beula), 1860: jugmaker.

Leopard, Robert (ca. 1830 [S.C.]–?)
Randolph County, Ala., 1840; Rusk County, Tex., 1860: jugmaker. Son of Emmanuel.

Leopard, Thomas
Edgefield District, 1810, 1830. Son of Emmanuel.

Long, James (1785 [Md.]–1869)
    Washington County, 1825, from Edgefield District?;
    Crawford County, 1826.

McGill, William
    York County, 1781: potter.
McKenon, Albert (ca. 1880–?) [black]
    Aiken County, 1900: laborer in pottery.
McPherson, Archie (1838 [S.C.]–1909)
    Randolph County, Ala. (Rock Mills), 1860: farmer;
    DeKalb County, Ala., 1870: mechanic; DeKalb
    County, Ala., 1880: potter. Md. [1] daughter of
    Edmund T. Belcher.
McPherson, Elijah (1808 [S.C.]–1854/55)
    Randolph County, Ala., 1850: farmer.
McPherson, Napoleon B. (ca. 1834 [S.C.]–1863/64)
    Randolph County, Ala. (Rock Mills), 1860. Son of
    Elijah.
McPherson, William (ca. 1836 [S.C.]–?)
    Randolph County, Ala. (Rock Mills), 1860. Son of
    Elijah.
Mason, Harry
    Jugtown, Spartanburg-Greenville County, early
    1900s: Irish immigrant potter; ran a pottery shop
    located on property owned by William Thomas Hen-
    son.
Massey, Abraham (ca. 1785 [N.C. or S.C.]–?)
    Edgefield District, 1814: witnessed deed in which
    Abner Landrum purchased Pottersville property;
    Washington County, Ga., 1820: stoneware manufac-
    turer.
Mathis, Robert W.
    Edgefield District, Pottersville, 1836–38: Ramey,
    Rhodes and Company; 1840: Phoenix Factory (co-
    owner with Collin Rhodes).
Matthews, B. C.
    Newberry County, ca. 1900.
Matthews, R. W.
    Edgefield District, 1840: living near potters Isaac
    Durham and Thomas Chandler; possibly a journey-
    man potter at the Phoenix Factory.
Meaders, Casey (1881–1945)
    White County, Ga., until 1920; Spartanburg County,
    ca. 1920–30; for George L. Clayton; Catawba, N.C.
    Son of John.
Merritt, Riley (1825 [S.C.]–?)
    Crawford County, Ga. Md. (1) Nancy Becham.

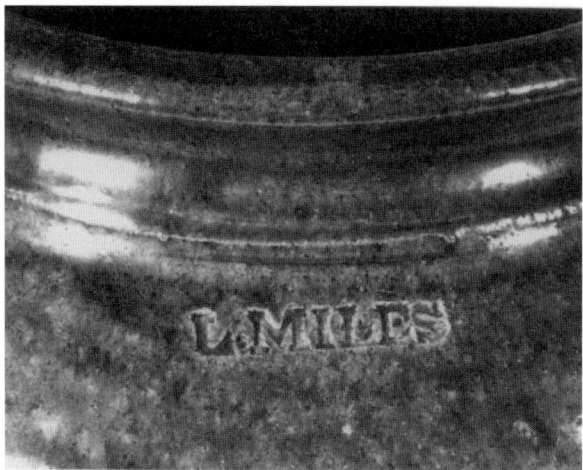

Detail of maker's mark L MILES. Alkaline-glazed
stoneware preserve jar, ca. 1860, Lewis Miles Pottery,
Edgefield District, S.C. Collection of the Charleston
Museum, Charleston, S.C.

Miles, John L. (ca. 1845–?)
    Edgefield County, 1870: manufacturing stoneware.
    Son of Lewis J.
Miles, Josh [black]
    Aiken County, 1880: Judge [Jug] Factory, Shaw's
    Creek (owner).
Miles, Lewis J. (ca. 1809–1868)
    Edgefield District, 1850: stoneware manufacturer;
    1860: stoneware maker. Son-in-law of John
    Landrum.
Miles, Moss [black]
    Benjamin F. Landrum Pottery, Edgefield County,
    late nineteenth century.
Miles, Oliver [mulatto]
    Seigler Pottery, Aiken County, late nineteenth cen-
    tury.
Miles, Philip (ca. 1820–?) [black]
    Edgefield County, 1870: turner.
Miles, Scott [black]
    Benjamin F. Landrum Pottery, Edgefield County,
    late nineteenth century.

Nash, Jefferson S.
    Edgefield District, 1849: appeared in newspaper
    notice as executor of Jasper Gibbs's estate. Marion
    County, Tex., 1850–60: J. S. NASH.

Ned [slave]

Kirksey's Crossroads, Edgefield District: listed as part of Thomas Chandler's property in a trust deed filed for Chandler's wife, Margaret, and their children.

Neville, James Francis

Enterprise Pottery, West Union, Oconee County, ca. 1875–1900. Brother of Jesse C., McCurry, and Samuel K.

Neville, Jesse Clarence

Enterprise Pottery, West Union, Oconee County, ca. 1875–1900. Brother of James F., McCurry, and Samuel K.

Neville, McCurry ("Mack")

Enterprise Pottery, West Union, Oconee County, ca. 1875–1900. Brother of James F., Jesse C., and Samuel K.

Neville, Samuel Knox

Enterprise Pottery, West Union, Oconee County, ca. 1875–1900. Brother of James F., Jesse C., and McCurry.

Odom, T. B.

Upshur County, Tex., 1880. No established Edgefield connection.

Oliver, Ross (ca. 1833–?)

Spartanburg County, 1870: potter.

Outen, Rufus Franklin (1905–1984)

Cheraw, Chesterfield County; Bethune, Kershaw County, ca. 1920–30; Matthews, Mecklenburg County, N.C. Son of William Franklin.

Outen, William Franklin (ca. 1860 [S.C.]–1946)

Lancaster, Lancaster County, ca. 1900; Catawba Junction, York County, by 1915. W. F. OUTEN / CATAWBA / SC; Matthews, Mecklenburg County, N.C., 1922. Brother-in-law of James C. ("Jug Jim") Broom of Union County, N.C.

Owensby [var. Ounsley, Ownsby], Joel (ca. 1820–?)

Spartanburg County, 1860: potter. Son of Thomas William.

Owensby [var. Owneby], Thomas (ca. 1823–?)

Union District, 1850: jugmaker. Son of Thomas William.

Owensby [var. Onsley, Ownsby], Thomas William (ca. 1794–1878)

Edgefield District, 1810; Spartanburg District, 1850: potter.

Parker, Francis (ca. 1821–?)

Union District, 1850: jugmaker. Brother-in-law of Thomas W. Owensby.

Peeler, Anson

Palmetto Fire Brick Works, Edgefield District, 1862–64 (co-owner with Thomas J. Davies).

Petty, Phillip G. (ca. 1847–?)

Cherokee County, 1900: farmer and jugmaker. Brother-in-law of Sarah Berthine Owensby Boyle.

Phil [slave]

Lewis Miles Factory, Edgefield District, ca. 1846.

Pickens, Francis W. (1805–1869)

Edgefield District, 1850: stoneware and brick factory.

Posey, Carey (see Carey Dickson)

Presley, Evan (1809 [S.C.]–?)

Autauga County, Ala. (Coosada), 1850; (Prattville), 1860: planter.

Presley, John

Edgefield District, 1820, 1830, 1840: stoneware manufactory; Winston County, Miss., 1850.

Ramey, Nathaniel

Edgefield District, 1836: Drake, Rhodes and Company; 1836–38: Ramey, Rhodes and Company; 1838–39: Rhodes, Ramey and Gibbs; 1839: N. Ramey and Company.

Ray, James (ca. 1827–?)

Greenville District, 1850: turner.

Ray, William

Union County, ca. 1880.

Rhodes, Coleman

Edgefield District, 1840: Phoenix Factory. Brother of Collin.

Rhodes, Collin (1811–1881)

Edgefield District, Pottersville, 1832–36: Drake and Rhodes Factory; 1836: Drake, Rhodes and Company; 1836–38: Ramey, Rhodes and Company; 1838–39: Rhodes, Ramey and Gibbs; Shaw's Creek, 1840: Phoenix Factory (co-owner with Robert Mathis); ca. 1843: Collin Rhodes Factory. Son-in-law of Amos Landrum.

Rodgers, Lee (ca. 1808 [Va.]–?) [black]

Edgefield County, 1870: works in pottery.

Rofs [var. Ross], Oliver (ca. 1833–?)

Spartanburg County, Campobello Township, 1870: potter.

Roundtree, W. D. (ca. 1855–1865)
  Edgefield District, Kirksey's Crossroads, ca. 1860–65 (stoneware factory owner).
Rushton, James
  Edgefield District, 1820, 1830.
Rushton, John
  Edgefield District, 1810.
Rushton, Joseph
  Edgefield District, ca. 1820; Randolph County, Ala., 1840, 1850; Rusk County, Tex., by 1870s.
Rushton, Moses (1793 [S.C.]–?)
  Montgomery County, Ala., 1850: churnmaker.

Samuel, John (ca. 1838–?) [black]
  Edgefield County, 1870: works in clay.
Seigler, G. P. (ca. 1860–?)
  Trenton, Aiken County, 1900: lumberman. "G. P. Seigler / Trenton / S.C."
Seigler, John W.
  Edgefield District, ca. 1860–80. "J.W.S. / Pine House / S.C."
Simkins, Henry [black]
  Edgefield District, Miles Mill, ca. 1850–60.
Simon [slave]
  Kirksey's Crossroads, Edgefield District: listed as part of Thomas Chandler's property in a trust deed filed for Chandler's wife, Margaret, and their children.
Sligh, John Nicholas (1807 [S.C.]–1897)
  Paulding County, Ga., by 1860: established Sligh Pottery.
Smith, John R.
  Spartanburg County: potter.
Smith, Julius L. (1872 [S.C.]–?)
  Atlanta area, 1900: potter.
Staubes, Jacob (ca. 1830 [Germany]–?)
  Edgefield District, 1860: stoneware maker; living in the household of John Staubes.
Staubes [var. Stobbs], Jno. [John] (ca. 1821 [Germany]–?)
  Edgefield District, 1860: stoneware maker; living next door to John Seigler.
Steen, Marion
  Bethune, Kershaw County, ca. 1950: assisted Edward ("Guy") Daugherty.

Stone, Edward
  Buncombe County, N.C., by ca. 1844, from Kirksey's Crossroads, Edgefield District.
Stork, Edward Leslie (1868/69–1925)
  Landrum Fire Brick Works, Richland County, 1880s; Ala.; Miss.; Elbert County, Ga.; Orange, Cherokee County, Ga.; Senoia, Coweta County, Ga.; Washington County, Ga.; Crawford County, Ga.; Alvaton, Meriwether County, Ga., 1907; Fayette County, Ga., 1908; Orange, Ga., 1909–25. Son of John J. Stork and Juliette Landrum.
Stork, John J. (1841–1915)
  Landrum Fire Brick Works, Richland County, 1870: works in pottery. Son-in-law of Abner Landrum.
Stork, Robert Manning (ca. 1875–1953)
  Landrum Fire Brick Works, Richland County, ca. 1880–1950. Son of John J. Stork and Juliette Landrum.
Stork, William H. ("Willie") (ca. 1848–?)
  Richland, 1880: laborer in pottery. Brother of John J.

Tapp, James Leroy (1875–1962)
  Spartanburg County.
Tapp, Moses Foster (ca. 1850–?)
  Spartanburg County.
Taylor, Wiley W. (1822 [S.C.]–?)
  Randolph County, Ala. (Rock Mills), 1860: potter (his son, William J., and potter John Lehman also living in household and working in pottery shop).
Terry, John H. (1810 [S.C.]–?)
  Bibb County, Ala., 1850: potter.
Thornwell, Archie (ca. 1860–?) [black]
  Aiken County, 1880: works in factory.
Thornwell, Jack (ca. 1833–?) [black]
  Aiken County, 1880: turning judges [jugs].
Thurman [var. Thurmond], Jack (ca. 1824–1908) [black]
  Aiken County, 1880: turning judges [jugs].
Tilman, Sanford (1829 [S.C.]–?)
  Lumpkin County, Ga., 1850: potter.
Tilman, Waldrip (ca. 1822–?)
  Greenville District, 1860: turner.
Towing [var. Towery, Lowery], William (1805 [S.C.]–?)
  Marion County, Ala., 1850: potter (living near Lloyds and Dorseys).

Trapp, John (?–1876)
  Kirksey's Crossroads, Edgefield District, 1843–ca. 1850 (co-owner of Trapp-Chandler factory with Thomas Chandler).
Trull, James Otis (1884–1958)
  Jugtown, Buncombe County, N.C.; Spartanburg County, ca. 1930, for George L. Clayton. Son of Benjamin Robert.
Turner, James (?–1870 [Fla.])
  Kirksey's Crossroads, Edgefield District, ca. 1840 (sold stoneware factory to W. D. Roundtree).

Vestall, Tilman (ca. 1816 [S.C.]–?)
  Lauderdale County, Miss., 1870.

Warwick, W. Asberry (1819 [S.C.]–1901)
  Mossy Creek, White County, Ga.
Watcher, Anthony (ca. 1879–?)
  Aiken County, 1900: laborer in pottery.
Waters, LeRoy
  Bethune, Kershaw County, ca. 1950, assisted Edward ("Guy") Daugherty.

Whatley, Isum (ca. 1827–?)
  Edgefield, 1870: works in pottery.
Whelchel [var. Welcher], Jesse (ca. 1827–?)
  Spartanburg, 1850: potter.
Whelchel, John (ca. 1816–?)
  Spartanburg District, 1860: potter.
Whelchel, Sam
  Cherokee County, 1875–ca. 1930: potter. Son of John.
Whelchel [var. Welcher], William (ca. 1814–?)
  Spartanburg District, 1850: potter. Son of Sam.
Willard, James W. (1841 [S.C.]–?)
  Jackson (now Barrow) County, Ga.: potter.
Williams, Milage (ca. 1835/1840–?) [black]
  Edgefield County, 1870: stoneware turner/stonemason; Aiken County, 1880: works in jug factory.
Williams, Richard ("Rich") (1849–?) [black]
  Greenville County, 1900: farmer (owned a pottery located south of Gowensville).
Wood, ———
  North Augusta, Aiken County, ca. 1900: bought out by Mark Baynham, Sr.

Index

References to South Carolina potters are printed in italic type.

229